The *Latest* ∧Illustrated
Book of
DEVELOPMENT
DEFINITIONS

NEW EXPANDED EDITION

About the Authors

HARVEY S. MOSKOWITZ, PP, FAICP, is a planning consultant and a former member and past president of the New Jersey Board of Professional Planners. He has a Ph.D. in urban planning and policy development from Rutgers University and an M.P.A. from New York University. Moskowitz was formerly on the board of directors of the American Planning Association and the New Jersey Site Improvement Advisory Board.

CARL G. LINDBLOOM, PP, AICP, is a planning and urban design consultant. He is a licensed professional planner in New Jersey and a former member of his local planning board. Early in his career he worked as an architect/planner in England for the London County Council and later with the Greater London Council. Lindbloom has an undergraduate degree in architecture and a graduate degree in city design from Miami University, Oxford, Ohio.

The *Latest* Illustrated Book of
Book of
DEVELOPMENT
DEFINITIONS

NEW EXPANDED EDITION

HARVEY S. MOSKOWITZ
and
CARL G. LINDBLOOM

CENTER FOR URBAN POLICY RESEARCH
EDWARD J. BLOUSTEIN SCHOOL OF PLANNING AND PUBLIC POLICY
RUTGERS, THE STATE UNIVERSITY OF NEW JERSEY
NEW BRUNSWICK, NEW JERSEY

Published by the Center for Urban Policy Research
Edward J. Bloustein School of Planning and Public Policy
Rutgers, The State University of New Jersey
Civic Square • 33 Livingston Avenue
New Brunswick, New Jersey 08901-1982

For purchasing information, contact CUPR PRESS at the above address, by telephone
at 732•932-3133, ext. 555, or by e-mail at cuprbook@rci.rutgers.edu

Printed in the United States of America

Library of Congress Cataloging-in-Publication Data

Moskowitz, Harvey S.
   The latest illustrated book of development definitions / Harvey S.
Moskowitz, Carl G. Lindbloom.—New expanded ed.
       p. cm.
Rev. ed. of: The new illustrated book of development definitions /
Harvey S. Moskowitz and Carl G. Lindbloom. c1993.
Includes bibliographical references.
   ISBN 0-88285-177-2 (paper : alk. paper)
   1. City planning—United States—Dictionaries. 2. Zoning—United
States—Dictionaries. 3. City planning and redevelopment law—United
States—Dictionaries. 4. Rural development—United
States—Dictionaries.   I. Lindbloom, Carl G.   II. Moskowitz, Harvey S.
New illustrated book of development definitions.   III. Rutgers
University. Center for Urban Policy Research. IV. Title.
HT167.M683 2004
307.1'216'0973—dc21   2003041033

Cover design: Helene Berinsky
Desktop production: Arlene Pashman

Contents

Illustrations

Preface

THE LATEST ILLUSTRATED BOOK OF DEVELOPMENT DEFINITIONS, like its predecessors (*The Illustrated Book of Development Definitions*, 1981; *The New Illustrated Book of Development Definitions*, 1993; both published by the Center for Urban Policy Research, Rutgers University) differs from a number of other books and publications containing development definitions in three major respects: (1) It is illustrated; (2) most of the definitions are designed to be used directly in ordinances with little or no change; and (3) the more complex definitions are accompanied by commentaries and annotations that explain how the definition may be used in an ordinance, along with background information pertinent to the definition.

The primary purpose of including illustrations is to aid in interpreting the definitions and to suggest that they have a place in local ordinances as well. With some exceptions, two of which are discussed in the next paragraph, illustrated definitions are rarely found in zoning and development ordinances. An occasional ordinance will show an angle-of-light or sky exposure plane diagram to establish the minimum dimension for interior courts or some similar complex and technical term. But by far, ordinances prefer the "thousand words" rather than the "single picture." Regardless of the reasons, the omission of illustrations, even if only to highlight a definition or standard, is strange since the first zoning ordinance (New York City, 1916) was a series of three graphic overlays regulating height, use, and bulk. Even today, the heart of a zoning ordinance is the district or zone map. Subdivision and site plan regulations are primarily concerned with design or graphic representations of what eventually will be three-dimensional products. Illustrations can greatly simplify how standards should be applied, particularly where the lot or parcel is irregularly shaped or where there are a number of variables present, each of which might have an impact on how the ordinance might apply in a specific situation.

Two examples of development ordinances that successfully use illustrations and integrate text and pictures are (1) the SmartCode© unified development ordinance recently developed by Duany Plater-Zyberk & Company and (2) the Coffee Creek Center *Design Code Book©* developed by the Lake Erie Land Co. of Chesterton, Indiana. The SmartCode effectively uses illustrations to provide a template for the built environment (including preserved and environmentally sensitive areas) in a variety of growth patterns from rural to urban, and to individual structures and their settings. The *Design Code Book* combines sketches, detailed drawings, and photographs along with the written text to illustrate specific site design details, including overall land planning, home types, siting, architectural details, building lines, parking, signs, landscaping, lighting, and infrastructure such as roads and drainage.

The original intent of the authors was to prepare a book of definitions that could be used directly, or with only slight modifications, in any zoning, subdivision, or land development ordinance. This presented certain obvious problems, such as attempting to write a single definition that would be appropriate in various kinds of municipalities in different states. In execution, however, this objective was not as difficult to achieve as it first appeared. One of the principles that the authors used and believe should be followed in writing any definition is not to include the standard that is being defined in the definition itself. Indeed, the standard itself may vary within the municipality by zoning district. For example, the definition for height can be constructed in such a manner that it can be applied universally while recognizing that the maximum or minimum standard will vary from municipality to municipality and even within municipalities. But how the height should be measured—from what point to what point—is equally applicable in New York City and East Alton, Illinois.

The attempt at universality and direct application broke down when the authors discovered two or even more equally adequate definitions covering the same word or term. For example, the definitions of *retail services*, *personal services*, *business services*, and *social services* overlap to a great extent, but the reader may find one more appropriate than another for a particular municipality.

Commentaries and annotations suggest how the definition is designed to be used in development regulations and offer some discussion pertinent to the definition. Although the commentaries are used primarily as a guide to the reader, the authors suggest that commentaries can be useful in local ordinances as well. Very often the background and legislative intent can be included, a device often used in state legislation but rarely, if ever, in local codes. A brief note could be inserted at the beginning of the ordinance that the commentaries are descriptive and explanatory only and are not part of the actual ordinance.

Since the publication in 1993 of the second edition, *The New Illustrated Book of Development Definitions*, significant changes have taken place in both the theory and the practice of planning. Many of the changes reflect greater awareness of the need to reexamine design concepts to make more efficient use of land, preserve open space, minimize traffic impacts, reduce environmental degradation, and make communities more attractive places to live, shop, and work. These changes are described in part by such terms as *agricultural zoning, smart growth, traditional neighborhood development*, and *traffic calming*, all of which are defined in this third edition.

In addition to changes in design concepts, changes affecting the use of land have taken place in retailing, industrial development, religion, and warehousing. Massive new retail establishments, supersized warehouses, mega-churches, and mixed-use planned developments, actually mini-cities, have appeared on the scene. The latest edition attempts to identify and define these uses.

The third edition also increases the number of commentaries and greatly expands the commentaries from the previous editions. The authors heard from planners who noted that the *Development Definitions* book was often the first step in researching planning problems, starting with the definition and then moving on to find out how the definition was applied in practice. The commentaries in the new edition further refine the practical applications, point out possible problems, and provide practical ways to avoid them. For example, the trend toward very large warehouses (1 million square feet and larger) and very large retail outlets has resulted in buildings with significant visual impacts on communities and adverse effects on the fabric and scale of development. The commentaries and illustrations have attempted to address those issues and offer practical solutions to minimize the impacts.

As a result, the third edition greatly expands the number of definitions, commentaries, and illustrations over the previous edition. The new book contains 1,955 definitions, or 172 more than the second edition; 787 commentaries, or 195 more than previously; and 102 illustrations, an increase of 27 over the 1993 edition. Furthermore, in the latest edition, many of the definitions and commentaries have been revised.

Throughout the book, the terms *zoning ordinance* and *land development ordinance* are used synonymously. Actually, a land development ordinance is much broader in scope and application, covering all aspects of development including, in addition to zoning, subdivision and site-plan regulations, stormwater management, environmental impact, and similar controls, standards, and requirements. Many municipalities recognize that, regardless of the type of ordinance, definitions, submission procedures, requirements for public hearings, data required for submissions, and improvements are the same. The trend is to combine the separate ordinances into a unified "land development ordinance."

A WORD OF CAUTION

The Latest Illustrated Book of Development Definitions expands significantly the references to legal decisions and statutes to analyze and explain how various definitions are applied, their limits, and their evolution. Neither of the authors is a lawyer; consequently, although we have relied on opinions from lawyers as well as on published legal sources, the reader is urged to consult with local counsel on specific questions of law and, in particular, how state enabling acts or court decisions affect the application of specific definitions in a particular jurisdiction.

Acknowledgments

Most zoning or land-development ordinance definitions are "borrowed," "inherited," or "stolen" from other ordinances. Indeed, most ordinances are written in this way. If a planner is particularly astute, early on he or she will start collecting definitions, then add, discard, or modify as the planner comes across new definitions or finds old ones not working. Many of the definitions in this book came about in this manner, but we would like to acknowledge the following contributions to this third edition.

1. A major source of many of the new definitions and assistance in developing more cohesive, insightful, and useful commentaries was the American Planning Association and its excellent publications. These include the well-researched and comprehensive material produced for the Planning Advisory Service (PAS), cases and commentaries in *Land Use Law and Zoning Digest*, and articles in *Planning* magazine and *Zoning News*. We sincerely appreciate the excellent cooperation and assistance of Frank So, then executive director of APA (now retired), and the following staff of APA: Jim Hecimovich, chief editor; Shannon L. Paul, librarian, Merriam Center Library; Shannon Armstrong and Michael Davidson, research associates; James C. Schwab, senior research associate; and Stuart Meck, senior research fellow.

2. The North American Industry Classification System (NAICS) supersedes the U.S. Standard Industrial Classification (SIC) system. Both the NAICS and SIC manuals contain the best source of definitions of all types of economic activity. More planners should use NAICS to allow definitions of various types of use activities to become standardized.

3. The New Jersey Site Improvement Advisory Board was established in 1993 to prepare uniform residential site improvement standards. The resulting Residential Site Improvement Standards (RSIS), N.J.A.C. 5:21, provides an excellent source for many

of the technical definitions relating to site improvements, including streets, sanitary sewers, stormwater management, and potable water supplies.

4. As was the case for the second (1993) edition, many of the references to court decisions used in the commentaries of the present edition are from William M. Cox and Donald M. Ross, *New Jersey Zoning and Land Use Administration* (Newark, NJ: Gann Law Books, 2003 and earlier editions).

5. Many of the definitions and commentaries, particularly as they apply to warehousing and distribution, impacts of large buildings, aesthetics, farmland preservation, conservation practices, and historic preservation are from the authors' experience in Cranbury Township (Middlesex County), New Jersey. A unique community of 10 square miles with a current population of about 3,400, Cranbury has a historic village, listed on the federal and state registers; much of its existing farmland has been preserved; and nearly 16 million square feet of warehouse, office, and distribution uses has been built or is planned.

   To the residents of Cranbury, ardent supporters of planning, we extend our thanks. We would also particularly like to thank Thomas B. Harvey, Planning Board chair, who encouraged the innovative thinking that has characterized planning in Cranbury; Joseph Stonaker, Planning Board attorney, who kept us out of trouble; and Cathy Marcelli, township engineer, who made sure the plans worked from an engineering perspective.

6. We also acknowledge the contribution of many people, including planners, lawyers, builders, developers, and colleagues who made important and timely recommendations and suggestions for this third edition. They include, in no particular order: Blaise Brancheau; Steven P. Moskowitz; Robert W. Burchell and David Listokin, codirectors of the Center for Urban Policy Research (CUPR) at Rutgers University; Robert Lake, editor in chief, CUPR Press; Richard Chaiken; Allan Maitlin; Jacob Lehrfeld; Kiersten Skog; Leonard J. Moskowitz; Jeff Toya; Marilyn Kasko; Walter D. LeVine; Bernard Searle; Fred Heyer; Susan Gruel; Deborah Moskowitz; Robert Kirkpatrick; William D. Kraft; Amy Greene; Peter Messina; Helen Forsa; David Karlbach; Tom Thomas; Elliot Semet, MD; Harvey Yesowitz; Susan B. Brecht; Dennis O'Neal; Jeff Speck; Kenneth Foster; Warren Stillwell; Dennis O'Brien; Richard Reading; Eric Tazelaar; John Madden; Karl Pehnke; Peter Steck; Kenneth Ochab; Allan Kehrt; Edward Klimek; Donald A. Krueckeberg; Demetri Baches; Kevin Warren; Thomas Troy, Sr.; and Shirley Bishop.

7. The authors particularly thank Alice Tomasulo, who typed many drafts of this third edition in her usual competent and expeditious manner.

xiv

8. Finally, special thanks and our deep admiration go to Arlene Pashman, senior editor, CUPR Press. Her impressive editing skills, uncommon common sense, sharp eye for detail, and willingness to accept copy long after deadlines have impressed us enormously. We are most grateful to this very special person.

To all who assisted, whether directly or indirectly, we give our thanks. Naturally, the authors alone accept the responsibility for any mistakes that may appear in the book.

Introduction

How much lighter is light industry than heavy industry? Is there a difference between an advertising sign and a business sign? Are the terms *floodplain*, *flood hazard area*, and *flood fringe area* interchangeable? The answers to these questions obviously depend on how we define our terms. Like it or not, all professional fields develop a language of their own. These "words of art" have meanings not anticipated by Webster. The purpose of *The Latest Illustrated Book of Development Definitions*, therefore, is to define some of the more common planning, development, and environmental terms.

THE PURPOSE OF DEFINITIONS

Webster defines *definition* as "a word or phrase expressing the essential nature of a person or thing or class of persons or of things, a statement of the meaning of a word or word group."[1] But definitions do more, and when used in complex legal documents such as zoning ordinances or other development regulations, they have a threefold purpose:[2]

1. *They simplify the text.* By defining our terms, it is possible to combine into a single word long phrases, lists of words, or similar terms that, from a zoning or control point of view, may be treated alike. For example, rather than repeat *application for site plan approval*, *permission to build in a floodplain*, *soil removal application*, or *application for subdivision* in an ordinance regulating development, the phrase *application for development* can be defined to mean all of the preceding terms. Similarly, the term *manufacturing* is defined to mean:

   > *Establishments engaged in the mechanical or chemical transformation of materials or substances into new products, including the assembling of component parts, the creation of products, and the blending of materials such as lubricating oils, plastics, resins, or liquors.*

   Think how long an ordinance would be if the definiens (the words used to describe the term to be defined) had to be repeated throughout the ordinance.

2. *Definitions precisely establish the meaning of a word or term that may be subject to differing interpretations.* The precise definition eliminates ambiguity and vagueness. It focuses on the essential elements of a word or phrase and clearly marks off and limits its application or interpretation. For example, a zone may permit light industrial uses. Everyone knows what light industry is—right? Industry is—well, work. Or is it manufacturing, and is warehousing included? Webster has five definitions of industry, and the Standard Industrial Classification system (now replaced by the North American Industry Classification System, or NAICS) includes retailing, finance, and real estate under the broad definition of industry. So it is not quite that apparent, and even experts can impart different meanings to the word.

   If we consider defining *industry* difficult, we must acknowledge the equally difficult problem of defining *light* in conjunction with it. Does *light* refer to the end product, the raw material, or the machines used in the process? Or does it refer to something else entirely?

   By precisely defining *light industry* in an ordinance, we eliminate the vagueness and ambiguity that, at best, result in confusion, and, at worst, end up in costly lawsuits and delays.

3. *Definitions translate technical terms into usable and understandable terminology.* Definitions enable us to convert sometimes abstract technical terms into meaningful standards to control and guide development. For instance, returning to our favorite example, the word *light* as used in *light industry* may be defined in terms of a number of variables, such as trip generation, bulk controls, and nuisance characteristics.[3] Each of these terms requires further definition to make the original *light industry* term meaningful and enforceable.

   Thus, one nuisance characteristic may be smoke emission, and the defined characteristic of *light industry* in terms of smoke emission is that the smoke density cannot exceed a certain level on the Ringlemann Chart, or some other authoritative standard, for measuring smoke density. Another nuisance characteristic is noise, and *light industry* can be further defined in terms of the maximum noise level as measured at the lot line.

WHAT DEFINITIONS ARE NOT

Given that definitions simplify, clarify, and translate, it might be wise to point out what definitions should not be. The most important limitation is that the definition should not contain the control elements or standards that regulate the defined word or phrase.

For example, most ordinances attempt to define home occupations in terms of the standards or controls under which the home occupation can be established. These controls usually include the percentage of floor area that can be occupied, limitations on nonresident employees, parking requirements, lot sizes, and sign controls. These controls belong in the body of the ordinance and may vary depending on the zone in which the home occupation is permitted. To locate the standards in the definition precludes this flexibility. Another example of misplaced standards is illustrated in our previously cited *light industry* example. The recommended definition of *light industry* reads as follows:

> **INDUSTRY, LIGHT**   Industrial uses that meet the performance standards, bulk controls, and other requirements contained in this ordinance.

The ordinance then spells out the performance standards and bulk controls to which *light industry* must conform. In fact, as illustrated below, the controls on *medium industry* and *heavy industry* also could be included, and the definition of *medium industry* and *heavy industry* need not be substantially different from *light industry*.[4]

A typical control chart, which would be part of the zoning chapter, might read as follows:

Control Elements, Industry	Light Industry	Medium Industry	Heavy Industry
MINIMUM LOT SIZE	No minimum	5 Acres	10 Acres
MAXIMUM LOT SIZE	5 Acres	10 Acres	No limit
MAXIMUM FAR	0.5	1.0	2.0
MAXIMUM BUILDING HEIGHT	2 Stories/30'	4 Stories/40'	6 Stories/60'
MAXIMUM NUMBER OF VEHICLE TRIPS PER PEAK HOUR	100	300	No limit
MAXIMUM NOISE LEVEL	70 dBA	75 dBA	82 dBA
MAXIMUM SMOKE DENSITY ON RINGLEMANN CHART	#1	#1	#2
VIBRATION	None permitted beyond building wall	None permitted beyond zone line	None permitted beyond zone line
AIR QUALITY	50% of maximum allowed by state law	75% of maximum allowed by state law	As permitted by state law
BUFFERS	25' around property line	40' around property line	50' around property line

Note: The list of control elements noted above is not complete, and standards suggested are for illustration purposes only. The chart does illustrate the point: The definition is only a few lines and simple; the standard in the ordinance may be long and detailed. We would also point out that some states do not permit a local ordinance to impose more stringent standards than permitted in the state law. This may be true of noise or air-quality standards.

Definitions also should not run counter to the generally accepted meaning of words and phrases. As pointed out, "If it quacks like a duck, walks like a duck . . . it must be a duck." Very often this problem manifests itself in a negative manner. A zoning ordinance may establish a retail commercial zone and then exclude an obvious retail use because of local pressures, fear of competition, or perceived impacts. The point is that the generally accepted meaning of words and phrases should not be radically altered in an ordinance. Cox (2003, p. 114) quotes a New Jersey case—*Essex County Retail, etc., v. Newark, etc. Beverage Control*, 77 N.J. Super. 70, 77 (App. Div. 1962):

> *Ordinances are to receive a reasonable construction and application, to serve the apparent legislative purpose. We will not depart from the plain meaning of language which is free of ambiguity, for an ordinance must be construed according to the ordinary meaning of its words and phrases. These are to be taken in the ordinary or popular sense, unless it plainly appears that they are used in a different sense.*

Similarly, common words and phrases often take on a specific meaning in a technical field, and these may differ substantially from the generally accepted or public definition. Some examples are *affordable housing*, *cellar*, *basement*, or *home occupation*. The courts also may restrict or expand commonly accepted definitions. The best illustration is the word *family*, which recent state court decisions have expanded to include an unlimited number of nonrelated individuals living as a single housekeeping unit.

REAL VERSUS NOMINAL DEFINITIONS

The American Planning Association's Planning Advisory Service (PAS) Report No. 72, *Zoning Ordinance Definitions* (1955), contains an excellent discussion on real and nominal definitions. It defines a nominal definition as " . . . one adopted more or less arbitrarily but which need not be a true description of the object denoted" (p. 8). A real definition attempts to describe precisely the object, use, or term.

Real definitions are preferred but are very often difficult to achieve. For example, the term *density* may be defined as the number of dwelling units per acre of land. For control or regulation purposes, it requires a further clarification to determine whether it is a net figure (excluding certain classes or types of land) or a gross figure (inclusive of the entire area within the described boundaries). Thus, the real definition of density requires two (or even more) nominal definitions to be utilized effectively in the ordinance.

To avoid the problem of whether a definition is real or nominal, most zoning or development ordinances usually preface the definition section with a phrase similar to the following: *Unless the context clearly indicates a different meaning, for the purposes of this ordinance, the following words and terms shall be defined as follows.*

SOME GENERAL OBSERVATIONS ABOUT
DEFINITIONS IN DEVELOPMENT ORDINANCES

1. *Don't define it if it is not used in the ordinance.* There are two schools of thought on whether to include a word or phrase that is not subsequently included in the ordinance. For example, in a rural farming municipality, should the term *high-rise apartment* be defined? Conversely, in a built-up urban area, should the term *farm* be defined?

Many drafters believe that if there is a possibility that the phrase will be used in the future, it should be included. The authors have a different opinion. If it is not used, either as a permitted use or one specifically excluded, it should not be defined. The reason is that it may confuse the intent of the framers. If high-rise apartments are not permitted, then there is no reason to include that term anywhere in the ordinance.[5] In addition, where there may be a question as to the intent of whether or not a particular use is allowed in a zone, the fact that it is defined gives credence to the position that the intent was to allow the use.

2. *Use federal, state, or county definitions if available.* More and more categories of land use are no longer under local control, or they may require federal, state, or county licenses or approvals even when the municipality exercises location control. To avoid conflicts, the local definition should agree with the "higher" definition, to the extent possible. It also more clearly defines the intent of the framers in allowing a specific type of use or activity in a zone. For example, all states license schools. If the local intent is to permit elementary schools in residential neighborhoods, then the definition can be "any school licensed by the State and which meets the State requirements for elementary education." This eliminates private business schools or vocational schools. County requirements and definitions relating to roads and streets are particularly appropriate for inclusion in local development codes. One word of caution, however. What may be appropriate on a federal or state level, and defined as such, may be inappropriate on a local level. This is particularly true of public utilities and essential services.

3. *Use nationally accepted definitions if available.* We noted in the introduction to the second edition of this book (*The New Illustrated Book of Development Definitions,* 1993) that, at that time, the best single source of use definitions was the *Standard Industrial Classification Manual.*[6] The SIC grouped all land-use activities in a series of categories from very broad activity classes (residential, manufacturing, trade, services, and so on) to very specific and detailed land-use categories. The SIC has been replaced by the North American Industry Classification System (NAICS).[7] It classifies business establishments into 20 two-digit broad categories as compared with the 10 divisions in the old SIC. The 20 broad categories are then further subdivided into 3-, 4-, 5-, and 6-digit categories. A total of 1,170 different industries and business activities are identified. It is

important to keep in mind that the NAICS defines uses; zoning controls are needed to regulate scale, intensity, and impacts.

4. *Words should be defined within the context of the legislative intent of the zone district and by the other examples of uses permitted in the district.* While these limitations may seem obvious, applicants may attempt to use uncommon or rare permutations of words in order to establish the legality of other uses. For example, a residential zone permitting single-family detached houses, home occupations, and studios as principal permitted uses does not contemplate professional office buildings or motion picture studios if one considers the legislative intent of the zone (residential) or the context of home occupations and studios in terms of scale and uses normally permitted in a single-family residential district.

5. *Legal and technical input is necessary in preparing definitions for development ordinances.* Legal review is needed to ensure that the definition does not run afoul of state or federal laws or counter to court decisions. Engineering, architectural, and environmental review is needed for definitions encompassing those fields.

SUMMARY

To summarize, and using in part the previously referenced PAS Report No. 72:

1. The term being defined

   a. Must be exactly equivalent to the definition.

   b. Should not appear in the definition.

   c. Cannot be defined by a synonym.

   d. Should not be defined by other indefinite or ambiguous terms.

2. Definitions phrased in positive terms are preferable to definitions in negative terms.

3. Definitions should not include standards, measurements, or other control regulations.

4. Anything not specifically included in a definition is automatically excluded.

5. A defined term can have none other but the defined meaning throughout the entire ordinance.

6. If a group of objects is being divided into two or more groups by definitions, be sure that all members of the group are included in one or the other of the groups.

7. Use particular care in the grammatical construction of definitions.

8. Do not define terms that are not used in the ordinance.

9. Check definitions in related local ordinances and make sure they do not conflict.

10. Use county, state, or federal definitions where appropriate.

11. Use standard definitions from national organizations or agencies when they are available.

12. Words can be further defined in context with other examples or in terms of the legislative intent of the zone where located.

13. Legal and technical review is needed to ensure the legality of terms and their technical correctness.

Notes

1. *Webster's Third New International Dictionary* (Springfield, MA: G. & C. Merriam Co., 1976).

2. The reader is referred to Planning Advisory Service Report No. 72, *Zoning Ordinance Definitions* (American Society of Planning Officials, now American Planning Association, 1955) for a more detailed discussion on the theory of zoning definitions. The material on the objectives of definitions is adopted from that publication.

3. It is not defined in terms of the end product, raw material, or the size of machines used in the process. See *Comment* under "light industry" in the text.

4. A municipality might want to allow outdoor storage in heavy industrial districts and amend the light industry definition accordingly.

5. The one exception may be in an ordinance that lists prohibited uses; then the definition of the prohibited use becomes important. Prohibitive-use ordinances generally are being replaced by permissive ordinances since, among other reasons, no ordinance could possibly list all the excluded uses.

6. *Standard Industrial Classification Manual* (Office of Management and Budget, Statistical Policy Division. Washington, DC: Government Printing Office, 1987).

7. North American Industry Classification System (NAICS) (Washington, DC: Executive Office of the President, Office of Management and Budget, 1997).

Abbreviations and Acronyms

Abbreviations and acronyms used in the definitions and comments.

AADT	average annual daily traffic
AASHTO	American Association of State Highway and Transportation Officials
ADT	average daily traffic
AICP	American Institute of Certified Planners
ANSI	American National Standards Institute
APA	American Planning Association
ASTM	ASTM International
	(formerly ASTM [American Society for Testing and Materials])
ATM	automated teller machine
ATV	all-terrain vehicle
B&B	bed-and-breakfast
BMP	best management practice
BOCA	Buildings Officials and Code Administrators (national building code)
	(*Editor's note:* In 1994, the International Code Council [**ICC**] was established, combining three organizations: **BOCA**, **ICBO** [International Conference of Building Officials], and **SBCCI** [Southern Building Code Congress International].)
BOD	biological oxygen demand
CAFO	concentrated animal feeding operation
CBD	central business district
CCRC	continuing care retirement community
CFS	cubic feet per second
CO	certificate of occupancy
CRDD	community residences for the developmentally disabled
dBA	A-weighted sound level
dB	decibel
DRI	development of regional impact
DO	dissolved oxygen
EIS	environmental impact statement
EMF	electromagnetic field
EPA	Environmental Protection Agency

FAR	floor area ratio
FCC	Federal Communications Commission
FIA	fiscal impact analysis
FIRM	flood insurance rate map
FIRE	finance, insurance, and real estate
GDP	general development plan
GFA	gross floor area
GHz	gigahertz
GIS	geographic information system
GLA	gross leasable area
Hz	hertz
HOV	high-occupancy vehicle
HUD	U.S. Department of Housing and Urban Development
ICF	intermediate care facility
IES	Illuminating Engineering Society
ITE	Institute of Transportation Engineers
ITS	Intelligent Transportation Systems
KHz	kilohertz
kV/m	kilovolts per meter
LRT	light rail transit
LUI	land-use intensity
MG	milligauss
MHz	megahertz
MSA	metropolitan statistical area
MXD	mixed-use development
NAICS	North American Industry Classification System
NEPA	National Environmental Policy Act
NRI	Natural Resources Inventory
NRPA	National Recreation and Park Association
ORV	off-road vehicle
PAS	Planning Advisory Service
PCD	planned commercial development
PD	planned development
PID	planned industrial development
PURD	planned-unit residential development

RHCF	residential health-care facility
ROW	right-of-way
RSIS	(NJ) Residential Site Improvement Standards
SID	special improvement district
SRO	single-room occupancy
TCC	technical coordinating committee
TDR	transfer of development rights
TLR	transit, light rail
TMA	transportation management association
TND	traditional neighborhood development
TOD	transit-oriented development
WQMP	water quality management plan

The *Latest* Illustrated Book of

Book of

DEVELOPMENT

DEFINITIONS

NEW EXPANDED EDITION

A

ABANDONED VEHICLE   *See* MOTOR VEHICLE, ABANDONED.

ABANDONMENT   The relinquishment of property, or a cessation of the use of the property, by the owner or lessee without any intention of transferring rights to the property to another owner or of resuming the use of the property.

Comment: In zoning, abandonment of a nonconforming use requires (1) a discontinuance of the use and (2) an intent to abandon (*Shack v. Trumble,* 28 N.J. 40 [1958]; *Marino v. Mayor and Council of Norwood,* 77 N.J. Super. 587, L.D. [1963]). Since intent is often difficult to prove, many zoning ordinances sidestep the issue by stating that a nonconforming use not exercised for a continuous period of time (one year, for example) cannot be resumed. Nonuse may not be enough, however, and absent any significant changes to suggest an intent to abandon the nonconforming use, the nonconforming rights remain. (Cox 2003) Conversion of a nonconforming use to a conforming one, though, is always indicative of an intent to abandon the use.

ABATEMENT   The method of reducing the degree and intensity of pollution.

ABATTOIR   A place where livestock are killed and prepared for distribution to butcher shops and food markets.

Comment: An abattoir is a very intensive use, often requiring a rail siding. It is usually a 24-hour operation, noisy and often odorous, with special solid and septic waste considerations. Some abattoirs have small retail operations selling directly to consumers.

ABSORPTION   (1) The penetration of one substance into or through another; (2) the length of time it takes for a product or real estate to be sold or rented.

Comment: Absorption in development terms is critical in determining whether a project is economically viable. Developers often speak of absorption rates of so many dwelling units (by type) per year or the square footage of floor area rented or leased over a fixed period of time.

ABSORPTION BED   A large pit or system of trenches containing coarse ag-
OR FIELD   gregate and distribution pipe through which the septic tank effluent may seep into the surrounding soil. (Toenjes 1989)

ABUT

To physically touch or border on; or to share a common property line but not overlap. *See* ADJOINING LOT OR LAND; CONTIGUOUS.

ABUTMENT

(1) A structure that supports the end of a bridge or arch; (2) the side of an earth bank that supports a dam. (Toenjes 1989)

ACCELERATION LANE

An added roadway lane that permits integration and merging of slower-moving vehicles into the main vehicular stream.

Comment: Frequently used in connection with the exit from a major traffic generator. *See Figure 1.*

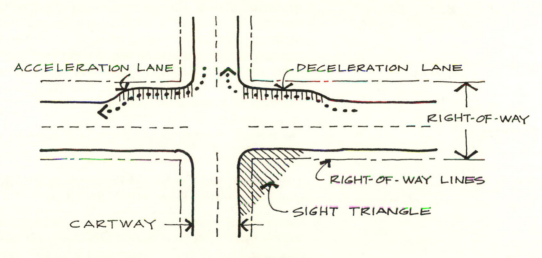

FIGURE 1

ACCESS

A way or means of approach to provide vehicular or pedestrian physical entrance to a property.

ACCESS CLASSIFICATION

A hierarchical rating system for streets and highways based on function, environment, and traffic characteristics, used to determine applicable access standards. *See* ACCESS CODE.

Comment: Part of a growing number of regulations governing access to state highways and, where applicable, to local and county roads. Access standards may include a minimum spacing of distance between driveways.

ACCESS CODE

The highway access management code adopted pursuant to appropriate legislation. *See* ACCESS CLASSIFICATION;

3

ACCESS LEVEL; ACCESS MANAGEMENT PLAN; ACCESS PERMIT; ALTERNATE WORK ARRANGEMENT PROGRAMS; EMPLOYEE TRANSPORTATION COORDINATOR; MAJOR TRAFFIC GENERATOR; PEAK-HOUR TRAFFIC; RATIONAL NEXUS; SIGNIFICANT INCREASE IN TRAFFIC; TRAFFIC GROWTH RATE; TRAFFIC IMPACT STUDY; TRANSPORTATION DEMAND MANAGEMENT PLAN; TRANSPORTATION MANAGEMENT ASSOCIATION.

Comment: Where permitted by states, municipalities and counties can adopt access codes providing for access management plans and standards of access to local and county roads.

ACCESS LEVEL

The allowable turning movements to and from access points on a highway segment based on the highway access classification.

ACCESS MANAGEMENT PLAN

A plan showing the design of access for every lot on a highway segment developed jointly by the state, the municipality in which the highway is located, and the county, if a county road intersects the segment.

Comment: In states with highway access regulations, counties and municipalities are permitted to enact access management plans for various categories of roads under their jurisdiction. These plans may include the minimum distance between road access points and the roadway design.

ACCESS PERMIT

A permit issued by the appropriate governmental agency for the construction, maintenance, and use of a driveway or public street or highway connecting to a highway.

ACCESS POINT

The location of the intersection of a highway or street or driveway with the highway.

ACCESS POINT OFFSET

The distance between the centerlines of access points on opposite sides of undivided highways and the distance between the centerlines of an access point and a median opening on a divided highway. *See Figure 2.*

ACCESS ROAD

See STREET, LOCAL.

ACCESSIBLE PRINCIPAL ARTERIAL

A roadway that is part of an interconnected network of continuous routes serving transportation corridors with high traffic volumes and long trips, the primary function of which is to provide safe and efficient service

4

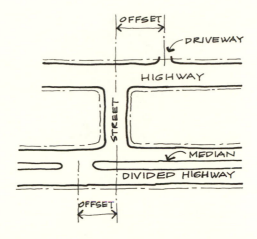

ACCESS POINT OFFSET

FIGURE 2

for major traffic movements in which access is subordinate.

ACCESSIBLE ROUTE

A continuous, unobstructed path connecting all accessible elements and spaces of a building or facility.

Comment: Accessible routes are required as part of the Americans with Disabilities Act of 1990. *See* AMERICANS WITH DISABILITIES ACT (ADA).

ACCESSORY APARTMENT

An independent dwelling unit that has been added onto, or created within, a single-family house.

Comment: The accessory apartment has separate kitchen, bathing, and sleeping areas. Accessory apartments are often occupied by elderly persons, with the main structure occupied by close relatives or friends. This option provides economic, social, and security benefits, since it allows older people to live independently but close to people who are concerned about their well-being.

Accessory apartments can be listed as permitted use in residential areas. Regulations vary from municipality to municipality but usually are concerned with health and safety issues, as well as maintaining the basic character of the neighborhood. These objectives can often be achieved by using designated minimum and maximum floor areas for the apartments, requiring off-street parking, and prohibiting any change in the basic single-family appearance of the structure.

5

ACCESSORY DWELLING

A dwelling unit either attached to a single-family principal dwelling or located on the same lot and having an independent means of access. *See* ACCESSORY APARTMENT.

Comment: An accessory dwelling differs from an accessory apartment in that, if permitted by local ordinance, it has a separate means of access and can be a separate structure on the lot.

ACCESSORY STRUCTURE

A structure detached from a principal building located on the same lot and customarily incidental and sub–ordinate to the principal building or use. *See Figure 3.*

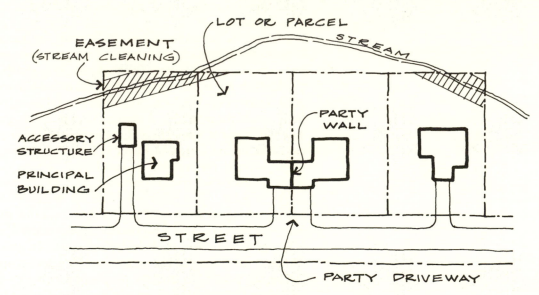

FIGURE 3

Comment: The accessory structure must be on the same lot as the principal structure unless the ordinance specifically permits it to be located on another lot. An example of this is a parking structure for a commercial establishment required to be located within a certain radius but not necessarily on the same lot as the establishment. It is desirable to place limits on the number and size of accessory structures, particularly in residential areas.

ACCESSORY USE

A use of land or of a building or portion thereof customarily incidental and subordinate to the principal use of the land or building and located on the same lot with the principal use.

Comment: A New Jersey case noted the following characteristics of an accessory use: commonly, habitually, and by long practice as being established or reasonably associated with the primary use. (*Charley Brown of Chatham v. Board of Adjustment*, 202 N.J. Super. 312, App. Div. [1985]) What constitutes an accessory use changes over time. For example, many ordinances now define a child-care facility as an accessory use to large-scale office or industrial buildings. Other facilities such as bank branches, gyms, restaurants, and gift shops, which primarily serve the employees in major office developments (and have the added benefit of reducing lunchtime vehicular trips), may also be defined as accessory uses.

It may be advisable to physically limit the accessory use to prevent it from becoming the principal use. For example, a retail outlet in a warehouse, selling those products stored in the warehouse, could be considered an accessory use. The local ordinance should limit the floor area of the retail use. A reasonable standard might be a maximum of 5 percent of the warehouse floor area, or 5,000 square feet, whichever is less. Other limits might include the number of employees. Where the accessory use is not confined to a specific physical area or the number of employees is difficult to establish, the approving agency might have to determine that the planning impacts of the proposed accessory use are, in fact, significantly less than the principal use. In other words, if the principal use generates 100 vehicle trips during the peak hour, and the proposed accessory use generates 125 trips, the accessory use can no longer be considered an accessory use.

ACCLIMATIZATION

The physiological and behavioral adjustments of an organism over time to changes in its environment.

ACCRETION

The creation of land by the recession of a lake or stream or by the gradual deposit of solid material by water.

ACRE

A measure of land containing 43,560 square feet.

Comment: Many ordinances use a "builder's acre" of 40,000 square feet. Other ordinances define a "net acre," which excludes existing rights-of-way, public use area dedications, easements, and similar limitations to development. *See* NET AREA OF LOT.

ACRE-FOOT

The volume of water 1-foot deep covering an acre of land.

Comment: This term is often used in defining storm or potable water storage capacity.

ACTIVATED SLUDGE PROCESS

The process of using biologically active sewage sludge to hasten the breakdown of organic matter in raw sewage during secondary waste treatment.

ACTIVE RECREATION

See RECREATION, ACTIVE.

ADAPTATION

A change in the structure or habit of an organism resulting from an adjustment to its environment.

ADAPTIVE REUSE

The development of a new use for an older building or for a building originally designed for a special or specific purpose.

Comment: Adaptive reuse is a particularly useful technique for preserving older buildings of historic or architectural significance. It also applies to the conversion of other special-use structures, such as gas stations, train stations, or school buildings, that are no longer needed for their original use.

ADDITION

(1) A structure added to the original structure at some time after the completion of the original; (2) an extension or increase in floor area or height of a building or structure.

Comment: "At some time after" is usually defined as after the certificate of occupancy has been issued for the original structure.

ADJACENT LAND

See ADJOINING LOT OR LAND.

ADJOINING LOT OR LAND

A lot or parcel of land that shares all or part of a common lot line with another lot or parcel of land. *See* ABUT; CONTIGUOUS.

ADMINISTRATIVE OFFICE

An establishment primarily engaged in overall management and general supervisory functions, such as executive, personnel, finance, legal, and sales activities, performed in a single location or building for other branches or divisions of the same company.

Comment: The term "administrative office" is obsolete, given changes in the way business is conducted. Moreover, in terms of impact, there is very little difference between an administrative office or other types of business offices, with the possible exception of a corporate headquarters office. Corporate headquarters offices usually have fewer employees per square foot and more conference rooms than other types of offices, but here again, bottom-line considerations are eliminating these differences as well.

ADMINISTRATIVE OFFICER

The designated governmental official charged with administering land development regulations.

Comment: The administrative officer is often identified as a specific official, such as the municipal clerk, planning commission secretary, or zoning officer. Many land development ordinances will often add in the definition section, "For purposes of this ordinance, the ad–ministrative officer shall be the. . . ."

ADULT BOOKSTORE

See ADULT USE.

ADULT RETIREMENT COMMUNITY

A planned development designed for active older people that emphasizes social and recreational activities but may also provide personal services, limited health facilities, and transportation. *See* RETIREMENT COMMUNITY.

Comment: Dwellings in adult retirement communities are generally for sale, but occasionally rental units are available. Dwellings may be in the form of detached and attached houses, duplexes, or apartments. Activities may include a clubhouse, tennis, golf, swimming, and other recreation resources appropriate for older residents. Services, such as transportation and limited medical care, may also be provided. A manager is usually responsible for the general maintenance and upkeep of the community, and a monthly fee is generally charged for these services. Regulations usually require a certain minimum entrance age. The 1988 amendment to the Federal Fair Housing Act provides some guidance on age restrictions.

ADULT USE

(*Note*: Much of the material used in defining Adult Use and the recommendations on regulations are adapted from Eric Damian Kelly, "Local Regulation of Lawful Sex Businesses," *Land Use Law & Zoning Digest* 51, 9, September 1999; and Eric Damian Kelly and Connie Cooper, *Everything You Always Wanted to Know About Regulating Sex Businesses*, Planning Advisory Service Report No. 495/496, December 2000. The authors are indebted to Professor Kelly and Ms. Cooper, as well as to the American Planning Association, for permission to use the material.)

An establishment consisting of, including, or having the characteristics of any or all of the following:

ADULT BOOKSTORE, NEWSSTAND, VIDEO STORE, OR COMBINATION: An establishment having more than 40 percent of its stock-in-trade, floor area, or display area used for the sale or rental of books, magazines, publications, tapes, or films that are distinguished or characterized by the emphasis on sexually oriented material depicting, describing, or relating to sexual activities or anatomical genital areas.

SEX SHOP: Any establishment offering, for sale or rent, items from any two of the following categories: sexually oriented books, magazines, and videos; leather goods marketed or presented in a context to suggest their use for sexual activities; sexually oriented toys and novelties; or video viewing booths; or an establishment that advertises or holds itself out in any forum as a sexually oriented business.

VIDEO VIEWING BOOTHS: Often referred to as peep shows and characterized by small private booths rented to individuals to view sexually explicit films or tapes.

ADULT MOTION PICTURE THEATER: A building used for presenting films distinguished or characterized by an emphasis on matter depicting, describing, or relating to sexual activities or anatomical genital areas.

ADULT CABARET: An establishment, either with or without a liquor license, offering sexually oriented live entertainment, which may include topless and go-go dancers, strippers, or male or female impersonators.

Comment: As noted earlier, many of the definitions and recommendations on regulations are from Kelly and Cooper's research work. (American Planning Association, Planning Advisory Service Report No. 495/496, 2000) Of particular relevance is the discussion in the report about various court decisions and how they influence the regulation of adult uses.

Kelly and Cooper establish the parameters of regulation of adult uses clearly and unequivocally by stating that ". . . local government clearly can regulate the location of sexually oriented businesses through zoning and, in many states, some or all local governments can also regulate the conduct of the business directly through licensing." (Kelly 1999, p. 3) But they also point out that ". . . some of the products handled by sexually oriented businesses—certain sexually oriented books, magazines, videos, and movies—enjoy First Amendment protection" (Kelly 1999, p. 3).

Some of the regulatory guidelines they suggest are as follows:

1. Dispersal ordinances or similar provisions in local zoning ordinances have been generally found to be legal. These ordinances establish minimum distances between adult uses and between adult uses and other uses such as child-oriented uses, houses of worship, and schools. The minimum distance figures vary from 500 to 1,500 feet. But Kelly points out that if the result is to eliminate all possible sites, the restriction can be considered unreasonable.

2. Licensing is probably the best way to control adult uses with on-premises entertainment. As Kelly (1999, p. 9) notes, " . . . zoning deals well with locational and basic design issues . . . [and] concerns about how customers will act when enjoying entertainment . . . [and] falls squarely within the scope of licensing laws."

3. General and content-neutral regulations have a better chance of being upheld, as opposed to content-based or content-oriented regulations. For example, not all business districts permit movies or cabarets. But trying to bar only sexually oriented movies or adult cabarets from districts that allow other types of movies or cabarets can be risky. Another example is the regulation of hours of operation. Such restrictions may be unreasonable if they apply only to adult uses and not to other uses in the zone.

4. Reasonable operating restrictions covering lighting, monitoring of booths, the age of customers, and displays are usually acceptable. But here again, licensing may be better than zoning to impose these controls.

5. Establishments that allow one-on-one interaction between patrons and employees, such as encounter booths, massage parlors (other than for licensed therapists), and escort services, may not enjoy First Amendment protection. (PAS Report 495/496 cited above) Note that none of the definitions of adult uses list one-on-one interaction activities. If a municipality wants to exclude such activities, it probably should list them as prohibited activities.

6. A clear delineation should be made between adult uses that feature predominantly on-site entertainment (such as movies and cabarets) and relatively benign uses

11

(such as adult bookstores or shops). In other words, there are good reasons to prohibit all types of on-premises entertainment in neighborhood business zones because of their potential adverse impact on the neighborhood. But it would be difficult to make the same case for a bookstore selling or renting adult books or tapes.

Finally, Kelly (1999, p. 9) makes a strong case that "findings in support of the action are important" and should be undertaken at the time the ordinance is enacted and not when the lawsuit is filed. The findings should clearly demonstrate that the proposed action is the minimum necessary to achieve the purposes. While local studies are best, material detailing the experience of other communities on the issue can also be used.

ADVANCED WASTE TREATMENT

Wastewater treatment beyond the secondary or biological state that includes removal of nutrients, such as phosphates and nitrates, and a high percentage of suspended solids.

Comment: Advanced waste treatment, known as tertiary treatment, is the "polishing state" of wastewater treatment and produces a high-quality effluent.

ADVERSE DRAINAGE CONDITION

The absence of stormwater maintenance facilities that would provide adequately for stormwater runoff, or that would prevent flooding, erosion, silting, or other damaging effects to a street, road, drainage structure, or property, or that would remove the threat of such damage. *See* STORMWATER MAINTENANCE FACILITIES.

ADVERSE IMPACT

A condition that creates, imposes, aggravates, or leads to inadequate, impractical, unsafe, or unhealthy conditions on a site proposed for development or on off-tract property or facilities.

Comment: Adverse impacts usually relate to circulation, drainage, erosion, potable water, sewage collection, and treatment. They may also relate to lighting and glare, aesthetics, quality of life, and impact on the environment.

ADVERSE POSSESSION

The right of an occupant to acquire title to a property after having continuously and openly used and maintained a property over a statutory period of time without protest from the owner of record.

ADVERTISING DISPLAY

See SIGN.

12

AERATION

The process of being supplied or impregnated with air.

Comment: Aeration is used in wastewater treatment to foster biological and chemical purification.

AERIAL MAP

A map created from a process involving the taking of photographs from the air with predetermined reference points marked on the ground.

AEROBIC

Life or processes that can occur only in the presence of oxygen.

AEROSOL

A suspension of liquid or solid particles in the air.

AESTHETIC

The perception of artistic elements or elements in the natural or created environment that are pleasing to the eye.

AESTHETIC ZONING

Regulations designed to preserve or improve building and/or site development design so as to reflect community design goals and objectives.

Comment: Planning has always had an aesthetic orientation. The origins of city planning were in the City Beautiful movement beginning with the 1893 World's Columbian Exposition held in Chicago. While early court decisions failed to sustain aesthetics as the sole basis for the exercise of the police power, later cases suggest a more pragmatic approach. In *City of Lake Wales v. Lamar Advertising Association of Lakeland*, 414 So.2d 1030 (Fla. 1982), the court noted: "Zoning solely for aesthetic purposes is an ideal whose time has come; it is not outside the police power." A New Jersey case (*State v. Miller*, 83 N.J. 402, A.2d 821, 1980) upheld aesthetics as a legitimate goal of zoning and ". . . no longer a matter of luxury or indulgence." In fact, the New Jersey *Municipal Land Use Law* (N.J.S.A. 40:55D-1 et seq.) lists as one of the purposes of the act: "To promote a desirable visual environment through creative development techniques and good civic design and arrangements." Finally, the U.S. Supreme Court in *Berman v. Parker* (348 U.S. 26, 1954) recognized the right of the legislature to determine that beauty is a valid objective of police power authority.

Ordinances that purport to regulate aesthetics, however, often have problems with standards upon which to judge the "aesthetics" of an application, particularly with respect to building design. Unless an area is an official historic district, architectural design control remains difficult to achieve unless ". . . the architectural standard . . . can be objectively administered and judiciously reviewed for arbitrariness, and yet not so confining as to unlawfully inhibit expression through architectural design." (Frizell & Pozycki 1989, p. 117) Even in historic districts, specific standards are required to allow applicants to know in advance the standard of review.

A well-prepared community design plan that provides supporting data and policy guidelines for design-related regulations offers the best chance for such ordinances to be upheld by the courts. As noted in Planning Advisory Service Report 489/490, "No trend is more clearly defined in planning law than that of courts upholding regulations whose primary basis is aesthetics. Only a few die-hard states do not permit local governments to adopt aesthetic-based police power regulations. While local governments must still proceed carefully in enacting and implementing aesthetic-based laws . . . they generally have great leeway in acting to protect community aesthetics." (American Planning Association, *Aesthetics, Community Character, and the Law,* Planning Advisory Service Report 489/490, 1999) *See* ARCHITECTURAL CONTROL; BUILDING MASS; BUILDING SCALE; COMMUNITY DESIGN PLAN; COMPATIBLE DESIGN; DESIGN CONTINUITY; DESIGN FIT; DESIGN REVIEW; DESIGN STANDARDS; DEVELOPMENT CONTEXT; HARMONIOUS RELATIONSHIP; HUMAN SCALE; URBAN CONTEXT; VIEW PROTECTION REGULATION.

AFFORDABLE

Housing with a sales price or rent within the means of a low-, middle-, or moderate-income household as defined by state or federal legislation.

Comment: "Affordable" may vary by state. In New Jersey, for example, affordable housing for moderate-income households is 80 percent of the median family income for a particular area, adjusted for household size and with not more than 30 percent of the income used for rent (including utilities) or 28 percent for purchase (including principal and interest, taxes, condo fees, and insurance). The applicable figure for low-income households is 50 percent of median family income. In Florida, on the other hand, affordable housing is defined as housing capable of being acquired with 30 percent of gross income.

While affordable housing is most often thought of as subsidized housing, this is not necessarily so. Market housing, meeting low- and moderate-income targets, with affordability controls in place, may also qualify.

14

AFFORESTATION

See FORESTRY.

AFTERBURNER

An air pollution abatement device that removes undesirable organic gases through incineration.

AGGRESSIVE SOILS

Soils that may be corrosive to metallic pipe or tubing. (N.J.A.C. 5:21-1.4)

AGRARIAN

Relating to land, particularly agriculture.

AGRICULTURAL BUILDING

A structure on agricultural land designed, constructed, and used to house farm implements, livestock, or agricultural produce or products grown or raised on the premises.

AGRICULTURAL LAND, PRIME

Land that qualifies for a rating as Class I in the U.S. Department of Agriculture (USDA) Soil Conservation Service land-use capability classification.

Comment: Capability classification is the grouping of soils that shows, in a general way, their suitability for various kinds of farming. It is a practical classification based on limitations of the soils, the risk of damage when they are used, and the way they respond to treatment. Capability classes are designated by roman numerals I–VIII. As the numerals increase, they indicate progressively greater limitations and narrower choices for practical use.

The best soils for agricultural use, Classes I and II, are described by the USDA as

Class I: Soils that have few limitations that restrict their use

Class II: Soils that have some limitations that reduce the choice of plants or require moderate conservation practices

The particular soil types for each class are detailed in the County Soil Surveys for each state.

AGRICULTURAL MARKET

See FARM STAND.

AGRICULTURAL POLLUTION

The liquid, gaseous, and solid wastes from all types of farming, including runoff from pesticides, fertilizers, and feedlots, erosion and dust from plowing, animal manure and carcasses, and crop residue and debris.

AGRICULTURAL SERVICES

Establishments primarily engaged in supplying soil preparation services, crop services, landscaping, horticultural services, veterinary and other animal services, and farm labor and management services.

AGRICULTURAL ZONING

Regulations that protect the agricultural land base by limiting nonagricultural uses, prohibiting high-density development, requiring houses to be clustered on small lots, and restricting subdivision of land into parcels that are too small to farm.

Comment: An example of agricultural zoning is in the Pinelands, an environmentally significant area in southern New Jersey. The area is preserved and regulated by the New Jersey Pinelands Commission. Farmers in designated agricultural areas may build only one house unrelated to farming on a 1-acre lot within each 40-acre agricultural section. In 1991, the New Jersey Supreme Court ruled that these regulations did not amount to an unconstitutional confiscation of property because the land could still be used for farming and had not, therefore, been rendered valueless. The Court added that ". . . there exists no constitutional right to the most profitable use of property" and also stated that the unique and ecologically fragile nature of the Pinelands justified the area's special treatment.

Conflicts between farmers and residents of new subdivisions are serious problems and can be expected to increase as new development expands into agricultural areas. Most new residents are attracted to these areas because of the bucolic impression created by farms. However, after moving into their new homes, many find that farming is an intensive industry, conducted mostly outdoors. These new residents find themselves subjected to noise from farm machinery, smells from livestock and animals, dust created by plowing, and chemicals from pesticides and fertilizers. Traffic bottlenecks created by slow-moving farm equipment are not uncommon.

On the other hand, farmers have legitimate complaints resulting from the encroachment of urban development, including having to respond to complaints from neighbors, vandalism to farm equipment, trespassing, and restrictions placed on farming operations.

Many of these problems can be addressed through smart planning and education. Some of the tools available to municipalities are noted below and are more fully discussed in "The Conflict at the Edge" (Thompson 1997a).

BUFFERS: Much of the conflict between farms and residential developments can be avoided by requiring wide buffers between new development and the farms. Minimum buffers would vary by type of farming. For example, the city of Napa, California, requires a minimum of 80 feet from the property line to any dwelling. The local ordinance also requires that at least 15 of the 80 feet be planted with trees, shrubs, berms, or fences. In addition, noise-reducing design and building construction includes window–door orientation and the use of double-pane windows. In San Luis Obispo County, California, buffer distances are 400 to 800 feet for vineyards, 300 to 800 feet for irrigated orchards, and 100 to 400 feet for field crops.

NUISANCE DISCLAIMERS: Disclaimers inform potential purchasers of homes adjacent to or near farms as to what they can expect from normal farming operations. While the disclaimer does not reduce the conflict, it does make it more difficult for the homeowner to claim he or she was not aware of the potential problems. In some cases, the disclaimer is noted on the deed and recorded, so that it becomes part of the official record describing the lot.

LARGE LOT ZONING: This technique is simply to zone land proposed to be preserved for farming into large parcels. This could be as "small" as 6 acres to as large as 40 acres. While this technique works, it often runs afoul of the farmer's ultimate goal of eventually selling out when retirement beckons and "the last crop is blacktop." Alternatives are participation in farmland preservation programs, now available in most states, in which the development rights are purchased, often through a cooperative program using state, county, and local funding, or through lot averaging or cluster planning. *See* CLUSTER SUBDIVISION; LOT AVERAGING.

RIGHT-TO-FARM ORDINANCES: All states have right-to-farm ordinances, which essentially protect farmers from nuisance suits resulting from normal farming operations. These educate the homeowner as to what can be expected in the new environment. Many municipalities require that a copy of the right-to-farm ordinance be made available to prospective purchasers of homes in farm areas.

COMMUNICATION: Laura Thompson (1997a) presents examples in which better communication can mitigate complaints and conflicts. Her article cites programs whereby farmers inform the municipality of plans to fertilize or lay down pesticide and this information is disseminated to surrounding residents, or where farmers inform surrounding residents of plowing and planting schedules.

AGRICULTURE

The production, storage, keeping, harvesting, grading, packaging, processing, boarding, or maintenance, for sale, lease, or personal use, of plants and animals useful to humans, including but not limited to: forages and sod crops; grains and seed crops; dairy animals and dairy products; poultry and poultry products; livestock, including beef cattle, sheep, swine, horses, ponies, mules, or goats or any mutations or hybrids thereof, including the breeding and grazing of any or all of such animals; bees and apiary products; fur animals; trees and forest products; fruits of all kinds, including grapes, nuts, and berries; vegetables; nursery, floral, ornamental, and greenhouse products; or lands devoted to a soil conservation or forestry management program. *See* AGRICULTURAL ZONING; HORSE FARM; HORTICULTURE.

Comment: The definition is contained in the *New Jersey Farmland Assessment Act* (Chapter 48, Laws of 1964) and is broadly applied. It includes intensive agricultural activities, such as feedlot operations, chicken farms, and agribusiness activities, some of which may not be appropriate in all areas. *See* CONCENTRATED ANIMAL FEEDING OPERATION.

The definition does not cover activities that are often connected with farms but are peripheral to the principal activities (for example, horse shows, mazes [in cornfields] and "pick your own"). Mazes and pick-your-own are not particularly intense operations and attract few participants over a short period of time. They can be easily accommodated with some consideration for parking.

Horse shows may take place two to four times a year and include the sale of horses, races, and similar activities. Horse shows can generate crowds of people, vehicles, and animals. Municipalities should decide whether these activities are accessory to the principal farm use or require special permits. The permits can specify the maximum number of shows per year and requirements for review of parking, circulation, and accommodations for crowds.

AGRICULTURE, HOME

The on-site production, principally for use or consumption of the property owner or tenant, of plants, animals, or their products, including, but not limited to, gardening, fruit production, poultry, and livestock production. This does not include the sale of products produced off-site but does include the sale of products produced on-site to others as long as such sales are incidental to the principal use of the property as a residence.

Comment: This definition requires that the agricultural products be produced on-site and that any sales to nonresidents or nontenants be of a minor or incidental use of the property.

AGRITOURISM

Agricultural uses, such as farms, ranches, and vine–yards that, through promotion and advertising, facilities, and activities, seek to attract visitors, guests, and vacationers.

Comment: Agritourism includes dude ranches on active cattle ranches; guest facilities, including eating and sleeping, in vineyards; and summer camps, particularly oriented to children, on active farms. *See* AGRI-CULTURE.

AIR PARK

A planned development that includes an airport, with accessory and support services.

AIR POLLUTION

The presence in the air of contaminants in concentrations beyond the normal dispensive ability of the air that interfere directly or indirectly with health, safety, or comfort or with the full use and enjoyment of property.

AIR POLLUTION EPISODE

The occurrence of abnormally high concentrations of air pollutants, usually resulting from low winds and temperature inversion, that may be accompanied by increases in illness and death. *See* INVERSION.

AIR QUALITY CONTROL REGION

An area designated by the federal government where two or more communities, either in the same or different states, share a common air pollution problem.

AIR QUALITY CRITERIA

The levels of pollution and length of exposure at which adverse effects on health and quality of life occur. *See* CRITERIA POLLUTANT.

AIR QUALITY STANDARDS

The prescribed level of pollutants in the outside air that cannot be exceeded legally during a specified time in a specified geographical area. *See* CRITERIA POLLUTANT.

AIR RIGHTS

The right to use space above ground level.

Comment: Many state enabling acts permit air rights to be shifted from one property to another. Air rights are actually a form of transfer of development rights. New York City's historic preservation program, for example, permits the purchase of air rights over historic structures, which then can be used to increase the height and/or intensity of development on nonhistoric properties. *See* TRANSFER OF DEVELOPMENT RIGHTS.

AIR TRANSPORTATION

Establishments engaged in transportation by air, including airports and flying fields, as well as terminal services.

AIRPORT

A place where aircraft can land and take off, usually equipped with hangars, facilities for refueling and repair, and various accommodations for passengers.

Comment: The U.S. Department of Transportation, in its National Plan of Integrated Airport Systems, defines five basic airport categories that reflect the type of public service provided:

1. PR: commercial service primary

2. CM: commercial service nonprimary

3. CR: commercial service airport that also serves as a reliever

4. RL: reliever airport

5. GA: general aviation airport

The five basic categories are further defined by role, which, in turn, affects the aircraft that can be accommodated and the roles and markets to be served.

From a zoning and planning perspective, allowing airports in a particular zone district calls for some consideration as to the type of airport, which, in turn, requires different types of accessory services or uses and has widely differing impacts on the municipality. *See* AIRPORT ZONING.

AIRPORT HAZARD

Any structure, vegetation, or use of land that would exceed federal airport obstruction standards or is otherwise hazardous to the landing or takeoff of aircraft.

AIRPORT ZONING

A specific set of controls intended to protect the integrity of an airport, its airspace, and its environs. *See Figure 4.*

Comment: While the major control is the height of buildings or structures near airports, with permitted maximums increasing with the distance from runways,

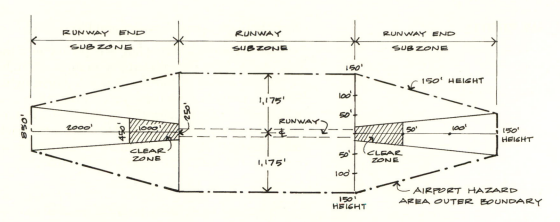

AIRPORT HAZARD AREA HEIGHT RESTRICTIONS

FIGURE 4

airport zoning also limits electronic interference with navigational equipment and some types of uses, primarily places of human assembly, to reduce accident risks. Many communities have, in addition, made special provisions for airport surroundings by zoning them for compatible uses (for example, warehousing, industry, and certain commercial uses) and excluding residential uses and places of assembly. (American Planning Association, *The Language of Zoning,* Planning Advisory Service Report No. 322, 1976)

AIRPORT-RELATED USE

A use that supports airport operations, including, but not limited to, aircraft repair and maintenance, flight instruction, and aircraft chartering.

AISLE

The traveled way by which cars enter and depart parking spaces. *See Figure 68.*

ALL-TERRAIN VEHICLE (ATV)

See VEHICLE, OFF-ROAD.

ALLEY

A service roadway providing a secondary means of access to abutting property and not intended for general traffic circulation. *See Figure 87.*

Comment: Found in many older, grid-pattern neighborhoods and providing access to garages, alleys have now found favor in traditional neighborhood designs by eliminating front-lot driveways, thereby improving the appearance of small lot layouts. In residential areas they are called "rear lanes" and are paved only in the center part of the right-of-way to a width of 10 to 12 feet. Commercial-area alleys tend to be paved over the entire right-of-way.

ALLUVION

That increase of land area on a shore or bank of a stream or sea by the force of the water, as by a current or by waves, that is so gradual that it is impossible to determine how much is added at each moment of time. *See* ACCRETION.

ALTERATION

Any change or rearrangement in the supporting members of an existing building, such as bearing walls, columns, beams, girders, or interior partitions, as well as any change in doors, windows, means of ingress or egress, or any enlargement to or diminution of a building or structure, whether horizontally or vertically, or the moving of a building or structure from one location to another. *See* ALTERATION, INCIDENTAL.

Comment: The definition of alteration is important because most ordinances do not permit any expansion of a nonconforming structure or use. All expansions are alterations, but not all alterations are expansions. This definition excludes normal repairs and maintenance, such as painting or roof replacement, but includes more substantial changes. *See* STRUCTURAL ALTERATION.

ALTERATION, INCIDENTAL

Modifications to an existing structure that are of a cosmetic nature, replacement of utilities, or rearrangement of non–load-bearing partitions.

ALTERNATE LIVING ARRANGEMENT

An arrangement in which households maintain private rooms yet share kitchen and bathroom facilities, central heat, and common areas. *See* SINGLE-ROOM OCCUPANCY.

Comment: Alternate living arrangements include boarding homes, residential health care facilities, group homes for the developmentally disabled and mentally ill, and congregate living arrangements.

ALTERNATE WORK ARRANGEMENT PROGRAMS

Programs that vary the traditional workday arrival and departure times for employees to avoid peak-hour congestion.

Comment: These programs may include flextime, compressed workweek, staggered hours, and job sharing.

ALTERNATIVE ACCESS

The ability to enter a highway indirectly through another improved roadway instead of from a direct driveway entrance from the principal highway frontage.

AMATEUR RADIO TOWER   *See* TOWER, AMATEUR RADIO.

AMBIANCE   The character of an area, as determined by building scale and design, amount and type of activity, intensity of use, location and design of open space, and related factors that influence the perceived quality of the environment.

AMBIENT AIR   Any unconfined portion of the atmosphere; the outside air.

AMBIENT AIR STANDARD   A maximum permissible air pollution standard. *See* CRITERIA POLLUTANT.

AMBIENT NOISE LEVEL   The normal or existing level of noise from existing conditions or activities at a given location.

AMBULATORY CARE FACILITY   *See* CLINIC.

AMENITY   A natural or created feature that enhances the aesthetic quality or visual appeal or makes more attractive or satisfying a particular property, place, or area.

AMERICANS WITH DISABILITIES ACT (ADA)   A 1990 federal law designed to bring disabled Americans into the economic mainstream by providing them equal access to jobs, transportation, public facilities, and services. ("Zoning and the Americans with Disabilities Act," *Zoning News*, February 1992) *See* ACCESSIBLE ROUTE; AREA OF RESCUE ASSISTANCE; CLEAR FLOOR SPACE; DISABILITY; MAJOR LIFE ACTIVITIES. *See Figure 5.*

Comment: The ADA has had a significant impact on planning and zoning activities, including public services, public accommodations, and commercial facilities. For example, every public meeting must be accessible. As the previously cited *Zoning News* states, a building or facility is accessible if it has no barriers to people with disabilities. This may mean a central location with public transportation, accessible rest rooms, signage, materials, and information a visually impaired person can use, and meetings in which people with hearing and speech impairments can participate and communicate. Posters announcing public hearings can be mounted in senior citizen housing and meal sites, group homes, and other public centers to reach more people with disabilities.

The *Zoning News* article also made an important point about zoning ordinances. Most communities continue to produce zoning ordinances only in written

23

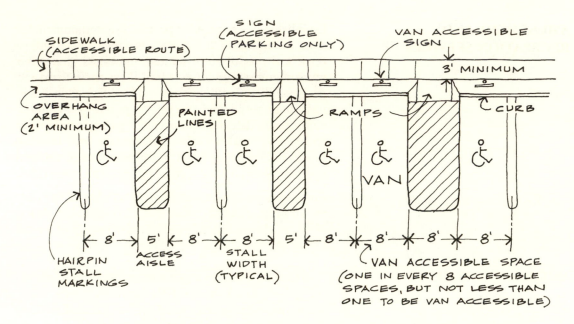

ACCESSIBLE PARKING SPACE STANDARDS

FIGURE 5

form, with limited availability to the public. Zoning administrators need to think carefully both about how zoning ordinances are published and about which citizens are excluded when the city is creating, modifying, and reviewing the ordinance. Under the ADA, other methods of communication must be adopted. Some cities use computer databases with a publicly accessible terminal to allow persons with disabilities to comment on proposed ordinance modifications. Cities will have to apply creative alternatives so that people with disabilities can read and use important documents, such as the city's zoning ordinance.

AMORTIZATION

A method of eliminating nonconforming uses by requiring the termination of the nonconforming use after a specified period of time.

Comment: The legality of requiring the amortization of nonconforming uses remains unclear. The most likely candidates for amortization are junkyards and signs that, in addition to not having a great deal of capital investment, are highly visible nuisances that may have significant adverse impacts on surrounding uses. *See* SIGN, NONCONFORMING.

AMUSEMENT AND RECREATION SERVICES

Establishments engaged in providing entertainment for a fee, including such activities as dance halls, studios, theatrical productions, bands, orchestras, and other musical entertainment; bowling alleys and billiard and pool establishments; commercial facilities, such as arenas, rings, rinks, and racetracks; public golf courses; coin-operated devices, amusement parks, membership sports and health clubs, amusement and bathing beaches, swimming pools, riding academies, carnival operations, expositions, game parlors, and horse rides.

Comment: The above definition is very broad and covers all types of amusement and recreational facilities. Many of the facilities listed are obviously not suited for all types of zones.

AMUSEMENT ARCADE

A primarily outdoor area or open structure, open to the public, that contains coin-operated games, rides, shows, and similar entertainment facilities and devices. *See* RECREATION FACILITY.

AMUSEMENT, COMMERCIAL, INDOOR

Amusement and recreation services that are wholly enclosed in a building.

AMUSEMENT, COMMERCIAL, OUTDOOR

Amusement and recreation services where any portion of the activity takes place outside a building.

AMUSEMENT MACHINE OR DEVICE

Any coin- or token-operated machine or device, whether mechanical, electrical, or electronic, that is ready for play by the insertion of a coin or token and operated by the public for use as a game, entertainment, or amusement.

Comment: Examples of an amusement machine or device are kiddie rides, games of chance, pool or billiards, pinball machines, shuffleboard, bowling, rotary merchandise, dartboards, target games, basket hoops, and electronic and video games.

AMUSEMENT PARK

A facility, primarily outdoors, that may include structures and buildings where there are various devices for entertainment, including rides, booths for the conduct of games or sale of items, as well as buildings for shows, entertainment, restaurants, and souvenir sales.

Comment: Amusement parks, better known as theme parks and family entertainment centers, are multiuse facilities often covering thousands of acres. Disney World is probably the best-known example of a theme park, but smaller ones include a variety of indoor and outdoor activities such as traditional rides (carousels, roller-coasters, Ferris wheels, and other "thrill rides"), shooting galleries, and games of skill and chance. Newer parks include music and craft shops, recreation (miniature golf, bowling, golf driving ranges, batting cages, and water sports), entertainment events, movie theaters, bumper boats, go-kart and roller rinks, arcades, and simulation and video games. Larger parks have hotels, retail stores, and many restaurants, ranging from typical fast-food operations to "silver service" establishments. Finally, theme parks host concerts, conventions, business meetings, and similar events.

Modern parks are mostly all-year-round facilities and can be an important boost to the local economy. They are difficult neighbors, however, often generating significant amounts of traffic, lights, noise, and other nuisance characteristics. These impacts need to be addressed in the local zoning ordinance by requiring adequate buffers, limits on the hours of operation, adequate parking facilities, and restrictions on fireworks, outdoor concerts, and similar activities.

In addition, larger parks can create major off-site demands for tourist-related facilities such as lodging, food, and retail uses, as well as impacts on services and utilities. Without proper planning and adequate controls, this can result in a "strip-city" environment.

ANAEROBIC

Refers to life or processes that occur in the absence of oxygen.

ANCHOR STORE

See ANCHOR TENANT; MAGNET STORE.

ANCHOR TENANT

The major store or stores within a shopping center.

Comment: The anchor tenant usually is a major department store, often in excess of 100,000 square feet. It is the most important tenant in a shopping center and the one that generates the customer traffic. Superregional centers (750,000 square feet or more) may have three or more anchor stores. *See* RETAIL STORE, LARGE SCALE.

ANCILLARY USE

See ACCESSORY USE.

ANIMAL

A living organism other than a plant or bacterium, including fish, amphibians, reptiles, birds, and mammals, excluding humans.

ANIMAL HOSPITAL

See VETERINARY HOSPITAL.

ANIMAL KENNEL

Any structure or premises in which animals are boarded, groomed, bred, or trained for commercial gain. *See* KENNEL.

ANIMAL SHELTER

A facility used to house or contain stray, homeless, abandoned, or unwanted animals and that is owned, operated, or maintained by a public body, established humane society, animal welfare society (such as the Society for the Prevention of Cruelty to Animals), or other nonprofit organization devoted to the welfare, protection, and humane treatment of animals.

ANIMAL UNIT

(1) A unit of measurement that compares various animal types based on the amount of waste that they generate (*Land Use and Zoning Digest*, Volume 55, No. 2, footnote, p. 5; S. Mark White, "Regulation of Concentrated Animal Feeding Operations: The Legal Context"); (2) the equivalent of 1 cow, 4 hogs, 10 sheep, 10 goats, 100 poultry, 1 horse, 1 pony, 1 mule, or 100 rabbits, or an equivalent combination thereof (Dade County, Wisconsin, ordinance).

Comment:

(1) The first definition is designed to control large feedlot and concentrated feeding operations (COFA). The basic standard used in determining animal units is the beef cow. Conversion factors are then used to compare various animal types, as shown in table A-1.

The maximum number of animal units permitted in a particular zone is used to determine the size of the animal feeding operation as well as the various bulk controls, size of parcel, distance to residences, minimum area required for manure distribution, and so on. *See* CONCENTRATED ANIMAL FEEDING OPERATION.

(2) The second definition is used to limit the number of animals on lots of 1 acre or more that are primarily residences and not farms in suburban areas. For example, not more than one animal unit per acre would be allowed in these districts. The standard is flexible enough to allow some negotiation between the enforcement officer and the homeowner to arrive at various combinations. In addition, the local ordinance can establish minimum setbacks from property lines for buildings that house animals, where animals are fed, and where they are permitted to graze, root, or wallow. (See "Living with Animals," *Zoning News*, January 1993, for complete discussion of animals and pets.)

TABLE A-1

Type of Livestock	U.S. EPA*	Illinois	Nebraska
Slaughter/feed cattle	1.0	1.0	1.0
Mature dairy cattle	1.4	1.4	1.4
Young dairy cattle	—	0.6	—
Swine	0.4[a]	0.4[a]	0.4
Swine (under 55 lbs.)	—	0.03	—
Sheep	0.1	0.1[b]	0.1
Horses	2.0	2.0	2.0
Turkeys	0.018	0.02	0.02
Ducks	0.2	0.2	0.2
Laying hens or broilers[c]	0.01	0.01	—
Laying hens or broilers[d]	0.03	0.03	—
Chickens	—	—	0.01

Notes:

* The Environmental Protection Agency's regulations do not specifically cite a conversion factor for poultry animals, but the numbers used here are inferred from the overall numbers used in defining COFAs.

[a] Factor is for swine over 55 lb.

[b] Factor includes goats.

[c] At facilities with continuous overflow watering.

[d] At facilities with liquid manure handling systems.

Source: Jim Schwab, *Planning and Zoning for Concentrated Feed Lot Operations,* Planning Advisory Service Report No. 482, December 1998; Jim Schwab, *Planning and Zoning for Concentrated Feed Lot Operations* (Chicago: Planners Book Service, 1999).

ANIMAL, DOMESTIC

Any animal that has been bred and/or raised to live in or about the habitation of humans and is dependent on people for food and shelter.

Comment: The ordinance might list the domestic animals acceptable to the community, or exclude by weight or other characteristics those animals deemed to be unacceptable. *See* HOUSEHOLD PET.

ANIMATED SIGN

See SIGN.

ANNEXATION

The incorporation of a land area into an existing community with a resulting change in the boundaries of that community.

Comment: Annexation may include newly incorporated land or land transferred from one municipality to another.

ANTENNA

A device used to transmit and/or receive radio or electromagnetic waves between terrestrially and/or orbitally based structures. *See* SATELLITE DISH ANTENNA; WIRELESS TELECOMMUNICATIONS TOWERS AND FACILITIES.

ANTIDEGRADATION CLAUSE

A provision in air quality and water quality laws that prohibits deterioration of air or water quality in areas where the pollution levels are currently below those allowed.

APARTMENT, GARDEN

See DWELLING, GARDEN APARTMENT.

APARTMENT, HIGH-RISE

See DWELLING, HIGH-RISE.

APARTMENT, MID-RISE

See DWELLING, MID-RISE.

APARTMENT HOTEL

A facility offering transient lodging accommodation to the general public and where rooms or suites may include kitchen facilities and sitting rooms in addition to the bedroom. *See* HOTEL.

Comment: The apartment hotel, also known as hotel suites, differs from the typical hotel in that transients are likely to rent rooms or suites for longer periods than the traditional one or two nights.

APARTMENT HOUSE

A structure containing three or more dwelling units. *See* DWELLING, MULTIFAMILY.

APARTMENT UNIT

One or more rooms with private bath and kitchen facilities constituting an independent, self-contained dwelling unit in a building containing three or more dwelling units.

APARTMENT UNIT, EFFICIENCY

See DWELLING UNIT, EFFICIENCY.

APPLICANT

A person submitting an application for development. *See* PERSON.

APPLICATION FOR DEVELOPMENT

The application form and all accompanying documents and exhibits required of an applicant by an approving authority for development review and approval purposes.

APPLICATION REVIEW COMMITTEE (ARC)

An advisory committee to a municipal agency or approving authority that provides nonbinding reviews of development applications. *See* TECHNICAL COORDINATING COMMITTEE.

APPRAISAL

An estimate or opinion of the value of real or personal property or an interest or estate in that property as determined by a qualified appraiser.

APPROVABLE SITE

(1) A site that meets all the bulk requirements of the local ordinance and is capable of accommodating permitted development; (2) a site that may be developed for low- and moderate-income housing in a manner consistent with the regulations of all agencies with jurisdiction over the site.

Comment: With respect to low- and moderate-income housing, a site may be approvable although not currently zoned for low- and moderate-income housing.

APPROVED PLAN

A plan that has been granted final approval by the appropriate approving authority.

APPROVED STREET

See STREET.

APPROVING AUTHORITY

The agency, board, group, or other legally designated individual or agency that has been charged with the review and approval of plans and applications.

APPURTENANCES

The visible, functional, or ornamental objects accessory to, and part of, buildings or structures. (American Planning Association, *Appearance Codes for Small Communities,* Planning Advisory Service Report No. 379, 1983)

AQUACULTURE

The propagation, rearing, and harvesting of aquatic organisms in controlled or selected environments, and the subsequent processing, packing, and marketing. (*New Jersey State Development and Redevelopment Plan* 2002)

AQUARIUM

A building where collections of fish, live water plants, and marine animals are exhibited.

AQUATIC ORGANISMS

Finfish, mollusks, crustaceans, aquatic plants, and similar creatures and species. (*New Jersey State Development and Redevelopment Plan* 2002)

AQUATIC PLANTS

Plants that grow in water either floating on the surface, growing up from the bottom of the body of water, or growing under the surface of the water.

AQUIFER

A geologic formation, group of formations, or part of a formation capable of storing and yielding ground water to wells or springs. *See Figure 6.*

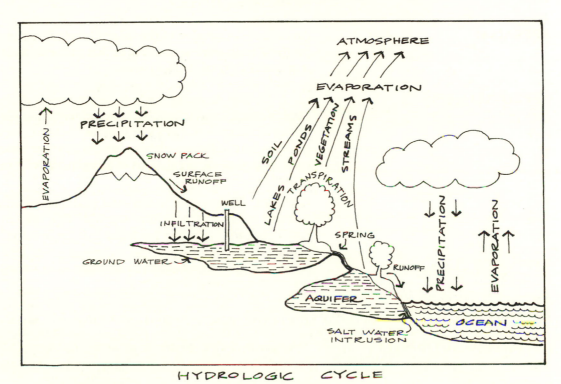

HYDROLOGIC CYCLE

FIGURE 6

AQUIFER RECHARGE AREA

The surface land or water area through which an aquifer is replenished. (*New Jersey State Development and Redevelopment Plan* 2002)

ARBORIST

An individual trained in arboriculture, forestry, landscape architecture, horticulture, or related fields and experienced in the conservation and preservation of native and ornamental trees.

ARCADE

A continuous passageway parallel to and open to a street, open space, or building, usually covered by a canopy or permanent roofing, and accessible and open to the public. *See Figure 17.*

31

ARCHAEOLOGICAL SITE

Land or water area that shows evidence of artifacts of human, plant, or animal activity, usually dating from periods of which only vestiges remain.

ARCHERY RANGE

An outdoor facility, which may include buildings or structures, used for target practice with bows and arrows. *See* AMUSEMENT, COMMERCIAL, OUTDOOR.

ARCHITECTURAL CONCEPT

The basic aesthetic idea of a building, or group of buildings or structures, including the site and landscape development that produce its distinctive character. (American Planning Association, *Appearance Codes for Small Communities,* Planning Advisory Service Report No. 379, 1983)

ARCHITECTURAL CONTROL

Public regulation of the exterior design of private buildings to preserve, enhance, or develop the character of a particular area.

Comment: Aesthetics is the major reason architectural controls are imposed. In all ordinances calling for architectural controls, the standards upon which to judge a particular building must be precise and carefully drawn to avoid charges of vagueness and improper delegation of authority. *See* AESTHETIC ZONING; DESIGN STANDARDS.

ARCHITECTURAL FEATURE

A prominent or significant part or element of a building, structure, or site. (APA, *Appearance Codes for Small Communities,* Planning Advisory Service Report No. 379, 1983)

ARCHITECTURAL PROJECTIONS

Building projections that are permitted to intrude into required front, rear, and side yards.

Comment: The text of the ordinance should indicate the extent to which the projection is permitted. For example, on dwellings, bay windows, chimneys, and roof overhangs might be limited to 2 feet into the yard. Unroofed steps and landings could extend up to 10 feet but could not occupy more than 20 percent of the building width. On nonresidential buildings, these projections may include the covered awning or canopy from the curb to the entrance.

ARCHITECTURAL STYLE

The characteristic form and detail of buildings of a particular historic period. (APA, *Appearance Codes for Small Communities,* Planning Advisory Service Report No. 379, 1983) *See* HISTORIC BUILDING STYLES.

AREA OF RESCUE ASSISTANCE

An area with direct access to an exit where people who are unable to use stairs may remain temporarily in safety to await further instructions or assistance during emergency evacuation.

Comment: Part of the Americans with Disabilities Act, 1990.

AREA PLAN

A plan that provides specific planning and design proposals for a defined geographic area.

Comment: Area, neighborhood, or district plans are urban design plans that are often prepared after the adoption of the local master plan. They provide the specific local planning detail, which may be adopted as amendments to the master plan.

AREA SCALE

A graphic display of the relationship between map areas and actual areas. *See* SCALE. *See Figure 7.*

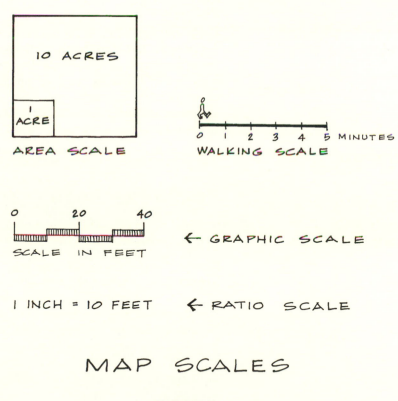

MAP SCALES

FIGURE 7

AREA SOURCE

In air pollution, any small individual fuel combustion source, including any transportation source. *See* POINT SOURCE.

Comment: This is a general definition; area source is

usually specifically set forth and precisely defined in appropriate federal statutes.

ARTERIAL STREET

See STREET, MAJOR ARTERIAL.

ARTESIAN AQUIFER

An aquifer in which water is confined under pressure between layers of impermeable (aquilude) material.

ARTICULATE

To divide into distinct and significant parts.

Comment: Design standards for large buildings can require that building walls over a certain length be "articulated," or divided into distinct and significant parts. *See* WAREHOUSE.

ARTIFICIAL RECHARGE

Adding water to an aquifer by artificial means, such as specially designed wells, ditches, or through other constructed methods.

ARTIST STUDIO

A place of work for an artist, artisan, or craftsperson, including persons engaged in the application, teaching, or performance of fine arts such as, but not limited to, drawing, vocal or instrumental music, painting, sculpture, and writing.

Comment: An artist's studio may include the dwelling of the artist.

ARTS CENTER

A structure or complex of structures for the visual and/or performing arts.

Comment: Arts centers are often owned and/or operated by public or semipublic agencies. In any zone permitting arts centers, accessory needs, such as parking, must be considered and adverse impacts, such as noise, lighting, traffic, and hours of operation, must be carefully evaluated and addressed.

ASSEMBLAGE

The merger of separate properties into a single tract of land. *See* CONSOLIDATION.

ASSESSED VALUATION

The value at which property is appraised for tax purposes. *See* ASSESSMENT RATIO.

ASSESSMENT RATIO

The relation between the assessed value of a property and its true market value.

Comment: For a number of reasons, the assessed value of property may not reflect market value. In some states, communities are permitted to assess at a percentage of true market value. In addition, in jurisdictions that do not reassess or revalue frequently, the discrepancy between assessed valuation and true market value often increases over time. To equalize all properties within a given taxing jurisdiction, some regional or state agency will assign an equalization ratio to a community's property. The planner must consider this equalization ratio in undertaking any cost-benefit analysis.

ASSIMILATION

The ability of a body of water to purify itself of organic pollution.

ASSISTED LIVING FACILITY

Residences for the frail elderly that provide rooms, meals, personal care, and supervision of self-administered medication. They may provide other services, such as recreational activities, financial services, and transportation. *See* RESIDENTIAL HEALTH CARE FACILITIES; RETIREMENT COMMUNITY.

Comment: Assisted living facilities (or assisted care facilities) range in size from a few rooms to more than a hundred. A typical development might be 110 to 115 units on 3 to 5 acres. The facilities are sometimes combined with other types of housing, such as congregate apartment housing for the elderly and residential health care facilities.

AT GRADE

See GRADE LEVEL.

ATMOSPHERE

The layer of air surrounding the earth. *See Figure 6.*

ATTACHED DWELLING UNIT

See DWELLING, ATTACHED.

ATTENTION-GETTING DEVICE

A device designed or intended to attract by noise; sudden, intermittent, or rhythmic movement; or physical change or lighting change, such as banners, flags, streamers, balloons, propellers, whirligigs, searchlights, and flashing lights.

ATTIC

That part of a building that is immediately below and wholly or partly within the roof framing. *See* STORY, HALF. *See Figure 8.*

ATTRIBUTES

Physical, natural, constructed, or demographic characteristics that define and describe a building, site, or entity.

Comment: Examples of attributes include physical characteristics of a building or structure, length and width of a road, and demographic data of a municipality or census tract.

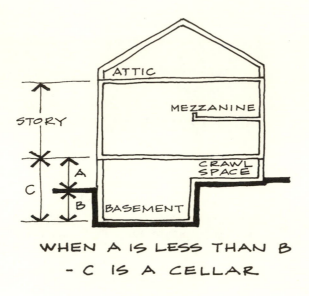

WHEN A IS LESS THAN B
- C IS A CELLAR

FIGURE 8

AUCTION HOUSE

A place where objects of art, furniture, and other goods are offered for sale to persons who bid on the object in competition with each other.

AUDIOMETER

An instrument for measuring hearing sensitivity.

AUTHORITATIVE SOURCE

A person, document, professional organization, or institution whose expertise, based on education, research, study, and experience of a given subject or in a given field is generally accepted by other experts on the subject or practitioners in the field.

Comment: Many ordinances allow flexibility and discretion in applying certain standards, particularly with respect to engineering and construction requirements. For example, an ordinance might require that all road improvements must meet AASHTO (American Association of State Highway and Transportation Officials) standards or standards from some other "authoritative source." One state enabling act, citing a specific document, allows changes or modifications ". . . in light of any recommended . . . standards promulgated under similarly authoritative auspices of any academic or professional institution or organization." (*New Jersey Municipal Land Use Law*, C. 40:55D-40.4, dealing with site improvement standards)

36

Many problems arise in attempting to differentiate between an authoritative source and a recognized source. While there is some overlap, a recognized source is one that has general acceptance but is not necessarily an authoritative source. The determination requires a case-by-case analysis. Other conflicts can arise when the authoritative source has a vested interest in the outcome. National organizations promoting education, libraries, or recreation, for example, or the use of certain materials such as plastic, concrete, or asphalt, often conduct research and publish recommended standards. These may be considered authoritative sources if the research used in developing the standards is carefully designed to remove any possible taint of bias. But the source still has to be considered, and the methods used in arriving at the standard should be examined.

AUTOMATED CONVENIENCE STORE

See VENDING MACHINE.

AUTOMATED TELLER MACHINE (ATM)

An automated device that performs banking financial functions at a location that may be separate from the controlling financial institution.

AUTOMATIC CAR WASH

A structure containing facilities for washing automobiles and automatic or semiautomatic application of cleaner, brushes, rinse water, and heat for drying.

Comment: Many gas stations are incorporating on-site automatic car wash facilities. Zoning considerations include drainage and possible freezing of runoff, water use, drying areas, vehicle stacking capacity, and litter and debris.

AUTOMOBILE

A self-propelled, free-moving vehicle, with four wheels, usually used to transport not more than six passengers and licensed by the appropriate state agency as a passenger vehicle.

AUTOMOBILE, COMPACT

See COMPACT CAR.

AUTOMOBILE DEALERSHIP, USED

See AUTOMOBILE SALES, USED.

AUTOMOBILE MALL

A single location containing more than one automobile dealership that provides display and sales space primarily for new motor vehicles, as well as centralized services, which may include vehicle servicing and repair, financing, insurance, leasing and rental, and other related services.

37

Comment: Auto malls are very large establishments, often consisting of several dealerships. They are the result of the increasing cost of retail auto sales and cost efficiencies from combining services facilities. Because of their size, they are usually located on the outside of the central business district and developed commercial areas. They require large tracts of land, often in excess of 30 or more acres with good access. Planning considerations include controls on lighting and signage and requirements for screening and landscaping. A major problem is that because of their large size and combined repair facilities, auto malls may generate significant environmental problems, including pollution and runoff. ("Acres of Automobiles," *Zoning News*, June 1997)

AUTOMOBILE REPAIR

See AUTOMOTIVE REPAIR SERVICES AND GARAGES; GARAGE, REPAIR.

AUTOMOBILE REPAIR SERVICES, MAJOR

General repair, rebuilding, or reconditioning of engines, motor vehicles, or trailers, including bodywork, welding, and major painting service.

AUTOMOBILE REPAIR SERVICES, MINOR

The replacement or repair of any automobile part that does not require removal of the engine head or pan, engine transmission, or differential but may include incidental body and fender work, minor painting, and upholstering service.

AUTOMOBILE SALES

The use of any building, land area, or other premise principally for the display, sale, rental, or lease of new or used automobiles (but may include light trucks or vans, trailers, or recreation vehicles), and including any vehicle preparation, warranty, or repair work conducted as an accessory use.

AUTOMOBILE SALES, USED

The use of land and buildings for the display and sale of primarily used motor vehicles and may include repair and service facilities as well as financing and leasing services.

Comment: The sale of used motor vehicles is customarily an accessory use to new car dealerships. Used-car superstores are a recent phenomenon, akin to the big box retailers. They usually provide one-stop shopping in the sale of used vehicles and include servicing, financing, and similar services. They occupy large land areas, usually on the outskirts of built-up areas. Good access and visibility are critical. As with auto malls, planning considerations include site design, landscaping, lighting, signage, and pollution. ("Acres of Automobiles," *Zoning News*, June 1997)

AUTOMOBILE SERVICE STATION

Any building, land area, or other premises, or portion thereof, used for the retail dispensing or sales of vehicular fuels; servicing and repair of automobiles; and including as an accessory use the sale and installation of lubricants, tires, batteries, and similar vehicle accessories.

Comment: The name "automobile service station" is probably a misnomer as more and more stations convert to fuel sales only and no longer undertake vehicle repairs. In addition, many gas-only stations are selling snack food, tobacco, drinks, newspapers, and similar convenience goods as accessory or appurtenant to the principal use. Some additional parking may be needed for shoppers other than those getting gas. At some point, the accessory use may become the principal use. Other zoning considerations include multiple use of the site, parking and circulation, signs, and landscaping. *See* MINIMART.

AUTOMOBILE WRECKING YARD

An establishment that cuts up, compresses, or otherwise disposes of motor vehicles. *See* JUNKYARD.

Comment: Wrecking yards may also store and sell salvaged auto parts, but if so, they function as junkyards.

AUTOMOTIVE REPAIR SERVICES AND GARAGES

Establishments primarily engaged in furnishing automotive repair, rental, leasing, and parking services to the general public.

Comment: This general category includes all major components of the automotive industry (except the dispensing of gas and oil directly into the vehicles), including parking lots and structures, all types of repairs, car washes, and rental and leasing activities.

AUXILIARY LANE

A part of the roadway striped for use but not for through traffic.

AVAILABLE SITE

A site with clear title, free of encumbrances that preclude development for low- and moderate-income housing. (New Jersey Council on Affordable Housing 1993)

AVERAGE ANNUAL DAILY TRAFFIC (AADT)

The total yearly traffic volume in both directions of travel divided by 365.

Comment: Generally replaced by Average Daily Traffic (ADT) counts. *See* AVERAGE DAILY TRAFFIC (ADT).

AVERAGE DAILY TRAFFIC (ADT)

Average daily traffic volumes at a given location over a 24-hour period.

Comment: ADT counts have generally replaced average annual daily traffic counts (AADT) as the norm. Traffic engineers usually will take a sample of 3 to 7 days of traffic to determine representative ADT counts.

AVERAGE FINISHED GRADE

See GRADE, FINISHED.

AVERAGE SETBACK

The average distance from the street right-of-way of buildings on both sides of a lot.

Comment: In built-up neighborhoods, many ordinances establish the prevailing setback as the standard to which new houses must conform. Thus, if the houses on both sides of a vacant lot are set back 20 and 30 feet, respectively, the average would be 25 feet. In some ordinances, all setbacks within a specific distance of the lot (200 to 300 feet) are averaged. Some ordinances will specify both a minimum and maximum setback.

AVERAGE VEHICLE RIDERSHIP (AVR)

A numerical value calculated by dividing the number of employees scheduled to start work between 6:00 A.M. and 10:00 A.M. by the number of vehicles arriving at the worksite between 6:00 A.M. and 10:00 A.M. *See* ACCESS CODE.

AVIARY

A place for the keeping of birds for the purpose of racing, exhibiting, or selling.

AVIATION EASEMENT

See EASEMENT, AVIATION.

AVULSION

A sudden and perceptible loss of or addition to land by the action of water.

Comment: Avulsion often occurs as the result of severe flooding or when a stream shifts course over a period of time.

A-WEIGHTED SOUND LEVEL (dBA)

The sound level in decibels as measured on a sound-level meter using the A-weighting network.

Comment: The A-weighting scale is "a scale for sound measurement that is meant to simulate the subjective response of the human ear." (American Planning Association, *Industrial Performance Standards for a New Century,* Planning Advisory Service Report No. 444, 1993)

AWNING

A rooflike cover that is temporary or portable in nature and that projects from the wall of a building for the purpose of shielding a doorway or window from the elements and is periodically retracted into the face of the building. *See Figure 9.*

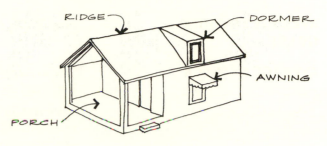

FIGURE 9

Comment: Awnings are temporary or portable devices. Once they become permanent, incapable of being retracted, then all setbacks should be measured from the end of the awning. Otherwise, most ordinances permit them to project into required yards.

AWNING, FIXED

An awning constructed with a rigid frame that cannot be retracted, folded, or collapsed.

AWNING, ILLUMINATED

A fixed awning covered with a translucent membrane that is, in whole or part, illuminated by light passing through the membrane from within the structure.

Comment: Illuminated awnings covering the width of a storefront can have a visually detrimental impact on a commercial streetscape and may be in violation of the local sign ordinance.

B

Definitions:

Back-to-back Lots
through
Buy-downs

Figures:

10. Block layout, illustrating lot categories
11. Intertidal area, showing beach, tide land, and low and high tides
12. Berm
13. Bikeway
14. Building footprint; yards; setbacks
15. Building height
16. Bulkhead line
17. Bus shelter and bus turnout area; kiosk; arcade; facade

BACK-TO-BACK LOTS Separate land parcels that have at least half of each rear lot line coterminous. *See Figure 10.*

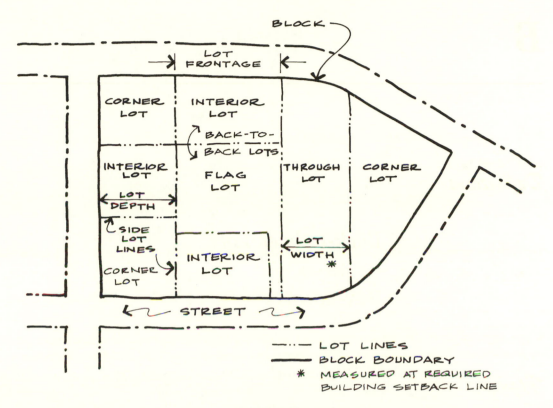

FIGURE 10

BACKFILL Material used to refill a ditch or other excavation, or the process of doing so.

BACKGROUND LEVEL Amounts of pollutants present in the ambient air.

Comment: Background level is also referred to as the ambient level and is the base from which measurements are calculated or made.

BAFFLE Any deflector device used to change the direction or the flow of water, sewage, products of combustion (such as fly ash or coarse particulate matter), or sound waves.

BALING A means of reducing the volume of solid waste by compaction.

BALLISTIC SEPARATOR

A machine that separates inorganic from organic matter in a composting process.

BANDWIDTH

In traffic analysis, the time in elapsed seconds between the passing of the first and last possible vehicle in a group of vehicles moving at the design speed of a progressive traffic signal system.

BANKED PARKING

See PARKING, BANKED.

BAR

See TAVERN.

BAR SCREEN

In wastewater treatment, a device that removes large floating and suspended solids.

BARRIER

A device that prevents traffic from crossing into the path of traffic flowing in an opposite direction. *See* MEDIAN ISLAND.

BARRIER ISLAND

Land area, separated on all sides by water; usually elongated and formed by the action of the sea on land, that protects the mainland from sea action.

BARRIER-FREE

An environment that will permit a disabled person to operate independently with comparative ease under normal circumstances and with little or no other assistance. *See* AMERICANS WITH DISABILITIES ACT; FACILITY FOR HANDICAPPED PEOPLE; HANDICAPPED PERSON; MINIMAL ACCESSIBILITY; NONAMBULATORY HANDICAP; NONSLIP; PHYSICAL HANDICAP; PRINCIPAL ENTRANCE; PUBLIC ASSEMBLY AREA; RAMP.

BASE FLOOD ELEVATION

The highest point, expressed in feet above sea level, of the level of floodwaters occurring in the regulatory base flood.

Comment: Flood elevations are calculated by engineering techniques, and observed experiences may be used to verify reliability. The base flood elevation represents the estimated height that waters will reach given a storm of certain magnitude; that is, 1-year, 2-year, 100-year, or 500-year. Regulations promulgated by various agencies, such as the U.S. Department of Housing and Urban Development, permit construction in certain flood-prone areas provided that the new construction is elevated or raised a given distance from the base flood elevation (usually 1 foot above the 100-year flood elevation) and that other flood damage prevention measures are taken.

BASE MAP

A map having sufficient points of reference, such as state, county, or municipal boundary lines, streets, easements, and other selected physical features, to allow the plotting of other data.

BASE STATION

In wireless communications, a fixed, local radio station used to communicate with a portable or mobile radio.

Comment: A base station includes equipment to receive and generate radio frequency signals and an antenna. *See* WIRELESS TELECOMMUNICATIONS TOWERS AND FACILITIES.

BASEMENT

A space having one-half or more of its floor-to-ceiling height above the average level of the adjoining ground and with a floor-to-ceiling height of not less than 6.5 feet. *See Figure 8.*

Comment: The Building Officials and Code Administrators (BOCA) Basic/National Building Code (1996) defines "basement" as that portion of a building that is partly or completely below grade. Use of this definition eliminates the distinction between basements and cellars. Ordinances should specify when the basement or cellar is counted as a story and when the floor space is used in computing the intensity of development.

Whether the basement is counted as a story depends on how great the vertical distance of the basement ceiling is over the average adjoining grade. Some ordinances call it a story if that distance is greater than 5 feet.

Generally speaking, if a basement is used only for heating, mechanical, and similar equipment and parking, it is not included in computing the intensity of development as measured by floor area ratio. The only exception is whether parking is also computed as part of the floor area ratio. If the basement is used for storage purposes for the principal use, for dwelling unit purposes, or for office space or a similar function, it is included in whatever standards are used to control the intensity of development.

BASIN

An area drained by the main stream and tributaries of a large river. *See* DETENTION BASIN; RETENTION BASIN.

BAYSCAPES

Areas that conserve water, create a diverse landscape and wildlife habitat, and use integrated (nonchemical) pest management.

Comment: Bayscapes are garden-type environments and are popular in bay areas, riverfront communities, and high-water locations. They provide an alternative to lawns and may include bogs, rock gardens, butterfly gardens, wildflower meadows, perennial gardens, ground cover and shrubs, all connected with paths. (Shirley 1999, p. 24)

BEACH

A nearly level stretch of pebbles and/or sand beside a body of water that may be artificially created or created by the action of the water. *See* INTERTIDAL AREA. *See* Figure 11.

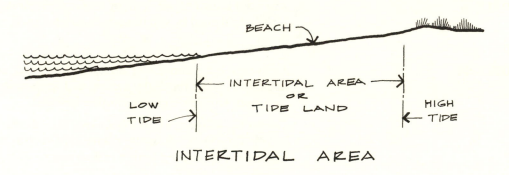

FIGURE 11

BED AND BREAKFAST

Overnight accommodations and a morning meal in a dwelling unit (B & B) provided to transients for compensation. *See* BOARDINGHOUSE.

Comment: Bed and breakfast accommodations, also referred to as tourist homes, differ from rooming and boardinghouses in that they are truly transient accommodations, with guests rarely staying more than a few days. In addition, the owner almost always lives in the facility. The impact of a B & B should not be much greater than that of a private home with frequent houseguests, with the exception of parking demand. Many B & Bs are not accessible by public transit and, consequently, guests usually arrive by auto. Zoning regulations should address parking requirements, the number of rooms that can be rented out, and signs, and require the owner or renter of the facility to live on the premises. Some ordinances limit meals (breakfasts to guests only) and limit the length of time a guest may stay—often a maximum of one week. Some municipalities permit B & Bs with accommodations for three or fewer guests as a matter of right, and as a conditional use for those renting to more than three guests. This recognizes that larger facilities have a greater impact on the neighborhood, requiring site plan approval and the opportunity for neighbors to comment on the application. Other municipalities require larger B & Bs to be licensed, with annual renewal requirements, to determine compliance with health and fire codes. ("Keeping Tabs on Bed and Breakfasts," *Planning*, August 1987; "Bed and Breakfasts: An Accommodating Neighbor," *Zoning News*, December 1989; both American Planning Association)

BEDROCK

Any solid body of rock, with or without fractures, that is not underlined by soil or unconsolidated rock material.

BEDROOM

A private room planned and intended for sleeping, separated from other rooms by a door, and accessible to a bathroom without crossing another bedroom.

Comment: When is a den a bedroom? The distinction may be important when other standards, such as parking, are based on the number of bedrooms.

BELGIAN BLOCK

Granite block curbing stones.

Comment: The minimum dimension for each block is 4" x 4" x 10". *See Figure 23.*

BELTWAY

A highway, usually of limited access, around a developed area. *See Figure 87.*

BERM

A mound of earth or the act of pushing earth into a mound. *See Figure 12.*

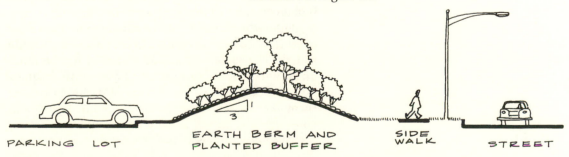

PARKING LOT   EARTH BERM AND PLANTED BUFFER   SIDE WALK   STREET

FIGURE 12

47

Comment: Berms are usually 2 to 6 feet high and are used to shield, screen, and buffer undesirable views and to separate incompatible land uses. They also provide visual interest, decrease noise, control the direction of water flow, and act as dams. Landscaping on berms, particularly on or near the top, often suffers from lack of water and needs an ensured water supply.

BEST MANAGEMENT PRACTICE (BMP)

State-of-the-art technology as applied to a specific problem and including a schedule of activities, prohibited practices, and maintenance procedures.

Comment: BMPs are often required as part of major land development projects. The BMP presents physical, institutional, or strategic approaches to environmental problems, particularly with respect to nonpoint-source pollution control.

BIFURCATED DRIVEWAY

A roadway with two separate road openings, one for ingress to, and one for egress from, a street or highway.

BIG BOX RETAIL

See RETAIL STORE, LARGE SCALE.

BIKE LANE

A corridor expressly reserved for bicycles, located on a street or roadway in addition to any lanes for use by motorized vehicles. *See Figure 13.*

BIKE PATH

A designated right-of-way for bicycles, separated from pedestrians and motor vehicles. *See Figure 13.*

BIKE ROUTE

A bicycle use corridor, shared with pedestrians and/or motor vehicular traffic. *See Figure 13.*

BIKEWAY

Any road, path, or way that is specifically designated for bicycle travel, regardless of whether such facilities are designated for the exclusive use of bicycles or are to be shared with other transportation modes. *See Figure 13.*

Comment: The bikeway has now become accepted as an important part of the circulation system. The U.S. Department of Transportation and various state highway departments have established specific standards for various classifications of bikeways. *See* BIKE LANE, BIKE PATH, and BIKE ROUTE for three suggested classifications.

BILLBOARD

See SIGN, BILLBOARD.

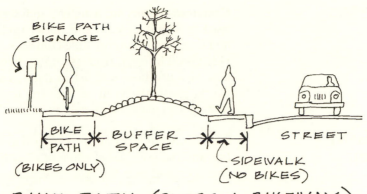

BIKE PATH SIGNAGE

BIKE PATH

BUFFER SPACE

STREET

(BIKES ONLY)

SIDEWALK (NO BIKES)

BIKE PATH (CLASS I BIKEWAY)

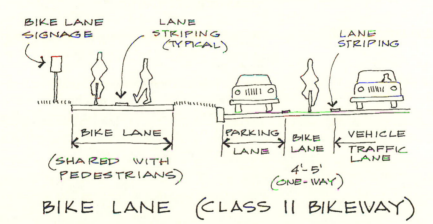

BIKE LANE SIGNAGE

LANE STRIPING (TYPICAL)

LANE STRIPING

BIKE LANE

(SHARED WITH PEDESTRIANS)

PARKING LANE

BIKE LANE

VEHICLE TRAFFIC LANE

4'-5' (ONE-WAY)

BIKE LANE (CLASS II BIKEWAY)

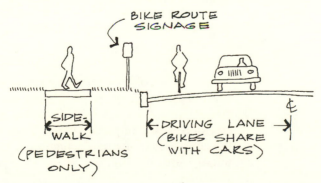

BIKE ROUTE SIGNAGE

SIDE-WALK

(PEDESTRIANS ONLY)

DRIVING LANE (BIKES SHARE WITH CARS)

BIKE ROUTE (CLASS III BIKEWAY)

FIGURE 13

49

BIOLOGICAL OXYGEN DEMAND (BOD)

A measure of the amount of oxygen consumed in the biological processes that break down organic matter in water.

Comment: Large amounts of organic waste use up large amounts of dissolved oxygen; thus, the greater the degree of pollution, the higher the BOD.

BIODEGRADABLE

Capable of being decomposed by the action of micro-organisms.

BIODIVERSITY

The variety of biological species within ecosystems together with the genetic variation within each species. (*New Jersey State Development and Redevelopment Plan* 2002)

BIOLOGICAL CONTROL

A method of controlling pests by means of introduced or naturally occurring predatory organisms, sterilization, or the use of inhibiting hormones, or similar methods rather than by mechanical or chemical means.

BIOLOGICAL OXIDATION

The process by which bacterial and other microorganisms feed on complex organic materials and decompose them. Also known as biochemical oxidation.

Comment: Biological oxidation is the basis for the self-purification of waterways and activated sludge and trickling filter wastewater treatment processes.

BIOMONITORING

The use of living organisms to test the suitability of effluent for discharge into receiving waters and to test the quality of such waters downstream from a discharge.

BIOSPHERE

That part of the earth and its atmosphere capable of supporting life.

BIOSTABILIZER

A machine used to convert solid waste into compost by grinding and aeration.

BIOTA

All the species of plants and animals occurring within a certain area.

BLANK WALL

An exterior building wall with no openings and generally constructed of a single material, uniform texture, and on a single plane. (Nelessen 1994, p. 271)

BLENDING

The joining of two or more materials that combine chemically to form a new product that differs chemically from either of the original materials.

Comment: The process of blending usually involves gases, liquids, or chemicals, but it may involve solids that are physically combined in a manner in which the individual components lose their original identities. Blending usually is classified as a manufacturing activity but is also typically part of small retail and service establishments, such as bakeries and restaurants.

BLIGHTED AREA

An area characterized by deteriorating and/or abandoned buildings; inadequate or missing public or community services; and vacant land with debris, litter, lack of utilities, accumulation of trash and junk and impacted by adverse environmental nuisances, such as odor, noise, and heavy traffic.

Comment: An alternative definition could refer to appropriate state enabling legislation. A blighted area has specific legal meaning in the application of federal and state funding. Under the Housing Act of 1949 as amended, and various state acts, an area that meets a blight definition can be acquired by public agencies by eminent domain and resold to private developers for the purpose of redevelopment and renewal. Blighted areas also may be eligible for certain favorable tax treatment and funding. An alternative, less derogatory term, "area in need of redevelopment," is used in more recent state enabling legislation.

BLOCK

A unit of land bounded by streets or by a combination of streets and public land, railroad rights-of-way, waterways, or any other barrier to the continuity of development. *See Figure 10.*

BLOCK STATISTICS

United States census information tabulated on a block basis.

BLOOM

A proliferation of living algae and/or other aquatic plants on the surface of lakes or ponds.

BOARD OF ADJUSTMENT

An officially constituted body whose principal duties are to hear appeals and, where appropriate, grant variances from the strict application of the zoning ordinance.

Comment: The name and work of boards of adjustment vary by state. In some states, boards of adjustment are called boards of standards and appeals or zoning hearing boards. In most states, the board of adjustment interprets the zoning ordinance and the zoning map, can grant variances from the bulk and dimensional requirements of the ordinance, and can grant a variance for a use not specifically permitted in the zone.

BOARDER

An individual other than a member of the family occupying a dwelling unit who, for a consideration, is furnished sleeping accommodations and meals and may be provided personal care, financial services, counseling, or other such services.

Comment: Many older zoning ordinances distinguished between roomers and boarders, the former being a person who did not receive meals. The distinction is not important from a zoning perspective. Older ordinances also made a distinction between temporary and permanent roomers or boarders, which is also not a particularly meaningful difference.

**BOARDING HOME
FOR SHELTERED CARE**

A nonprofit or for-profit group home for the sheltered care of persons with special needs, which, in addition to providing food and shelter, may also provide some combination of personal care, social or counseling services, and transportation. *See* ASSISTED LIVING FACILITY; BOARDINGHOUSE; COMMUNITY RESIDENCES FOR THE DEVELOPMENTALLY DISABLED; COMMUNITY SHELTERS FOR VICTIMS OF DOMESTIC VIOLENCE; FAMILY; HANDICAP.

Comment: The sheltered care facility serves as a substitute for the residents' own homes, furnishing facilities and comforts normally found in a home but providing, in addition, such service, equipment, and safety features as are required for safe and adequate care of the residents. These may include: (1) supervision and assistance in dressing, bathing, and in the maintenance of good personal hygiene; (2) care in emergencies or during temporary illness; (3) supervision in the taking of medications; and (4) other services conducive to the residents' welfare. Group homes for sheltered care should be treated as boardinghouses in zoning terms unless they qualify under state licensing requirements as houses for battered spouses and children or community residences for the developmentally disabled.

Group homes for the developmentally disabled are subject to the provisions of the federal Fair Housing Act (42 U.S.C.A. §3601). The Fair Housing Act, as amended, prohibits municipalities from "applying different rules to the handicapped than are applied to others" (49 ZD 131, *Land Use Law*, April 1997, p. 17). Spacing requirements (minimum distance between homes) and limits on the number of residents would not be permitted.

BOARDING STABLE

A structure designed for the feeding, housing, and exercising of horses not owned by the owner of the premises and for which the owner of the premises may receive compensation. *See* HORSE FARM.

BOARDINGHOUSE

A dwelling unit or part thereof in which, for compensation, lodging and meals are provided and personal and financial services may be offered. *See* BOARDING HOME FOR SHELTERED CARE; PERSONAL SERVICES.

Comment: Over the years, the distinction between boarding and rooming houses has narrowed. Traditionally, rooming houses provided only rooms and boardinghouses rooms and meals, but this distinction is no longer meaningful. The principal concern from a zoning point of view is how many rooms should be permitted to be rented as a matter of right, beyond which the rooming or boardinghouse would be restricted to certain zones with controls, permitted only as a conditional use or licensed. Another concern is how to ensure that the rooming houses and boardinghouses remain safe and sanitary.

Communities have addressed these problems by licensing boarding and rooming houses, requiring periodic inspections, limiting the number of guests, prohibiting cooking facilities in guest rooms, requiring adequate parking (in terms of both number and location of spaces), and establishing a minimum floor area for guest rooms. For boardinghouses in residential zones, communities require the owners or operators to maintain their residence on-site and personally collect rents to ensure that the structure remains principally a private dwelling unit.

Concerns over abuses of residents, especially the poor, aged, or special groups, have prompted some states to require state licenses for boardinghouses. In New Jersey, accommodations for two or more unrelated boarders require a state license, and a distinction is made between rooming houses, which provide only rooms or rooms and meals, and boardinghouses, which provide personal or financial services as well. However, the location and conditions of approval still remain local prerogatives.

Some boarding homes serve special populations, and these homes may be referred to as assisted living facilities, boarding homes for sheltered care, community residences for the developmentally disabled, and community shelters for the victims of domestic violence.

BOARDWALK

An elevated public pedestrian walkway constructed over a public street or along an oceanfront or beach.

BOAT RAMP

A facility designed to launch and retrieve recreational watercraft from a trailer.

BOAT SLIP

A space designed for the mooring of a single watercraft.

BOATEL

A combination of a motel and marina that is accessible to boats as well as automobiles and may include boat sales and servicing facilities, overnight accommodation for transients, and eating and drinking facilities.

BOATHOUSE

An enclosed or partially enclosed structure designed for the use and storage of private watercraft.

BOATYARD

See MARINA.

BOG

Wet, spongy land, usually poorly drained, highly acid, and rich in plant residue.

BOLLARD

A short post used to divert or block vehicular traffic.

Comment: Originally designed to secure ships, bollards are a useful and decorative street furniture element. They often incorporate low-level lighting and can restrict vehicular travel while permitting unimpeded pedestrian movement.

BONUS ZONING

See INCENTIVE ZONING.

BOROUGH

An incorporated, self-governing municipality.

BOULEVARD

A collector street that includes landscaped medians.

Comment: The most attractive boulevards are those with landscaping in the medians and a double row of trees, framing the sidewalks, along the outside of each roadway. For additional information on boulevards, *see* Allan Jacobs, Elizabeth MacDonald, and Yodam Rofe, *The Boulevard Book: History, Evolution, Design of Multiway Boulevards* (Cambridge, MA: MIT Press, 2002).

BRACKISH WATER

A mixture of fresh and salt water.

BREAKAWAY WALL

A wall that is not part of the structural support of a building and is intended, through its design and construction, to collapse under specific lateral loading forces without causing damage to the elevated portion of the building or supporting foundation system.

BREAKWATER

A protective structure, usually built offshore for the purpose of protecting the shoreline or harbor areas from wave action.

BREEDING FARM

An agricultural establishment where animals are impregnated either naturally or by artificial insemination and whose principal purpose is to propagate the species.

BREW PUB

A restaurant that prepares handcrafted natural beer intended for consumption on the premises as an accessory use.

Comment: Also known as a microbrewery. Some ordinances place limitations on the yearly production of beer, and/or on the percent of gross floor area of the primary restaurant occupied by the brewery operation.

BRIDGE

A structure having a clear span of more than 20 feet designed to convey vehicles and/or pedestrians over a watercourse, railroad, public or private right-of-way, or any depression.

Comment: Structures having a clear span of less than 20 feet are usually designated as culverts.

BRITISH THERMAL UNIT

The amount of heat required to raise the temperature of one pound (BTU) of water at one atmosphere one degree Fahrenheit.

BROADCAST APPLICATION

The application of a chemical or seeds over an entire field, lawn, or other area.

BROOK

A small stream or creek.

BROWNFIELDS

Abandoned, idled, or underutilized industrial and commercial facilities where expansion or redevelopment is complicated by real or perceived environmental contamination. (U.S. EPA, cited in PAS Report 491/492)

Comment: The term "brownfields" is often applied to sites with confirmed levels of contamination as well as to sites that are believed to be contaminated although actual contamination is unverified. Brownfields, often located in older urban areas but also evident in rural areas, offer potential opportunities for redevelopment in areas with a scarcity of vacant land. Recent changes in federal regulations allow for a variety of cleanup methods and standards, depending on the reuse of the property. For example, brownfield sites to be used only for parking can be rendered usable by paving the site.

BUFFER STRIP

Open spaces, landscaped areas, fences, walls, berms, or any combination thereof used to physically separate or screen one use or property from another so as to visually shield or block noise, lights, or other nuisances. *See Figure 68.*

Comment: Basic criteria for buffers are the width of the buffer and the type of material to be planted or installed. In design of buffers, the ordinance should allow flexibility and permit fences and berms to be used in conjunction with the landscaping. (American Planning Association, *Zoning News*, February 1990) *See* BERM.

BUFFER ZONE

See TRANSITION ZONE.

BUILDABLE AREA

The area of a lot remaining after the minimum yard and open space requirements of the zoning ordinance have been met. *See Figure 14.*

Comment: The buildable area should be actually buildable. If a lot is largely wetlands, very steep slopes, or easements, it may be difficult to locate a building or improvements on the land. The zoning regulations should specify that a minimum building area must be available to accommodate a building, driveway, and where required, a well and septic system.

BUILDING

Any structure having a roof supported by columns or walls and intended for the shelter, housing, or enclosure of any individual, animal, process, equipment, goods, or materials of any kind.

BUILDING, ACCESSORY

A subordinate structure on the same lot as the principal or main building or use. *See* ACCESSORY STRUCTURE.

BUILDING, PRINCIPAL

A building in which is conducted the principal use of the lot on which it is located. *See Figure 3.*

BUILDING COVERAGE

The ratio of the horizontal area, measured from the exterior surface of the exterior walls of the ground floor, of all principal and accessory buildings on a lot to the total lot area.

Comment: In single-family residences, porches and decks usually are excluded. For multifamily and nonresidential structures, more meaningful controls over the intensity and environmental impact of development are limits on impervious surfaces and floor area ratio, coupled with open-space requirements.

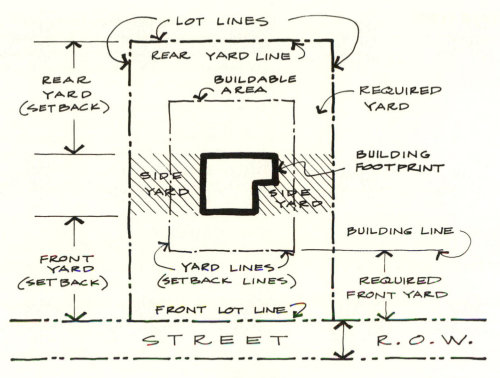

FIGURE 14

BUILDING ENVELOPE	*See* ZONING ENVELOPE.
BUILDING FOOTPRINT	The area encompassed by a building's outer wall at ground level. *See Figure 14.*
BUILDING HEIGHT	The vertical distance from finished grade to the top of the highest roof beams on a flat or shed roof, to the deck level on a mansard roof, and the average distance between the eaves and the ridge level for gable, hip, and gambrel roofs. (BOCA National Building Code, slightly modified) *See Figure 15. See* GRADE, FINISHED.

Comment: Mechanical equipment, chimneys, air conditioners, elevator penthouses, church spires and steeples, water towers, and similar appurtenances are usually exempted from height restrictions. However, the exclusion should apply only to those elements that are usually appurtenant to a building. For example, antennas are often excluded from height restrictions. This might result in radio broadcasting antennas, often 200 feet or higher, to be placed on the roof of a building in a zone with a maximum height of 35 feet. One way to preclude this is to specify that the excluded elements cannot exceed the maximum height by more than 25 feet.

Note, however, that the FCC regulations affecting amateur radio and satellite antennas may override local controls. *See* SATELLITE DISH ANTENNA; TOWER, AMATEUR RADIO.

Measuring height on sloping ground can be a problem; consequently, some limit on the number of stories is needed, at least in residential zones. Although height measurements are usually taken from the average finished grade, without a story limitation a building on sloping land could result in the situation shown in *Figure 15A*. With a typical limit of 35 feet or two and one-half stories, whichever is less, the result would be as shown in *Figure 15B*. *See* GRADE, FINISHED.

BUILDING INSPECTOR

The individual designated by the appointing authority to enforce the provisions of the building code.

Comment: Also referred to as the construction official.

BUILDING LINE

A line parallel to the street right-of-way line touching that part of a building closest to the street. *See* SET-BACK LINE. *See Figure 14*.

Comment: The building line is important because many ordinances prohibit parking or other uses between the street and the building line.

BUILDING MASS

The three-dimensional bulk of a structure: height, width, and depth.

BUILDING PERMIT

Written permission issued by the proper municipal authority for the construction, repair, alteration, or addition to a structure.

BUILDING SCALE

The relationship of a particular building, in terms of building mass, to other nearby and adjacent buildings.

BUILDOUT ANALYSIS

An estimate of the projected population, employment, traffic, utilities, and types/sizes of land uses in a project area or other designated area in accordance with the current zoning ordinance and other applicable regulations.

Comment: A buildout analysis can also include the consideration of other impacts. For example, the local regulations might require, for large projects, an analysis of visual impacts, specific utility demands, school impacts, and recreation needs.

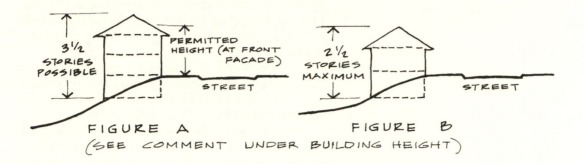

3½ STORIES POSSIBLE

PERMITTED HEIGHT (AT FRONT FACADE)

STREET

FIGURE A

2½ STORIES MAXIMUM

STREET

FIGURE B

(SEE COMMENT UNDER BUILDING HEIGHT)

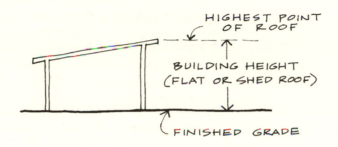

HIGHEST POINT OF ROOF

BUILDING HEIGHT (FLAT OR SHED ROOF)

FINISHED GRADE

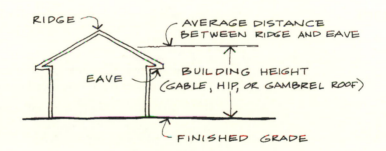

RIDGE

AVERAGE DISTANCE BETWEEN RIDGE AND EAVE

EAVE

BUILDING HEIGHT (GABLE, HIP, OR GAMBREL ROOF)

FINISHED GRADE

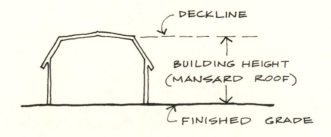

DECKLINE

BUILDING HEIGHT (MANSARD ROOF)

FINISHED GRADE

BUILDING HEIGHT

FIGURE 15

BUILT ENVIRONMENT

Artificially created fixed elements, such as buildings, structures, utilities, roads, and surfaces, that together create the physical character of an area. *See* URBAN AREA.

BUILT-UP AREA

An area where less than 25 percent of the land is vacant.

Comment: While the figure of 25 percent is somewhat arbitrary, it is at this figure (75 percent developed) that an area gives the observer the impression of being totally developed.

BULK ENVELOPE

See ZONING ENVELOPE.

BULK PLANE

See SKY EXPOSURE PLANE.

BULK REGULATIONS

Standards applying to individual lots that control the placement, intensity, and character of development and include the amount of open space on the lot, the height of structures, setbacks from property lines and public rights-of-way, impervious coverage, floor area ratio, and density. (*Designing New Jersey*. Trenton, NJ: Office of State Planning, Department of Community Affairs, 2000)

BULK STORAGE

The storage of chemicals, petroleum products, grains, and other materials in structures for subsequent resale to distributors or retail dealers or outlets.

Comment: Bulk storage is essentially a warehousing and wholesaling operation. The products are primarily sold for eventual resale and not directly to the consuming public.

BULKHEAD

A retaining wall created along a body of water behind which fill is placed. *See Figure 16.*

BULKHEAD LINE

A line along a navigable waterway offshore of which no fill or structure is permitted. *See Figure 16.*

Comment: The bulkhead line defines the permanent shoreline of navigable waterways or lakes. The top is usually stated in feet above sea level. *See* PIERHEAD LINE.

BULLETIN BOARD SIGN

See SIGN, BULLETIN BOARD.

BUMPERS

Permanent devices in each parking stall that block the front wheels of a vehicle.

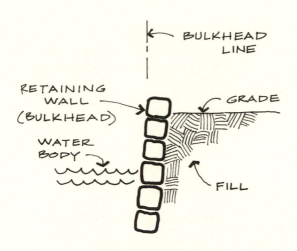

BULKHEAD LINE

FIGURE 16

Comment: Typical precast concrete wheel stops can be a problem in that they crack easily, make it difficult to clear parking areas of snow, trap debris, and are a hazard to pedestrians. They should not be used. A better arrangement is to widen the adjacent walkways or parking lot islands, install curbing, and permit the cars to overhang the curb.

BUS LANE

A designated part of a roadway intended primarily for bus use during specified periods.

BUS POOL

A bus service, usually administered by an employer, with limited pickup and destination stops, guaranteed seats, and advance ticket purchase.

BUS SHELTER

A small, roofed structure, usually having three walls, located near a street and designed primarily for the protection and convenience of bus passengers. *See Figure 17.*

Comment: Shelters are often constructed of see-through materials for safety reasons.

BUS TERMINAL OR BUS STATION

Any premises for the storage or parking of motor-driven buses and the loading and unloading of passengers.

Comment: Bus terminals may include ticket purchase facilities, toilets, restaurants, and stores.

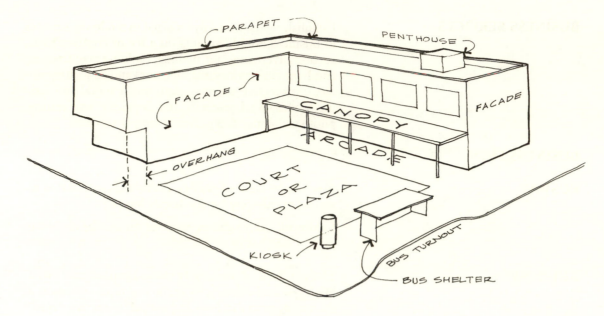

FIGURE 17

BUS TURNOUT   A paved indentation at the side of a roadway designed to allow buses to pick up and discharge passengers. *See Figure 17.*

BUSINESS CLUSTER ANALYSIS   An economic development technique that analyzes the economic base of a region as part of the economic element of the local master plan.

Comment: Business cluster analysis is designed to provide insight into a region's economic activities as a basis for attracting new firms and activities. It does so by defining the existing business clusters that share infrastructure, suppliers, business services, support facilities, and distribution facilities. It provides a focus for future efforts in attracting and keeping industries and employment in an area. A community can then develop land-use policies and capital programs to strengthen the base that initially attracted these business clusters.

BUSINESS IMPROVEMENT DISTRICT   *See* SPECIAL IMPROVEMENT DISTRICT.

62

BUSINESS SERVICES

Establishments primarily engaged in rendering services to business establishments on a fee or contract basis, such as advertising and mailing; building maintenance; employment services; management and consulting services; protective services; equipment rental and leasing; commercial research, development, and testing; photo finishing; and personal supply services.

BUSINESS SIGN

See SIGN, BUSINESS.

BUSWAY

A vehicular right-of-way or portion thereof that is reserved exclusively for the use of buses.

Comment: The exclusive reservation may be limited to peak traffic hours.

BUY-DOWNS

The purchase of previously owned market-rate dwelling units and offering of them in sound condition at affordable prices to low- and moderate-income households.

Comment: A buy-down program, if permitted by state and local enabling legislation, is a fast and efficient way municipalities can provide low- and moderate-income housing. Since the buy-down program buys existing units, it addresses community concerns with growth, increased densities, or the lack of available land for new housing. In addition, it is particularly cost-effective when the housing market is soft and mortgage rates are low. When purchases are in existing developments with homeowners associations, exterior maintenance is provided. A buy-down program provides for instant scattered-site housing without concerns about too many low- and moderate-income units in a single location. (McGowan and Richter-Reba 1998)

C

Definitions:

Cafeteria
through
Cutoff-type Luminaire

Figures:

CAFETERIA

A restaurant in which patrons wait on themselves, carrying their food from counters, where it is displayed and served, to their tables.

CALIPER

The diameter of a tree trunk. *See Figure 18.*

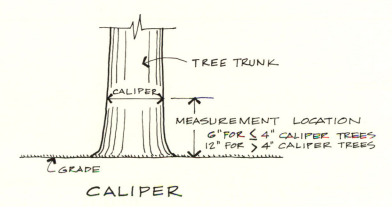

CALIPER

FIGURE 18

Comment: The measurement distance from ground level should be specified. The usual distance is 6 inches for trees up to 4 inches in diameter and 12 inches for larger-diameter trees (American Association of Nurserymen standard). The diameter standard, which may be used to require certain mature trees to remain on a site or require planting of minimum-age trees, will vary with the species. Certain trees, such as birches or dogwoods, are normally thinner; consequently, the standard for such trees would be different from that for other species.

CAMP

See CAMPGROUND; CAMPING UNIT.

CAMPER

Any individual who occupies a campsite or otherwise assumes charge of, or is placed in charge of, a campsite.

CAMPGROUND

A plot of ground on which two or more campsites are located, established, or maintained for occupancy by camping units as temporary living quarters for recreation, education, or vacation purposes. *See* CAMPING UNIT.

Comment: Most states regulate campgrounds under a state campground code or sanitary code. Any state definition should be used in the local ordinance. The state code also may prescribe minimum standards, including the amount of space required for each campsite, provision of sanitary facilities, and similar requirements. Local ordinances usually are required to be as strict as the state's, but in some states, they may be stricter. Many state or local ordinances also prohibit occupancy for longer than a specified period of time, often 90 continuous days, in order to prevent these temporary accommodations from becoming permanent.

CAMPING UNIT

Any tent, trailer, cabin, lean-to, recreational vehicle, or similar structure established or maintained and operated in a campground as temporary living quarters for recreation, education, or vacation purposes.

CAMPING VEHICLE

See RECREATIONAL VEHICLE.

CAMPSITE

Any plot of ground within a campground intended for exclusive occupancy by a camping unit or units under the control of a camper.

CAMPUS

The grounds and buildings of a public or private college, university, school, or institution.

CANAL

An artificial waterway for transportation or irrigation.

CANDLEPOWER

Luminous intensity expressed in candelas.

Comment: Candlepower is a measure of illuminating power that has generally been replaced by the footcandle. For those technically inclined, the luminous intensity is defined as the luminous flux per unit solid angle in a given direction. *See* FOOTCANDLE; LUMEN.

CANOPY

See AWNING.

CAPACITY, ROADWAY

The maximum hourly rate at which vehicles can reasonably be expected to traverse a point or uniform section of a lane or roadway during a given time period under the prevailing roadway, traffic, and control conditions. (Transportation Research Board 2000) *See* LEVEL OF SERVICE.

Comment: Roadway capacity is defined in terms of levels of service. Six levels of service are described, designated from A through F, with A representing the best operating conditions and level F the worst. Level C is usually designated as the level minimally uncongested.

Briefly, the level of service A represents free flow, B stable flow, and C also stable but starting to be affected by other drivers. Level of service D starts to experience some congestion, with speed and freedom to maneuver restricted. Level of service E is a level in which the road is operating at or near capacity; speed is slow; and comfort and convenience are poor. Level F is forced or breakdown flow, with severe congestion.

CAPACITY ANALYSIS

Determining and evaluating the capacity of natural systems, infrastructure, and social and fiscal systems to define the carrying capacity for existing development and future growth of a municipality or region. (*New Jersey State Development and Redevelopment Plan* 2000)

Comment: Capacity analysis is a useful planning tool for evaluating the impacts of alternative growth scenarios.

CAPITAL FACILITIES

The land, buildings, and other physical facilities under public ownership or operated or maintained for public benefit that are necessary to support development and redevelopment and to protect the public health, safety, and welfare.

CAPITAL IMPROVEMENT

An acquisition of real property, major construction projects, or acquisition of expensive equipment expected to last a long time. *See* IMPROVEMENT.

Comment: Capital improvements are usually large, nonrecurring items. They are often financed by the sale of bonds. Many ordinances specify a minimum expenditure or cost to qualify as a capital improvement.

CAPITAL IMPROVEMENTS PROGRAM

A timetable or schedule of all future capital improvements to be carried out during a specific period, listed in order of priority, together with cost estimates and the anticipated means and sources of financing each project.

Comment: The capital improvements program is usually a six-year program, with the first year being the capital improvements budget.

CAPPED SYSTEM

A completed water supply and/or sewerage system, put in place for future use, rather than to meet immediate development needs.

Comment: The capped system may be needed to accommodate a proposed expansion of the development or the installation or the expansion of treatment or supply facilities.

CAR WASH

Any building or premises used for washing motor vehicles.

Comment: Car wash establishments usually perform polishing, and many provide detailing and minor body repair services. Some car washes have vacuum machines to allow owners to clean the interior of their vehicles. *See* AUTOMATIC CAR WASH.

CARBON DIOXIDE (CO$_2$)

A colorless, odorless, nonpoisonous gas that is a normal part of the ambient air and is a product of fossil fuel combustion.

CARBON MONOXIDE (CO)

A colorless, odorless, highly toxic gas that is a normal by-product of incomplete fossil fuel combustion.

CARPOOL, CARPOOLING

Two or more people commuting on a regular basis to and from work by means of a privately owned vehicle, either using one car and sharing expenses or alternating vehicles so that no money changes hands.

Comment: Carpooling is similar to vanpooling but differs in that in carpooling, the driver is usually the car owner. In vanpooling, the vehicle is usually owned by the employer and the driver rides free in return for maintaining the van and serving as driver. From a zoning perspective, carpooling reduces the number of parking spaces needed for any use that employs the system. Zoning regulations might permit an applicant with a viable carpooling program to request relief from installing all of the required off-street parking. The site plan would show the required parking for which relief is requested, but it would not have to be installed unless a new occupant without a carpooling plan moved into the premises.

CARPORT

A roofed structure providing space for the parking of motor vehicles and enclosed on not more than three sides.

CARRYOUT RESTAURANT

An establishment that by design of the physical facilities, service, or packaging, sells prepared ready-to-eat foods intended primarily to be consumed off the premises. *See* RESTAURANT, TAKE-OUT.

Comment: Zoning and site design considerations should include drive-up facilities, circulation, queuing space for stacking, and parking requirements. Many primarily carryout restaurants also have tables, further blurring the distinction between conventional restaurants and carryout places. If space for parking is limited, the number of tables should be restricted.

CARTWAY

The paved area of a street between the curbs, including travel and parking lanes and acceleration and deceleration lanes, but not including shoulders, curbs, sidewalks, or swales. *See Figure 1.*

Comment: Where there are no curbs, the cartway is that part between the edges of the paved, or hard-surface, width.

CASINO

A room or rooms in which legal gaming is conducted.

CASINO HOTEL

See HOTEL, CASINO.

CATALYTIC CONVERTER

An air pollution abatement device that removes organic contaminants by oxidizing them into carbon dioxide and water through chemical reaction and that is used to reduce nitrogen oxide emissions from motor vehicles.

CATCH BASIN

An inlet designed to intercept and redirect surface waters.

CELLAR

A space with less than one-half of its floor-to-ceiling height above the average finished grade of the adjoining ground or with a floor-to-ceiling height of less than 6.5 feet. *See Figure 8.*

Comment: Cellars should be used only for mechanical equipment accessory to the principal structure or for unhabitable space. As such, they are not counted as a story or in the computation of the intensity of land use, such as floor area ratio.

CELLS

With respect to solid waste disposal, earthen compartments in which solid wastes are dumped, compacted, and covered over daily with layers of earth.

CELLULAR TOWER SITE

See WIRELESS TELECOMMUNICATIONS TOWERS AND FACILITIES.

CEMETERY

Property used for the interment of the dead.

Comment: Most development ordinances do not include provisions for cemeteries. They are so unusual a use that they are generally handled by variance. When cemeteries are regulated in the development ordinance, height and setback standards should be established for crematories and mausoleums, where the bodies are interred above ground in stacked vaults. In areas with high water tables, this is a fairly common type of burial.

CENSUS

An official periodic enumeration of a designated geographic area's population, housing, and related characteristics.

CENSUS TRACT

Small areas into which large cities and adjacent areas have been divided for statistical purposes.

CENTER ISLAND NARROWING

See TRAFFIC CALMING.

CENTERLINE OFFSET

The distance between the centerline of roads intersecting a common road, as measured along the centerline of the common road. *See* ACCESS POINT OFFSET.

CENTRAL BUSINESS DISTRICT (CBD)

The largest, most intensively developed mixed-use area within a city, usually containing, in addition to major retail uses, governmental offices; service uses; professional, cultural, recreational, and entertainment establishments and uses; residences; hotels; appropriate industrial activities; and transportation facilities.

Comment: There is no hard-and-fast rule as to what the CBD may include. In fact, all uses are appropriate, providing they do not adversely infringe on other uses or diminish the traditional retail, office, cultural, and entertainment functions. Controls on industry in the CBD, for example, might restrict them from prime, first-floor locations, which should be used for retail activities. Even open space and passive recreational facilities have a place in the CBD.

CERTIFICATE OF APPROPRIATENESS

A certificate issued by the approving authority on approval of the exterior architectural features of any new building construction or alterations to an existing building located within a historic zone.

Comment: Certificates of appropriateness are typically required in historic or other special design districts before the issuance of a building or zoning permit. In some historic district ordinance procedures, the application review is carried out by a special design review committee of local experts, and their nonbinding recommendations are forwarded to the approving authority for consideration and action.

In a historic district, the review is usually limited to architectural features that are visible from a public street. For a special design district (a central business district, for example), the basis for review is the conformance of the development proposal to the adopted area design plan. *See* CERTIFICATE OF COMPLIANCE.

70

CERTIFICATE OF COMPLIANCE

A document issued by the proper authority certifying that the plans for a proposed use meet all applicable codes and regulations.

CERTIFICATE OF NEED

A document required to be obtained before certain facilities can be constructed or expanded.

Comment: Certificates of need are usually required before a health facility can be constructed and/or an existing one expanded. Certificates of need may also be required for subsidized housing facilities and may be a condition for certain other public uses. In many states, when a certificate of need is required, it provides the critical proof for the grant of a variance or approval of a conditional use.

CERTIFICATE OF OCCUPANCY (CO)

A document issued by a governmental authority allowing the occupancy or use of a building and certifying that the structure or use has been constructed and will be used in compliance with all the applicable municipal codes and ordinances.

Comment: One of the questions with respect to COs is whether a temporary CO is a viable regulatory device. In theory, if an applicant does not meet certain conditions of approval by certain dates, the CO is lifted. In practice, once issued, COs are difficult to revoke. A better arrangement is to require the posting of bonds or a letter of credit to guarantee the completion of all required improvements. *See* TEMPORARY PERMIT.

CERTIFICATION

A written statement by the appropriate officer that required constructions, inspections, tests, or notices have been performed and comply with applicable requirements.

CESSION DEED

The conveyance to a local governmental body of private property street rights.

CESSPOOL

A covered pit with open, jointed lining where untreated sewage is discharged, the liquid portion of which is disposed of by seepage or leeching into the surrounding porous soil, the solids, or sludge, being retained in the pit.

CFS

Cubic feet per second.

Comment: The measure of the amount of liquid or gas passing a given point.

CHAIN

A lineal measure equal to 66 feet.

Comment: This surveyor's measure is no longer in use. Many street right-of-way widths were laid out as 33 feet, or half a chain.

CHAIN STORE

Retail outlets with the same name, selling similar types of merchandise, operating under a common merchandising policy, and usually owned or franchised by a single corporate entity.

CHANGE OF USE

Any use that substantially differs from the previous use of a building or land.

Comment: Change of use is important in that any such change usually requires site plan approval. Most courts have indicated that a change of occupancy or a change of ownership in and by itself should not be construed as a change of use. To be considered a change, a new use has to be substantially different from the previous use. Thus, a retail clothing store selling men's clothes would not be substantially different from a retail clothing store selling women's clothes. Whether a retail clothing store would be substantially different from a drugstore is debatable. One possibility is to define "substantially different" as a use that is in a different sector level (two-digit code) as set forth in the *North American Industry Classification System (NAICS),* which replaced the old *Standard Industrial Classification (SIC)* system in 1997. *See* NORTH AMERICAN INDUSTRY CLASSIFICATION SYSTEM.

From a zoning perspective, change of use is important only if it affects any of the usual elements involved in site plan review: parking, drainage, traffic, circulation, landscaping, signage, building arrangements, and nuisance factors, such as lighting and noise. If they remain the same, it is questionable as to why a new site plan is needed, and a waiver of that requirement may be appropriate.

A New Jersey Supreme Court case (*Belleville v. Parrillo's, Inc.*, 83 N.J. 309 [1980]) provides further insight as to when a change of use takes place. Cox (2003) writes:

> In that case a restaurant was changed to a "disco" and a proceeding was brought in the Municipal Court charging violation of the zoning ordinance. The defendant's conviction was reversed by the Appellate Division, which held that there was not a change of use, but the Supreme Court disagreed. The Appellate Division had found that each aspect of the "new" business

72

had been conducted previously, e.g., food had been served previously and continued to be; there had been music in the restaurant and continued to be; there was serving of alcoholic beverages previously and continued to be. The Supreme Court held that this quantitative analysis was improper and that the focus in cases of this type must be on the quality, character and intensity of the use viewed in their totality and with regard to the overall effect on the neighborhood and zoning plan (83 N.J. 309 at 314). As a restaurant it had been open every day but now was open only one day and three evenings; the primary use of the dance hall had been incidental to dining but was now a primary use; the music was formerly provided by live bands and was now recorded; admission charges were now made whereas there had been none; the bulk of the prior business was food catering, which now was discontinued. The Court concluded that there had indeed been a change of use and that the defendant was properly convicted. . . . The Supreme Court [also] noted that "an increase in the time period during which a conforming use is operated may justifiably be the basis for finding an unlawful extension thereof, just as changes in the functional uses of the land or increases in the area of use have been."

(*Belleville v. Parrillo's, Inc.* at 317–18)

CHANNEL

A watercourse with a definite bed and banks that confine and conduct the normal continuous or intermittent flow of water.

CHANNELIZATION

(1) The straightening and deepening of channels and/or the surfacing thereof to permit water to move rapidly and/or directly; (2) a traffic control device that forces vehicles into certain traffic flows or turning movements.

CHARACTER

Special physical characteristics of a structure or area that set it apart from its surroundings and contribute to its interest and/or individuality.

Comment: Examples of an area's character might include: a pattern of residential gridiron, tree-lined streets with alleys for garage access and trash removal; a business district with uniformity in building scale, materials, setbacks, street furniture, and sign design; or a waterfront promenade with fountains, public art, and design-coordinated street furniture of benches, light standards, and trash receptacles.

CHARGING STATION

The physical device that provides a connection from a power source to an electric vehicle.

CHARITABLE USE

A use that provides essential goods or services, such as food, housing, clothing, counseling, aid, or assistance to those in need, for no fee or compensation or at a fee recognized as being significantly less than the cost of the goods or services.

CHARRETTE

A highly focused, broad-based public work effort to develop consensus on a variety of design issues, usually as part of a master plan study.

Comment: A charrette is named after the horse-drawn cart that, during the Beaux-Arts period, collected the elaborate drawings and models prepared by French architecture students for their design projects. Even though their projects were imminently due, the students would often ride in the cart with their drawings, adding finishing touches as they and their work were conveyed across town to be judged by the faculty. (Lardner/Klein Landscape Architects 1998)

CHATTEL

Personal property as contrasted with real estate.

CHECKERBOARDING

Undersized adjoining lots being owned alternately by two individuals.

Comment: Cox tells of the case of a husband and wife who owned a number of adjoining lots as tenants by the entirety. Prior to a new zoning amendment that upgraded minimum lot sizes, they conveyed the lots alternately to each other in an attempt to circumvent the upgrading requirements. The local board of adjustment rejected an application for a variance since adjacent land was available at a reasonable price to bring the lots up to the minimum required by the ordinance. In addition, any hardship would be considered self-created. (Cox 2003)

CHEMICAL OXYGEN DEMAND (COD)

A measure of the amount of oxygen required to oxidize organic and oxidizable inorganic compounds in water.

Comment: The COD test, like the BOD (biological oxygen demand) test, is used to determine the degree of pollution in an effluent.

CHICANES

See TRAFFIC CALMING.

CHILD-CARE CENTER

An establishment providing for the care, supervision, and protection of children.

Comment: Child care emerged as one of the critical planning issues of the 1980s and will continue to be because of the number of women in the workforce with children under the age of six years. The general definition is all-inclusive and requires further refinement for zoning use. Some of these refinements are suggested below.

EXEMPT CHILD-CARE CENTER:
Many states permit child care in private residences as permitted uses for a specified number of children—five or fewer, for example. This type of child care is the most widely used and, according to some experts, the preferred method. It is referred to as family day care because it is provided in a private residence occupied by the provider of the day care.

FAMILY DAY-CARE CENTER/HOME OCCUPATION:
New Jersey and some other states use a different approach and require municipalities to treat family day-care centers as any home occupation is treated. If home occupations are allowed in residential zones, family day-care centers must also be permitted. No additional or more restrictive controls are permitted. (N.J.S.A. 40:55D-66.4) The problem in using general home occupation criteria for family day-care centers is that they often limit the amount of square footage that the home occupation can occupy. The home occupation requirements must be carefully reviewed to ensure that they are not onerous.

Typically, family day-care centers are defined as a private residence, approved by a public or nonprofit agency, in which child-care services are regularly provided to no less than three and no more than five children for no less than 15 hours per week. Children legally related to the provider are not included in the care limits nor are children who are part of a cooperative agreement between parents for the care of their children by one or more of the parents and where no payment for the care is being provided.

LICENSED CHILD-CARE CENTER:
A third category of child-care centers is the licensed center that is regulated by a governmental agency (usually the state) and that by definition meets stringent licensing requirements. The requirement for state licensing is often triggered by the number of children in the center.

The planner has to decide in which zones licensed centers are appropriate. They could be permitted in residential zones, for instance, as conditional uses. In nonresidential districts, many states have followed the lead of New Jersey, which makes child-care centers permitted uses in all nonresidential districts, eliminates all off-street parking requirements, and exempts the floor area from any density or floor area ratio limits. (N.J.S.A. 40:55D-66.6)

Recent unpublished court cases have also recognized child-care centers in nonresidential zones as customary accessory uses.

CHIMNEY

A structure containing one or more flues for drawing off emissions from stationary sources of combustion. *See* STACK.

CHLORINATED HYDROCARBONS

A class of usually long-lasting, broad-spectrum insecticides.

Comment: The best known of the chlorinated hydrocarbons is DDT, first used for insect control during World War II. The characteristics of persistence and effectiveness against a wide variety of insect pests were long regarded as highly desirable in agriculture, public health, and home uses. Later research has revealed that these same qualities may represent a potential hazard through accumulation in the food chain and persistence in the environment.

CHLORINATION

The application of chlorine to drinking water, sewage, or industrial waste for disinfection or oxidation of undesirable compounds.

CHLORINATOR

A device for adding a chlorine-containing gas or liquid to drinking or wastewater.

CHLOROSIS

Yellowing or whitening of normally green plant parts caused by disease organisms, lack of oxygen or nutrients in the soil, or various air pollutants.

CHOKERS

See TRAFFIC CALMING.

CHRISTMAS TREE FARM

A land area cultivated for the growing, harvesting, and marketing of evergreen trees.

CHURCH

See MEGACHURCH; PLACE OF WORSHIP; RELIGIOUS USE.

CINEPLEX

See MEGAPLEX; MOTION PICTURE THEATER.

CIRCULATION

Systems, structures, and physical improvements for the movement of people, goods, water, air, sewage, or power by such means as streets, highways, railways, waterways, towers, airways, pipes, and conduits and the handling of people and goods by such means as terminals, stations, warehouses, and other storage buildings or transshipment points.

CISTERN

A tank or reservoir used for storing rainwater.

CITIZEN PARTICIPATION

Public involvement in governmental policy formation and implementation.

CITY PLANNING

The decision-making process in which goals and objectives are established, existing resources and conditions analyzed, strategies developed, and legislation and policies enacted and adopted to achieve the goals and objectives as they relate to cities and communities.

CIVIC CENTER

A building or complex of buildings that houses government offices and services and that may include cultural, recreational, athletic, convention, and entertainment facilities.

Comment: Broadly speaking, ownership and operation by a governmental agency is no longer a critical element in the definition of a civic center. Governmental participation and/or sanction of a private endeavor would still meet the definition.

CLARIFICATION

In wastewater treatment, the removal of turbidity and suspended solids by settling, often aided by centrifugal action and chemically induced coagulation.

CLARIFIER

In wastewater treatment, a settling tank that mechanically removes settled solids from water.

CLEAN AIR ACT

A federal act establishing national air quality standards.

CLEAR-CUTTING

The large-scale, indiscriminate removal of trees, shrubs, and undergrowth with the intention of preparing real property for nonagricultural development purposes. (American Planning Association, *A Survey of Planning Definitions,* Planning Advisory Service Report No. 421, 1989)

Comment: In a tree preservation ordinance, the removal of dead trees and selective cutting in accordance with a forest management plan (often required to be prepared by a certified forester) is usually permitted. The

77

approving agency, in considering any development plan for a heavily wooded tract, should require submission of a tree retention plan. In addition to the removal of trees and vegetation, changes in grades and other significant cutting and filling can have deleterious impacts on the remaining trees. Many agencies require that trees to be retained be marked and protected by placing fencing around them at the drip line. This protects them, at least in theory, from construction activities. *See Figure 98.*

CLEAR FLOOR SPACE

The minimum unobstructed floor or ground space required to accommodate a single, stationary wheelchair and occupant. *See* AMERICANS WITH DISABILITIES ACT.

CLEAR VISION TRIANGLE

See SIGHT TRIANGLE.

CLERGY

Men and women who conduct religious services and undertake the duties prescribed by religious orders or denominations.

CLERGY RESIDENCE

The home of a member of the clergy and located on the same parcel as the house of worship.

Comment: Also referred to as a parsonage, vicarage, manse, or rectory. When located on the same lot as the house of worship, the clergy residence is a customary accessory use. When located on a separate lot, it is a single-family home. When the house is a clergy residence, bible studies, prayer meetings, counseling, committee meetings, and similar activities in the clergy residence are customary accessory uses.

CLINIC

An establishment where patients are admitted for examination and treatment on an outpatient basis by physicians, dentists, other medical personnel, psychologists, or social workers and where such examination and treatment generally require a stay of less than 24 hours.

Comment: The clinic, often associated with a hospital, is now more accurately described as an ambulatory health care facility in which outpatient treatment is provided.

CLOVERLEAF

A grade-separated, multiple-highway intersection that, by means of curving ramps from one level to another, permits traffic to move or turn in any of four directions without interference. *See Figure 87.*

Comment: Partial cloverleafs permit traffic movements in fewer than four directions.

CLUB

A group of people organized for a common purpose to pursue common goals, interests, or activities and usually characterized by certain membership qualifications, payment of fees and dues, regular meetings, and a constitution and bylaws.

Comment: Older zoning ordinances usually permitted clubs in residential neighborhoods under the phrase "clubs, lodges, and social buildings." Such clubs were assumed to draw their membership from the neighborhood. Today, clubs have become much more regionally oriented; consequently, there is little reason to permit them in low-density residential areas. A distinction also should be made between nonprofit clubs organized for religious, social, cultural, or educational purposes and those that usually are commercial in nature and primarily recreational, such as tennis and racquetball clubs. *See* FRATERNAL ORGANIZATION.

CLUBHOUSE

A building, or portion thereof, used by a club.

CLUSTER

A development design technique that concentrates buildings on a part of the site to allow the remaining land to be used for recreation, common open space, and preservation of environmentally sensitive features.

CLUSTER SUBDIVISION

A form of development that permits a reduction in lot area and bulk requirements, provided there is no increase in the number of lots permitted under a conventional subdivision or increase in the overall density of development, and the remaining land area is devoted to open space, active recreation, preservation of environmentally sensitive areas, or agriculture. *See Figure 19.*

Comment: The cluster subdivision is an excellent planning concept that has been used successfully in many communities. Some communities require the developer to submit a conventional subdivision plan to establish the number of developable lots possible and a cluster subdivision plan to determine the appropriateness of cluster design for the site. Cluster should not be used to subsidize a developer who buys a piece of land with development constraints, such as steep slopes, wetlands, and floodplains, and expects the yield to be the same as if the land were completely developable. *See* CRITICAL AREA.

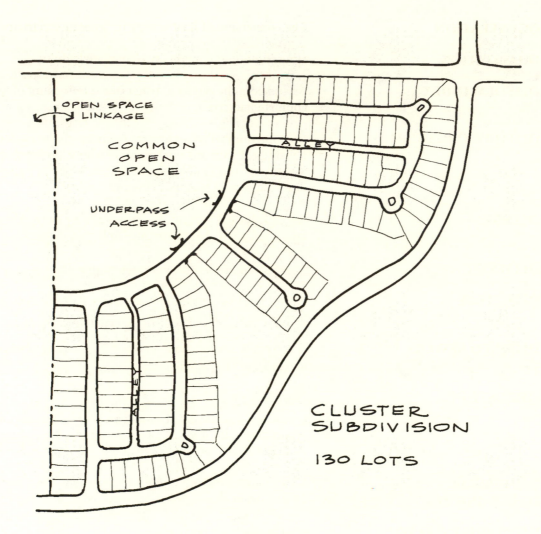

OPEN SPACE LINKAGE

COMMON OPEN SPACE

UNDERPASS ACCESS

ALLEY

ALLEY

CLUSTER SUBDIVISION

130 LOTS

FIGURE 19

The cluster subdivision technique can be used in conjunction with an areawide plan for a system of pathways and bikeways or the conservation of wildlife corridors or riverside areas. This approach means that implementation of a circulation system, recreation program, or the conservation of environmentally sensitive areas can be achieved through the development process. Cluster subdivisions can also be used to preserve lands in agricultural uses, thus serving as an alternative to the purchase of development rights. *See* CONSERVATION AREA.

COGENERATION

The conversion of heat energy to generate electricity.

COHABITATION

Household that contains two unrelated adults.

COLIFORM INDEX

An index of the purity of water based on a count of its coliform bacteria.

COLIFORM ORGANISM

Any of a number of organisms common to the intestinal tract of humans and animals whose presence in wastewater is an indication of pollution and of potentially dangerous bacterial contamination.

COLLEGE

An educational institution authorized by the state to award associate, baccalaureate, or higher degrees.

COLLIERY

A coal mine, its buildings, and equipment.

COLOSSEUM

A large enclosed and roofed structure used for spectator sports, exhibitions, and cultural events.

COMBINED SEWERS

A sewerage system that carries both sanitary sewage and stormwater runoff.

COMBUSTION

Burning.

Comment: Technically, combustion is a rapid oxidation accompanied by the release of energy in the form of heat and light.

COMMERCIAL CONDOMINIUM

See CONDOMINIUM.

COMMERCIAL GARAGE

See GARAGE, PUBLIC.

COMMERCIAL GREENHOUSE

A structure in which plants, vegetables, flowers, and similar materials are grown for sale.

COMMERCIAL USE

Activity involving the sale of goods or services carried out for profit.

COMMERCIAL VEHICLE

Any motor vehicle licensed by the state as a commercial vehicle.

Comment: Current practice is to permit only certain types of commercial vehicles in residential zones, such as passenger vehicles licensed as commercial vehicles, or vans or small trucks of up to a certain carrying capacity or gross vehicle weight limitation.

COMMINUTION

Mechanical shredding or pulverizing of waste, converting it into a homogeneous and more manageable material.

Comment: Used in solid waste management and in the primary stage of wastewater treatment.

COMMINUTOR

A device that grinds solids to make them easier to treat.

COMMON ELEMENTS

Land amenities; certain areas of buildings, such as lobbies, corridors, and hallways; central services and utilities; and any other elements and facilities owned and used by all condominium unit owners and designated in the master deed as common elements.

COMMON LATERAL

A pipe carrying sewage from more than one dwelling unit. (N.J.A.C. 5:21-1.4)

COMMON OPEN SPACE

See OPEN SPACE, COMMON.

COMMON OWNERSHIP

Ownership by one or more individuals in any form of ownership of two or more contiguous lots.

COMMON PASSAGEWAY

A commonly shared or used pedestrian or vehicular way that connects or serves two or more properties. *See* PARTY DRIVEWAY.

COMMUNICATION USE

Establishments furnishing point-to-point communication services, whether by wire or wireless means, either aurally, visually, or by radio frequency, including radio and television broadcasting stations and the exchange or recording of messages. *See* WIRELESS TELECOMMUNICATIONS TOWERS AND FACILITIES.

Comment: Some care must be exercised in permitting all communication uses, since the term covers a wide range of uses and impacts. For example, radio broadcast stations often include high, multitower antennas covering large areas. Point-to-point communication services using cable, on the other hand, may be indistinguishable from a typical office use.

COMMUNITY ASSOCIATION

A homeowners association organized to own, maintain, and operate common facilities and to enhance and protect their common interests.

COMMUNITY CENTER

A facility used for recreational, social, educational, and cultural activities.

COMMUNITY CHARACTER

The image of a community or area as defined by such factors as its built environment, natural features and open space elements, type of housing, architectural style, infrastructure, and the type and quality of public facilities and services.

COMMUNITY DESIGN PLAN

An element or subplan element of a local master plan that provides supporting data and policy guidelines for the enactment of design-related land development regulations and for the review of community development proposals.

Comment: The end product of the urban planning process is the built environment. If that end product is to be a visual as well as social, economic, and functional success, there must be three-dimensional design input into that process. Depending on community size and needs, community design plan proposals may range from a set of general policy statements or guidelines to detailed urban design plans and standards for every neighborhood. In addition, the community design plan may also provide design guidelines for development application review by the municipal planner and planning board; provide design guidelines for all municipal departments, agencies, and commissions in decisions affecting community design in their own operations; inform architects, builders, and developers of design guidelines for development that are considered important to the community; and provide general education in community design to increase public awareness of the issues, focus the efforts of improvement groups, and influence the many small design decisions that collectively affect the character of the community. *See* COMPATIBLE DESIGN.

COMMUNITY DEVELOPMENT BOUNDARY

See URBAN GROWTH BOUNDARY; URBAN SERVICE BOUNDARY.

COMMUNITY FACILITY

A building or structure owned and operated by a governmental agency to provide a governmental service to the public.

COMMUNITY IMPACT STUDY

See IMPACT ANALYSIS.

COMMUNITY OF PLACE

A dynamic, diverse, compact, and efficient center that has evolved and been maintained at a human scale, with an easily accessible central core of commercial and community services, residential units, and recognizable natural and built landmarks and boundaries that provide a sense of place and orientation. (*New Jersey State Development and Redevelopment Plan* 2000) *See* HUMAN SCALE; SENSE OF PLACE.

COMMUNITY RESIDENCES FOR THE DEVELOPMENTALLY DISABLED (CRDD)

Residential facilities, licensed by the state, providing food, shelter, and personal guidance, with supervision, to developmentally disabled or mentally ill persons who require assistance, temporarily or permanently, in order to live in the community. (Adapted from the New Jersey *Municipal Land Use Law* [N.J.S.A. 40:55D-66.2]) *See* BOARDING HOME FOR SHELTERED CARE.

Comment: CRDDs normally include group homes, halfway houses, intermediate care facilities, and supervised apartment living arrangements.

COMMUNITY RESIDENTIAL HOME

A dwelling unit licensed to provide a living environment for unrelated residents who operate as the functional equivalent of a family, including such supervision and care by supportive staff as may be necessary to meet the physical, emotional, and social needs of an aged person, a physically disabled or handicapped person, a developmentally disabled person, an undangerous mentally ill person, and a child as defined in the appropriate statute. *See* CONGREGATE RESIDENCES.

Comment: A community residential home is similar to congregate residences. In both cases, the residents served may be defined under a specific state statute. It would be important to cite the statute to provide a more specific definition of whom the home is designed to serve.

COMMUNITY SHELTERS FOR VICTIMS OF DOMESTIC VIOLENCE

A residence providing food, shelter, medical care, legal assistance, personal guidance, and other services to persons who have been victims of domestic violence, including any children of such victims, and who temporarily require shelter and assistance in order to protect their physical or psychological welfare. (Adapted from the New Jersey *Municipal Land Use Law* ([N.J.S.A. 40:55D-66.1])

Comment: *See* COMMUNITY RESIDENCES FOR THE DEVELOPMENTALLY DISABLED.

COMPACT CAR

Any motor vehicle that does not exceed 15 feet in length, bumper to bumper, and 5 feet, 9 inches in width.

COMPACTION

Reducing the bulk of solid waste by rolling, tamping, and compression.

COMPATIBLE DESIGN

The visual relationship between adjacent and nearby buildings and the immediate streetscape, in terms of a consistency of materials, colors, building elements, building mass, and other constructed elements of the urban environment, such that abrupt or severe differences are avoided.

Comment: Two of the major problems facing planners today with respect to compatible design are "teardowns" and "poptops" (American Planning Association, *Planning*, October 1999). Teardowns are buildings (usually dwellings) purchased for the specific purpose of replacement, almost always on a larger scale than the original. Poptops are second-story additions, usually considerably higher than the surrounding structures.

Many planners would agree that residential teardowns are part of the natural evolutionary process that takes place within neighborhoods. As noted by Charles Crook, planning director of Lake Forest (Illinois), in the previously cited planning article, "Some houses deserve to be torn down . . . [but] . . . you need to control what you put up in their place." (ibid, p. 7)

A number of different techniques have been suggested to ensure that replacement homes or major expansions still remain compatible with the surrounding homes and reflect the neighborhood fabric. These techniques include FAR (floor area ratio) limits, building scale calculations, encroachment planes, and similar methods. With the exception of FAR limits, these techniques appear to be complicated and labor-intensive.

Generally speaking, the techniques that seem to work include making house size a function of lot size, that is, smaller houses on smaller lots. Thus, a 5,000-square-foot lot with a maximum FAR of .30 would permit a 1,500-square-foot house. Larger lots would allow larger houses, but the FAR would probably have to be reduced in order to keep the houses compatible with the neighborhood. A 15,000-square-foot lot with the same FAR as the one permitted for the 5,000-square-foot lot (.30) would result in a house with 4,500 square feet. This probably would be inconsistent with the overall neighborhood design. A FAR of between .20 and .25 would probably be appropriate. The exact FAR would have to be determined after more detailed studies of the prevailing FAR in the neighborhood, possibly as part of the design element of the master plan.

More important, however, new houses or expansions of existing houses should take place on the lot only in such a manner that the character of the existing streetscape is not seriously affected. This requires that the existing front yard and side yard setbacks remain the same, or in the case of the side yards, any encroachment take place toward the rear of the lot. Building heights can be increased, but that part of the roof that is raised should be set back farther from the front building line.

One additional point worth noting is that most houses are not built to existing setback requirements, except on very small lots. In other words, on moderately sized and larger lots, with the exception of the front building line, many houses can be expanded to the rear and sides and still conform to existing codes. But this type of expansion or new house will be significantly different from the existing neighborhood character. A detailed survey of the existing development characteristics is needed to establish a realistic and effective set of controls. This type of survey can best be done by the use of aerial photography. *See* COMMUNITY DESIGN PLAN; DESIGN FIT.

COMPATIBLE LAND USE

A use of land and/or building(s) that, in terms of development intensity, building coverage, design, bulk and occupancy, traffic generation, parking requirements, access and circulation, site improvements, and public facilities and service demands, is consistent with and similar to neighboring uses and does not adversely affect the quality of life of persons in surrounding or nearby buildings. *See* QUALITY OF LIFE; COMPATIBLE DESIGN.

Comment: The definition spells out the specific criteria that should be examined but also includes a determination as to whether the use adversely affects the quality of life of the neighborhood residents. Compatible land uses may include different land uses that are mutually supportive and necessary, providing goods and services, economic opportunities, and a healthy and safe environment.

COMPLETE APPLICATION

An application for development completed as specified by ordinance and the rules and regulations of the approving authority and the provisions of all required documents.

Comment: Most states require that a determination of completeness be made within a specific period of time and on the meeting of all requirements specified in the ordinance and in the rules and regulations of the approving authority. On the day it is so certified by the administrative officer, the time period for action by the approving authority begins. Problems occasionally occur when a required document, on initial review, does not appear to substantially meet the ordinance requirements. For example, a landscaping plan showing only foundation plants surrounding a building on a 10-acre site may be rejected outright as incomplete. However, a better way to handle questionable submissions is to certify them as complete but, after detailed review, to reject the questionable or unacceptable element as not in conformance with the technical or design standards set forth in the ordinance.

COMPONENT FACTORS

The various parts of a road, including right-of-way, grading, surface and subsurface drainage provisions, curbs, gutters, catch basins, foundations, shoulders and slopes, wearing surfaces, bridges, culverts, retaining walls, intersections, private entrances, guide rails, trees, illumination, guideposts and signs, ornamentation, and monuments.

COMPOST

Relatively stable decomposed organic matter.

COMPOSTING

A controlled process of degrading organic matter by microorganisms.

Comment: Composting may be achieved by several methods: (1) mechanical—a method in which the compost is continuously and mechanically mixed and aerated; (2) ventilated cell—compost is mixed and aerated by being dropped through a vertical series of ventilated cells; and (3) windrow—an open-air method in which compostable material is placed in windrows, piles, or ventilated bins or pits and occasionally turned or mixed. The process may be anaerobic or aerobic.

COMPREHENSIVE PLAN

See MASTER PLAN.

COMPRESSED WORKWEEK PROGRAM

A program that allocates the working hours into fewer than 5 days per week or fewer than 10 days per two-week period, such as a 4-day workweek or a 9-day, 80-hour schedule.

CONCENTRATED ANIMAL FEEDING OPERATION (CAFO)

A parcel of land, with or without buildings, used or intended to be used for the confined feeding, breeding, raising, or holding of animals in excess of 200 animal units and specifically designed to store and accumulate animal manure and other waste products in holding areas and lagoons.

Comment: Concentrated (the term "confined" is also used) animal feeding operations (also known as feedlots) are industrial operations with enormous potential for air, water, and soil pollution. While experts agree that the most serious problems come from hog operations, all CAFOs can have major adverse impacts over large areas in proximity to the operation unless careful management procedures and processes are undertaken and implemented. These might include large setbacks to residential areas, injection of manure rather than spraying, and the use of covered lagoons. The topic is complex and calls for the assistance of qualified agricultural engineers to address these potential problems. In addition, many states have included CAFOs under their "right to farm" legislation, making it difficult to apply zoning as a means of controlling these uses. In these states, as well as in states where zoning is used, some controls have been included as part of local health and environmental legislation.

While the definition specifically calls for a maximum of 200 animal units, the local ordinance may establish higher or lower limits. The definition of ANIMAL UNIT notes each swine over 55 pounds constitutes 0.4 animal units. A typical family farm might have 500 swine (Barrette 1996) or 200 animal units. An ordinance allowing up to a maximum of 200 animal units on a farm would then clearly preclude CAFOs.

One approach recommended by James Duncan and Associates (1996) for Minnesota communities divides agricultural uses into limited agricultural and general agricultural zones. The limited agricultural category does not permit any livestock production, while the general agricultural permits large-scale uses and feedlots. Obviously, the requirements for each are significantly different, and the general agricultural zones can be located in areas where their impact on existing or potential new development is minimized.

In addition to controlling the operation of these uses, some provision should be included for returning the soil to a viable, non-feedlot agriculture use when the CAFO is discontinued or abandoned. This may call for escrow or bonds to avoid the creation of "rural brownfields." (Schwab 1998)

The best and most comprehensive discussion of CAFO is the American Planning Association's Planning Advisory Service Report No. 482, *Planning and Zoning for Concentrated Animal Feeding Operations,* by Jim Schwab, December 1998. The October 1996 issue of APA's *Zoning News* also discusses feedlots in the Barrette article. *See* FEEDLOT.

CONCEPT PLAN

A schematic or conceptual design for land development, prepared for informal review purposes, that carries no vesting rights or obligations on any party. *See* PLAT, SKETCH.

Comment: Many approving authorities use the informal concept plan review process to alert applicants to problems and requirements before the submission of a formal development application. Use of the concept plan review can save time and money for all parties.

CONCURRENCY

A finding by the approving authority that basic services are adequate to serve a proposed development.

Comment: Concurrency requirements may be very stringent, such as in Florida, which requires that public facilities must be in place before a development can be built; or less stringent, such as in Colorado, which requires only a finding as to the adequacy of sewer, water, and access before approval.

Basic services may include water, sewers, roads, schools, parks, and recreation facilities. The definition of "adequate" requires that, to the extent possible, objective standards be established to measure any deficiencies so that the applicant can be required to provide his or her fair share of bringing these services up to the standard.

The three objectives of requiring adequacy standards are to (a) ensure that new development actually has adequate services; (b) prevent totally inappropriate subdivision in areas with poor services; and (c) increase the cost of marginal subdivisions on remote land, making development closer to urbanized areas more attractive. (Kelly 1999) *See* PRO RATA.

CONDEMNATION

The exercise by a governmental agency of the right of eminent domain. *See* EMINENT DOMAIN.

CONDITIONAL USE

A use permitted in a particular zoning district when it is shown that such use in a specified location will comply with all the conditions and standards for the location or operation of the use as specified in the zoning ordinance and authorized by the approving authority.

Comment: Conditional uses are permitted uses and are appropriate in the zoning district only when all conditions are met. For example, houses of worship may be desirable in a residential area, but controls over parking, circulation, setbacks, and landscaping may be needed to prevent them from adversely affecting surrounding residences. By classifying them as conditional uses, separate regulations can be imposed to mitigate the adverse impacts. In some states, conditional uses are classified as special-exception uses. In all cases, the conditions must be specific.

CONDITIONAL USE PERMIT

A permit issued by the approving authority stating that the conditional use meets all conditions set forth in local ordinances.

CONDITIONS OF APPROVAL

Requirements established by the approving authority before preliminary or final approval of an application for development becomes effective.

Comment: Applications for development are often approved by the responsible authority subject to certain changes, corrections, or compliance with other agency reviews or approval. These changes and corrections, usually minor in nature, and compliance with other agency reviews or approvals, usually statutory, must be achieved before the application is deemed approved. Required signatures, for example, are withheld until the municipal engineer or planner certifies that all conditions are met. Any time limits for appeals, building permits, and so on run from the time all conditions of approval have been met.

CONDOMINIUM

A building, or group of buildings, in which dwelling units, offices, or floor area are owned individually and the structure, common areas, and facilities are owned by all the owners on a proportional, undivided basis.

Comment: By definition, a condominium has common areas and facilities, and there is an association of owners organized for the purpose of maintaining, administering, and operating the common areas and facilities. It is a legal form of ownership of real estate and not a specific building style. The purchaser has title to his or her interior space in the building and an undivided interest in parts of the interior, the exterior, and other common elements. The property is identified in a master deed and recorded on a plat with the local jurisdiction. The common elements usually include the land underneath and surrounding the building, certain improvements on the land, and such items as plumbing, wiring, and major utility systems, the interior areas between walls, public interior spaces, exterior walls, parking areas, private roads, and recreational facilities.

Most states do not permit zoning ordinances to differentiate among various forms of ownership. Thus, an ordinance could not limit the principal use as a condominium or cooperative as opposed to rental housing or leased space.

CONDOMINIUM ASSOCIATION

The community association that administers and maintains the common property and common elements of a condominium.

Comment: Condominium associations differ from other forms of community associations in that the condominium association does not have title to the common property and facilities. These are owned by the condominium owner on a proportional, undivided basis.

CONDOMINIUM HOTEL

A building constructed, maintained, and operated and managed as a hotel in which each room is individually owned and in which some or all of the rooms are available to transients for rent, and where the structure, common areas, and facilities are owned by all the owners on a proportional, individual basis.

CONFERENCE CENTER

A facility used for conferences and seminars, with accommodations for sleeping, food preparation and eating, recreation, entertainment, resource facilities, meeting rooms, fitness and health center, and retail stores and services primarily for conference center guests.

Comment: The definition could also include a minimum and maximum number of rooms and a minimum floor area for seminar and conference facilities related to the number of rooms. An informal study of conference centers found approximately 90 square feet of meeting and seminar room space per sleeping room. A 100-room conference inn would have about 9,000 square feet of meeting rooms.

Communities also must decide whether or not to allow conference centers to rent rooms and facilities to transients other than those attending conferences. Very often a specific percentage of rooms must be reserved for conference participants, with the remainder available for transients.

CONFERENCE INN

A hotel with a primary focus on conference center activities. *See* CONFERENCE CENTER; HOTEL.

CONGREGATE RESIDENCES

Apartments and dwellings with communal dining facilities and services, such as housekeeping, organized social and recreational activities, transportation services, laundry, and other support services appropriate for the residents and designed to provide a relatively independent lifestyle. *See* COMMUNITY RESIDENTIAL HOME.

91

Comment: Congregate apartment residences are often developed in conjunction with assisted living facilities. Long-term care is sometimes added as well, so that a range of accommodations and a continuum of care can be provided.

Congregate residences may also function as boarding homes for sheltered care, community residences for the developmentally disabled, and community shelters for the victims of domestic violence. For these groups, specialized on-site support services may also be provided. *See* ASSISTED LIVING FACILITY; BOARDING HOME FOR SHELTERED CARE; COMMUNITY RESIDENCES FOR THE DEVELOPMENTALLY DISABLED; COMMUNITY SHELTERS FOR VICTIMS OF DOMESTIC VIOLENCE; CONTINUING CARE RETIREMENT COMMUNITY; LONG-TERM CARE FACILITY.

CONSERVATION AREA

Environmentally sensitive areas with characteristics such as steep slopes, wetlands, floodplains, high water tables, forest areas, endangered species habitat, dunes, or areas of significant biological productivity or uniqueness that have been designated for protection from any activity that would significantly alter their ecological integrity, balance, or character. (American Planning Association, *A Survey of Zoning Definitions,* Planning Advisory Service Report No. 421, 1989) *See* CLUSTER SUBDIVISION; CRITICAL AREA.

Comment: Local ordinances could specify more specific standards, such as the percentage of slope considered steep (often 20 percent) or how high a water table (less than 3 feet). Environmentally sensitive areas may also have been mapped as part of the open space and conservation element of a comprehensive plan.

CONSERVATION DISTRICT

See SOIL CONSERVATION DISTRICT.

CONSERVATION DISTRICT, HISTORIC

See HISTORIC AREA.

CONSERVATION EASEMENT

See EASEMENT, CONSERVATION.

CONSIDERATION

An inducement to a contract.

CONSISTENCY

A requirement that all land development regulations be consistent with the comprehensive or master plan of the municipality, county, or state.

Comment: New Jersey, as do many other states, requires that all zoning "either be substantially consistent with the land use plan element and the housing plan element of the master plan, or designed to effectuate such plan element" (N.J.S.A. 40:55D-62a, NJ *Municipal Land Use Law*) In states with consistency requirements, ordinance amendments that are inconsistent can be successfully attacked in court. In some states, where inconsistent amendments are permitted, they may require a supermajority (a majority of the fully authorized membership of the governing body, as opposed to a majority of the members present), and a statement citing the reasons for the inconsistency.

In states where a separate written comprehensive plan is not required and a municipality has chosen not to adopt one, consistency may have to be evaluated in terms of municipal goals and objectives, adequate findings, and consideration of neighboring land uses. (Dennison 1996)

CONSOLIDATION

The removal of lot lines between contiguous parcels.

Comment: Consolidation of several lots into a single lot or tract is usually considered an exempt subdivision. *See* ASSEMBLAGE; SUBDIVISION.

CONSTRUCTION OFFICIAL

See BUILDING INSPECTOR.

CONSTRUCTION PERMIT

Legal authorization for the erection, alteration, or extension of a structure.

CONTEXT

See DEVELOPMENT CONTEXT.

CONTIGUOUS

Next to, abutting, or touching and having a boundary, or portion thereof, that is coterminous. *See* ABUT; ADJOINING LOT OR LAND.

CONTINUING CARE RETIREMENT COMMUNITY (CCRC)

An age-restricted development that provides a continuum of accommodations and care, from independent living to long-term bed care, and enters into contracts to provide lifelong care in exchange for the payment of monthly fees and an entrance fee in excess of one year of monthly fees.

Comment: What distinguishes a CCRC from other types of mixed residential development is (1) a contract for lifelong care; (2) monthly maintenance fees; and (3) a substantial entrance fee always greater than one year of monthly fees. Because of the substantial amounts of money required to enter a CCRC and the long-term commitment, many states have established stringent controls over CCRCs, including licensing, certificates of need, and full financial disclosure.

A CCRC typically includes independent living units, congregate residences, assisted care units, and a long-term bed care section. All units are age restricted. The independent living units may be single-family detached or attached housing or apartments.

CCRCs include health care services and meals, with common dining facilities, physical therapy facilities and activities, meeting rooms, social activities, recreation facilities, on-site services and shops, and other ancillary services customarily accessory to the principal permitted use.

From a zoning perspective, CCRCs should be designated as conditional uses. Public water and sewer are necessary and the appropriate location is within, or at the edge of, a residential area. Since the traffic generation of a CCRC is significantly lower than nonage-restricted housing, a higher density can be accommodated. Setbacks typical of multifamily uses are also appropriate for CCRCs. *See* ASSISTED LIVING FACILITY; CONGREGATE RESIDENCES; RETIREMENT COMMUNITY.

CONTINUING EASEMENT

See EASEMENT, CONTINUING.

CONTOUR LINE

A line on a map that connects all points of the same ground elevation. *See* TOPOGRAPHIC MAP.

Comment: Contour maps are the standard way of representing ground form. The contour lines on topographic maps indicate the slope of the land. The closer the lines are to each other, the steeper the slope. Conversely, the farther apart the contour lines, the flatter the slope. The contour lines represent a vertical interval. In relatively flat areas, a topographic map using a 1- or 2-foot contour interval is necessary for planning design and review purposes. For areas with steep slopes, a 5- or 10-foot contour interval may be adequate. *See Figure 20.*

CONTRACTOR'S STORAGE YARD

A lot or portion of a lot or parcel used to store and maintain construction equipment and other materials and facilities customarily required in the building trade by a construction contractor.

CONVALESCENT CENTER

A facility that provides short-term, primarily in-patient care, treatment, and/or rehabilitation services for persons recovering from illness or injury who do not require continued hospitalization. *See* INTERMEDIATE CARE FACILITY.

94

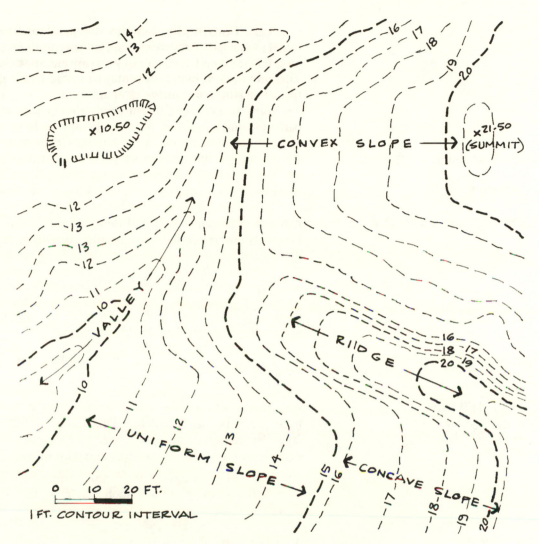

FROM GRADE EASY, BY RICHARD K. UNTERMANN

CONTOUR MAP

FIGURE 20

All points on a contour line have the same elevation. A contour line connects points of the equal elevation.

A contour line that closes on itself is either a summit or a depression. Both are indicated by a spot elevation at the highest or the lowest point. A depression is also indicated by placing hachure marks on the low side of the contour line.

Contour lines never cross other contours except where there is an overhanging cliff, natural bridge, or similar condition.

On a convex slope (gentler slope at the summit), the higher contours are spaced farther apart than the lower ones. On a concave slope (steeper slope at the summit), the lower contour lines are spaced farther apart than the higher ones.

Source: Richard K. Untermann, *Grade Easy* (American Society of Landscape Architects, 1989).

Comment: Convalescent centers are now generally referred to as rehabilitation centers. Unlike nursing homes and similar extended and long-term care facilities, convalescent homes are similar to short-term care facilities that assist patients in physical rehabilitation and recovery from illness or injury. They may also include outpatient services.

CONVENIENCE STORE

See RETAIL STORE, CONVENIENCE.

CONVENT

The dwelling of female members of a religious order.

CONVENTION FACILITY

A building or portion thereof designed to accommodate 300 or more people in assembly. *See* CONFERENCE CENTER.

Comment: The definition is admittedly broad, and the figure 300 is arbitrary. It is designed to give the municipality as much control over these very intensive uses as possible. Most municipalities restrict them to central business districts. Standards have to be established relating to parking, setbacks, signs, landscaping, and circulation.

**CONVENTIONAL
ENERGY SYSTEM**

Any energy system, including supply elements, furnaces, burners, tanks, boilers, related controls, and energy-distribution components, that uses any source(s) of energy other than solar energy and windmills.

Comment: The sources of conventional energy systems include the usual fossil fuels, such as gas, oil, and coal, as well as nuclear fuels.

CONVERSION

A change in the use of land or a structure.

COOLING TOWER

A device to remove excess heat from water used in industrial operations, notably in electric power generation.

CORNER LOT

See LOT, CORNER.

CORNICE

Any horizontal member, structural or nonstructural, projecting outward from the exterior walls at the roofline, including eaves and other roof overhang. *See Figure 21.*

CORRECTIONAL FACILITY

A public or privately operated facility housing persons awaiting trial or persons serving a sentence after being found guilty of a criminal offense.

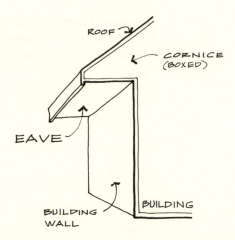

FIGURE 21

COST-BENEFIT ANALYSIS

An analytical method whereby the primary and secondary costs of a proposed project are measured against the benefits to be received from the project.

Comment: The field of cost-benefit analysis is complex. For instance, some cost-benefit analyses consider only primary costs and benefits. Others may include secondary and tertiary costs and benefits. (Burchell and Listokin 1980)

COTTAGE

A small, detached dwelling unit.

Comment: A cottage is usually an outbuilding on a larger tract of land. Originally, the cottage may have been a seasonal dwelling without heat but later converted to an all-year-round dwelling. Local ordinances should specify minimum standards for space, heating, and sanitary facilities as a condition of conversion.

COTTAGE INDUSTRY

A home occupation.

Comment: "Cottage industry" is an obsolete term previously used to describe manufacturing and assembly carried out in the home, often on a contract basis, with the entire family working. In later years, cottage industry was accessory to the principal residential use and was often carried out in an outbuilding or accessory structure. It is now used to describe start-up businesses or occupations carried out by single practitioners in their homes.

COUNCIL OF GOVERNMENTS

A regional planning and review authority whose membership includes representation from all communities in the designated region.

COUNTRY CLUB

A recreational facility, usually restricted to members and their guests, which generally includes a clubhouse, dining and eating establishments, and recreational facilities such as golf course(s), tennis courts, and swimming pools.

Comment: While most country club facilities are restricted to members and their guests, some clubs make available their facilities to nonmembers for weddings, banquets, golf tournaments, dances, conferences, and so forth. In addition, the restaurants may be open to the general public, and some country clubs offer limited memberships for specific facilities such as golf, swimming, or tennis. The expanded use of the country club to nonmembers often creates a year-round, active, and heavily patronized facility. When these clubs are located in residential areas, the heavy use can create friction between surrounding residents and club patrons.

Another factor to be considered is the fact that the golf course, almost always a feature of a country club, is a significant user of water and is heavily dependent on pesticides and fertilizers. New clubs should be required to indicate water sources and a best-management protocol limiting the use of chemical pesticides and fertilizers.

COUNTY MASTER PLAN

The official master plan for the physical development of a county.

COURT

Any open space, unobstructed from the ground to the sky, that is bounded on two or more sides by the walls of a building that is on the same lot. *See* PLAZA; SQUARE. *See Figure 17.*

COURT, INNER

An open area, unobstructed from the ground to the sky, that is bounded on more than three sides by the exterior walls of one or more buildings. *See Figure 22.*

COURT, OUTER

An open area, unobstructed from the ground to the sky, that is bounded on not more than three sides by the exterior walls of one or more buildings. *See Figure 22.*

COVE

A small bay or inlet or a sheltered recess in a cliff face.

COVENANT

See RESTRICTIVE COVENANT.

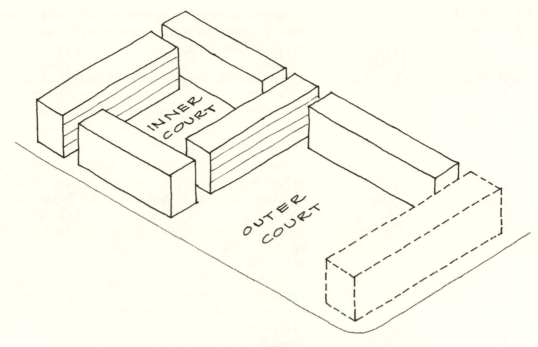

FIGURE 22

COVER MATERIAL Soil that is used to cover compacted solid waste in a sanitary landfill.

COVERAGE *See* BUILDING COVERAGE; LOT COVERAGE.

COVERED EMPLOYMENT Employees covered by the state's unemployment compensation law.

Comment: In some states, covered employment and covered employment trends are used in formulas to determine lower-income housing needs. The amount of change is measured by a linear regression equation over a time span sufficiently long—seven years, for example—to minimize the impact of short-term fluctuations.

CRAFTSPERSON An individual having creative skills in manufacturing or arrangement of materials resulting in a finished product or commodity such as wearing apparel, home decorations, jewelry, toys, furniture, leather goods, dried flowers, or similar products.

CRAWL SPACE A space between the ceiling of one story and floor of the next story, which usually contains pipes, ducts, wiring and lighting fixtures, and permits access but is too low for an individual to stand. *See Figure 8.*

Comment: The crawl space may be a cellar area no more than 4.5 feet high or, if between a ceiling and a flat or shed roof, a cockloft.

CREEK

A small stream somewhat larger than a brook.

CRITERIA POLLUTANT

One of the six air pollutants used by the federal Environmental Protection Agency to measure ambient air quality under the Clean Air Act.

Comment: The six air pollutants are nitrogen dioxide, sulfur dioxide, particulate matter, lead, ozone, and carbon monoxide. *See* PERFORMANCE ZONING.

CRITICAL AREA

An area with one or more of the following environmental characteristics: (1) steep slopes; (2) floodplain; (3) soils classified as having high water tables; (4) soils classified as highly erodible, subject to erosion, or highly acidic; (5) land incapable of meeting percolation requirements; (6) land formerly used for landfill operations or hazardous industrial use; (7) fault areas; (8) stream corridors; (9) estuaries; (10) mature stands of native vegetation; (11) aquifer recharge and discharge areas; (12) wetlands and wetland transition areas; and (13) habitats of endangered species. *See* CONSERVATION AREA.

Comment: The purpose of classifying certain lands as critical areas is to focus attention on these lands and to set standards to regulate development in these areas. Local ordinances should specify standards within these general categories, such as the percentages of slope considered steep (often 20 percent) or water table height. The additional requirements may also include the preparation and submission of an environmental impact statement or requirement that the applicant specifically address what measures will be taken with respect to the critical elements. Local development ordinances can also provide for shifting development from critical areas to non-critical areas of the site. This transfer provision often results in greater cooperation from builders since the development potential of the site is preserved. *See* CLUSTER SUBDIVISION.

CRITICAL HABITATS

Biologically diverse areas containing habitats of endangered or threatened plant or animal species; contiguous freshwater wetland systems, defined as the zone of biological diversity primarily supported by wetlands and wetland systems; and prime forested areas, including mature stands of native species. *See* BIODIVERSITY.

CROP

A harvestable product, planted, grown, and cultivated in the soil.

CROSSWALK

Any portion of a roadway distinctly indicated for pedestrian crossing by lines or other surface markings or by a change in surface material.

CUBIC CONTENT

The volume of space contained within the walls of a room or building found by multiplying the height, width, and length.

CUL-DE-SAC

See STREET, CUL-DE-SAC; STREET, DEAD-END.

CULTURAL EUTROPHICATION

Acceleration of the natural aging process of bodies of water.

Comment: Eutrophication often takes place because of runoff from cultivated lawns or the use of septic systems that introduce nutrients into the water, thus hastening the growth of algae and underwater plants.

CULTURAL FACILITIES

Establishments that document the social and religious structures and intellectual and artistic manifestations that characterize a society and include museums, art galleries, and botanical and zoological gardens of a natural, historic, educational, or cultural interest. (*New Lexicon Webster Dictionary* 1989)

Comment: While these activities may charge admission fees, the bulk of their expenses are usually borne by public agencies, foundations, or donations.

CULVERT

A drain, ditch, or conduit, not incorporated in a closed system, that carries drainage water under a driveway, roadway, railroad, pedestrian walk, or public way, or other type of overhead structure.

CUMULATIVE IMPACT

The total impact that results from an individual action under consideration, when added to the impacts of other past, present, and reasonable foreseeable future actions. (*New Jersey State Development and Redevelopment Plan* 2002)

Comment: The cumulative impact analysis is particularly important in assessing traffic and utility capacities. *See* CAPACITY ANALYSIS.

CUPOLA

A small roof tower, usually rising from the roof ridge. (Nelessen 1994)

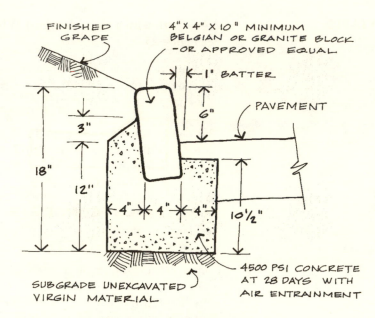

FINISHED GRADE

4" X 4" X 10" MINIMUM BELGIAN OR GRANITE BLOCK —OR APPROVED EQUAL

1" BATTER

PAVEMENT

6"

3"

18"

12"

4" 4" 4"

10½"

SUBGRADE UNEXCAVATED VIRGIN MATERIAL

4500 PSI CONCRETE AT 28 DAYS WITH AIR ENTRAINMENT

BLOCK CURB

FIGURE 23

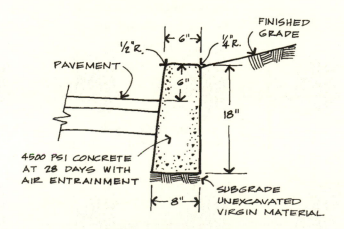

FINISHED GRADE

6"

½"R.

¼"R.

PAVEMENT

6"

18"

4500 PSI CONCRETE AT 28 DAYS WITH AIR ENTRAINMENT

SUBGRADE UNEXCAVATED VIRGIN MATERIAL

8"

CONCRETE CURB

FIGURE 24

CURB

A stone, concrete, or other improved boundary marking the edge of the roadway or paved area. *See Figures 23 and 24.*

102

CURB, MOUNTABLE

A low curb with a slope designed to be crossed easily. *See Figure 25.*

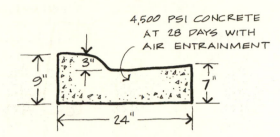

MOUNTABLE CONCRETE CURB

FIGURE 25

CURB CUT

The opening along the curb line at which point vehicles may enter or leave the roadway. *See Figure 68.*

CURB LEVEL

The permanently established grade of the curb top in front of a lot.

CURB RETURN

The connecting link between the street curb and the ramp or driveway curb. *See Figure 26.*

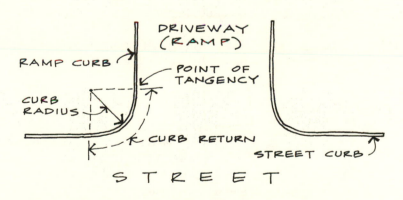

FIGURE 26

CURRENT

(1) The volume of water passing a given point measured in cubic feet per second; (2) the part of any body of water that has more or less steady flow in a definite direction for certain periods during the day.

CURRENT PLANNING CAPACITY (CPC)

A measure of the ability of a region to accommodate growth and development within the limits set by existing infrastructure and natural resource capabilities. *See* CAPACITY ANALYSIS; CUMULATIVE IMPACT.

Comment: Generally, CPC is defined by water supply, water and air quality, sewage capability, highway capacity, and available community facilities. Some development ordinances award points for various infrastructure improvements and subtract them when certain environmental constraints are noted. The higher the number of points, the higher the permitted development density.

In Florida, a "CPC-like" point system, included in an Urban Area Residential checklist (part of the County Comprehensive Plan), permits applicants to request higher densities based on the following: proximity to commercial or employment centers; vehicular access to an arterial; access to mass transit; fire protection; water supply and sewers; percentage of affordable housing to be provided; access to schools; and proximity to parks and recreation.

It is important to keep in mind that CPC does not necessarily yield appropriate or desired densities or levels of development. It often represents a cap.

CURTAIN WALL

A nonstructural exterior building wall, usually window or window panel dominated.

CURVILINEAR STREET SYSTEM

A pattern of streets that is curved. *See Figure 27.*

CUT

A portion of land surface or area from which earth has been removed or will be removed by excavation; the depth below the original ground surface or excavated surface. *See Figure 42.*

CUTOFF

The point at which all light rays emitted by a lamp, light source, or luminaire are completely eliminated at a specific angle above the ground. (Kendig et al. 1980)

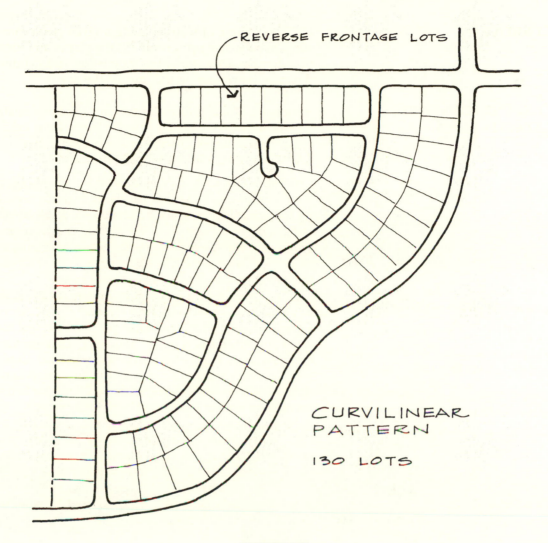

REVERSE FRONTAGE LOTS

CURVILINEAR
PATTERN

130 LOTS

FIGURE 27

CUTOFF ANGLE	The angle formed by a line drawn from the direction of light rays at the light source and a line perpendicular to the ground from the light source, above which no light is emitted. (Kendig et al. 1980)
CUTOFF-TYPE LUMINAIRE	A lamp or source of illumination with elements such as a shield, reflector, or refractor panels that direct and cut off the light at a cutoff angle less than 90 degrees. (Kendig et al. 1980)

D

DAM

An artificial dike, levee, embankment, or other barrier, with appurtenances, for the purpose of impounding or retaining water. *See* EMBANKMENT.

DATUM

A reference point, line, or plane used as a basis for measurements.

DAY-CARE CENTER/ DAY NURSERY

See CHILD-CARE CENTER.

DAY-CARE CENTER, ADULT

A facility providing care for the elderly and/or functionally impaired adults in a protective setting for part of a 24-hour day.

DE MINIMIS

A minimal deviation from the norm or standard.

Comment: A *de minimis* exception is often used to justify the grant of a design waiver or variance. In fact, Black says *de minimis* is "Of a fact or thing so insignificant that a court may overlook it in deciding an issue or case" (*Black's* 1999). In planning and zoning, *de minimis* means that the approval will not affect the basic standard and may not even be noticed, if granted. No attempt has been made to quantify what minimal means, and it varies with each application.

DEAD-END STREET

See STREET, DEAD-END.

DECELERATION LANE

An added roadway lane that permits vehicles to slow down and leave the main vehicle stream. *See Figure 1.*

DECIBEL

A unit of sound pressure level measuring the amplitude of sound.

Comment: The decibel (abbreviated dB) is used to express noise level. The reference level is a sound pressure of 20 micronewtons per square meter. Zero decibels, the starting point of the scale of noise level, is about the level of the weakest sound that can be heard by someone with very good hearing in an extremely quiet location. The noise level in an average residence is about 50 decibels; 20 feet from a subway train the noise level is about 90 decibels; and 200 feet from a jet, it is 120 decibels. *See* table D-1.

DECIDUOUS

Plants that drop their foliage annually before becoming dormant.

Comment: In specifying landscaping for buffer areas, there should be a mix of deciduous and evergreen trees, with the predominant emphasis on evergreens, which provide an all-year-round buffer.

TABLE D-1: SOUND LEVELS AND HUMAN RESPONSE

Common Sounds	Noise Level	Effect
Carrier deck Jet operation Air raid siren	140	Painfully loud
Jet takeoff (200 feet) Thunderclap	130	
Discotheque Auto horn (3 feet)	120	Maximum vocal effect
Pile drivers Chain saw (2 feet)	110	
Garbage truck (50 feet) Power lawn mower (4 feet)	100	
Heavy truck (50 feet) City traffic (8 hours)	90	Very annoying Hearing damage
Alarm clock (2 feet) Hair dryer Vacuum cleaner (5 feet)	80	Annoying
Noisy restaurant Freeway traffic Man's voice (3 feet)	70	Telephone use difficult
Air-conditioning unit (20 feet)	60	Intrusive
Light auto traffic (100 feet)	50	
Living room Bedroom Quiet office	40	Quiet
Library Soft whisper (15 feet)	30	Very quiet
Broadcasting studio	20	
	10	Just audible
	0	Hearing begins

Source: City of Chula Vista, California, *Noise Control Ordinance.*

DECK

(1) An unroofed platform, either freestanding or attached to a building, that is supported by pillars or posts; (2) a pier or landing for a boat.

DECK LINE

The intersection of two roof surfaces of a mansard roof forming the highest horizontal line of the steeper roof slope. *See Figure 73.*

DECOMPOSITION

Reduction of the net energy level and change in chemical composition of organic matter because of the actions of aerobic or anaerobic microorganisms.

DEDICATION

The transfer of property by the owner to another party.

Comment: Such transfer is conveyed by written instrument and is completed with an acceptance. The dedication is often for a specific use. Typically, dedication of land for roads, utilities, and open space is a requirement of subdivision or site plan approval. Where dedication is impractical because of costs or other reasons, an easement may suffice. *See* EASEMENT.

DEDICATION, FEE IN LIEU OF

Payments in cash as an alternative to dedication of land or construction of improvements.

Comment: In some states, mandatory construction of improvements or dedication of land for open space, recreation, services, or utilities may be a requirement for development approval. Where such construction or dedication is physically impossible or untimely, a fee in lieu of dedication may be substituted, based on a formula established by ordinance.

DEED

A legal document conveying ownership of real property.

DEED RESTRICTION

See RESTRICTIVE COVENANT.

DEFENSIBLE SPACE

Design or redesign of the built environment to reduce opportunities for crime.

Comment: Defensible space or "crime prevention through environmental design" is based on three principles: natural surveillance by placing physical features, activities, and people to maximize visibility; natural access control through the judicial placement of entrances, exits, fencing, landscaping, and lighting; and territorial reinforcement using buildings, fences, pavement, signs, and landscaping to express ownership. (Brennan et al. 1997; Newman 1996)

DEFICIENT UNIT

A housing unit that is not decent, safe, or sanitary, as determined through census surrogates or on-site inspection, and that does not comply with local codes or other housing standards. *See* SURROGATE.

Comment: Surrogates for deficient housing include age of structure, overcrowding, lack of central heat, shared bathroom facilities, inadequate kitchen facilities, inadequate access, and lack of elevators in mid- and high-rise buildings.

DEMOGRAPHY

The study of population and its characteristics.

DEMOLITION PERMIT

Official authorization to remove part, or all, of a building or structure.

Comment: Demolition permits are usually authorized by the construction official or building inspector. The grant of a demolition permit may be contingent on fulfilling certain requirements, such as rodent control, insurance in place, and protection against erosion.

DENSITY

The number of families, individuals, dwelling units, households, or housing structures per unit of land.

Comment: The most common standard is dwelling units per acre. Ordinances regulating density must make it clear as to whether the standard is stated in net or gross density. Gross density includes all the area within the boundaries of the specific area. Net density usually refers to the developable areas only, excluding streets, easements, water areas, lands with environmental constraints, parklands, and undevelopable lands. Table D-2 shows some typical gross densities for various types of housing.

Allowable densities may vary, depending on occupancy characteristics. For example, senior citizen apartments are typically built at higher densities than nonage-restricted units, since overall impact of such factors as vehicle trip generation, schoolchildren, persons per acre, and so forth is less. Mixed-type structures containing townhouses and flats, for instance, may have densities somewhere between the two types. Single-family detached variations, such as zero lot line homes, are often built at densities of about 6 to 10 dwelling units per net acre.

Stuart Meck, principal investigator for the American Planning Association's *Growing Smart* project, suggests that low density is 1 to 7 dwelling units per acre; medium density is 7 to 14 dwelling units per acre; and high density is 14 or more dwelling units per acre. He

TABLE D-2: GROSS DENSITY RANGES FOR HOUSING TYPES

Type of Unit	Typical Density Ranges (units per gross acre)		
	Suburban Area	Town	Urban Center
Single-family detached	1–4	4–8	8–15
Two-family	6–8	8–12	20–40
Town houses	6–10	10–20	20–30
Flats, two- and three-story	10–18	15–30	25–40
Mid-rise	20–40	30–50	40–60
High-rise	—	50–60	70+

notes that in an article on density by Ruth Eckdish Knack ("Dense, Denser, Denser Still," *Planning*, August 2002), the densities are similar to Lynch and Hack's (1994) categories in *Site Planning. See* CRITICAL AREA; NET AREA OF LOT.

DENSITY BONUS

The granting of additional floor area or dwelling units, beyond the zoned maximum, in exchange for providing or preserving an amenity at the same or a separate site.

Comment: For a residential site the amenity might be the preservation and restoration of a historic home or site; for a commercial development the amenity might be the inclusion of a generous plaza dedicated to use by the public. The methodology for calculating the amount of the bonus should be specified in the ordinance, perhaps as a maximum allowable percentage increase in gross floor area or dwelling units per acre.

DENSITY MODIFICATION FACTOR

See CLUSTER SUBDIVISION.

DENSITY TRANSFER

The transfer of all or part of the permitted density on a parcel to another parcel.

Comment: "Density transfer" is also known as the transfer of development rights (TDR). TDR must be permitted by a state enabling act and then enacted in the local ordinance. Usually, density transfers are made from designated sending districts to designated receiving districts. Both types of districts must be identified in the zoning ordinance. Density transfer may be used to preserve farmland, open space, historic areas, and critical areas. *See* AIR RIGHTS; LOT AVERAGING; NONCONTIGUOUS PARCEL CLUSTERING; TRANSFER OF DEVELOPMENT RIGHTS.

DENSITY ZONING

Averaging residential density over an entire parcel without restriction as to lot sizes. (American Planning Association, *The Language of Zoning*, Planning Advisory Service Report No. 322, 1976)

Comment: Density zoning is often confused with cluster development. Technically, it is more akin to lot averaging, in which the size of the lots may vary if the number of dwelling units remains the same. Density zoning may also be used to permit any housing type, provided the number of units does not exceed the maximum density permitted in the ordinance. *See* LOT AVERAGING.

DESALINIZATION

Salt removal from seawater or brackish water.

DESIGN CONTINUITY

A unifying or connecting theme or physical feature for a particular setting or place, provided by one or more elements of the natural or created environment.

DESIGN FIT

Consistency in scale, quality, or character between new and existing development so as to avoid abrupt and/or severe differences. *See* COMPATIBLE DESIGN; COMPATIBLE LAND USE.

DESIGN FLOOD

The magnitude of a flooding event that a facility is designed to accommodate.

Comment: The design flood can be used as a basis for a water surface elevation or for the delineation of a flooding and flood hazard area.

DESIGN REVIEW

Site or building design review by a design review body constituted to comment or make recommendations on the design or to grant approval. *See* SITE PLAN REVIEW.

Comment: Three American Planning Association Planning Advisory Service (PAS) publications offer a most useful overview on the background, legality, and function of the design review process, with suggestions for the preparation and implementation of design review guidelines. These include: Robert Lee Fleming, *Saving Face: How Corporate Franchise Design Can Respect Community Identity*, PAS Report Number 452 (1994); Mark L. Hinshaw, *Design Review*, PAS Report Number 454

(1995); and Christopher J. Duerksen and R. Matthew Goebel, *Aesthetics, Community Character and the Law*, PAS Report Number 489/490 (1999). *See also* Hamid Shirvani, *Urban Design Review: A Guide for Planners* (Washington, DC: Planners Press, 1981).

DESIGN STANDARDS

A set of guidelines defining parameters to be followed in site and/or building design and development. *See* DESIGN REVIEW.

Comment: Design standards can be quite specific and required in a historic or other special design district. They can also be more general guidelines, adopted as part of the local master plan, to provide direction to decision makers, design professionals, and the public regarding site, building, landscaping, and infrastructure design in the preparation and review of development applications.

DETENTION BASIN (POND)

A facility for the temporary storage of stormwater run-off.

Comment: Detention basins or ponds differ from retention basins in that the water storage is only temporary, with water often released by mechanical means at such time as downstream facilities can handle the flow. Basins are generally designed to regulate the rate of flow to predevelopment conditions. Usually the basins are planted with grass and, if large enough, can be used for open space or recreation in periods of dry weather. Basins also serve to recharge ground water and are not considered impervious surfaces.

DETERIORATION

The marked diminishing of the physical condition of structures or buildings. *See* DEFICIENT UNIT; SURROGATE.

DEVELOPABLE LAND

Parcels or sites free of constraints to development such as, but not limited to, wetlands, steep slopes, water bodies, unstable soils, easements, and legal impediments and that have frontage on or access to an improved roadway and can be served by public or private utilities and facilities such as sewer, water, electricity, and gas.

DEVELOPER

The legal or beneficial owner or owners of a lot or of any land included in a proposed development, including the holder of an option or contract to purchase or other persons having enforceable proprietary interests in such lands. *See* APPLICANT.

DEVELOPMENT

The division of a parcel of land into two or more parcels; the construction, reconstruction, conversion, structural alteration, relocation, or enlargement of any structure; any mining, excavation, landfill, or land disturbance; or any use or extension of the use of land.

DEVELOPMENT, CONVENTIONAL

Development other than planned development or cluster development.

DEVELOPMENT, MAJOR

Any development involving more than three lots and/or involving a land area of more than 5 acres.

DEVELOPMENT, MINOR

Any development involving three or fewer lots and/or involving a land area of less than 5 acres and not requiring the extension of any new streets or other municipal or governmental facilities. *See* DEVELOPMENT.

Comment: The definition of development is sufficiently broad to cover all types of activity relating to land and building. The designation of an application as a minor development relieves the applicant of the need to meet the more stringent requirements of a major application, including advertising, notification of neighbors, and a public hearing. The number of lots and land area is strictly a local determination. In many built-up communities, where the streets and major infrastructure are already installed, five lots or less may be considered a minor subdivision. In urban areas, the 5-acre standard for site plans may be too large, and a smaller minimum may be desirable.

There are two recurring problems with respect to minor developments. The first is the danger that the land will come in at some subsequent time for another minor—"the creeping major." This problem can be addressed by requiring any application involving land previously approved as a minor development to be submitted as a major application. The second problem is how the developer proposes to use the remaining land. While applicants will often claim that they have no intention of developing the remainder, the prudent board will require at least a concept plan for the remaining land to ensure that the minor development does not pose future problems.

DEVELOPMENT, PLANNED

See PLANNED DEVELOPMENT.

DEVELOPMENT ANALYSIS STUDY

An analysis of potential uses and markets, whether permitted by zoning or not, for a parcel of real estate to determine the type and intensity of development. *See* FEASIBILITY STUDY.

Comment: Development analysis differs from impact analysis, which analyzes the impact of a specific development in terms of water and sewer use, traffic, and impact on community facilities, such as schools, recreation, environment, and public services. The development analysis study is often called a feasibility study.

DEVELOPMENT CONTEXT

The three-dimensional character of the buildings, structures, streetscape, and immediate surroundings of a given building or site.

Comment: An important consideration in site plan review is how the proposed site development respects the contextual character of its location. Contextual elements include building design (roof shape, mass, fenestration, materials, and color), setbacks, street furniture, street and sidewalk width, fences, street trees, street lighting, open spaces, and the like. *See* CHARACTER; COMMUNITY CHARACTER; COMPATIBLE DESIGN; COMPATIBLE LAND USE; DESIGN FIT; URBAN CONTEXT.

DEVELOPMENT REGULATION

Any zoning, subdivision, site plan, official map, floodplain or wetlands regulation, or other governmental regulation that affects the use and intensity of land development.

Comment: The current trend is to combine all development regulations into a single land development ordinance since procedures, informational requirements, public hearings, and notices are the same or similar for all development applications.

DEVELOPMENT REVIEW COMMITTEE

See TECHNICAL COORDINATING COMMITTEE.

DEVELOPMENT RIGHT

The right to develop property.

Comment: Fee simple ownership of property involves a bundle of rights, including but not limited to mineral rights, air rights, easements, and such. These may be sold, dedicated, or transferred in their entirety or in part. Purchase of development rights has become a method to preserve farmland, open space, or historic structures. Usually a governmental agency purchases the development rights to the property at a fair appraisal price. The owner keeps title to the property and may continue to farm the land and live on the property. Development rights can also be transferred. *See* DENSITY TRANSFER.

115

DEVELOPMENT TIMING

Regulating the rate and geographic sequence of development.

Comment: Large-scale developments are often phased in terms of the number of units and geographic area. The approving authority has to ensure that each phase can stand on its own in terms of circulation, utilities, and drainage, in the event subsequent phases are delayed or canceled. This can be done by requiring that facilities designed to serve a specific project phase are built at the same time as that phase or by requiring a performance guarantee.

DEVELOPMENTS OF REGIONAL IMPACT (DRI)

Projects or development activities that have impacts that extend beyond local government borders or that affect more than one community.

Comment: The impacts can be traffic, stormwater flow, aesthetics, noise, glare, and similar development characteristics. Some ordinances classify any development activity within 100 yards of another municipality as a DRI. States that have specific standards and review procedures for DRIs include Colorado, Florida, Georgia, Maine, Massachusetts, Minnesota, Vermont, and Washington.

DIAGONAL DIVERTERS

See TRAFFIC CALMING.

DILAPIDATION

A deterioration of structures or buildings to the point of being unsafe or unfit for human habitation or use.

DILUTION RATIO

The ratio of the volume of water of a stream to the volume of incoming waste.

Comment: The capacity of a stream to accept wastewater is partially dependent on the dilution ratio.

DISABILITY

In reference to an individual, a physical or mental impairment that substantially limits one or more of the major life activities; a record of such an impairment; or being regarded as having an impairment. *See* AMERICANS WITH DISABILITIES ACT; MAJOR LIFE ACTIVITIES.

DISCOTHEQUE

A nightclub for dancing to recorded music; broadly, a nightclub often featuring psychedelic and mixed-media attractions, such as slides, movies, and special lighting effects. (*New Lexicon Webster Dictionary* 1989)

DISCOUNT CENTER

A single store, or group of stores, offering merchandise for sale at lower-than-usual retail prices.

Comment: Discount centers or stores are now major forces in retailing. Discount centers are characterized by very large structures, often converted warehouses, and merchandise offered for sale on steel industrial shelving in original shipping boxes. Many require customers to join and pay an annual fee (the club concept). From a zoning perspective, they have a market area larger than a shopping center of the same size. In addition, their major traffic impact is usually on weekends. *See* RETAIL OUTLET STORE; RETAIL STORE, LARGE-SCALE; RETAIL WAREHOUSE OUTLET.

DISCOVERY

(1) The act or process of finding or learning something that was previously unknown; (2) compulsory disclosure, at a party's request, of information that relates to the litigation. (*Black's* 1999)

Comment: Black notes that "[t]he primary discovery devices are interrogatories, depositions, and requests for production" (p. 478). Since many planners will testify in a court of law at some time or other during their careers, they will most likely experience the discovery process. Except for privileged communications, usually from or to attorneys, all material in the planner's file used to prepare reports or opinions is subject to discovery. The planner's attorney should be consulted as to what files, letters, and notes must be produced for the discovery process.

DISPOSAL AREA

The entire area used for underground dispersion of the liquid portion of sewage.

Comment: The disposal area usually consists of the seepage pit or a disposal field or a combination of both.

DISPOSAL BED

That part of a disposal field used for sanitary sewage.

Comment: The disposal bed is an area from which the entire earth contents have been removed and the excavation partially filled with satisfactory filtering material in which distribution lines have been laid. The entire area is then covered with topsoil and suitable vegetative cover.

DISPOSAL FIELD

An area consisting of a combination of disposal trenches and a disposal bed. *See Figure 28.*

Comment: The disposal field is used for dispersion of the liquid portion of sanitary sewage into the ground as close to the surface as possible. *See* SEPTIC SYSTEM.

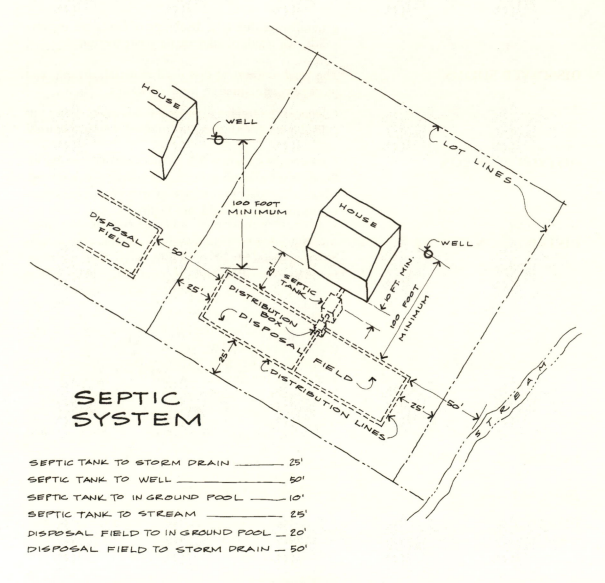

SEPTIC
SYSTEM

SEPTIC TANK TO STORM DRAIN ———— 25'
SEPTIC TANK TO WELL ——————— 50'
SEPTIC TANK TO INGROUND POOL ——— 10'
SEPTIC TANK TO STREAM ———————— 25'
DISPOSAL FIELD TO INGROUND POOL — 20'
DISPOSAL FIELD TO STORM DRAIN — 50'

FIGURE 28

DISPOSAL TRENCH

A shallow ditch with vertical sides and a flat bottom partially filled with a satisfactory filtering material in which a single distribution line has been laid and covered with topsoil and a suitable vegetative cover.

DISSOLVED OXYGEN (DO)

The oxygen dissolved in water or sewage.

Comment: Adequate DO is necessary for the life of fish and other aquatic organisms. Low DO concentrations generally are due to a discharge of excessive organic solids, the result of inadequate waste treatment.

DISSOLVED SOLIDS

The total amount of dissolved material, organic and inorganic, contained in water or wastes.

Comment: Excessive dissolved solids make water unpalatable for drinking and unsuitable for industrial uses.

DISTRIBUTION BOX

A watertight structure that receives sanitary sewage effluent from a septic tank and distributes such sewage effluent in equal portions to two or more pipelines leading to the disposal field. *See Figure 28.*

DISTRIBUTION CENTER

An establishment engaged in the receipt, storage, and distribution of goods, products, cargo, and materials, including transshipment by boat, rail, air, or motor vehicle. *See* TRUCK TERMINAL; WAREHOUSE.

Comment: Breakdown of large orders from a single source into smaller orders and consolidation of several orders into a single large one for distribution to several recipients is a key part of the function of a distribution center. The functions of distribution centers and warehouses often overlap, but retail sales, assembly, or product processing are not considered part of the distribution process.

DISTRIBUTION LINES

A series of open, jointed, or perforated pipes used for the dispersion of sewage into disposal trenches or disposal beds. *See Figure 28.*

DISTRICT

A part, zone, or geographic area within the municipality within which certain zoning or development regulations apply. *See* OVERLAY ZONE.

Comment: District regulations must be uniform for all uses within the district. For example, if a municipality wants to apply a larger lot size to service stations within a district compared to other uses, it has to make such uses conditional or special exception uses.

DIVERSION CHANNEL

A channel constructed across or at the bottom of a slope.

DIVIDED HIGHWAY

(1) A highway having access on only one side of the direction of travel; (2) a highway having a median island or other barrier separating opposing moving lanes. *See* STREET, DUAL.

DOMICILE

A residence that is a permanent home to an individual.

DONATION

A voluntary gift for which no valuable consideration is given in exchange.

DORMER

A projection from a sloping roof that contains a window. *See Figure 9.*

DORMITORY

A building used as group living quarters for a student body or religious order as an accessory use to a college, university, boarding school, convent, monastery, or similar institutional use.

Comment: Recent court cases on the definition of family (for instance, *State of N.J. v. Dennis Baker,* A-59, Supreme Court of New Jersey) make the distinction between dormitories and households of unrelated individuals less precise. Regulations based on living space or other performance standards may offer the most positive method of control. The basic difference between dormitories and dwelling units is that: (1) a dormitory is an accessory use to an institutional use while a dwelling unit is a principal use; and (2) a dwelling unit is designed to be occupied by one or more persons functioning as a household. Dormitories do not usually include individual kitchen facilities or private bathroom facilities as do dwelling units.

DOUBLE-WIDE UNIT

Two manufactured housing components, attached side by side, to make one complete housing unit.

DOWNZONE

To increase the intensity of use by increasing density or floor area ratio or otherwise decreasing bulk requirements.

Comment: Developers and some landowners consider this term to have the opposite meaning. *See* UPZONE.

DRAINAGE

(1) Surface water runoff; (2) the removal of surface water or groundwater from land by drains, grading, or other means, which include runoff controls to minimize erosion and sedimentation during and after construction or development.

DRAINAGE AREA

That area in which all of the surface runoff resulting from precipitation is concentrated into a particular stream.

DRAINAGE DISTRICT

A district established by a governmental unit to build and operate facilities for drainage.

DRAINAGE SYSTEM

Pipes, swales, natural features, and constructed improvements designed to carry drainage.

Comment: The system may carry the drainage to storage or treatment facilities, streams, or retention or detention basins.

DRAINAGEWAY

Any natural or artificial watercourse, trench, ditch, swale, or similar depression into which surface water flows.

DREDGE AND FILL

A process that creates land by dredging material from the bottom of a body of water and depositing this material on land, usually adjacent to the water.

DREDGING

A method of deepening streams, swamps, or coastal waters by removing solids from the bottom.

Comment: Dredging and filling can disturb natural ecological cycles. For example, dredging can destroy shellfish beds and other aquatic life; filling can destroy the feeding and breeding grounds for many fish species. The dredging and filling of navigable waterways and most wetland areas are regulated by the federal government.

DRIP LINE

The ground line around a tree that defines the limits of the tree canopy. *See Figure 97.*

DRIVE-IN THEATER

See THEATER, DRIVE-IN.

DRIVE-IN USE

An establishment that by design, physical facilities, service, or packaging procedures encourages or permits customers to receive services, obtain goods, or be entertained while remaining in their motor vehicles.

DRIVEWAY

A private roadway providing access to a street or highway.

Comment: Driveways may be paved or unpaved and are not considered streets, roads, or highways.

DRIVEWAY WIDTH

The narrowest width of driveway measured perpendicular to the driveway.

DRUGSTORE

A store where the primary business is the filling of medical prescriptions and the sale of drugs, medical devices and supplies, and nonprescription medicines but where nonmedical products may be sold as well.

Comment: A drugstore may be distinguished from a pharmacy, which deals primarily with preparing and dispensing drugs and medicines. The non–medicine-related products may be cards, candy, and cosmetics. In recent years, however, the variety of nonmedical products has expanded substantially, particularly with the advent of national drugstore chains. *See* PHARMACY.

DRY LINES   *See* CAPPED SYSTEM.

DRY WELL   A covered pit with an open, jointed lining through which water is piped or directed from roofs, basement floors, other impervious surfaces, swales, or pipes to seep or percolate into the surrounding soil. *See Figure 29.*

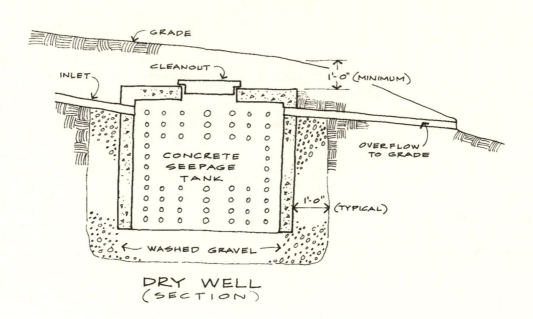

DRY WELL
(SECTION)

FIGURE 29

DUMP   A land site used primarily for the disposal by dumping, burial, burning, or other means and for whatever purposes of garbage, sewage, trash, refuse, junk, discarded machinery, vehicles or parts thereof, and other waste, scrap, or discarded material of any kind.

DUMPSTER™   An exterior waste container designed to be mechanically lifted by and emptied into or carted away by a collection vehicle.

Comment: The unregulated placement and control of trash bins or containers, particularly in commercial and

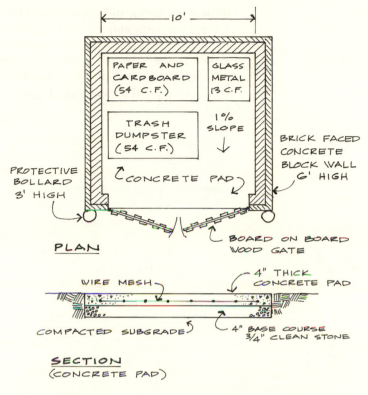

FIGURE 30

multifamily developments, can be visually detrimental to the urban environment. Site plan regulations should include standards for trash bin size, placement, screening, and maintenance. In multifamily developments, bins should be housed in fully enclosed, roofed structures that match the architectural character of the development. *See Figure 30.*

DUPLEX

A building containing two single-family dwelling units totally separated from each other by an unpierced wall extending from basement to roof. *See* DWELLING, TWO-FAMILY.

Comment: One major advantage of a duplex is that each dwelling unit can be sold in fee simple. The two-family type with one apartment over another requires condominium ownership. In some areas, the duplex is known as a twin.

DWELLING

A structure or portion thereof that is used exclusively for human habitation.

DWELLING, ATTACHED

A one-family dwelling with ground floor outside access, attached to two or more one-family dwellings by common vertical walls without openings.

Comment: Also known as a town house.

DWELLING, DETACHED

A dwelling that is not attached to any other dwelling by any means.

Comment: The detached dwelling does not have any roof, wall, or floor in common with any other dwelling unit.

DWELLING, GARDEN APARTMENT

One or more two- or three-story, multifamily structures, generally built at a gross density of 10 to 15 dwelling units per acre, with each structure containing 8 to 20 dwelling units and including related off-street parking, open space, and recreation facilities. *See* DWELLING, MULTIFAMILY. *See Figure 31.*

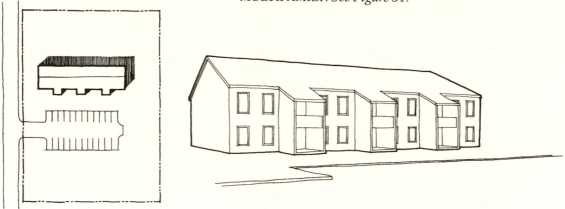

DWELLING, GARDEN APARTMENT

FIGURE 31

Comment: A garden apartment is actually a multifamily development. Development controls should define the commonly accepted configuration of a garden apartment in terms of density (usually 10 to 15 dwelling units per acre in a suburban community, somewhat higher in an urban area and lower in a rural area), height (usually a maximum of three stories or 35 feet, with a maximum of three levels of dwelling units), and maximum length of a structure (usually between 150 and 200 feet). Access is usually from a common hall, although

124

individual entrances can be provided. Dwelling units can be located back-to-back, adjacent, and one on top of another.

DWELLING, HIGH-RISE

An apartment building of eight or more stories. *See Figure 32.*

Comment: High-rise apartment buildings often have health club facilities and other services for the residents.

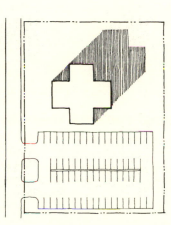

DWELLING, HIGH-RISE

FIGURE 32

DWELLING, MID-RISE

An apartment building containing from three to seven stories. *See Figure 33.*

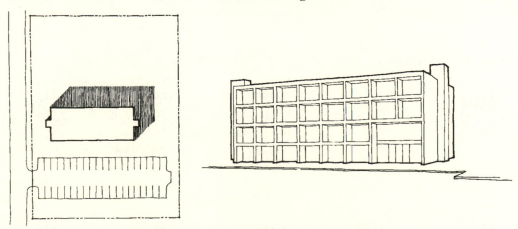

DWELLING, MID-RISE

FIGURE 33

125

**DWELLING,
MULTIFAMILY**

A building containing three or more dwelling units, including units that are located one over another.

Comment: Multifamily buildings include garden apartments and mid- and high-rise apartment buildings.

DWELLING, PATIO HOME

A dwelling on a separate lot with open space setbacks on three sides. *See* DWELLING, ZERO LOT LINE. *See Figure 34.*

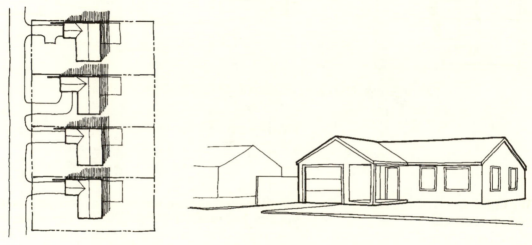

DWELLING, PATIO HOME

FIGURE 34

**DWELLING,
QUADRUPLEX**

Four attached dwellings in one building in which each unit has two open-space exposures and shares one or two walls with adjoining unit or units. *See Figure 35.*

DWELLING, SEASONAL

A dwelling unit that is not used as a principal residence and may be occupied weekends and for brief periods during the year.

Comment: "Brief period" is difficult to define. Seasonal dwellings in oceanfront or lake areas may be occupied for three to four months. In ski areas, six months may be the norm.

At one time, seasonal units often lacked heat and insulation. Today, most municipalities do not make any distinction between seasonal and all-year-round units; both must meet the same standards.

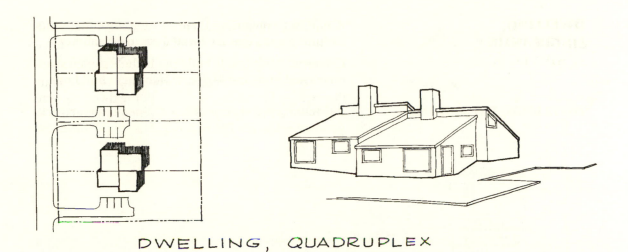

DWELLING, QUADRUPLEX

FIGURE 35

**DWELLING,
SINGLE-FAMILY
DETACHED**

A building containing one dwelling unit and that is not attached to any other dwelling by any means and is surrounded by open space or yards. *See* DWELLING, DETACHED. *See Figure 36.*

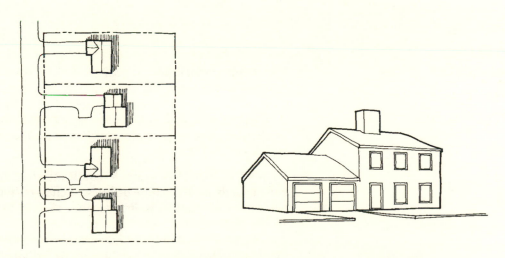

DWELLING, SINGLE-FAMILY DETACHED

FIGURE 36

**DWELLING,
SINGLE-FAMILY
SEMIDETACHED**

A one-family dwelling attached to one other one-family dwelling by a common vertical wall, with each dwelling located on a separate lot. *See* DUPLEX. *See Figure 37.*

Comment: The semidetached dwelling is most commonly a two-family structure with the dwelling units side by side as opposed to one on top of the other.

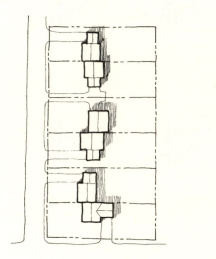

DWELLING, SEMIDETACHED

FIGURE 37

**DWELLING,
TOWN HOUSE**

A one-family dwelling in a row of at least three such units in which each unit has its own front and rear access to the outside, no unit is located over another unit, and each unit is separated from any other unit by one or more vertical common fire-resistant walls. *See Figure 38.*

Comment: Town houses (single-family attached dwellings) usually have separate utilities, such as individual hot water and heating systems, separate electric meters, and so forth. However, in some condominium developments, the condominium association may arrange for bulk purchase of certain utilities and distribute them to individual dwelling units. Consequently, the definition normally would not contain a requirement for separate utility systems. In some states—Florida, for example—one-story single-family attached dwellings are called "villas." *See* DWELLING, ATTACHED.

DWELLING, TOWN HOUSE

FIGURE 38

DWELLING, TRIPLEX

A building containing three dwelling units, each of which has direct access to the outside or to a common hall.

DWELLING, TWO-FAMILY

A building on a single lot containing two dwelling units, each of which is totally separated from the other by an unpierced wall extending from ground to roof or an unpierced ceiling and floor extending from exterior wall to exterior wall, except for a common stairwell exterior to both dwelling units.

DWELLING, ZERO LOT LINE

A building located on a lot in such a manner that one or more of the dwelling's sides rests on a lot line.

DWELLING UNIT

One or more rooms, designed, occupied, or intended for occupancy as separate living quarters, with cooking, sleeping, and sanitary facilities provided within the dwelling unit for the exclusive use of a single family maintaining a household. *See* ECHO HOUSING; HOUSING UNIT.

DWELLING UNIT, EFFICIENCY

A dwelling unit consisting of not more than one habitable room, together with kitchen or kitchenette and sanitary facilities.

Comment: Efficiency units, also known as studio apartments, typically contain between 200 and 400 square feet.

DYSTROPHIC LAKES

Lakes between eutrophic and swamp stages of aging.

Comment: Such lakes are shallow and have high humus content, low nutrient availability, and high BOD (biological oxygen demand). They are heavily stained and are commonly referred to as brown-water lakes.

E

EASEMENT

A grant of one or more of the property rights by the property owner to and/or for use by the public, a corporation, or another person or entity. *See Figure 3.*

Comment: An easement may be a more acceptable and less expensive way to achieve certain public goals, since not all of the property rights are being purchased. For instance, where property owners are reluctant to donate land for road-widening purposes, an easement may be an acceptable alternative. The property owner keeps the title but the road can be widened. This is particularly important in rural areas where land is sold by the acre. Another example is slope rights to permit roadway grading.

EASEMENT, AFFIRMATIVE

An easement that gives the holder a right to make some limited use of land owned by another. *See* EASEMENT IN GROSS.

EASEMENT, APPURTENANT

An easement benefiting, attaching to, and running with a designated parcel of land.

EASEMENT, AVIATION

An air rights easement that protects air lanes around airports.

EASEMENT, CONSERVATION

The grant of a property right requiring that the described land will remain in its existing natural state in perpetuity.

Comment: Conservation easements are useful tools to preserve open space, environmentally sensitive areas, scenic views, or wetlands and wetlands buffers. But while approving agencies usually identify those areas suitable for easement protection, follow-up is often lax. In a survey of 322 easements on 33 properties in Hopewell Township, New Jersey, easement violations were found on 80 percent of the sites by the Stony Brook-Millstone Watershed Association. (Watershed Watch, June 2001) The association recommended a number of steps that municipalities could take to monitor conservation easements effectively:

- Ensure that all easements are referenced by lot and block number and the details of restrictions are shown in the master plan. If a municipality has an official map, the easements should be shown on the map.

- Ensure that easements are shown on the documents filed with the official filing agency. For example, in New Jersey, easements are filed with the county and not the municipality.

132

- Establish a routine by which all easements are inspected on a regular basis and, if practical, photographed to guard against any violations.

- Provide a regular funding source to provide for effective and routine monitoring.

In addition to the monitoring of easements, another major problem is providing for the maintenance and/or replacement of vegetation. A typical example is where a stream cuts across a parcel proposed to be subdivided. Good platting practice would have the rear lot lines follow the stream course, and the stream, wetlands, and vegetation on both sides of the stream course should be included as part of a conservation easement. But trees and vegetation die, often some plants crowd out others, noxious plants grow, and storm and insect infestation can significantly alter the original character of the area proposed to be conserved.

Property owners should be permitted to undertake minor maintenance and replacement of vegetation in conservation easements. The minor maintenance includes removal of dead or diseased plants, undergrowth thinning that does not reduce shielding or buffering, and the removal of noxious or poisonous plants. Minor maintenance should be limited to hand tools, excluding electric, motor, or engine-powered tools. Removal of dead trees should be considered major maintenance.

Where major maintenance or changes are proposed, the municipality should be informed and a municipal official, often the municipal engineer or planner, should be given the opportunity to review and comment on the changes. In addition, the changes should be indicated on a written document so that the official approval of the site plan or subdivision can be properly amended.

It is also important that neighbors be given notice of any proposed major changes to a conservation easement area. The existence of the easement may have been a factor in their purchase of the property and changes to the easement could affect their views, drainage, or their privacy.

If a conservation easement is under the ownership and control of a homeowners association, they should also have the right to review and approve any major changes to the easement.

Finally, in some cases, conservation easements along streams can be linked together to form scenic greenways. In order to do this, however, the original conservation easement should specify that the municipality (or other governmental agency) has the right to construct a pathway through the conservation easement.

EASEMENT, CONTINUING

An easement that is self-perpetuating and runs with the land.

EASEMENT, CROSS

See EASEMENT, PRIVATE ACCESS.

EASEMENT, DISCHARGE

The grant of a property right to allow runoff in excess of the previous quantity and/or rate of flow.

EASEMENT, DRAINAGE

Land required for the installation of stormwater sewers or drainage ditches and/or required for the preservation or maintenance of a natural stream or watercourse or other drainage facility.

EASEMENT, EXPRESS

An easement that is expressly created by a deed or other instrument.

EASEMENT, FACADE

An easement that prohibits or restricts any changes in the facade of a building that would alter or damage its historic integrity or architectural character.

EASEMENT, MAINTENANCE

A part of a lot free of structures reserved to an adjacent lot to allow access to repair or maintain a structure located on the adjacent lot.

EASEMENT, NEGATIVE

An easement that precludes the owner of the land from doing that which the owner would be entitled to do if the easement did not exist.

Comment: Negative easements historically have been limited to easements for light, air, views, and conservation.

EASEMENT, PRIVATE ACCESS

An easement created for the purpose of providing vehicular or pedestrian access to a property.

EASEMENT, SCENIC

An easement that allows a public agency to use private land for: (1) scenic enhancement, such as roadside landscaping; (2) vista preservation.

EASEMENT, UTILITY

The right-of-way acquired by a utility or governmental agency to locate utilities, including all types of pipelines, telephone and electric cables, and towers.

Comment: Most utility easements have restrictions on their use; however, some can be used as walkways and bike paths, buffer areas, and transition areas.

EASEMENT, VIEWSHED

An easement that places restrictions on the development of private land in order to preserve a viewshed. *See* VIEWSHED. *See Figure 100.*

EASEMENT IN GROSS

An easement created for the personal benefit of the holder and not benefiting, attaching to, and running with a designated parcel of land.

EATING AND DRINKING PLACES

Retail establishments selling food and drink for consumption on the premises, including lunch counters and refreshment stands selling prepared foods and drinks for immediate on-site consumption.

Comment: Eating and drinking places are a specific type of food establishment. They differ from take-out places where food is ready for consumption but eaten off the premises. Restaurants, lunch counters, and drinking places operated as a subordinate service facility or accessory use in other establishments, such as the cafeteria of a large company, are not regarded as separate permitted uses but as accessory to the principal use. *See* RESTAURANT, TAKE-OUT.

EAVE

The projecting lower edges of a roof overhanging the wall of a building. *See Figure 21.*

ECHO HOUSING

A small, removable modular cottage on a concrete foundation or slab in the rear or side yard of a dwelling.

Comment: Echo housing is also known as "granny" flats or elder cottage housing. It permits an older person to live independently but close to relatives. The cottage consists of one bedroom, a bathroom, living room, and kitchen and is connected to the utility system of the main unit.

ECOLOGICAL IMPACT

The total effect of an environmental change, either natural or man-made, on the ecology of an area.

ECOLOGY

The interrelationship of living things to one another and to their environment, or the study of such relationships.

ECONOMETRICS

Statistical analysis and techniques applied to economic information and used for modeling and projection.

ECONOMIC BASE

The system of production, distribution, and consumption of goods and services within a planning area.

Comment: "Economic base," as the term is used in planning, is the sum of all activities that result in income

135

for the area's inhabitants. The definition, however, is significantly broad to include all geographic and functional elements that may have an impact on the planning area even if not physically part of the area. Economic base analysis identifies and measures the components of an area's economic base and highlights strengths and weaknesses of the local economy. "Economic base" is different from "base economy," which is a term used by economists to identify that part of a region's economy that is sold outside the region.

ECOSYSTEM

The interacting system of all living organisms and the physical environment in a geographic area.

Comment: An ecosystem can be the entire biosphere, an ocean, a parcel of land, or an aquarium, depending on the context of use.

EDGE CLEARANCE

The distance measured along the curb line from the extended property lot line to the driveway. *See Figure 39.*

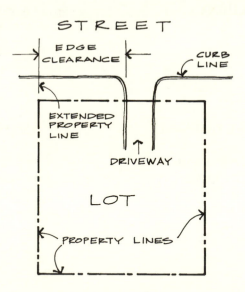

EDGE CLEARANCE

FIGURE 39

EDGE DEFINITION

A way of identifying the traveled way as distinguished from the nontraveled way.

Comment: The edge may be defined by the use of railings, bollards, wheel stops, curb, or edge plantings.

EDUCATIONAL INSTITUTION

A college or university authorized by the state to award degrees.

Comment: The term as defined is applicable only to colleges and universities. Elementary, middle, and high schools are defined under schools. The purpose in limiting the definition is to recognize the significant difference in impacts between the two types of facilities (schools and educational institutions). The development ordinance must consider the fact that colleges and universities are actually minicities with concerns relating to circulation, services, utilities, on-campus housing, and significant impacts for special events, such as athletics. The educational institution may require and support a major number of off-campus goods and service establishments. Educational institutions can also impose severe impacts on surrounding areas and generate increased competition for housing.

EFFICIENCY UNIT

See DWELLING UNIT, EFFICIENCY.

EFFLUENT

A discharge of liquid waste, with or without treatment, into the environment.

Comment: The term is generally used to describe discharges into water.

EGRESS

An exit.

ELDER HOUSING

See HOUSING FOR THE ELDERLY.

ELECTROMAGNETIC FIELD (EMF)

Fields that arise whenever electrons are moved through a conducting medium. ("APA Recommends Proactive Regulation of Electromagnetic Fields," *Zoning News*, August 1992, p. 13)

Comment: EMFs have two components, one electric and the other magnetic. They move with regular periodicity and are measured in hertz (Hz). ("APA Recommends . . . ," *Zoning News*, 1992) The electric fields come directly from the strength of the charge. Magnetic fields result from the motion of the charge. EMFs are measured in kV/m, or kilovolts per meter. A significant amount of research is now under way on the biological effects of EMF, particularly 60 Hz EMF, the type of electric power used in the United States. Most experts believe that "prudent avoidance" of 60 Hz electric and magnetic fields represents sound policy. (Morgan 1989) Several states have established maximum field strength standards for transmission line rights-of-way, as shown in table E-1:

TABLE E-1: STATE REGULATIONS THAT LIMIT FIELD STRENGTHS ON TRANSMISSION LINE RIGHTS-OF-WAY

State	Field Limit
Montana	1 kV/m at edge of ROW in residential areas
Minnesota	8 kV/m maximum in ROW
New Jersey	3 kV/m at edge of ROW
New York	1.6 kV/m at edge of ROW
North Dakota	9 kV/m maximum in ROW
Oregon	9 kV/m maximum in ROW
Florida	10 kV/m (for 500 kV), 8 kV/m (for 230 kV) maximum in ROW
	2 kV/m at edge of ROW all new lines, 200 mG (for 500kV single circuit, 250 mG (for 500 kV double circuit), and 150 mG (for 230 kV) maximum at edge of ROW

Notes: kV = kilovolt; kV/m = kilovolts per meter; MG = milligauss; ROW = right-of-way.

Source: M. Granger Morgan, *Electric and Magnetic Fields from 60 Hertz Electric Power: What Do We Know About Possible Health Risks?* (Pittsburgh, PA: Department of Engineering and Public Policy, Carnegie-Mellon University, 1989).

According to the August 1992 *Zoning News* article, municipalities can mitigate EMF emissions by requiring various configurations of the transmission lines to take advantage of the cancellation effects of positive and negative charges. The authors also noted that earth is not an effective shield against EMF emissions, so that burying lines is not effective.

ELEEMOSYNARY OR PHILANTHROPIC INSTITUTION

A private or public organization that is organized and operated for the purpose of providing a service or carrying on a trade or business without profit and for charitable purposes.

Comment: Eleemosynary or philanthropic organizations generally provide services or goods to disadvantaged persons. Their nonprofit aspects are recognized by the Internal Revenue Service. However, these uses should be located in areas according to their specific function without reference to their nonprofit status. The type of use, the service it provides, and the actual impacts on the surrounding area are the primary factors in locating these uses. For example, a nonprofit fund or foundation that distributes grants functions as an office use, but a nonprofit organization that provides furniture restoration and repair training and employment for the handicapped would be located in an industrial area.

ELEVATION

(1) A vertical distance above or below a fixed reference level; (2) a fully dimensioned drawing of the front, rear, or side of a building showing features such as windows, doors, and relationship of grade to floor level.

EMBANKMENT

An elevated deposit of soil, rock, or other materials either constructed or natural. *See* DAM.

EMERGENCY SHELTER

A facility providing temporary housing for one or more individuals who are otherwise temporarily or permanently homeless.

Comment: Emergency shelters are usually provided by governmental agencies and religious, eleemosynary, or philanthropic institutions. In addition to housing, some shelters provide food, clothing, and other ancillary services. Emergency shelters generally serve the poor, primarily indigent, or needy; however, persons displaced by emergencies (such as fire and natural disasters) may also be temporarily housed in emergency shelters.

EMERGENCY SPILLWAY

See SPILLWAY, EMERGENCY.

EMINENT DOMAIN

The authority to acquire or take or to authorize the taking of private property for public use or public purpose. *See* TAKING; JUST COMPENSATION.

Comment: While eminent domain is largely the prerogative of government, utilities and independent agencies may also have the right of eminent domain if permitted under state law. The U.S. Constitution requires just compensation for any taking, and the taking must be for a public purpose.

EMISSION

A discharge of pollutants into the air.

EMISSION FACTOR

The average amount of a pollutant emitted from each type of polluting source in relation to a specified amount of material processed.

Comment: The emission factor is used in establishing a performance standard. Most of the factors and standards

139

themselves are now specified and regulated by state or federal agencies.

EMISSION STANDARD

The maximum amount of a pollutant legally permitted to be discharged from a single source, either mobile or stationary.

EMPLOYEE TRANSPORTATION COORDINATOR

The person who develops, implements, and administers an employee transportation program.

Comment: Also referred to as a rideshare coordinator; duties may include registering employees for a ride-match program, coordinating the formation of car, van, and bus pools, promoting the use of public transit, and monitoring employee participation in the program.

ENABLING ACT

A legislative act authorizing a county, municipal, or other governmental agency to undertake activities.

ENCROACHMENT

Any obstruction or illegal or unauthorized intrusion in a delineated floodway, right-of-way, or on adjacent land. *See Figure 43.*

ENDANGERED SPECIES

Wildlife species whose prospects for survival are in immediate danger because of a loss of or change in habitat, overexploitation, predation, competition, disease, disturbance, or contamination and designated as such by a governmental agency.

ENLARGEMENT

An increase in the size of an existing structure or use, including the physical size of the property, building, parking, and other improvements.

Comment: What constitutes an enlargement is especially critical when it comes to nonconforming uses. While a physical expansion always constitutes an enlargement, other changes, such as alterations, may or may not be considered an enlargement. This was noted in a New Jersey Supreme Court (the state's highest court) decision (*Burbridge v. Mine Hill Twp.*, 117 N.J. 376 [1990]), in which the court said: "Applications to expand nonconforming uses offer boards opportunities to impose conditions, frequently aesthetic, which will help integrate the use with its surroundings." (Cox 2003)

ENRICHMENT

The addition of nitrogen, phosphorus, and carbon compounds or other nutrients to a lake or other waterway.

Comment: Enrichment greatly increases the growth potential for algae and aquatic plants. Most frequently,

140

enrichment results from the inflow of sewage effluent or from fertilizer runoff.

ENVIRONMENT

All external conditions and influences affecting the life, development, and ultimately the survival of an organism.

ENVIRONMENTAL IMPACT STATEMENT (EIS)

A statement of the effect of proposed development and/or other major private or governmental actions on the environment.

Comment: The purpose of an EIS is to provide the community with information needed to evaluate the effects of a proposed project upon the environment. The statement usually consists of an inventory of existing environmental conditions at the project site and in the surrounding area. The inventory includes air and water quality, water supply, hydrology, geology, soil type, topography, vegetation, wildlife, aquatic organisms, ecology, demography, land use, aesthetics, history, and archaeology. An EIS also includes a project description and may include a list of all licenses, permits, or other approvals required by law. The EIS assesses the probable impact of the project on all the inventory items and includes a listing of adverse environmental impacts that cannot be avoided. The statement also includes what steps the applicant proposes to take to minimize adverse environmental impacts during construction and operation and whether there are alternatives to any part of the project.

ENVIRONMENTAL RESOURCE INVENTORY

See NATURAL RESOURCES INVENTORY.

ENVIRONMENTALLY SENSITIVE AREA

The natural resources of an area that are important to its ecology, including natural habitats, steep slopes, wetlands, tree canopies, and endangered plant or animal species. *See* CRITICAL AREA.

EROSION

The detachment and movement of soil or rock fragments or the wearing away of the land surface by water, wind, ice, and gravity.

EROSION CONTROL PLAN

A plan designed to minimize erosion, ensure proper waste disposal, and protect trees on a building site.

Comment: The objectives of the erosion control plan can be achieved by implementing a number of important measures. These include requiring that grading and excavation be confined to the smallest site area as possible and protecting exposed areas with vegetation,

141

sod, tarps, or seeding and covered with mulch soon after the ground is turned. Other measures include the requirement that fill be kept clean of topsoil, organic matter, and rocks and stored away from any protected vegetation and stabilized by mulching, vegetation, or tarps. An erosion control plan should also provide for sedimentation basins for disturbed areas of more than 10 acres and silt filter fences or straw bales to be employed to keep the soil from moving off the site. The plan should provide for "no-disturbance setbacks" from streams or ponds, with appropriate vegetation in place filtering stormwater before it enters water bodies. An important measure to achieve erosion control is to design the grading plan to minimize the importing of fill or the removal of material from the site.

Other measures call for gravel or paved driveways into and out of the site to prevent mud from being tracked onto public roads, with construction vehicles to be cleaned and scraped before leaving the site. Any mud on public roads from the site is the responsibility of the contractor and should be swept up, rather than washed away.

The erosion control plan should also address waste disposal and specifically prohibit construction debris and other waste from being buried on the site. Finally, an important element of the plan should be the saving of as many trees on the site as possible and providing adequate protection for the saved trees during the construction period. Compaction, grading, and excavation around the root system should be avoided by protecting these areas with fencing. It may also be necessary to prune the tree crown to reduce the demand on the roots for nutrients and water.

The erosion control plan should include a construction schedule; maintenance plan for keeping erosion control equipment in good repair; maps showing proposed locations for temporary and permanent channels, fencing, vegetation, and fill areas; drawings of erosion control devices and where they are to be located on the site; and cut-and-fill calculations.

ESCROW

A deed, bond, cash, or other security delivered to a third person or agency and delivered by the third person to the grantee only upon fulfillment of a condition.

Comment: Applicants for development are often required to post escrows to ensure payment of review and inspection fees.

ESSENTIAL SERVICES

Services and utilities needed for the health, safety, and general welfare of the community, such as underground, surface, or overhead electrical, gas, telephone, steam, water, sewerage, and other utilities and the equipment and appurtenances necessary for such systems to furnish an adequate level of service for the area in which they are located.

Comment: The definition of essential services is limited to utility-type services as opposed to other, equally important services, such as police, fire, and transportation. Essential services are either permitted or conditional uses in all zones, but some distinction is necessary for the equipment, facilities, and appurtenances associated with the service. For example, sewer lines and lift stations may be located in residential areas, but the treatment facility is not appropriate next to dwellings. *See* PUBLIC UTILITY.

ESTABLISHMENT

An economic unit where business is conducted or services or industrial operations are performed.

Comment: Establishments are generally at a single physical location but not necessarily so. An establishment may include, for example, one or more manufacturing plants and several retail sales outlets.

ESTUARIES

Areas where fresh water meets salt water, such as bays, mouths of rivers, salt marshes, and lagoons.

EUTROPHIC LAKES

Shallow water bodies, often weed-choked, and very rich in nutrients.

Comment: Eutrophic lakes are characterized by large amounts of algae, poor water transparency, low dissolved oxygen, and high BOD (biological oxygen demand).

EUTROPHICATION

The normally slow aging process by which a lake evolves into a bog or marsh and ultimately assumes a completely terrestrial state and disappears.

EVALUATION

A process to measure the success of an activity and how closely the results meet the anticipated outcome defined as part of the initial phase of the activity.

EVAPORATION PONDS

Shallow, artificial ponds where sewage sludge is pumped, permitted to dry, and either removed or buried by more sludge.

EVERGREEN

A plant with foliage that remains green year-round.

EXACTION

Contributions or payments required as an authorized precondition for receiving a development permit. (American Planning Association, *The Language of Zoning*, Planning Advisory Service Report No. 322, 1976)

Comment: Exactions may refer to mandatory dedications, such as for road widenings or low-income housing. In all cases, there must be some relationship between the amount of the exaction and the purpose for which it is used. Thus, an exaction fee from an office use, based on the number of square feet, could be used for improvements to roadways that are directly impacted by the added office area.

EXCAVATION

Removal or recovery by any means whatsoever of soil, rock, minerals, mineral substances, or organic substances other than vegetation from water or land, on or beneath the surface thereof, or beneath the land surface, whether exposed or submerged.

EXCEPTION

Permission to depart from the design standards in the ordinance. *See* WAIVER.

Comment: Exceptions often refer to design standards such as length of cul-de-sacs, location and type of improvements, and landscaping requirements. They are dictated by the circumstances related to the specific application that makes the design requirement for which the exception is requested unnecessary or unreasonable.

As in the case of waivers, the approving agency must make findings and conclusions before granting the exception.

EXCLUSIONARY ZONING

Development regulations that result in the exclusion of low- and moderate-income and minority families from a community.

Comment: Exclusionary zoning may also serve to keep out, or limit, additional development. Exclusionary zoning provisions include allowing only large-lot, single-family detached dwellings; bulk regulations in excess of those needed for health and safety; limiting or barring of multifamily development; and excessive improvement requirements that generate unnecessary costs.

EXCLUSIVE-USE DISTRICT

A zoning district that allows only one use or a limited range of uses.

EXECUTIVE HEADQUARTERS

An office building occupied almost entirely by the principal office of a business or corporation.

144

Comment: Usually, the executive headquarters (or corporate headquarters) bears the name of the corporation and is designed to project a favorable corporate image. The buildings are often of a higher quality and cost more to construct than multitenanted or speculative office buildings. Headquarters buildings have fewer employees per square foot since the executives typically have large offices and the buildings have a significant number of meeting rooms. From a planning and zoning perspective, there is no guarantee that a headquarters building will always remain so. Corporations are sold, functions change, and cost cutting requires economies. The fewer parking spaces allowed for a headquarters building may not be sufficient when the building no longer functions as originally approved.

EXISTING GRADE OR ELEVATION

The vertical location above some elevation point of the ground surface before excavating or filling.

EXISTING USE

The use of a lot or structure at the time of the enactment of a zoning ordinance.

Comment: Some municipalities, at the time a new zoning or development ordinance is adopted, will attempt to survey existing uses in order to provide an accurate record of preexisting nonconforming uses. The preexisting nonconforming use, legal at the time of the passage of the ordinance but made nonconforming as a result of the ordinance, has a legal right to continue. Future problems arise because of confusion as to the extent and nature of the uses at the time of passage. Hence, an inventory is often necessary to ensure that nonconforming uses do not expand illegally.

EXIT RAMP, ENTRANCE RAMP

Access lanes leading to and from a limited access highway.

EXPERT

A person who, through education or experience, has developed skill or knowledge in a particular subject so that he or she may form an opinion that will assist the fact finder. (*Black's* 1999)

Comment: Other tests as to the qualifications of an individual are whether the expert has been accepted by his or her peers as an expert or whether the individual has been qualified as an expert before other courts or agencies.

EXTENDED CARE FACILITY

A long-term facility or a distinct part of a facility licensed or approved as a nursing home, infirmary unit

145

of a home for the aged, or a governmental medical institution. *See* LONG-TERM CARE FACILITY.

EXTENDED PROPERTY LOT LINE

A line, radial or perpendicular to the street centerline, at each end of the frontage, extending from the right-of-way line to the curb line. *See Figure 39.*

EXTENSION

(1) An increase in the amount of existing floor area beyond the exterior wall; (2) extending the length of time an approving authority can act on an application for development.

EXTERIOR WALL

Any wall that defines the exterior boundaries of a building or structure.

EXTRACTIVE INDUSTRIES

Excavating and removing rock, stone, ore, soil, gravel, sand, minerals, and similar materials from the surface and/or subsurface.

Comment: Extractive industries are quarries, sand and gravel pits, mines, and soil removal operations. They are intensive operations, generating large amounts of truck traffic, noise (including blasting), and dust. Much of the activity takes place outdoors, and the result can be a continuing, unaesthetic scar on the landscape with ore, gravel, sand, and rock piled high on the property. In addition, customary accessory uses provide their own special nuisance impacts, such as odors from asphalt plants, noise and dust from sifters, crushers, and loading and unloading trucks, as well as runoff from washing material and cleaning operations and water sprayed to keep the dust down. Blasting, an integral part of quarry operations, can be particularly bothersome to adjacent properties and at times, due to miscalculation, dangerous as rock is exploded and thrown beyond the boundaries of the site.

In addition, extractive industries are governed by special rules. As Cox (2003) notes, "Since by the very nature of the use they must continually expand over a larger area, the "'diminishing asset theory' provides that such an industry may expand to the boundaries of its property. . . ." However, Cox also quotes a court decision (*Mt. Bethel Humus v. State*, 273 N.J. Super, 421 Appellate Div. 1994) in which the court noted that nonconforming uses of this type are still subject to the regulations adopted by the municipality such as soil removal regulations and applicable state laws such as, for example, wetlands protection regulations.

While development regulations may prohibit such uses in all zones or restrict them to only appropriate industrial districts, annual or biennial licensing requirements by the municipality appear to be the most effective way of regulating and controlling these uses. The licensing can require that a reuse plan be presented to the approving authority and that all activities be directed to the ultimate implementation of the plan. The licensing requirement can require adherence to a program of material extraction, showing locations where the material is to be extracted and time schedules. At the time of license renewal, the applicant would have to demonstrate, through aerial maps and surveys, that the locations and schedules have been followed. In addition, adequate buffered setbacks from surrounding areas should be established, and special routing for trucks can be required. Hours of operation and limits on blasting, with adequate insurance in place in case of a mishap, can also be part of the licensing requirement. The licensing requirement can also specify that piles of materials, asphalt plants, rock crushers, conveyers, and truck loading and unloading areas be located on the site in such a way as to minimize their impact on surrounding properties. Finally, some municipalities levy an escrow fee at the time of license renewal to cover inspection costs and necessary repairs to roads resulting from the heavy truck use on local roads. Others levy a per-cubic-yard extraction fee to cover the same costs.

EXURBAN AREA

The fringe area between a suburbanized area and rural area, subject to development pressures.

F

FABRICATION AND ASSEMBLY

The manufacturing from standardized parts of a distinct object differing from the individual components.

Comment: The term "fabrication and assembly" is often used to describe a general class of permitted uses. It usually involves materials with form and substance (as opposed to liquid or gas), with a physical (as opposed to chemical) mating or joining of the individual parts.

FACADE

The exterior walls of a building exposed to public view or that wall viewed by persons not within the building. *See Figure 17.*

FACADES, PRINCIPAL

Exterior walls of a building or structure that are adjacent to or front on a public street, park, or plaza.

FACILITY

A place where an activity occurs.

Comment: The word "facility" (or "facilities") is a general term describing one or more buildings, structures, locations in, on, or at which something, other than a random occurrence, is happening. Land development ordinances provide controls on the facility in terms of where in the municipality it is permitted and on such physical characteristics as size, height, setbacks, and similar bulk controls. The land development ordinance may also establish controls on the activity itself, such as how many parking spaces are required, the location of lighting, how many signs are allowed, and similar characteristics.

FACILITY FOR HANDICAPPED PEOPLE

Any ramp, handrail, elevator, door, specially treated surface and similar design, convenience, or device that facilitates the health, safety, or comfort of a handicapped person.

FACTORY

A building in which raw material and semifinished or finished materials are converted to a different form or state or where goods are manufactured, assembled, treated, or processed.

FACTORY-BUILT HOUSING

Structures designed for long-term residential use. For the purpose of these regulations, factory-built housing consists of three types: modular, mobile homes, and manufactured homes. (American Planning Association, *Manufactured Housing: Regulation, Design Innovations, and Development Options,* Planning Advisory Service Report No. 478, 1998) *See* MANUFACTURED HOME; MOBILE HOME; MODULAR HOME.

149

FAIR MARKET VALUE

The price of a building or land that would be agreed upon voluntarily in fair negotiations between a knowledgeable owner willing, but not forced, to sell and a knowledgeable buyer willing, but not forced, to buy.

Comment: The definition describes an ideal abstract situation. In real-life situations, brokers use a variety of methods to establish the fair market value, including comparable sales, income capitalization, and replacement value.

FAIR SHARE PLAN

A plan or proposal by which a municipality would satisfy its obligation to create a realistic opportunity to meet its fair share of the low- and moderate-income housing needs of its region and which details the affirmative measures the municipality proposes to undertake to achieve its fair share of low- and moderate-income housing.

Comment: The above definition was derived from New Jersey's Supreme Court *Mt. Laurel II* case, *Southern Burlington County NAACP v. Mt. Laurel Township*, 92 N.J. 158 (1983).

FALLOW LAND

Farmland left uncultivated.

FAMILY

A group of individuals not necessarily related by blood, marriage, adoption, or guardianship living together in a dwelling unit as a single housekeeping unit. For purposes of this ordinance, "'family' does not include any society, club, fraternity, sorority, association, lodge, federation, or like organizations; or any group of individuals who are in a group living arrangement as a result of criminal offenses." (Merriam and Sitkowski 1999) *See* HOUSEHOLD.

Comment: The key words in the definition are "single housekeeping unit," which is defined as "common use and access to all living and eating areas, bathrooms, and food preparation and serving areas." In addition to the single housekeeping unit, a family also represents an intentionally structured relationship and implies a permanent and long-term voluntary relationship as opposed to one that is short-term, transient, and mandated by law.

The above definition places no limit on the number of unrelated individuals that may occupy the dwelling unit, save the specific exceptions noted. However, a limitation on unrelated individuals living together is legal under the U.S. Supreme Court decision in the *Village of Belle Terre v. Boraas* case (416 U.S. 1 [1974]). In

150

that case, a maximum of two unrelated individuals was deemed to constitute a family. However, as Merriam and Sitkowski note, ". . . a law can be legal under the U.S. Constitution but not under that of a state constitution."

Several states did just that; they amended their own constitutions or passed laws pursuant to their own constitutions to prohibit limits on unrelated individuals living together as a family. For example, in *State v. Baker* 81 N.J. 99, 108–09 (1979), the state Supreme Court invalidated a local ordinance that established a limit on the number of unrelated individuals. It suggested that by limiting the number of unrelated individuals it prohibited much reasonable occupancy, such as unrelated widows, bachelors, or "even judges." The decision said that the municipality could regulate density by relating the number of occupants to the number of bedrooms, bathrooms, or a minimum number of square feet per occupant. It also said that traffic could be restricted by limiting the number of vehicles.

That decision anticipated a U.S. Supreme Court decision, *City of Edmonds v. Oxford House*, 524 U.S. 725 (1995), 47 ZD 212. As Susan M. Connor noted, "The Court addressed whether the zoning regulation (single-family zoning defining "'family' to include no more than five unrelated individuals was a reasonable occupancy restriction that is exempt from the Federal Fair Housing Act. . . .The Supreme Court recognized a distinction between land use restrictions and maximum occupancy restrictions . . . [and] that . . . maximum occupancy restrictions cap the number of occupants per dwelling, typically in relation to available floor space or the number of any type of rooms . . . and these restrictions ordinarily apply uniformly to all residents of all dwellings. . . ." (Connor 1998) For a detailed and extensive discussion of the entire issue of "family" and recommendations on alternate definitions, see the previously cited article by Merriam and Sitkowski.

FAMILY ENTERTAINMENT CENTER

See AMUSEMENT PARK; THEME PARK.

FARM OR FARMLAND

A parcel of land used for agricultural activities. *See* AGRICULTURE; AGRICULTURAL ZONING; HORSE FARM.

FARM STAND

A structure for the display and sale of farm products primarily grown on the property upon which the stand is located.

Comment: In farming communities or municipalities where farms exist, farm stands are customary accessory uses and very much part of the farming operation. Reasonable restrictions are appropriate, however, to ensure the stands are operated in a safe manner and do not constitute a nuisance to surrounding nonfarm properties. Controls include maximum size of the stand, setbacks from the road and side property lines, signage, parking, and litter control.

Farm stands should be a maximum of 250 square feet in order to reflect their temporary and accessory nature. Setbacks of 25 feet from the side property lines and road provide some nuisance protection for adjacent properties and allow cars to safely pull off the road. The local zoning officer or planner should review a sketch plan to determine that adequate parking is provided and that provisions are made to control litter.

Some municipalities impose the additional restriction that the farm products sold at the stand must be raised on the farm or the land on which the stand is located. In actual practice, this has proven to be impractical and difficult to enforce. On the other hand, most towns would not like to see "garden centers" on each farm. The definition requires the products to be "primarily grown on the property, etc." This allows some flexibility and also provides an indication of the intent of the ordinance.

FARM STRUCTURE

Any building or structure used for agricultural purposes.

FARMER'S MARKET

The seasonal selling or offering for sale at retail of vegetables or produce, flowers, orchard products, and similar nonanimal agricultural products, occurring in a predesignated area, where the vendors are individuals who have raised the vegetables or produce or have taken the same on consignment for retail sale.

Comment: Municipalities or local business associations usually sponsor farmers' markets. They are probably best regulated by licensing and a separate farmer's market ordinance, which would include general regulations establishing who can sell and what may be sold, hours and days of operation, responsibilities for cleanup, fees for the rental of spaces and stalls, liability requirements, and so on. The land development ordinance should establish the zones where farmers' markets could be located and provide for site plan review to ensure adequate circulation, safe access, and controls over signage and lighting. If permitted by the local ordinance, farmers' markets may also include home-produced crafts and restaurants.

Farmers' markets are usually held in business areas, often on existing parking lots and/or closed-off streets. They can be important elements of an overall plan to revitalize urban areas. They serve to attract more people into these areas and increase the market for existing merchants. Observers of farmers' markets have noted "they encourage community interaction, establish community cohesion, and evoke a community spirit." (Linowes 1985) For a recent book dealing with organizing, maintaining, and selling in a farmer's market, see Corum et al. 2001.

FAST-FOOD RESTAURANT

An establishment whose principal business is the sale of pre-prepared or rapidly prepared food directly to the customer in a ready-to-consume state for consumption either within the restaurant building, in vehicles on the premises, or off the premises.

Comment: The distinction between the fast-food restaurant and other types of restaurants is rapidly becoming blurred. The major objections to fast-food restaurants come from circulation concerns and the potential adverse impacts of high traffic generation, glare, garish design, litter, and noise. In the past, they often became hangouts. With stringent performance standards, these problems can be controlled, and there appears to be little reason to differentiate between fast-food restaurants and other types of restaurants.

However, the "take-out" place is a distinctive use. Usually orders are called in and then picked up. Parking requirements are not as high as for eat-in restaurants. *See* RESTAURANT, DRIVE-IN; RESTAURANT, TAKE-OUT.

FEASIBILITY STUDY

An analysis of a specific project or program to determine if it can be successful.

Comment: Feasibility studies can cover a wide range of subjects. The most common is the financial feasibility study to determine whether the project will turn a profit. Other feasibility studies may cover law and various elements of planning, such as traffic, environment, building size, and so forth. The feasibility study relates capacity to demand but may also cover political and social benefits and costs. Banks may require feasibility studies to determine the estimated rate of return on investment. *See* COST-BENEFIT ANALYSIS; MARKETABILITY STUDY.

FEE SIMPLE ABSOLUTE   The most complete set of private property land rights, including mineral rights below the surface, surface rights, and air rights. *See* EASEMENT.

FEEDLOT   A confined area or structure, pen, or corral, used to fatten livestock prior to final shipment. *See* CONCENTRATED ANIMAL FEEDING OPERATION.

FENCE   An artificially constructed barrier of any material or combination of materials erected to enclose, screen, or separate areas.

Comment: Development regulations should include provisions for fences. Generally, they should be divided into categories of open, semiopen, and closed fences, and regulations should establish maximum heights and setbacks for the different categories. For example, an open fence, such as a split rail fence, might be permitted anywhere on a particular lot. Solid fences, such as brick, might be restricted to a maximum height of 6 feet and be required to meet all setback requirements for principal structures in the zone. A fence may or may not include a gate, but a gate does not include a fence. *See* GATE.

FENCE, OPEN   A fence constructed with openings between the materials used in its construction. *See Figure 40.*

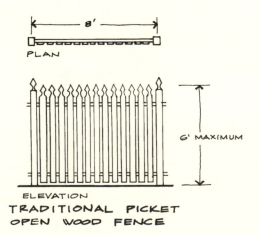

ELEVATION
TRADITIONAL PICKET
OPEN WOOD FENCE

FIGURE 40

FENCE, SOLID   A fence, including any gates, constructed of solid material, wood or masonry, through which no visual images may be seen. *See Figure 41.*

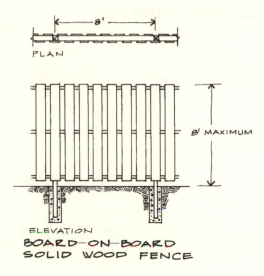

PLAN

8' MAXIMUM

ELEVATION

BOARD-ON-BOARD
SOLID WOOD FENCE

FIGURE 41

FENESTRATION

Windows and other openings on a building facade.

FESTIVAL MARKETPLACE

An anchorless retail center with a mix of small specialty shops offering one-of-a-kind merchandise, with an emphasis on gifts and crafts supplied locally and food offerings, often located in a unique architectural setting. (Sawicki 1989)

Comment: Sawicki notes that these shops are not primary retail centers but more like entertainment centers anchored by restaurants. Underground Atlanta is often cited as a prime example of a festival marketplace.

FIELD CHANGES

Adjustments to approved plans based on actual conditions found during construction.

Comment: Field changes are usually approved by the municipal engineer, municipal planner, or construction official. They are minor in nature, such as the need to shift a pipe a few feet, change the location of a catch basin, or substitute a plant or tree species. Field changes do not require variances or design waivers. After approval, a field change memo is usually prepared by the approving official and placed in the project file. The actual change is reflected in the final "as-built" plans submitted by the applicant.

FILL

Sand, gravel, earth, or other materials of any composition whatsoever placed or deposited by humans. *See Figure 42.*

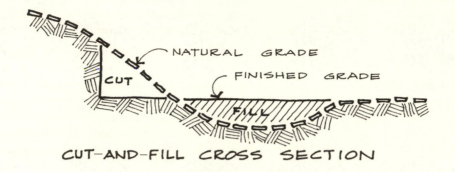

CUT-AND-FILL CROSS SECTION

FIGURE 42

FILLING

The process of depositing fill in a low-lying area. *See* LAND RECLAMATION; MADE LAND.

Comment: Many municipalities restrict the amount of fill that can be spread on a construction site. They often require a "balanced" job where the grading eliminates the need to bring in fill or requires the removal of soil from the property. If fill is required, municipalities often require that the fill be from a virgin source and free from any contamination. Filling does not include placing fill in wetlands, marshy areas, or water bodies. Filling of these sites is governed by state and/or federal statutes.

FILLING STATION

See AUTOMOBILE SERVICE STATION.

FILTRATION

In wastewater treatment, the mechanical process that removes particulate matter from water, usually by passing it through sand.

FINAL APPROVAL

The last official action of the approving agency taken on a development plan that has been given preliminary approval after all conditions and requirements of preliminary approval have been met and the required improvements have either been installed or guarantees properly posted for their installation, or approval conditioned on the posting of such guarantees.

Comment: Final approval permits the applicant to sell lots and construct houses or buildings.

156

FINAL PLAN

See PLAT, FINAL.

FINANCE, INSURANCE, AND REAL ESTATE (FIRE)

Establishments such as banks and financial institutions, credit agencies, investment companies, brokers of and dealers in securities and commodities, security and commodity exchanges, insurance agents, lessors, lessees, buyers, sellers, agents, and developers of real estate.

Comment: Often referred to as FIRE in use groupings.

FINANCIAL SERVICE CENTER

A non-bank entity that does not accept deposits or make loans like traditional banks or financial institutions but that provides monetary services that include the sale or redemption of travelers checks or money orders, money wire transfers, check cashing, and currency exchange.

Comment: Financial service centers may also provide electronic bill payments, automatic teller machine access, sale of debit and phone cards, deposit acceptance services, public transportation fare and token sales, postage stamp sales, fax and copy services, and electronic tax preparation. They are characterized by mostly on-site customer service.

FINGER-FILL CANALS

In waterfront residential developments, deep, narrow canals created by the dredging and filling of shallow bays and estuaries and interspersed with fingerlike projections of land on which the housing is erected.

FINISHED ELEVATION

The proposed elevation of the land surface of a site after completion of all site preparation work. *See* GRADE, FINISHED. *See Figure 42.*

FINISHED PRODUCT

The end result of a manufacturing process that is ready for utilization or consumption by the ultimate consumer. (NAICS 1997) *See* SEMIFINISHED PRODUCT.

FIRE HAZARD ZONE

An area where, because of slope, fuel, weather, or other fire-related conditions, the potential loss of life and property from a fire necessitates special fire protection measures and planning before development occurs.

FIRE LANE

An unobstructed paved or improved surface area clearly defined by pavement markings and signs, at least 12 feet wide, and designed to provide access for fire-fighting equipment.

Comment: Fire lanes are recommended for shopping centers and larger office buildings to ensure access to the building for fire-fighting equipment. The lanes should not be used for parking but may be part of the overall circulation system.

FIRE ZONE

An area clearly delineated and marked to facilitate access to hydrants and buildings as designated by the chief of the fire district in which the building, structure, or use is situated.

FISCAL IMPACT ANALYSIS (FIA)

An analysis of the costs and revenues associated with a specific development application. *See* COST-BENEFIT ANALYSIS.

Comment: FIAs are also known as cost-revenue analyses. They can be simple or sophisticated, depending in part on whether secondary and tertiary impacts are considered.

FISH FARM

An area devoted to the cultivation of fish and other seafood for commercial sale. *See* AQUACULTURE.

FISHING, HUNTING, TRAPPING

Establishments primarily engaged in commercial fishing, including shellfish marine products, operating fish hatcheries, and fish and game preserves, and the killing of animals by shooting or the capture in mechanical or other types of devices for commercial gain.

FITNESS CENTER

See HEALTH CLUB.

FLAG LOT

See LOT, FLAG.

FLEA MARKET

An occasional or periodic market held in an open area or structure where groups of individual sellers offer goods for sale to the public.

Comment: Flea markets often are regularly scheduled—such as on weekends and holidays–and while most are held outdoors or under sheds, a recent trend is to utilize large, vacant buildings or vacant shopping centers. What differentiates flea markets from other retail stores or shopping centers is that there are no long-term leases between the sellers and owners, or lessors, of the site and that often the sellers use their own vehicles for display or set up temporary tables for their wares. While some flea markets are temporary in nature and are established on lands or in buildings not customarily used for such a purpose, others are more or less permanent. These long-term flea markets should be subject to site plan review to ensure appropriate circulation, safety, and off-street parking, lighting, landscaping, signage, and trash storage.

FLEXTIME

The ability of an employee to determine his or her starting and finishing times.

Comment: Flextime is used to spread peak-hour traffic loads and may be required as part of traffic management systems. Employers usually determine a range of starting and finishing times, such as 6:30 A.M. to 9:30 A.M. and 3:30 P.M. to 6:30 P.M., and core hours when all employees have to be on the premises.

FLOATING ZONE

An unmapped zoning district where all the zone requirements are contained in the ordinance and the zone is fixed on the map only when an application for development meeting the zone requirements is approved.

Comment: Floating zones (or overlay zones) have generally declined in popularity because of charges that they closely resemble spot zoning or contract zoning, both illegal under current case law. The most appropriate application appears to be in rural communities, where large tracts of land may be developed in accordance with planned development regulations providing the ordinance requirements are met for conversion of the land from the previous rural designation to a development zone. Some of these ordinance regulations might require direct access to major roads, availability of public water and public sewer, and proximity to other municipal facilities and services.

In recent years, floating zones have also been used to provide lower-income housing in built-up municipalities. Such floating zones typically require that when previously unavailable land (such as a farm, surplus municipal land, or redevelopment areas) above a minimum area (for example, 2 acres) is proposed to be developed for residences, a percentage of the units must be reserved for low- and moderate-income households. An alternative to floating zones is to make the planned development or lower-income housing conditional uses in those zones deemed appropriate.

FLOCCULATION

In wastewater treatment, the process of separating suspended solids by chemical creation of clumps or floes.

FLOOD

The temporary overflowing of water onto land that is usually devoid of surface water. *See* BASE FLOOD ELEVATION; FLOOD-PRONE; FLOOD, REGULATORY BASE; FLOOD, REGULATORY BASE DISCHARGE; FLOOD FRINGE AREA; FLOOD HAZARD AREA; FLOOD HAZARD DESIGN ELEVATION; FLOOD INSURANCE RATE MAP; FLOOD OF RECORD; FLOODPLAIN; FLOODWAY; FLOODWAY, REGULATORY.

FLOOD, BASE FLOOD ELEVATION	*See* BASE FLOOD ELEVATION.
FLOOD DAMAGE POTENTIAL	The susceptibility of a specific land use at a particular location to damage by flooding and the potential of the specific land use to increase off-site flooding or flood-related damages.
FLOOD FRINGE AREA	That portion of the flood hazard area outside of the floodway based on the total area inundated during the regulatory base flood plus 25 percent of the regulatory base flood discharge. *See* FLOOD, REGULATORY BASE; FLOOD, REGULATORY BASE DISCHARGE; FLOODWAY. *See Figure 43.*

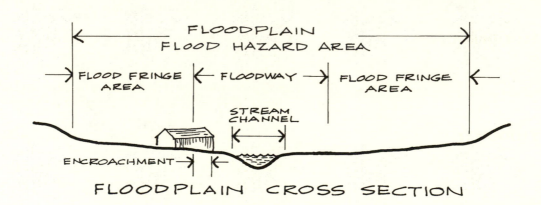

FIGURE 43

FLOOD HAZARD AREA	The floodplain consisting of the floodway and the flood fringe area. *See* FLOODPLAIN. *See Figure 43.*
FLOOD HAZARD DESIGN ELEVATION	The highest elevation, expressed in feet above sea level, of the level of floodwaters that delineates the flood fringe area.
FLOOD INSURANCE RATE MAP (FIRM)	The official map on which the Federal Insurance Administration has delineated both the areas of special flood hazards and the risk premium zones applicable to the community.
FLOOD OF RECORD	A past flood for which there are accurate local records available and that is used as the reference flood.

160

FLOOD, REGULATORY BASE

A flood with a 1 percent chance of being equaled or exceeded in any given year.

Comment: This is often referred to as a 100-year flood.

FLOOD, REGULATORY BASE DISCHARGE

The rate of flow produced by the regulatory base flood measured in cubic feet per second (CFS).

FLOODPLAIN

The channel and the relatively flat area adjoining the channel of a natural stream or river that has been or may be covered by floodwater. *See Figure 43.*

FLOOD-PRONE

A land area adjoining a river, stream, watercourse, or lake for which a floodway and floodplain have not been determined with respect to any specific flood frequency, but for which the potential for flooding can be identified by soils, geological evidence, or other data.

FLOODPROOFING

A combination of structural provisions and changes or adjustments to properties and structures subject to flooding for the reduction or elimination of flood damage to properties, water and sanitary facilities, and other utilities, structures, and the contents of buildings.

FLOODWAY

The channel of a natural stream or river and portions of the floodplain adjoining the channel, which are reasonably required to carry and discharge the floodwater or flood flow of any natural stream or river. *See* FLOODWAY, REGULATORY. *See Figure 43.*

FLOODWAY, REGULATORY

The channel and the adjacent land areas that must be reserved in order to discharge the regulatory base flood without cumulatively increasing the water surface elevation more than 0.2 feet.

FLOOR AREA, GROSS (GFA)

The sum of the gross horizontal areas of all enclosed floors of a building, including cellars, basements, mezzanines, penthouses, corridors, and lobbies from the exterior face of exterior walls, or from the centerline of a common wall separating two buildings, but excluding any space with a floor-to-ceiling height of less than 6 feet 6 inches. (Institute of Real Estate Management 1985)

FLOOR AREA, NET

The total of all floor areas of a building, excluding stairwells and elevator shafts, equipment rooms, interior vehicular parking or loading; and all floors below the first or ground floor, except when these are used or intended to be used for human habitation or service to the public.

161

Comment: Very often, for ease of administration, net floor area is expressed as gross floor area minus a certain percentage. Stairwells, elevator shafts, equipment rooms, and utility rooms generally average out to about 15 percent of the gross floor area. Thus, net floor area may be defined as gross floor area minus 15 percent.

FLOOR AREA, USAGE

See FLOOR AREA, NET.

FLOOR AREA RATIO (FAR)

Representing the gross floor area of all buildings or structures on a lot divided by the total lot area. *See Figure 44.*

Comment: Some care should be exercised in applying this definition. It includes all buildings and structures and the *entire* lot area. The New Jersey cases (*Manalapan Builders v. Tp. Committee*, 290 N.J. Super. 295 [App. Div. 1992] and *Crow—New Jersey 32 Ltd v. Township of Clinton*, 718 F. Supp. 378 [D. N.J. 1980]) set aside FAR definitions that excluded environmentally sensitive land from the ordinance definition of FAR. In the Manalapan case, the judge noted that, if the site had extensive environmentally constrained areas, the FAR should be adjusted accordingly.

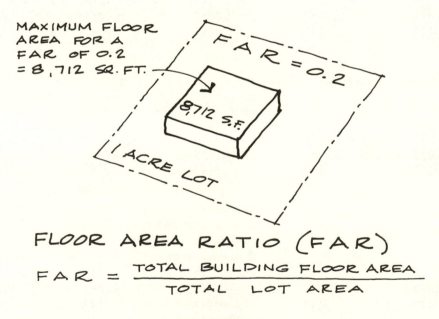

FIGURE 44

162

FLORICULTURE	The cultivation of ornamental flowering plants.
FLOWMETER	In wastewater treatment, a meter that indicates the rate at which wastewater flows.
FLUE GAS	A mixture of gases resulting from combustion that emerges from a chimney.
FLUME	A constructed channel that carries water.
FLY ASH	All partially incinerated solids that are carried in a gas stream.
FLY-IN DEVELOPMENT	A residential development planned and integrated with airport facilities and directly accessible to recreational flyers.
FOOD COURT	An area in which a variety of prepared meals, beverages, and desserts are available from one or more establishments for purchase and for consumption within a common seating area on the premises.
	Comment: These establishments are found in regional shopping malls, major office and retail complexes, resort and entertainment centers, gambling casinos, and the like. Appropriate accessory or adjacent uses often include entertainment, recreation, child care facilities, and rest rooms. When located within a shopping mall or other major complex, food courts will typically provide, in addition to interior access, direct access to the exterior of the facility.
FOOD STORE	*See* RETAIL FOOD ESTABLISHMENT; RETAIL STORE, CONVENIENCE.
FOOD-PROCESSING ESTABLISHMENT	An establishment in which food is processed or otherwise prepared for eventual human consumption but is not consumed on the premises.
	Comment: A food-processing establishment covers a wide range of businesses, all involved with food. It may be a caterer or a flour mill. The zoning implications are based on impacts and size of the establishment.
FOOTCANDLE	(1) The unit of illumination when the foot is the unit of length. *See Figure 45.* (2) A unit of illumination produced on a surface, all points of which are one foot from a uniform point source of one candle. (Kendig et al. 1980)

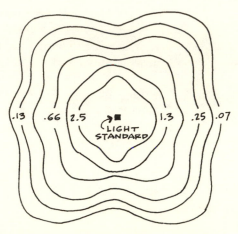

250-WATT / HIGH-PRESSURE SODIUM
20-FOOT MOUNTING HEIGHT

TYPICAL LIGHTING PATTERN
(SHOWN IN FOOTCANDLES)

0   40   80

SCALE IN FEET

FIGURE 45

Comment: Local ordinances usually establish a minimum and sometimes maximum footcandle level required for different areas. These are shown in subdivision or site plans as isofootcandle diagrams, where all the points on the line represent the same level of illumination. The diagrams are often drawn around light standards to show the level and extent of lighting on the site.

Recommended levels of illumination for various activities are contained in the Illuminating Engineering Society of North America's *IES Lighting Handbook* (1987). Typical levels, as listed in Listokin and Walker (1989), are shown in table F-1.

FORCED-TURN ISLANDS

See TRAFFIC CALMING.

FOREST

Areas or stands of trees, the majority of which are greater than 12 inches caliper, covering an area greater than one-quarter acre; or groves of mature trees, without regard to minimum area, consisting of substantial numbers of individual specimens.

Comment: The 12-inch requirement does not apply to certain species, such as birches and dogwoods, and trees

164

TABLE F-1: ILLUMINATION GUIDELINES FOR STREET, PARKING, AND PEDESTRIAN AREAS

A. Street Illumination

Street Hierarchy	AREA CLASSIFICATION		
	Commercial Footcandles	Intermediate Footcandles	Residential Footcandles
Major	1.2	0.9	0.6
Collector	0.8	0.6	0.4
Local	0.6	0.5	0.3

B. Parking Illumination (Open Parking Facilities)

Level of Activity	ILLUMINATION OBJECTIVE	
	Vehicular Use Area Only Footcandles	General Parking and Pedestrian Safety Footcandles
Low activity	0.5	0.2
Medium activity	1.0	0.6
High activity	2.0	0.9

C. Pedestrian Way Illumination

Walkway and Bikeway Classification	Minimum Average Horizontal Levels Footcandles	Average Levels for Special Pedestrian Security Footcandles
Sidewalks (roadside) and Type A Bikeways[a]		
Commercial Areas	1.0	0.2
Intermediate Areas	0.6	0.1
Residential Areas	0.6	0.5
Walkways distant from roadways and Type B Bikeways[b]		
Walkways, Bikeways, and Stairways	0.5	0.5
Pedestrian tunnels	4.3	5.4

Notes:
    a. Type A bikeways are on-street areas reserved for bikes.
    b. Type B bikeways are separate designated bikeways.

Source: David Listokin and Carole Walker, *The Subdivision and Site Plan Handbook* (New Brunswick, NJ: Center for Urban Policy Research, 1989).

found in pinelands. The minimum caliper should represent a mature tree. "Substantial numbers" is difficult to define. It represents more of a visual impression than a specific number.

FOREST MANAGEMENT PLAN

A plan establishing best conservation and management practices, including schedules and responsible agencies.

FORESTRY

The operation of timber tracts, tree farms, forest nurseries, the gathering of forest products, or the performing of forest services.

FOSSIL FUELS

Fuels derived from the remains of ancient plant and animal life, such as coal, oil, and gas.

FRANCHISE

The right or authority to provide specified goods or services to a defined geographic area.

Comment: The most common use of franchise in planning is with respect to utility franchises. Exclusive franchises are often granted to utility companies to provide service to a geographic area.

FRATERNAL ORGANIZATION

A group of people formally organized for a common interest, usually cultural, religious, or entertainment, with regular meetings, rituals, and formal written membership requirements.

Comment: Examples of such groups are Masons or the Knights of Columbus. The clubhouses for fraternal organizations were usually located in residential neighborhoods, but newer ordinances properly locate them in business areas or classify them as conditional uses with carefully drawn requirements for parking, buffering, lighting, and solid waste disposal because they usually draw their membership from a wide geographic area. In addition, the club facilities often are used for weddings, bingo, and weekend catering and can become nuisances to surrounding residences. *See* CLUB; MEMBERSHIP ORGANIZATION.

FRATERNITY HOUSE

A building containing sleeping rooms, bathrooms, common rooms, and a central kitchen and dining room maintained exclusively for fraternity members and their guests or visitors and affiliated with an institution of higher learning.

Comment: A fraternity house is a distinct and separate use. It is not a dwelling unit or multifamily structure. The members do not constitute a family in the zoning sense since they do not function as a single household unit. *See* FAMILY.

FREEWAY

See STREET, FREEWAY.

FREIGHT FORWARDING

Establishments primarily engaged in the transshipment of goods from shippers to receivers for a charge, covering the entire transportation route and, in turn, making use of the services of other transportation establishments in effecting delivery.

FREIGHT-HANDLING FACILITIES

Terminals with the capability of handling a large variety of goods involving various forms of transportation and providing multimodal shipping capabilities, such as rail to truck and truck to air.

Comment: Freight-handling facilities are terminals that have a variety of equipment and storage facilities and space to handle shipboard, truck, rail, and air freight containers and often liquid and raw agricultural products. They differ from warehouses in that they do not usually store the freight for any period of time, although they may have warehouses associated with them. (Schultz and Kasen 1984)

FRESHWATER WETLAND

See WETLAND, FRESHWATER.

FRINGE AREA

The area of transition between two different dominant land uses or other recognizable characteristics, including social, economic, or cultural. (Schultz and Kasen 1984)

FRONT FOOT

A measure of land width, being 1 foot along the front lot line of a property.

Comment: Front foot measurements are usually used in assessment formulas.

FRONT LOT LINE

See LOT LINE, FRONT.

FRONT YARD

See YARD, FRONT.

FRONTAGE

That side of a lot abutting on a street; the front lot line. *See Figure 14.*

Comment: On corner or through lots, the frontage may be designated by the owner, but it should be consistent with the orientation of buildings on the other lots and improvements on the same side of the street. On improved lots, the frontage is usually the side where the main building entrance is located and in the general direction in which the principal building faces.

FRONTAGE ROAD

A service road, usually parallel to a highway, designed to reduce the number of driveways that intersect the highway.

FUEL DISPENSER

The vertical structure(s) at gasoline stations that contains the hoses from which fuel is dispensed directly into motor vehicles.

Comment: Formerly referred to as gas pumps, they did, at one time, contain the pump that transferred fuel from storage tanks into motor vehicles. Now, all pumps are located in the underground storage tanks. Modern fuel dispensers may have up to three hoses on each side of the structure for regular, plus, and high-octane fuel. But in all cases, only two motor vehicles can be serviced at any time. Older ordinances often specified the number of "gas pumps" on a site to limit the size of the station.

FUEL PUMP

See FUEL DISPENSER.

FULL CLOSURES

See TRAFFIC CALMING.

FUNERAL HOME

A building used for the preparation of the deceased for burial and the display of the deceased and rituals connected therewith before burial or cremation.

Comment: Funeral homes are generally very stable uses and are extremely well maintained. The only potential problem is the necessity for adequate off-street parking and stacking room for cars lined up for the funeral procession.

G

**GAME OR
GAMBLING GAME**

Any banking or percentage game played for money, property, or any representative of value with cards, dice, or any device or machine and located exclusively within a facility licensed for such activity.

**GAMING
OR GAMBLING**

The dealing, operating, carrying on, conducting, maintaining, or exposing for pay of any game.

**GAMING OR GAMBLING
ESTABLISHMENT**

Any premises wherein or whereon gaming is done. *See* CASINO.

**GAMING DEVICE OR
GAMING EQUIPMENT**

Any device, contrivance, or machine used in connection with gaming or any game.

GAP ANALYSIS

The study of available time between vehicles in a stream of traffic to determine the potential capacity of traffic turning to or from a roadway or crossing.

GARAGE

A deck, building, or parking structure, or part thereof, used or intended to be used for the parking and storage of vehicles.

Comment: A distinction should be made between parking, short- and long-term, and storage, such as that associated with auto sales and unregistered vehicles.

GARAGE, MUNICIPAL

A structure owned or operated by a municipality and used primarily for the parking and storage of vehicles owned by the general public.

**GARAGE,
PRIVATE CUSTOMER
AND EMPLOYEE**

A structure that is accessory to a nonretail, commercial, or manufacturing establishment, building, or use and is primarily for the parking and storage of vehicles operated by the customers, visitors, and employees of such building and that is not available to the general public.

**GARAGE, PRIVATE
RESIDENTIAL**

A structure that is accessory to a single- or two-family dwelling, is used for the parking and storage of vehicles owned and operated by the residents thereof, and is not a separate commercial enterprise available to the general public.

Comment: The combination of narrow lots and two-car attached garages can result in visually unattractive "snout houses" or "garage door" streetscapes. Solutions include using detached garages set back from the house with street access or fronting on an alley. In both cases, a covered walkway to the house can be provided. Side-entry garages are another possibility but usually require at least a 115-foot lot width. Another solution is sharing the driveway access and necessary turning courts with the adjacent lot. In this last example, three-bay side-entry garages can be accommodated with no detriment to the streetscape. *See* SNOUT HOUSE.

GARAGE, PUBLIC

A structure or portion thereof, other than a private customer and employee garage or private residential garage, used primarily for the parking and storage of vehicles and available to the general public.

GARAGE, REPAIR

Any building, premises, and land in which or upon which a business, service, or industry involving the maintenance, servicing, repair, or painting of vehicles is conducted or rendered. *See* AUTOMOTIVE REPAIR SERVICES AND GARAGES.

GARAGE, SHARED RESIDENTIAL

A garage used exclusively for the parking and storage of vehicles owned or operated by residents of nearby dwelling units and their guests, which is not available to the general public.

GARAGE SALE

The sale or offering for sale to the general public of items of personal property by the owner or tenant of an improved lot in a residential district, whether within or outside any building.

Comment: This definition limits sales to residential districts, appropriate to the noncommercial nature of this occasional activity. Some local regulations require a permit and fee, with restrictions on hours of operation, a limit of two sales per household per year, and requirements for the removal of signs after the sale.

GARBAGE

Animal and vegetable waste resulting from the handling, storage, sale, preparation, cooking, and service of foods. *See* SOLID WASTE.

GARDEN APARTMENT

See DWELLING, GARDEN APARTMENT.

GARDEN CENTER

See NURSERY, RETAIL.

GAS PUMP

See FUEL DISPENSER.

GASOLINE STATION

See AUTOMOBILE SERVICE STATION.

GASOLINE STATION AND CONVENIENCE CENTER (TRAVEL CENTER)

A gasoline station, fast-food restaurant, and convenience store located on the same lot and planned, operated, and maintained as an integrated planned development.

Comment: A natural extension of the combination gas station and convenience store, gasoline and convenience centers (travel centers) take the concept one step further by allowing fast-food restaurants on the same site.

If a particular zone permits a variety of uses, there is no reason why the various uses cannot be combined on a single parcel and developed as an integrated entity. Indeed, by combining the various uses, the result is efficiency in travel and better site design with fewer driveway openings, less impervious coverage, and with closer attention to landscaping and signs. But the site ". . . (must be) . . . designed in a manner that enables each business to function without internal congestion." (Thompson 1997b, p. 2)

Site-planning issues for the combined site are complex and include circulation, parking, landscape and buffering, and signage. Many municipalities classify these uses as conditional uses, requiring detailed traffic studies that include on-site circulation, stacking requirements, parking, and attention to potential conflicts between pedestrians and vehicles. Site plan review should consider noise and other nuisances resulting from "increased traffic, car radios, and loudspeakers from order menus as well as an increase in vehicle exhaust and cooking odors." (Thompson 1997b) Because of the increased activity, buffers and landscaping considerations become critical. In one ordinance, the article noted minimum setbacks of 30 feet, heavily landscaped with an opaque screen or fencing. In addition, if residential development is in close proximity, ordinance regulations can establish reasonable hours of operation and prohibit around-the-clock activity. As a general rule, separate signs should be sharply restricted, relying on a single freestanding sign for the site and single, smaller identification signs for each tenant on their building walls. (Thompson 1997b) *See* RETAIL STORE, CONVENIENCE; MINIMART.

GATE

(1) An opening in a fence; (2) an artificial barrier capable of being opened and closed, permitting or denying access across a driveway or path.

GATED COMMUNITIES

Residential developments that limit access to residents, invited guests, and authorized service and delivery vehicles.

Comment: Gated communities are often high-end residential subdivisions and multifamily enclaves, located largely in the suburbs. The type of gates can range from

172

elaborate guard houses to simple electronic barriers. Residents may enter by electronic cards, identification stickers, codes, or remote-control devices. Visitors and service and delivery vehicles must stop to be verified for entry. ("Gated Communities," *Planning and Zoning News*, March 1999)

Gated communities can be a disruptive force to the functional continuity of a neighborhood. If permitted, they should be located only in areas that are already physically or geographically isolated from the larger community. For a full discussion of gated communities, see Blakeley and Snyder 1997.

GATEWAY

A major entrance or point of access into a neighborhood, district, community or region. (*New Jersey State Development and Redevelopment Plan* 2002)

Comment: Gateways are often defined or reinforced by features that emphasize the transition and create a sense of arrival and departure. Gateway features are often vertical elements and can be constructed, such as taller buildings, pylons, or arches; or they may be natural, such as a river gorge or a valley. (*New Jersey State Development and Redevelopment Plan* 2002)

GAZEBO

An accessory building consisting of a detached, covered, freestanding, open-air structure not exceeding 300 square feet.

Comment: The limitation on the size of a gazebo is important to maintain its accessory-use status. The public use of a gazebo as, for example, a bandstand, may require a size exemption.

GENERAL DEVELOPMENT PLAN (GDP)

A plan showing general land use, circulation, open space, utilities, stormwater management, environmental factors, community facilities, housing, and phasing for parcels of land in excess of 100 acres and proposed to be constructed as a planned development.

Comment: The GDP is a concept plan that vests for up to 20 years the right of the applicant to submit various phases for preliminary and final site plan approval. Both the vesting period and minimum acreage are usually set by local ordinances in accordance with state enabling legislation.

The GDP differs from concept plans in that the latter provides no vesting. Most GDP legislation calls for sufficient detail to allow the approving agency to determine that the plan as submitted will work. The long vesting period is needed because of the high upfront investment in improvements. The applicant requires assurances that the zoning will not be amended or rescinded before the project is completed.

GENERAL PUBLIC

Any and all individuals without prior qualifications.

Comment: When a facility is "open to the general public," there are no restrictions or limitations other than a possible admissions fee for the persons attending.

GEOGRAPHIC INFORMATION SYSTEM (GIS)

A computer-generated mapping system for collecting, storing, analyzing, and integrating information about physical and man-made features on maps.

GLARE

The effect produced by light from a luminaire with an intensity sufficient to cause annoyance, discomfort, or loss in visual performance and visibility.

Comment: The definition is subjective but can be applied in a given situation by establishing a reference line (usually the lot or zone line) and maximum footcandle reading. See FOOTCANDLE.

GOLF COURSE

A tract of land laid out for at least nine holes for playing the game of golf that may include a clubhouse, dining and snack bars, pro shop, and practice facilities. *See* COUNTRY CLUB.

Comment: Golf courses are fairly intensive uses. They require significant quantities of water for irrigation and make extensive use of pesticides and fertilizers. Most golf courses have clubhouses that include dining rooms, locker facilities, and pro shops. Many dining rooms are open to the public and, if permitted, may be rented for weddings and other social events. Adequate parking for all functions, some of which overlap, must be considered. Maintenance, storage sheds, and garages are typically part of a golf course.

The Middlesex County, New Jersey, *Open Space and Recreation Plan 2003* has standards for county golf courses that are generally applicable to all golf courses, as follows:

Golf courses can be one of three types:

1. Regulation golf courses have a minimum par of 72 and a minimum of 6,000 yards as measured from the middle tees.

2. Executive golf courses have a total par ranging from 55 to 68 and an average of 3,000 to 4,500 yards.

3. *Par 3 golf courses have a par on each hole of 3 and an average of 2,000 to 2,500 yards.*

Typical ancillary facilities include a practice range, a clubhouse with dining facilities, and a pro shop. Other recreation activities may occur on portions of the property not developed for golf. The minimum acreage for each type of course is:

Regulation:	*150 acres*
Executive:	*40–75 acres*
Par 3:	*30 acres*

A total land area of 250 acres or more is preferred to accommodate 27 holes at each course. Potential for possible future expansion should be considered. The site should have topography, soils, and a configuration that will efficiently support golf course development. The site should be capable of withstanding intensive public use and should include adequate parking facilities to accommodate employees and guests. The course should be capable of being developed and operated in a fashion compatible with any significant environmental features. Land uses within or adjacent to the site should not unduly constrain the site or golf course operation. An adequate water supply for irrigation is required.

[Adapted from the *Open Space and Recreation Plan 2003*, Middlesex County, New Jersey]

GOVERNING BODY

The chief legislative body of the municipality. *See* LOCAL AUTHORITY; MUNICIPALITY.

GOVERNMENT AGENCY

Any department, commission, independent agency, or instrumentality of the United States, of a state, county, incorporated or unincorporated municipality, township, authority, district, or other governmental unit.

GRADE

(1) The average elevation of the land around a building; (2) the percent of rise or descent of a sloping surface. *See* SLOPE.

Comment: Grade is usually described as finished or natural and measured in feet above sea level. There is a distinction between percentage of slope and degree of slope. For example, a 45-degree slope is a 100 percent grade. *See Figures 15 and 46.*

GRADE, FINISHED

The final elevation of the average ground level adjoining a building at all exterior walls after development. (BOCA 1996, p. 55) *See* FINISHED ELEVATION. *See Figure 15.*

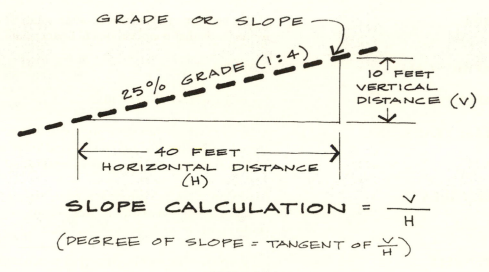

SLOPE CALCULATION = $\dfrac{V}{H}$

(DEGREE OF SLOPE = TANGENT OF $\dfrac{V}{H}$)

FIGURE 46

GRADE, NATURAL

The elevation of the ground level in its natural state, before construction, filling, or excavation. See NATURAL GROUND SURFACE. *See Figure 42.*

GRADE LEVEL

Roads, buildings, or structures built on the ground.

Comment: "Grade level" (or "at grade") differs from "below grade" or "above grade." All use the existing grade, whether finished or natural, as the reference.

GRADE REQUIREMENTS

Engineering standards establishing minimum and maximum slopes and geometry of roads, such as radii, and horizontal and vertical curves.

GRADE SEPARATION

Structures that physically separate various modes of transportation and intersecting flows of traffic from one another.

GRADED AREA

Pertaining to streets, land within the right-of-way, adjacent and parallel to the cartway, that must be flattened or leveled to the same width and cross-slope as a sidewalk, if a sidewalk is located or required at that location.

GRADING

Any stripping, cutting, filling, or stockpiling of earth or land, including the land in its cut or filled condition, to create new grades.

GRANITE BLOCK

See BELGIAN BLOCK.

GRANT

(1) An instrument that conveys some estate or interest in the lands that it embraces; (2) financial aid.

GRAPHIC SCALE

See SCALE.

GRAVEL PIT

See EXTRACTIVE INDUSTRIES.

GREASE TRAP

A device in which the grease present in sewage is intercepted and congealed by cooling and from which it may be skimmed of liquid wastes for disposal.

GREEN AREA

Land shown on a development plan, master plan, or official map for conservation, preservation, recreation, landscaping, or park. *See* OPEN SPACE.

GREENBELT

An open area that may be cultivated or maintained in a natural state surrounding development or used as a buffer between land uses or to mark the edge of an urban or developed area. *See* OPEN SPACE, NATURAL.

Comment: The famous greenbelt surrounding the metropolitan area of London, England, includes large-scale open recreation areas and low-intensity public and semipublic facilities and uses.

GREENFIELD

Farmland and open areas where there has been no previous industrial or commercial activity.

GREENHOUSE

A building or structure whose roof and sides are made largely of glass or other transparent or translucent material and in which the temperature and humidity can be regulated for the cultivation of fragile or out-of-season plants for subsequent sale or for personal enjoyment. *See* NURSERY, RETAIL.

GREENWAY

(1) A linear open space established along either a natural corridor, such as a riverfront, stream valley, or ridge line, or over land along a railroad right-of-way converted to recreational use, a canal, a scenic road, or other route; (2) any natural or landscaped course for pedestrian or bicycle passage; (3) an open-space connector linking parks, natural reserves, cultural features, or historic sites with each other and with populated areas; (4) locally, certain strip or linear parks designated as a parkway or greenbelt. (Little 1990)

GREYWATER

Wastewater from domestic sinks and tubs, but excluding that part of the plumbing waste stream that includes human wastes.

GRID SYSTEM

A map coordinate system that allows identification of a land area by using two coordinate figures. *See Figure 47.*

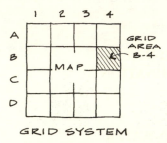

FIGURE 47

GRIDIRON PATTERN

A street and block system of formal, regular rectangular blocks and resulting four-way intersections.

Comment: The gridiron pattern, characteristic of older city neighborhoods, fell into disfavor because of its insensitivity to topography, the excessive areas required for streets, and inflexible platting. It was replaced in the late 1930s by the curvilinear layout. Recently completed traditional neighborhood developments have shown that the gridiron system deserves reexamination because of its pedestrian orientation and scale, ease of access, multipathway opportunities, and mixed-use potential. *See* TRADITIONAL NEIGHBORHOOD DEVELOPMENT.

GROSS FLOOR AREA

See FLOOR AREA, GROSS and FLOOR AREA, NET.

GROSS HABITABLE FLOOR AREA

See FLOOR AREA, NET.

GROSS LEASABLE AREA (GLA)

The total floor area for which the tenant pays rent and that is designed for the tenant's occupancy and exclusive use, including any basements and mezzanines.

Comment: GLA does not include public or common areas, such as utility rooms, stairwells, and malls.

GROUND COVER

Grasses or other low-growing plants and landscaping.

GROUND COVERAGE

See LOT COVERAGE.

GROUND FLOOR

The first floor of a building other than a cellar or basement.

178

GROUND WATER

(1) The supply of fresh water under the surface in an aquifer or geologic formation that forms the natural reservoir for potable water; (2) the water contained within the interconnected pores, cracks, or fractures located below the water table of a confined or unconfined aquifer. *See Figure 6.*

GROUND-WATER CONTAMINATION

The presence in excess of the maximum allowable contaminant level of any substance designated by federal or state authorities as a primary or secondary water-quality parameter.

GROUND-WATER RECHARGE

The natural process of infiltration and percolation of rainwater from land areas or streams through permeable soils into water-holding strata or soils that provide underground storage.

GROUND-WATER RUNOFF

Ground water that is discharged into a stream channel as spring or seepage water.

GROUP CARE FACILITY

See BOARDING HOME FOR SHELTERED CARE.

GROUP HOME

See BOARDING HOME FOR SHELTERED CARE.

GROUP LIVING QUARTERS

See BOARDINGHOUSE; DORMITORY; FRATERNITY HOUSE.

GROUP RESIDENCES

See BOARDING HOME FOR SHELTERED CARE; BOARDINGHOUSE; DORMITORY; FRATERNITY HOUSE.

GROWTH MANAGEMENT

Techniques used by the government to control the rate, amount, location, timing, and type of development.

GUARANTEES

Cash, letters of credit, bonds, or similar financial instruments deposited with the municipality to ensure that required improvements will be constructed or installed.

Comment: Guarantees are required before a development application receives final approval or before a governmental agency accepts an improvement. They are designed to ensure that all streets, sidewalks, utility lines, street lighting, and similar improvements are completed and in place before certificates of occupancy are issued. Performance guarantees protect the municipality against a developer who may go bankrupt or be unable to complete the improvements for any reason. Maintenance guarantees ensure that the improvement will function for a period of time (usually 18 months

179

to two years); if not, the developer is responsible for correcting the problem. *See* MAINTENANCE GUARANTEE; PERFORMANCE GUARANTEE.

GUIDE RAIL

A safety barrier designed to protect motor vehicles from hazardous areas. *See Figure 48.*

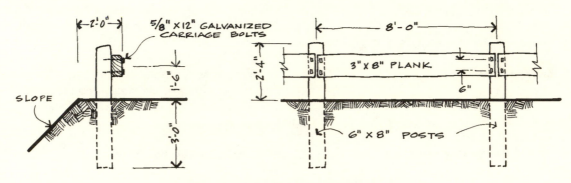

WOOD GUIDE RAIL

FIGURE 48

GUTTER

A shallow channel, usually set along a curb or the pavement edge of road, for purposes of catching and carrying off runoff water. (N.J.A.C. 5:21-1.4)

GYM

See HEALTH CLUB.

H

Definitions:

Habitable Floor Area
through
Hydrophytic Vegetation

Figures:

HABITABLE FLOOR AREA   The total floor area of all the habitable rooms in a dwelling unit.

HABITABLE ROOM   Any room in a dwelling unit other than a kitchen, bathroom, closet, pantry, hallway, cellar, storage place, garage, or unfinished basement, cellar, or attic.

HABITAT   The sum total of all the environmental factors of a specific place that is occupied by an organism, population, or a community.

HABITAT PROTECTION AREA   The site where a protected species of flora or fauna lives and grows.

HAIRPIN MARKING   A double-painted line separating parking stalls. *See Figure 49.*

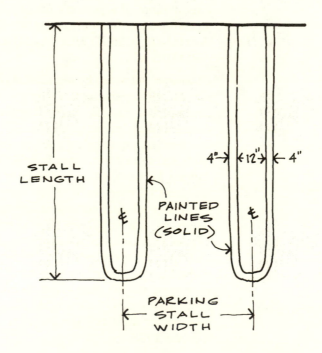

HAIRPIN MARKING

FIGURE 49

HALF-CLOSURES   *See* TRAFFIC CALMING.

HALF-STORY   *See* STORY, HALF.

HALFWAY HOUSE   *See* BOARDING HOME FOR SHELTERED CARE.

HAMLET   A small settlement or village.

Comment: *The New Jersey State Development and Redevelopment Plan* (2002) defines hamlet as a small-scale, compact residential settlement with one or more community-related functions that accommodates development in a compact form.

HAMMERMILL   A broad category of high-speed equipment that uses pivoted or fixed hammers or cutters to crush, grind, chip, or shred solid wastes.

HANDICAP   Physical or mental impairment that substantially limits one or more of a person's major life activities. (1988 amendments to the Fair Housing Act, 42 U.S.C. §3602[h]) *See* HANDICAPPED PERSON; AMERICANS WITH DISABILITIES ACT.

Comment: As noted by Mandelker (1994), the act ". . . affects land use restrictions on group homes that are contained in statutes and local ordinances. The act includes as discrimination the refusal *to make reasonable accommodations* in rules, policies, and practices where such accommodations are necessary to afford handicapped persons an opportunity to use and enjoy a dwelling"(Mandelker 1994, p. 3). A number of court cases have interpreted "reasonable accommodation" to mean that municipalities have to amend zoning regulations to accommodate people with disabilities. For example, ramps needed by persons in wheelchairs should be considered exceptions to front-yard setback requirements. Treating group homes differently from other residences, for example, would be discriminatory under the Fair Housing Act. (Mandelker 1994; Connor 1998)

HANDICAPPED PERSON   A person or persons who may be classified as having a physical impairment that manifests itself in one or more of the following ways: nonambulatory; semiambulatory; visually impaired; deaf or hard-of-hearing; having faulty coordination; and having reduced mobility, flexibility, coordination, or perceptiveness due to age or physical or mental conditions. *See* AMERICANS WITH DISABILITIES ACT; HANDICAP.

HARDSCAPE

Nonliving components of a landscape design, such as walls, sculpture, paved walkways, patios, stone and gravel areas, benches, fountains, and similar hard-surface areas and objects.

HARDSHIP VARIANCE

See VARIANCE, HARDSHIP.

HARMONIOUS RELATIONSHIP

The design, arrangement, and location of buildings or other created or natural elements of the urban environment that are sufficiently consistent in scale, character, and siting with other buildings or created or natural elements in the area to avoid abrupt or severe differences. *See* DEVELOPMENT CONTEXT.

Comment: The objective of a harmonious relationship is appropriate as part of the total quality of life. It applies equally to residential and nonresidential areas.

HAZARDOUS AIR POLLUTANT

A pollutant for which no ambient air quality standard is applicable and which may cause or contribute to an increase in mortality or serious illness.

Comment: Examples of hazardous air pollutants are asbestos, beryllium, and mercury.

HAZARDOUS SUBSTANCE

Any substance or material that, by reason of its toxic, caustic, corrosive, abrasive, or otherwise injurious properties, may be detrimental or deleterious to the health of any person handling or otherwise coming into contact with such material or substance.

Comment: The U.S. Environmental Protection Agency (EPA) has developed a list of hazardous wastes based upon corrosiveness, reactivity, and toxicity. Hazardous substances include but are not limited to inorganic mineral acids or sulfur, fluorine, chlorine, nitrogen, chromium, phosphorous, selenium, and arsenic and their common salts; lead, nickel, and mercury and their inorganic salts, or metallo-organic derivatives; coal; tar acids, such as phenol and cresols and their salts; and all radioactive materials.

HAZARDOUS SUBSTANCE DISPOSAL

A method for the safe disposal of hazardous substances.

HAZARDOUS USE

A building or structure or any portion thereof that is used for the storage, manufacture, or processing of highly combustible or explosive products or materials that are likely to burn with extreme rapidity or that may produce poisonous fumes or explosions; for storage

184

or manufacturing that involves highly corrosive, toxic, or noxious alkalies, acids, or other liquids or chemicals producing flame, fume, or poisonous, irritant, or corrosive gases; and for the storage or processing of any materials producing explosive mixtures of dust or that result in the division of matter into fine particles subject to spontaneous ignition.

HEALTH CARE FACILITY

A facility or institution, whether public or private, principally engaged in providing services for health maintenance and the treatment of mental or physical conditions. *See* HEALTH CARE SERVICES.

Comment: Health care facilities include general or special hospitals, public health centers, diagnostic centers, treatment centers, rehabilitation centers, extended care facilities, long-term care facilities, residential health care facilities, outpatient clinics, and dispensaries. Accessory uses include laundries, restaurants, gift shops, laboratories, pharmacies, and medical offices.

HEALTH CARE SERVICES

Establishments providing support to medical professionals and their patients, such as medical and dental laboratories, blood banks, oxygen, and miscellaneous types of medical supplies and services.

HEALTH CLUB

An establishment that provides facilities for aerobic exercises, running and jogging, exercise equipment, game courts, swimming facilities, and saunas, showers, massage rooms, and lockers.

Comment: Health clubs may also include eating facilities and shops selling a variety of sports equipment and clothing. Instruction programs, aerobic classes, and weight control programs may be offered. Clubs are usually open only to members and their guests.

HEALTH PLANNING

The study of the provision, distribution, and financing of health facilities and services for present and future populations.

HEAT ISLAND EFFECT

An air circulation problem peculiar to urban areas whereby heat from buildings, structures, pavements, and concentrations of pollutants creates a haze dome that prevents rising hot air from being cooled at its normal rate.

HEAVY INDUSTRY

See INDUSTRY, HEAVY.

HEIGHT

The vertical distance of a structure measured from the average elevation of the finished grade surrounding the structure to the highest point of the structure.

Comment: The highest point of the structure will vary with the type of roof. *See* BUILDING HEIGHT; GRADE, FINISHED. *See Figure 15.*

HELIPORT

An area, either at ground level or elevated on a structure, licensed by the federal government or an appropriate state agency and approved for the loading, landing, and takeoff of helicopters and including auxiliary facilities, such as parking, waiting room, fueling, and maintenance equipment.

HELISTOP

A heliport but without auxiliary facilities, such as parking, waiting room, fueling, and maintenance equipment.

Comment: Helistops are often constructed by major office and industrial uses and can be considered an accessory to the principal use. Many municipalities ban them because of concerns relating to nuisance and safety. From a planning point of view, controls relating to hours of operation and the number of daily flights may be reasonable. A single helistop in an office park or industrial park may be a more viable alternative than one for each building.

HERTZ (Hz)

A unit that measures frequency in all physical systems that have a wave pattern.

HIGH-OCCUPANCY VEHICLE (HOV)

A vehicle carrying more than a specified number of people.

HIGH-RISE

See DWELLING, HIGH-RISE.

HIGH-SPEED RURAL ROADWAY

The access classification for roadways in rural environments where the posted speed limit is 50 miles per hour or greater. *See* HIGH-SPEED URBAN ROADWAY.

HIGH-SPEED URBAN ROADWAY

The access classification for roadways in urban environments where the posted speed limit is 45 miles per hour or greater.

Comment: Both the "high-speed rural" and "high-speed urban" classifications are part of highway access codes that establish standards for driveway access to roads. *See* HIGH-SPEED RURAL ROADWAY.

186

HIGHEST AND BEST USE

An appraisal concept that determines the use of a particular property likely to produce the greatest net return in the foreseeable future. (Johnsich 1991, p. 76)

Comment: The term "highest and best use" has little validity in planning or zoning studies. Its major application is as a comparison between several uses to determine which is more profitable.

HIGHWAY

See STREET.

HIGHWAY CAPACITY

See CAPACITY, ROADWAY.

HIGHWAY-ORIENTED BUSINESS

A use dependent on both a large flow of traffic and convenient access.

Comment: Typical highway-oriented business uses include hotels and motels, restaurants, automobile service uses, auto sales (new and used), and retail centers. These uses often require large land parcels for vehicle storage and circulation that may be disruptive or unavailable in many urban settings. Zoning controls for such areas might preclude the individual small user, unless part of a larger complex of related uses. Site design standards for highway access spacing, landscaping, signage, and site design objectives are essential to avoid the clutter and unattractive commercial highway strip development found at the entrances to many cities.

HISTORIC AREA

A district, zone, or area designated by a local, state, or federal authority within which the buildings, structures, appurtenances, and places are of basic and vital importance because of their association with history; or because of their unique architectural style and scale, including color, proportion, form, and architectural detail; or because of their being a part of or related to a square, park, or area, the design or general arrangement of which should be preserved and/or developed according to a fixed plan based on cultural, historical, or architectural motives or purposes. *See* NATIONAL REGISTER OF HISTORIC PLACES.

Comment: Local historic districts or zones are usually implemented as overlay zones, that is, the historic district often covers several use districts, and the overlay zone usually regulates only the exterior appearance of the property and its existing and proposed structures, not its use. These zones usually require local agency design review and approval for any exterior building changes or new construction. Local historic district regulations must conform to state enabling legislation, and the district may include nonhistoric properties if such properties are essential to the preservation and protection of the district. The delineation of historic districts, and their design standards, should be supported by appropriate studies and incorporated in the local master plan. *See* HISTORIC BUILDING STYLES; NATIONAL REGISTER OF HISTORIC PLACES; OVERLAY ZONE.

HISTORIC BUILDING

Any building or structure that is historically or architecturally significant.

HISTORIC BUILDING STYLES

Recognized architectural styles, such as Colonial, Early and Late Georgian, Federal, Greek Revival, Victorian, Victorian Gothic, Carpenter Gothic, Italianate, Tudor, Mission, and Art Moderne. *See Figures 50–55.*

Comment: The definition is actually a partial listing of major American historic building styles. For purposes of historic district zoning for a particular area, this listing might be revised as appropriate and detailed architectural definitions of each style added.

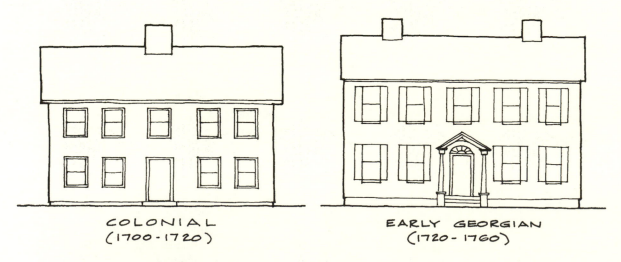

COLONIAL
(1700-1720)

EARLY GEORGIAN
(1720-1760)

Spartan design; large central chimney; narrow clapboards (bricks in the South); simple frames around doors and windows; small window-panes (often 12-over-12)

Symmetrical design; set on high foundation, with emphasis on entrance bay; columns frame entry, with pediment above; often classical features in cornice; executed in brick or wood

FIGURE 50

188

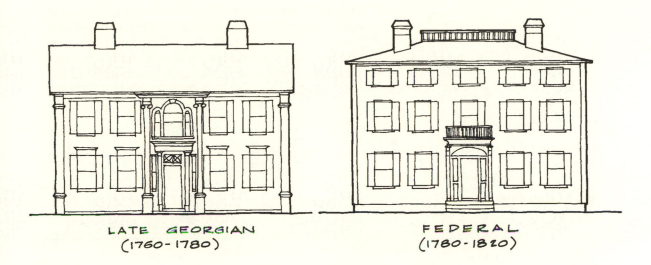

LATE GEORGIAN
(1760-1780)

FEDERAL
(1780-1820)

Lavish use of classical details; doorways surrounded with pilasters or columns; Palladian window on second floor in center, cornice on window caps; corners marked with quoins or pilasters

Doorways with pilasters and columns, often topped with flat entablature; elliptical fanlight over entry; simple window frames; hipped roofs, often with balustrade

FIGURE 51

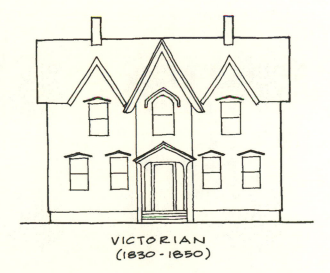

GREEK REVIVAL
(1820-1840)

VICTORIAN
(1830-1850)

Emphasis on columns, capitals, and low triangular gabled pediment to create Greek temple appearance; strong vertical windows, with six-over-six panes; simple lines

Emphasis on vertical effect, with many sharply pointed gables; steeply pitched roofs; slender, tall windows; decorated woodwork

FIGURE 52

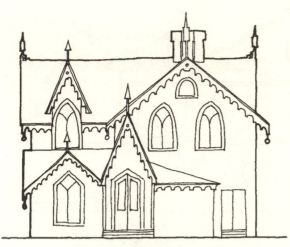

VICTORIAN GOTHIC
(1850-1880)

Medieval building characteristics; heavy use of decoration; tall windows with leaded panes

CARPENTER GOTHIC
(1880-1910)

Sawn-wood ornament at peaks of gables, in verge boards under gables, and on porches; sawn brackets on porch posts and on cornice

FIGURE 53

ITALIANATE
(1850 - 1880)

Two or three stories; low-pitched hip roof with widely overhanging eaves supported by large brackets; a center cupola or tower; balanced facades; decorative lintels over narrow-hung windows; double doors

TUDOR
(1920-1940)

Steeply pitched end-gabled roofs; gabled entryway; multi-paned narrow windows in bands of three; tall chimneys; masonry stuccoed construction; half-timbering

FIGURE 54

MISSION
(1885 - 1915)

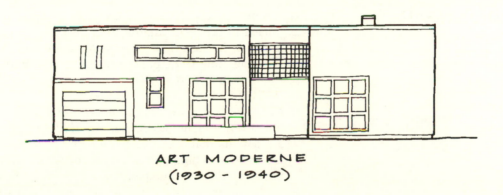

ART MODERNE
(1930 - 1940)

(Mission, top)   Stucco walls; round arches supported by piers; continuous wall surface forming parapets; hip roof of red tiles; overhanging eaves with exposed rafters

(Art Moderne, bottom)   Streamlined appearance; smooth wall surfaces with rounded corners; little ornamentation; flat roof; windows that wrap around corners; often a curved canopy over the front door

FIGURE 55

HISTORIC DISTRICT *See* HISTORIC AREA.

HISTORIC PRESERVATION The identification, evaluation, protection, rehabilitation, and restoration of districts, sites, buildings, structures, and artifacts significant in history, architecture, archaeology, or culture.

191

Comment: Historic preservation includes managing, stabilizing, and at times sensitive reuse of historic buildings. It also includes conserving scenic views and natural landscapes. (New Jersey Office of State Planning 1996)

HISTORIC SITE

A structure, place, natural object, or configuration, or portion thereof, of historical, archaeological, cultural, or architectural significance and designated as such by federal, state, county, or municipal government.

HI-VOLUME (HI-VOL) SAMPLER

A device used in the measurement and analysis of suspended particulate pollution.

HOLDING ZONE

A zone established in the zoning ordinance on a temporary basis awaiting applications for rezoning to desired uses. *See* INTERIUM ZONING.

HOME OCCUPATION

Any activity carried out for gain by a resident and conducted in the resident's dwelling unit. ("When Home Is Where the Business Is," *Zoning News*, December 1991; *Planning*, June 1993, p. 16; Julie Bennett, "Home Bodies," *Planning*, May 1999)

Comment: The above definition is the broadest possible one covering all home occupations. It simply states that any activity that is carried out for gain by a resident in his or her dwelling unit is a home occupation. It does not mean that a municipality must permit home occupations or that controls and limits cannot be placed on home occupations. Home occupations are best controlled through performance standards rather than listings of permitted home occupations or professions. In those zones where home occupations are permitted, the development ordinance may impose reasonable restrictions, including the number of nonresident employees (usually a maximum of two), sign control (one sign, with the name of the resident and the home occupation and not to exceed the size of any residential identification sign permitted in the zone), and a maximum on the amount of square footage that may be used for the home occupation (25 percent or 400 feet, whichever is less).

Other controls are also appropriate. These include:

- The home occupation must be carried out indoors without any outdoor storage.
- The residential appearance of the structure may not be altered.

- Any commercial vehicles for the use must be garaged.
- Noise, glare, fumes, odors, or electrical interference are prohibited.
- Not more than one client, customer, or patron is permitted on the premises at any time.
- Deliveries and pickups by tractor-trailers are prohibited.

An applicant for a home occupation should be required to submit a site plan to the appropriate municipal official (engineer, planner, or zoning official) to ensure that all zoning requirements are met. If additional parking is required, a site plan should be submitted to the approving authority to determine what landscaping and setback requirements are needed.

The home occupation should also be customary, incidental, and accessory to the principal residential use. "Customary" is subject to change, however, as modern technology reduces the need for face-to-face communication.

HOME OFFICE

See HOME OCCUPATION.

HOME PROFESSIONAL OFFICE

A home occupation consisting of the office of a practitioner of a recognized profession. *See* HOME OCCUPATION.

Comment: The major question is defining a recognized profession. The granting of a state license in and by itself is not an indication of a recognized profession. Customary home professional offices usually include attorneys, medical practitioners, engineers, and architects. As noted in the definition of "home occupation," performance standards are preferable to distinctions between occupations and professions and/or listings of acceptable occupations.

HOMELESS SHELTER

A facility providing temporary housing to indigent, needy, or homeless persons.

HOMEOWNERS ASSOCIATION

A community association, other than a condominium association, that is organized in a development in which individual owners share common interests and responsibilities for costs and upkeep of common open space or facilities.

Comment: The homeowners association usually holds title to certain common property, manages and maintains the common property, and enforces certain covenants and restrictions. Condominium associations

193

differ from homeowners associations in that condominium associations do not have title to the common property.

HOMES FOR THE AGED

See ADULT RETIREMENT COMMUNITY; ASSISTED LIVING FACILITY; CONGREGATE RESIDENCES; CONTINUING CARE RETIREMENT COMMUNITY; HOUSING FOR THE ELDERLY; RESIDENTIAL HEALTH CARE FACILITIES; RETIREMENT COMMUNITY.

Comment: An obsolete term no longer used.

HORSE FARM

A farm that is primarily used for the breeding and boarding of horses. *See* BOARDING STABLE; AGRICULTURE.

Comment: Under the principal definitions of "farms" and "agriculture," horse farms would be permitted uses. The problem is that horse farms often have as accessory to their principal use of breeding and boarding such activities as races, horse shows, auctions, and riding classes. Races, shows, and auctions can generate significant amounts of traffic and crowds where food and drinks are sold. Consequently, many ordinances identify horse farms as conditional uses and limit the number of horse shows, races, and other events. They may even require site plans to show how access, parking, circulation, and sanitary facilities are proposed to be accommodated. Some towns require special permits regulating the maximum number of shows and length of time for each show.

HORTICULTURE

The cultivation of a garden or orchard. *See* AGRICULTURE.

HOSPICE

A facility for terminally ill persons.

Comment: The hospice facility is more than a physical location. It is a program designed to assist patients with a life expectancy of six months or less. The facility itself may be the patient's home, a nursing home, or a separate place for hospice patients.

HOSPITAL

An institution providing primary health services and medical or surgical care to persons, primarily inpatients, suffering from illness, disease, injury, deformity, and other abnormal physical or mental conditions and including as an integral part of the institution related facilities, such as laboratories, outpatient facilities, training facilities, medical offices, and staff residences.

Comment: State agencies usually regulate the size, scale, type, and location of hospitals. Before one can be built, a "certificate of need" or similar instrument is required. In most urban and suburban areas, new hospital construction is rare as state agencies attempt to reduce costs by limiting new facilities. However, reconstruction, rehabilitation, and new construction for older hospitals to meet new demands are increasing.

From a zoning perspective, hospitals are extremely intensive uses. They operate 24 hours per day, generate significant traffic volumes, and have many employees on different shifts. Some estimates indicate that the average hospital has three employees per bed, plus volunteers, visitors, and doctors. Because hospitals are often located in residential areas, particular attention should focus on entrances and exits; location of power plants, laundries, and other support uses; parking; and overall neighborhood impact.

Hospital care is changing rapidly, and this will have an impact on the future design of hospital campuses. For instance, outpatient surgery, which accounted for less than 3 percent of all surgery 20 years ago, now constitutes more than 75 percent of all surgical procedures. The result is a general downsizing of bed and long-term functions and more outpatient facilities.

Another change is the construction of medical office buildings on hospital campuses. They bring doctors closer to hospitalized patients, reduce traffic and congestion, and offer some taxes from otherwise tax-exempt facilities.

HOSTEL

See YOUTH HOSTEL.

HOTEL

A facility offering transient lodging accommodations to the general public and which may include additional facilities and services, such as restaurants, meeting rooms, entertainment, personal services, and recreational facilities. *See* BED AND BREAKFAST; BOARDINGHOUSE; CONFERENCE CENTER; INN; MOTEL; RESORT; TOURIST HOME.

Comment: Hotels can generally be classified as limited service or full service. Limited-service hotels provide only lodgings and do not provide any restaurant or food service, recreation facilities, and the like. Full-service hotels always have restaurants and possibly a bar or lounge with entertainment, personal services, health club, and retail stores.

Hotels can also be classified as extended-stay facilities or traditional hotels. As a general rule, extended-stay facilities are limited-service hotels but with larger rooms (approximately 425 square feet) and with refrigerators, cooktops, microwave ovens, dishes, utensils, and with washers and dryers on premises. The extended-stay facility is for transients staying 5 or more days, with an average of 7–10 days. The average stay for traditional transient facilities (non-extended stay) is 1.5 days. Extended-stay hotels will have a variety of room types, including studios and one- and two-bedroom suites.

Another type of hotel, which can be a full- or limited-service hotel, is an all-suites hotel. These can be extended-stay or traditional but, as the name implies, consist mostly of suites.

The principal zoning concern is whether the extended-stay hotels can, with very long-term occupancies, become apartment houses. According to representatives of the industry, this is highly unlikely because the average room rental, on a monthly basis, is too expensive for long-term occupancy. In addition, the BOCA National Building Code classifies hotels with occupancies of 30 days or more as apartment houses and requires significantly greater and more expensive materials and construction techniques.

Other concerns relate to the number and size of ancillary facilities, such as restaurants, bars and lounges, and health clubs. For example, a full-service hotel might be too intensive a use for a residential neighborhood. But an extended-stay facility, without any restaurant, bar, or lounge, might easily be accommodated.

HOTEL, CASINO

Establishments primarily engaged in providing short-term lodging in hotel facilities with a gambling casino on premises.

Comment: The casino on premises includes table wagering games and other gambling activities, such as slot machines and sports betting. These establishments generally offer a range of services and amenities, such as food and beverage services, entertainment, valet parking, swimming pools, spas, and personal services.

HOUSE OF WORSHIP

See PLACE OF WORSHIP.

HOUSE TRAILER

See MANUFACTURED HOME.

HOUSEHOLD

A family living together in a single dwelling unit, with common access to and common use of all living and eating areas and all areas and facilities for the preparation and serving of food within the dwelling unit. *See* FAMILY.

196

HOUSEHOLD PET

An animal, not exceeding 100 pounds, residing within a dwelling unit and not raised for the production of products or for sale. *See* ANIMAL, DOMESTIC.

Comment: The real problem is not in defining household pets but in limiting the number and size to prevent them from becoming nuisances. The 100-pound limit prevents large animals, such as large pigs and goats, from becoming household pets. A reasonable number of household pets, excluding fish and birds, might be not more than three per dwelling unit.

For lots in excess of an acre outside of urban areas but used primarily as residences, as opposed to farms, a different standard, limiting the number of "animal units," can be used. For example, on lots of 1 acre or more, 1 animal unit per acre could be permitted. An animal unit would be defined as the equivalent of 1 cow, 4 hogs, 10 sheep, 10 goats, 100 poultry, 1 horse, 1 pony, 1 mule, or 100 rabbits, or combinations thereof.

HOUSING, RETIREMENT

See HOUSING FOR THE ELDERLY.

HOUSING, SHARED

Two or more unrelated persons living in a single dwelling unit.

Comment: Shared housing is primarily used to reduce housing costs and provide housing for seniors but can be used to increase the housing supply for all age groups. Some municipalities have set up formal mechanisms where persons with extra room in their dwelling units are matched up with individuals seeking housing.

A distinction can be made between shared housing and boardinghouses. Boardinghouses generally lease a specific room to the tenant, and kitchen privileges are not usually available. Shared housing allows for much greater use of all rooms (except bedrooms). It is clearly not a fraternity house. *See* FRATERNITY HOUSE.

HOUSING ELEMENT

That portion of the master plan consisting of reports, statements, proposals, maps, diagrams, and text designed to meet the municipality's fair share of its region's present and prospective housing needs, particularly with regard to low- and moderate-income housing.

Comment: Housing elements usually include a good deal of other information as required by state law. In New Jersey, for example, the following information is required in a housing element:

- An inventory of the municipality's housing stock by age, condition, purchase or rental value, occupancy characteristics, and type, including the number of units affordable to low- and moderate-income households and substandard housing capable of being rehabilitated;

- A projection of the municipality's housing stock, including the probable future construction of low- and moderate-income housing, for the next six years, taking into account, but not necessarily limited to, construction permits issued, approvals of applications for development, and probable residential development of lands;

- An analysis of the municipality's demographic characteristics, including, but not limited to, household size, income level, and age;

- An analysis of the existing and probable future employment characteristics of the municipality;

- A determination of the municipality's present and prospective fair share for low- and moderate-income housing and its capacity to accommodate its present and prospective housing needs, including its fair share for low- and moderate-income housing; and

- A consideration of the lands that are most appropriate for construction of low- and moderate-income housing and of the existing structures most appropriate for conversion to, or rehabilitation for, low- and moderate-income housing, including a consideration of lands of developers who have expressed a commitment to provide low- and moderate-income housing.

HOUSING FOR THE ELDERLY

Multifamily housing designed for older people. *See* ADULT RETIREMENT COMMUNITY; ASSISTED LIVING FACILITY; CONGREGATE RESIDENCES; CONTINUING CARE RETIREMENT COMMUNITY; RETIREMENT COMMUNITY.

HOUSING REGION

That geographic area surrounding or adjacent to a municipality from which the bulk of the employment within the municipality is drawn; or the area surrounding or adjacent to the municipality where most of the residents of the municipality are employed.

Comment: The issue of housing region has assumed even greater importance in recent years because of its application in exclusionary housing cases. In the *Mt. Laurel I* case (*Southern Burlington County NAACP v.*

Township of Mt. Laurel, 67 N.J. 151, 1975), the court determined the *Mt. Laurel* housing region as a 20-mile radius from Camden but stopping at the state boundary. Norman Williams, Jr., in *After Mt. Laurel: The New Suburban Zoning* (Rose and Rothman 1977), defined the housing region as "the area of continuous settlement which coincides roughly with the area within which substantial numbers of people commute to work in the old center." In *Oakwood at Madison v. Township of Madison* (72 N.J. 481), the court noted the region as "the area from which, in view of available employment and transportation, the population of the township would be drawn absent invalidly exclusionary zoning. . . ." In many other exclusionary zoning cases, the work/resident/trip destination forms the basis of the housing region from which fair share allocations could then be made.

HOUSING UNIT

A room or group of rooms used by one or more individuals living separately from others in the structure, with direct access to the outside or to a public hall and containing separate bathroom and kitchen facilities. *See* DWELLING UNIT.

Comment: The Census 2000 definition of "housing unit" drops the requirement for cooking facilities and allows above-the-garage quarters and group homes to be defined as housing units. The census defines a housing unit as a house, an apartment, a mobile home, a group of rooms, or a single room that is occupied as separate living quarters.

HUMAN SCALE

The proportional relationship of a particular building, structure, open space enclosure, or streetscape element to the human form and function.

HUMUS

Decomposed organic material.

HYDROLOGY

The science dealing with the properties, distribution, and circulation of water and snow.

HYDROPHYTIC VEGETATION

Wetlands vegetation consisting of plant life adapted to growth and reproduction under periodically saturated-root-zone conditions during at least a portion of the growing season.

I

ILLUMINATED SIGN

See SIGN, ILLUMINATED.

IMPACT ANALYSIS

A study to determine the potential direct or indirect effects of a proposed development on activities, utilities, stormwater runoff, circulation, surrounding land uses, community facilities, environment, and other factors.

Comment: The impact analysis also can include fiscal, aesthetic, social, and legal impacts. The impact analysis serves a variety of functions. It should point out what impact the proposed development will have on the factors considered and what steps are needed to mitigate the impact. This is particularly true for environmental considerations, stormwater management, and utility needs. For projects that require variances, the impact analysis can be used to determine whether substantial detriment would result—an important criterion in the granting of a variance. Finally, impact analysis allows the municipality to plan. If, for example, a development of houses is expected to generate a given number of school-age children, an impact analysis can alert the local board of education to the need to accommodate the additional load.

IMPACT FEE

A fee imposed on a development to help finance the cost of improvements or services.

Comment: Developers have long been required to pay for the cost of improvements necessitated by a development. These improvements include on- and off-site roads, utilities, and stormwater management facilities. Developers have also been required to pay for their fair share of off-tract facilities that are needed as a result of their development. Through this method, off-tract intersections may be improved, water and sewer mains enlarged, and additional off-tract drainage basins constructed.

Impact fees are an extension of the philosophy that developments should pay their own way. Thus, where permitted by state legislation and local ordinance, an impact fee may be imposed on development for roads, schools, parks, fire stations, libraries, and other such public facilities. Where impact fees are permitted, they must be specific, based on a reasonable formula, and uniformly applied.

IMPERMEABLE

Not permitting the passage of water.

IMPERVIOUS COVERAGE

See LOT COVERAGE.

IMPERVIOUS SURFACE

A surface that has been compacted or covered with a layer of material so that it is highly resistant to infiltration by water. *See Figure 56.*

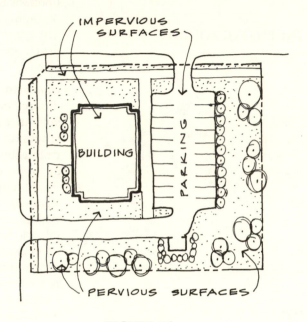

FIGURE 56

Comment: One method by which impervious surfaces can be defined is in terms of a percolation rate in minutes per inch. For example, the New Jersey State Standards for Construction of Individual Subsurface Sewage Disposal Systems define impervious formations as having a percolation rate slower than 120 minutes per inch. Retention and detention basins and dry wells allowing water to percolate directly into the ground usually are not considered impervious surfaces. Graveled areas initially allow a significant amount of percolation, but with heavy traffic and use they become less pervious. Local ordinances often allow not more than 50 percent of graveled areas to be counted as pervious. *See* DETENTION BASIN; RETENTION BASIN.

IMPLEMENTATION

Carrying out or fulfilling plans and proposals.

IMPOUNDMENT

A body of water, such as a pond, confined by a dam, dike, floodgate, or other barrier.

202

IMPROVED PUBLIC STREET

See STREET, IMPROVED PUBLIC.

IMPROVEMENT

Any permanent structure that becomes part of, is placed upon, or is affixed to real estate.

INCENTIVE ZONING

The granting by the approving authority of additional development capacity in exchange for the developer's provision of a public benefit or amenity.

Comment: In urban areas, developers are granted additional height and floor area in exchange for the development of public plazas and similar urban open spaces. In some developing suburbs and urban areas, developers are offered additional dwelling unit density if lower-income housing units are created.

Incentive zoning should not be confused with off-tract improvements or impact fees. These represent attempts to correct deficiencies in infrastructure or to ensure that infrastructure needs created by a project are adequate. Incentive zoning is a quid pro quo—more development for some benefit, the need for which may not necessarily be created by the development itself. The local ordinance would have to clearly spell out the bonuses and the benefits.

INCIDENTAL

Subordinate and minor in significance and bearing a reasonable relationship to the primary use.

INCINERATION

The controlled process by which solid, liquid, or gaseous combustible wastes are burned and changed into gases and residue containing little or no combustible material.

INCINERATOR

A device for burning waste substances in which all the combustion factors—temperature, retention time, turbulence, and combustion air—can be controlled.

INCLUSIONARY DEVELOPMENT

A residential housing development in which a percentage of the dwelling units is affordable to low- and moderate-income households.

Comment: Depending on state law, inclusionary developments may include specific percentages of lower-income dwelling units (20 percent, for example) and specify a reasonable affordable income range (low income, up to 50 percent of median family income; moderate, up to 80 percent of median family income).

INCLUSIONARY ZONING

Regulations that increase housing choice by establishing requirements and providing incentives to construct housing to meet the needs of low- and moderate-income households.

Comment: Inclusionary techniques include specific requirements for a minimum percentage of low- and moderate-income housing as part of any development and density bonuses for building low- and moderate-income units. Another technique designed to provide more affordable housing is the removal or modification of regulations to eliminate requirements unrelated to or in excess of those needed for safe and sanitary housing. (For a fuller discussion of this complex subject, see Babcock and Bosselman 1973; Listokin 1976; Mallach 1984.)

INDIGENOUS NEED

Existing deficient housing units within a municipality that are occupied by low- and moderate-income households. *See* SURROGATE.

Comment: Indigenous need refers to those dwelling units in a municipality that are deemed deficient (formerly known as dilapidated) and occupied by lower-income households. In fair share programs, indigenous housing is part of the present need, as opposed to a prospective need.

INDIRECT SOURCE

An indirect pollution source that by its nature attracts large numbers of polluting sources while not actually releasing the pollutant itself.

Comment: Indirect sources of pollution may include parking lots, roofs, and retention and detention basins.

INDIVIDUAL SEWAGE DISPOSAL SYSTEM

A system for the treatment and disposal of sanitary sewage in the ground on the lot upon which the primary use is located. *See Figure 28.*

Comment: Septic systems are designed and constructed to treat sewage in a manner that will retain most of the settleable solids in a septic tank and discharge the liquid portion to a disposal field.

INDOOR RECREATION CENTER

A permanent structure containing facilities for recreational activities such as tennis, platform games, swimming, exercise rooms, handball, and similar activities.

Comment: The definition does not differentiate between recreational centers operated by public or semipublic agencies such as a local board of education, YMCA, or commercial recreation centers. Recreation centers may also include facilities for lectures, arts and crafts, and special events. They may include child-care centers, snack bars, retail shops, and instruction in various games. Zoning and site design considerations include parking, circulation, aesthetics, hours of operation, and impact on surrounding areas. (Schultz and Kasen 1984)

INDOOR TENNIS FACILITY

A building or structure containing one or more roofed and enclosed tennis courts.

INDUCED DEMAND

In traffic engineering, the creation of traffic demand by adding highway capacity.

Comment: Proponents of mass transit point out that widening roads actually increases congestion by inducing demand. In addition, development often follows road improvements, further adding to traffic volumes.

INDUSTRIAL PARK

A tract of land that is planned, developed, and operated as a coordinated and integrated facility for a number of separate industrial uses, with consideration for circulation, parking, signage, utility needs, aesthetics, and compatibility.

Comment: Modern industrial parks include support facilities for the principal uses, such as hotels, restaurants, recreation, banking and business services, child care centers, and telecommunications facilities. Individual uses are often subdivided for financing purposes but cross easements are required to ensure that circulation, utilities, signage, parking, and other facilities are maintained and available to all uses in the industrial park. A good reference for industrial park development standards is the 2001 *Business Park and Industrial Development Handbook*, published by the Urban Land Institute (Frej et al. 2001). *See* WAREHOUSE.

INDUSTRIAL PROPERTY

Any parcel of land containing an industrial use defined in this ordinance, or any building containing such uses.

INDUSTRIAL SEPARATOR

An air pollution control device that uses the principle of inertia to remove particulate matter from a stream of air or gas.

INDUSTRIAL WASTE

Liquid, gaseous, chemical, and solid residue or byproducts of an industrial process.

INDUSTRY

Those fields of economic activity including forestry, fishing, hunting, and trapping; mining; construction; manufacturing; transportation, communication, electric, gas, and sanitary services; and wholesale trade.

INDUSTRY, HEAVY

Industrial uses that meet the performance standards, bulk controls, and other requirements contained in this ordinance.

Comment: See comments under INDUSTRY, LIGHT.

INDUSTRY, LIGHT

Industrial uses that meet the performance standards, bulk controls, and other requirements contained in this ordinance.

Comment: Most zoning ordinances define light industry in terms of the finished product, raw materials, size of the machinery used in the process, or number of employees. A typical definition of light industry might require that the finished product consist of small machine parts or electronic equipment. Another common definition would prohibit motors in excess of 10 horsepower. The Institute of Transportation Engineers (ITE) describes "general light industrial" as employing fewer than 500 persons with emphasis on activities other than manufacturing (ITE 1997).

Light industry (and heavy industry, for that matter) should be defined in terms of intensity and impact, as well as use. With the advent of stricter environmental laws regulating noise, air pollution, glare, water quality, and waste treatment, the difference between light and heavy industry essentially narrows down to traffic generation, building bulk, and intensity of site development.

The recommended definition states that all light industry is required to meet the performance and bulk standards established in the ordinance. Light industrial standards would restrict the intensity of development in terms of floor area ratio (FAR), impervious coverage, size of the building, and number of vehicles, including those for employees as well as those for deliveries and pickups. It would prohibit outdoor storage and require that all activities be carried on within the principal building. This latter provision would rule out, for example, those facilities that require large structures outside principal buildings, such as refineries. By establishing a maximum impervious coverage of 55 percent, a maximum height of two stories, and a FAR of .35 or less, the municipality would be assured that the light industry would generate an acceptable level of traffic and have limited impact on the surrounding area.

Additional requirements could be established to further define light and heavy industry. For instance, many states allow municipalities to impose higher performance standards than those required by state law. Noise standards could be established to prohibit any noise above a certain decibel rating beyond the walls of the building, with a different standard for light and heavy industrial zones. Air quality requirements could similarly be increased. Given the difficulty in enforcing the standards and determining when violations take place, the most practical approach is to establish bulk and intensity standards that limit the size and bulk of the building and consequently the impact.

Finally, specific use categories can be included to rule out certain uses that would not be permitted regardless of intensity or impact. For example, manufacturing of certain toxic gases or chemicals would not be a permitted use regardless of the size of the facility.

INFILL

The development of new housing or other uses on scattered vacant sites in a built-up area.

INFILTRATION

(1) The flow of water into soil; (2) unplanned and unwanted stormwater flow into a sanitary sewer system.

INFRASTRUCTURE

Facilities and services needed to sustain all land-use activities.

Comment: Infrastructure includes water and sewer lines and other utilities, streets and roads, communications, and public facilities, such as firehouses, parks, and schools.

INGRESS

Access or entry.

INHERENTLY BENEFICIAL USES

(1) Uses that clearly promote the public good; (2) use of land or buildings having well-recognized value or benefit to a community and that therefore deserve special consideration in the administration of local zoning.

Comment: Inherently beneficial uses are those uses that are essential to society. These uses include schools, child-care centers, medical facilities and nursing homes, public housing, lower-income housing, public utility installations, sewage treatment plants, and places of worship.

Since ordinances do not often zone for many types of inherently beneficial uses, they may require use variances in order to locate in the municipality. In New Jersey, the designation as an inherently beneficial use relieves the applicant of the obligation of proving special reasons for the use. The use still must meet the negative criteria that it will not be substantially detrimental to the public good and will not substantially impair the intent and purpose of the zone plan and zoning ordinance (N.J.S.A. 40:55D-70d). In addition, in *Kohl v. Fair Lawn* (50 NJ 265 [1967]), the court

207

noted: ". . . there must be a finding that the use is particularly fitted to the particular location for which the variance is sought."

Because of the potential diversity, size, and complexity of such uses, a recommended approach to their regulation is to classify them as conditional uses in the local development ordinance and include appropriate development standards for each use.

INN

An establishment for the housing and feeding of transients.

Comment: An inn is commonly distinguished from a hotel or motel by its size and its purportedly more personal atmosphere. Inns often are contained in whole or in part in buildings that were previously private residences. *See* BED AND BREAKFAST; HOTEL; MOTEL.

INOPERABLE VEHICLE

Any vehicle at present inoperable but capable of being repaired to place it in operating condition without exceeding its present estimated value and repair cost.

INSTITUTIONAL USE

A nonprofit, religious, or public use, such as a religious building, library, public or private school, hospital, or government-owned or -operated building, structure, or land used for public purpose.

INTELLIGENT TRANSPORTATION SYSTEM (ITS)

A method to maximize the efficiency of the existing roadway system by using computer-based interactive management elements that provide information to motorists and/or are responsive to changing demands. (Adapted from the *New Jersey State Development and Redevelopment Plan* 2002)

INTENSITY OF USE

The number of dwelling units per acre for residential development and floor area ratio (FAR) for nonresidential development, such as commercial, office, and industrial.

Comment: In small- to medium-sized-lot residential development (lots under 1 acre), FAR is a very useful tool in maintaining an appropriate relationship between building bulk and lot size.

INTERBASIN TRANSFER

Moving water from one watershed to another. (*New Jersey State Development and Redevelopment Plan* 2002)

INTERMODAL

A facility or system that transfers people, goods, or information between two or more transport modes or networks between an origin and destination. (*New Jersey State Development and Redevelopment Plan* 2002)

208

INTERCEPTOR DRAIN

Underground drainage system designed to catch and divert stormwater runoff away from a slope or other area sensitive to water erosion or impact.

INTERCEPTOR SEWER

Sewers used to collect the flows from main and trunk sewers and carry them to a central point for treatment and/or discharge.

INTERCHANGE

A grade-separated, bridged system of access to and from highways where vehicles may move from one roadway to another without crossing streams of traffic. *See* GRADE SEPARATION. *See Figure 87.*

INTERESTED PARTY

(1) In a criminal or quasi-criminal proceeding, any citizen of the state; (2) in a civil proceeding, in any court, or in an administrative proceeding before a municipal agency, an individual, whether residing within or without the municipality, whose right to use, acquire, or enjoy property is or may be affected by any action taken under any law of the municipality or state or the United States.

INTERIOR LOT

See LOT, INTERIOR.

INTERIUM ZONING

A zoning device to freeze or severely restrict development for a short period during which a comprehensive plan for an area or a new set of zoning regulations is prepared.

Comment: Interium zoning has three main purposes: It permits planning and ordinance preparation to proceed relatively free of development pressures; it prevents uses that will not conform to the adopted ordinances; and it engenders public debate on the issues. When interium zoning controls have been found to be a subterfuge for a more-or-less permanent effort to halt growth, the courts have thrown them out. (American Planning Association, *The Language of Zoning,* Planning Advisory Service Report No. 322, 1976)

INTERMEDIATE CARE FACILITY (ICF)

A facility that provides, on a regular basis, personal care, including dressing and eating and health-related care and services, to individuals who require such assistance but who do not require the degree of care and treatment that a hospital or skilled nursing facility provides.

Comment: Most states regulate ICFs, which are often grouped under the general term nursing home or long-term care facility. Unlike nursing homes or hospitals, ICFs provide only limited medical supervision, such as the administration of medication or medical treatment by qualified personnel. *See* LONG-TERM CARE FACILITY.

INTERMITTENT SOUND

Sound that is not continuous or that is of cyclic or repetitive nature.

INTERMITTENT STREAM

A stream that normally flows for at least 30 days after the last major rain of the season and is dry a large part of the year. (*California General Plan Glossary* 1997)

INTERSECTION

The location where two or more roadways cross at grade without a bridge. *See* JUNCTION. *See Figure 87.*

INTERSTATE HIGHWAY

A countrywide, federally supported network of controlled and limited-access highways.

INTERSTATE WATERS

(1) Rivers, lakes, and other waters that flow across or form a part of state or international boundaries; (2) waters of the Great Lakes; (3) coastal waters, including ocean waters seaward to the territorial limits and waters along the coastline (including inland streams) influenced by the tide.

INTERTIDAL AREA

The land area between high and low tide, also called a beach. *See* BEACH. *See Figure 11.*

INTRUSIVE SOUND

Noise that is over and above the existing ambient noise level.

Comment: Noise that is intrusive is obviously "louder" than the ambient noise level. Other factors affecting the intrusive nature include amplitude, duration, frequency, and time of occurrence.

INVERSE CONDEMNATION

The taking or reduction in value of private property as a result of governmental activity without any formal direct exercise of eminent domain.

Comment: An example of an inverse condemnation is the expansion of an airport flight path that brings airplanes so low over residences as to make them uninhabitable.

INVERSION

An atmospheric condition in which a layer of cool air is trapped by a layer of warm air so that it cannot rise.

Comment: Inversions spread polluted air horizontally rather than vertically so that contaminating substances cannot be dispersed widely.

210

ISLAND

(1) A land area totally surrounded by water; (2) in parking lot design, built-up structures, usually curbed, placed at the end or middle of parking rows as a guide to traffic and for landscaping, signing, or lighting.

ISOLATED LOT

An undeveloped substandard lot in separate ownership from surrounding property and not meeting area or bulk requirements for the zone in which it is located. (Cox 2003)

Comment: The isolated lot invariably becomes the subject of a variance application. Many ordinances address the issue by "grandfathering" such lots or allowing such lots to be developed with any use permitted in the zone, provided that the applicant does not own any adjacent land or has not owned any adjacent land since the ordinance made the lot nonconforming. Where "grandfathering" is not permitted, a New Jersey Supreme Court decision (*Chirichello v. Zoning Board of Adjustment, Borough of Monmouth Beach*, 78 N.J. 544, 1979) offers some guidelines on how to deal with the problem, as follows:

- Did the owner purchase the property knowing either in fact or constructively of the deficiency? For example, if the lot became nonconforming by reason of a change in the zoning regulations after the property was purchased, the owner could not have known of the potential disablement.

- Was an offer made to purchase the property at a fair price? If so, there is no hardship. (The court indicated that the fair market value should be based on the assumption that the variance would be granted. Otherwise, the value of the unusable lot would be zero.)

- Conversely, can vacant land be purchased at a fair price that would make the lot conforming?

In addition to proving hardship, the applicant also must satisfy that what is being proposed will not have an adverse impact on surrounding properties or the neighborhood and that the proposed development is consistent with the intent and purpose of the zone plan and ordinance.

J

JET SKI	*See* PERSONAL WATERCRAFT.
JETTY	*See* BREAKWATER.
JOINT OWNERSHIP	The equal estate interest of two of more persons.
JOURNEY TO WORK	The worker's daily trip from residence to place of employment and back, by whatever mode of transportation. *See Figure 57.*

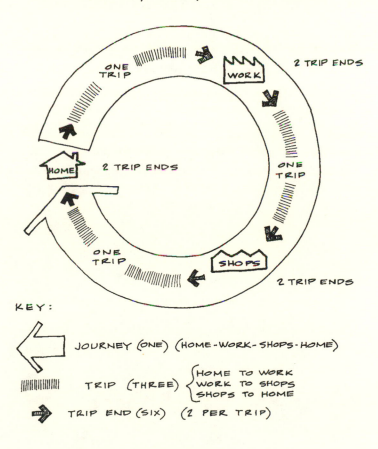

FIGURE 57

JUNCTION

A place of joining or crossing of streets or railroads. *See* INTERSECTION.

JUNK

Any scrap, waste, reclaimable material, or debris, whether or not stored, for sale or in the process of being dismantled, destroyed, processed, salvaged, stored, baled, disposed of, or for other use or disposition.

Comment: The definition can also include examples of what constitutes junk, such as unregistered and inoperable vehicles, tires, vehicle parts, equipment, paper, rags, metal, glass, building materials, household appliances, machinery, brush, wood, and lumber. *See* GARBAGE; SOLID WASTE.

JUNK VEHICLE

See VEHICLE, JUNK.

JUNKYARD

Any lot, land, parcel, building, or structure, or part thereof, used for the storage, collection, processing, purchase, sale, salvage, or disposal of junk.

Comment: Junkyards are intensive uses, and since they are usually operated outdoors, appropriate setbacks, screening, and buffering are required.

JUST COMPENSATION

Payment made to a private property owner by an agency with power of eminent domain when the private property is taken for public use. *See* EMINENT DOMAIN; TAKING.

K

KENNEL

An establishment in which dogs or domesticated animals are housed, groomed, bred, boarded, trained, or sold, all for a fee or compensation.

Comment: Since kennels include animal runs, care must be taken to locate them away from residential areas and provide noise buffers or barriers. Many communities license kennels, establishing a minimum number of animals after which a license is required.

KENNEL, PRIVATE

The keeping, breeding, raising, showing, or training of four or more dogs over six months of age for personal enjoyment of the owner or occupant of the property.

Comment: This provision identifies individuals who breed, raise, train, and show dogs. Because of the potential nuisance and neighborhood impact, the primary control should be the size of the property where permitted.

KIOSK

A freestanding structure upon which temporary information and/or posters, notices, and announcements are posted. *See Figure 17.*

Comment: A kiosk may incorporate a public pay phone and a trash receptacle. Its design should reflect community character. *See Figure 58.*

KIOSK

FIGURE 58

KNOLL

A small, natural round hill or mound.

L

Definitions:

Labor Force
through
Luminaire

Figures:

LABOR FORCE

All the population 16 years of age or older having the potential for active work for wages.

LAGOON

In wastewater treatment, a shallow, artificial pond where sunlight, bacterial action, and oxygen interact to restore wastewater to a reasonable state of purity.

LAKE

An inland water body fed by springs or surrounding runoff.

LAND

Ground, soil, or earth, including structures on, above, or below the surface.

LAND BANK

Government-purchased land held for future use.

LAND DISTURBANCE

Any activity involving the clearing, cutting, excavating, filling, or grading of land or any other activity that alters land topography or vegetative cover.

LANDLOCKED

A lot or parcel of land without direct access to a public road.

Comment: Local development regulations should preclude approval of any subdivision or site plan that results in any property becoming landlocked.

LAND RECLAMATION

Increasing land-use capability by changing the land's character or environment through drainage, fill, or regrading. *See* FILLING.

Comment: Land reclamation is often associated with landfills and quarries.

LAND SURVEYOR

One who is licensed by the state as a land surveyor and is qualified to make accurate field measurements and to mark, describe, and define land boundaries.

LAND USE

A description of how land is occupied or used.

LAND-USE INTENSITY (LUI) STANDARDS

A system of bulk regulations, designed primarily for large-scale developments, and based on the physical relationships between specific development factors.

Comment: LUI standards attempt to correlate the land area, floor area, open space, recreation space, and car storage of a project. Details of the system were first published in the Federal Housing Administration's *Land Planning Bulletin No. 7, Land Use Intensity Rating* (1996). They have never been fully appreciated or gained wide-scale acceptance.

218

LAND-USE PLAN

A basic element of the community master plan containing proposals for the physical, economic, and social development of the community.

Comment: The land-use plan takes into account the other master plan elements and shows the existing and proposed location, extent, and intensity of development of land to be used for residential, commercial, industrial, open space, agricultural, recreational, educational, and other public and private purposes. In many state jurisdictions, the local zoning ordinance must be consistent with the adopted land-use plan element of the local master plan.

LANDFILL

A disposal site in which refuse and earth, or other suitable cover material, are deposited and compacted in alternating layers of specified depth in accordance with an approved plan. *See* SANITARY LANDFILL.

Comment: Landfills are usually regulated and licensed by the state or other regional agency to accept certain types of waste. Landfills differ from dumps in that refuse is compacted and covered in the landfill.

LANDMARK

(1) Any site, building, structure, or natural feature that has visual, historic, or cultural significance; (2) a permanent marker, usually called a "monument," designating property boundaries.

LANDSCAPE

(1) An expanse of natural scenery; (2) lawns, trees, plants, and other natural materials, such as rock and wood chips, and decorative features, including sculpture, patterned walks, fountains, and pools.

Comment: As noted in the definition, landscaping treatment can include some elements of street furniture. It does not include artificial trees or other artificial plants. Natural materials often are referred to as "soft" landscape, and other materials are known as "hard" landscape.

LANDSCAPE PLAN

A component of a development plan on which are shown:
- proposed landscape species (such as number, spacing, size at time of planting, and planting details)
- proposals for protection of existing vegetation during and after construction
- proposed treatment of hard and soft surfaces
- proposed decorative features
- grade changes
- buffers and screening devices

219

- any other information that can reasonably be required for an informed decision to be made by the approving authority

See Figures 59 and 60.

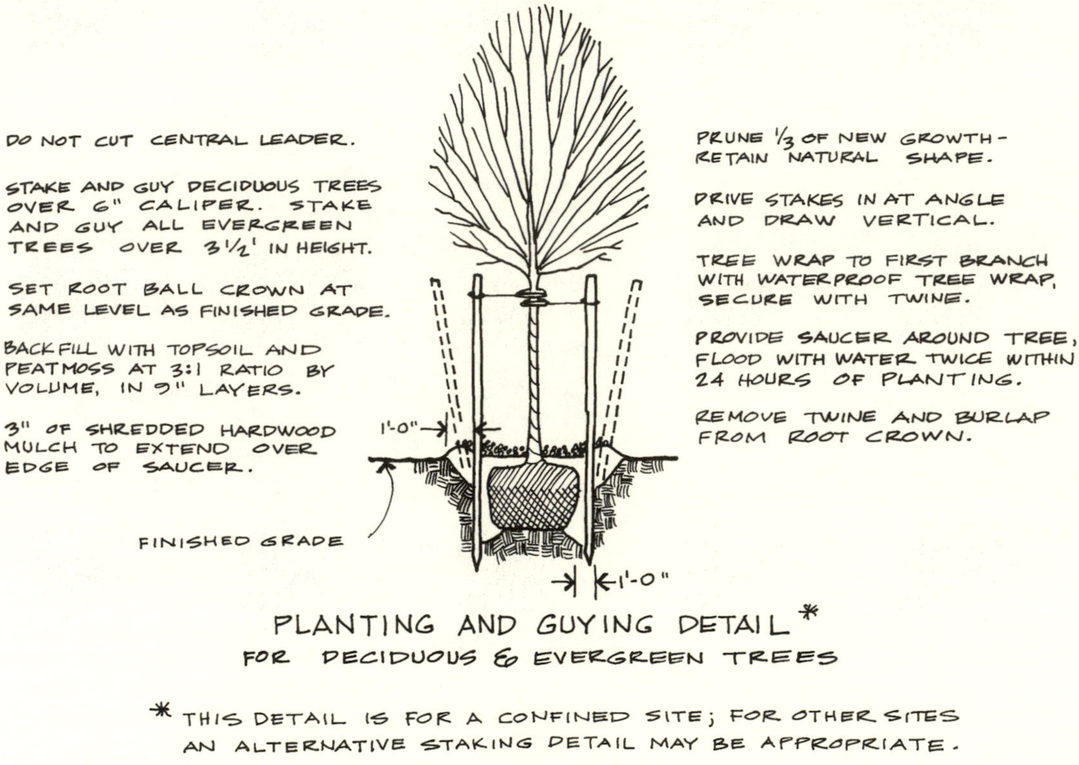

DO NOT CUT CENTRAL LEADER.

STAKE AND GUY DECIDUOUS TREES OVER 6" CALIPER. STAKE AND GUY ALL EVERGREEN TREES OVER 3½' IN HEIGHT.

SET ROOT BALL CROWN AT SAME LEVEL AS FINISHED GRADE.

BACKFILL WITH TOPSOIL AND PEATMOSS AT 3:1 RATIO BY VOLUME, IN 9" LAYERS.

3" OF SHREDDED HARDWOOD MULCH TO EXTEND OVER EDGE OF SAUCER.

FINISHED GRADE

PRUNE ⅓ OF NEW GROWTH – RETAIN NATURAL SHAPE.

DRIVE STAKES IN AT ANGLE AND DRAW VERTICAL.

TREE WRAP TO FIRST BRANCH WITH WATERPROOF TREE WRAP, SECURE WITH TWINE.

PROVIDE SAUCER AROUND TREE, FLOOD WITH WATER TWICE WITHIN 24 HOURS OF PLANTING.

REMOVE TWINE AND BURLAP FROM ROOT CROWN.

1'-0"

1'-0"

PLANTING AND GUYING DETAIL *
FOR DECIDUOUS & EVERGREEN TREES

* THIS DETAIL IS FOR A CONFINED SITE; FOR OTHER SITES AN ALTERNATIVE STAKING DETAIL MAY BE APPROPRIATE.

FIGURE 59

LANE

A private street or easement providing vehicular and service access to the rear of individual lots. *See* ALLEY.

LARGE-LOT ZONING

Low-density residential development that requires a large parcel of land for each dwelling.

Comment: While there is no set definition on what constitutes a "large parcel," low density usually refers to development on lots of 1 acre or more.

LATENT DEMAND

In traffic engineering, the increase in traffic demand as highway congestion decreases.

LATERAL SEWERS

Pipes conducting sewerage from individual buildings to larger pipes called "trunk" or "interceptor" sewers.

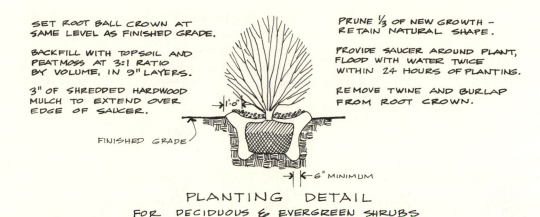

SET ROOT BALL CROWN AT SAME LEVEL AS FINISHED GRADE.

BACKFILL WITH TOPSOIL AND PEATMOSS AT 3:1 RATIO BY VOLUME, IN 9" LAYERS.

3" OF SHREDDED HARDWOOD MULCH TO EXTEND OVER EDGE OF SAUCER.

FINISHED GRADE

PRUNE ⅓ OF NEW GROWTH – RETAIN NATURAL SHAPE.

PROVIDE SAUCER AROUND PLANT, FLOOD WITH WATER TWICE WITHIN 24 HOURS OF PLANTING.

REMOVE TWINE AND BURLAP FROM ROOT CROWN.

1'-0"

6" MINIMUM

PLANTING DETAIL
FOR DECIDUOUS & EVERGREEN SHRUBS

FIGURE 60

LAUNDROMAT^{SM}

An establishment providing washing, drying, or dry-cleaning machines on the premises for rental use to the general public.

LEACHATE

Liquid that has percolated through solid waste or other mediums from which dissolved or suspended materials have been extracted.

LEACHING

The process by which soluble materials in the soil, such as nutrients, pesticide chemicals, or contaminants, are washed into a lower layer of soil and are dissolved and carried into ground water.

LEASE

A contractual agreement for the use of lands, structures, buildings, or parts thereof for a fixed time and consideration.

LEAST-COST HOUSING

Housing that sells for prices substantially below median housing prices in an area and built in accordance with local codes and ordinances that have been carefully screened to eliminate cost-generating provisions and any requirements not related to health, safety, and welfare. *See* MANUFACTURED HOME.

Comment: Some of the cost-generating requirements found to be unrelated to health, safety, and welfare include large-lot zoning, unrealistic densities for various housing types, minimum building areas, garages, and oversized utilities or infrastructures (36-foot-wide local streets, for example). However, the appropriate minimum standards for lot size, density, utilities, and other requirements may vary between municipalities

221

and even within them, depending on existing natural and created constraints and the character of local development.

Many of the impediments to least-cost housing are identified in the 1991 report of the President's Advisory Committee on Regulatory Barriers to Affordable Housing, *Not in My Back Yard: Removing Barriers to Affordable Housing* (Kemp Report).

LEISURE SERVICES

Activities for people other than employment or mandatory functions and including activities relating to recreation, social and cultural events, religion, and education.

LESS-THAN-FEE ACQUISITION

See EASEMENT.

LETTER OF CREDIT

A letter issued by a bank permitting the person or agency named in it to draw a certain amount of money from another specified bank. (Adapted from Johnsich 1991, p. 121)

Comment: Letters of credit are now accepted in the same manner as cash or bonds to ensure the installation or construction of required improvements. *See* PERFORMANCE GUARANTEE.

LEVEE

A structure designed and constructed to contain, control, or divert the flow of water so as to provide protection from temporary flooding.

LEVEL OF SERVICE

A quality measure describing operational conditions within a traffic stream, generally in terms of such service measures as speed and travel time, freedom to maneuver, traffic interruptions, and comfort and convenience. (Transportation Research Board 2000, p. 2-2)

Comment: The level of service ranges from A (free flow of traffic with minimum intersection delay), which is the best, to F (forced flow, jammed intersections, long delays), which is the worst. It reflects factors such as speed, travel time, freedom to maneuver, traffic interruptions, and delay. *See* CAPACITY, ROADWAY.

LIBRARY

A place containing books for reading, study, and research.

Comment: The above definition is the classical and largely outdated definition of a library. If most people can't define a library, everyone can probably describe one and how it functions. Libraries today still have books for reading, study, and research on-site or to borrow. They now

TABLE L-1: FLOOR SPACE RECOMMENDATIONS FOR PUBLIC LIBRARIES

Population to be Served	Minimum Square Feet of Floor Space			
Less than 10,000	3,500 ft.^{2}	+ 0.70 ft.^{2} per capita	>	5,000 population
10,000 – 24,999	7,000 ft.^{2}	+ 0.60 ft.^{2} per capita	>	10,000 population
25,000 – 49,999	16,000 ft.^{2}	+ 0.45 ft.^{2} per capita	>	25,000 population
50,000 – 99,999	27,250 ft.^{2}	+ 0.35 ft.^{2} per capita	>	50,000 population
100,000 – 199,999	44,750 ft.^{2}	+ 0.25 ft.^{2} per capita	>	100,000 population
200,000 – 499,999	69,750 ft.^{2}	+ 0.20 ft.^{2} per capita	>	200,000 population
500,000 +	129,750 ft.^{2}	+ 0.15 ft.^{2} per capita	>	500,000 population

Source: New Jersey State Library, Trenton, New Jersey

also have newspapers, magazines, artwork, books on tape, videos, and CDs. Libraries feature lectures, classes, concerts, and recitals. They may include day-care centers, homework centers, and meeting facilities for clubs, neighborhood associations, and outreach groups. Most have Internet access.

Libraries play key roles as community centers. They are strong anchors for downtowns and neighborhoods, and planners have found them important in revitalization efforts. They have returned to their original roles as social centers and promote and schedule conferences, exhibits, and shows. Many, going toe to toe with some of the large book retailers, have restaurants and snack bars.

Libraries can be located anywhere, but they obviously function best near schools, particularly high schools, retail locations, and other central places with people. As noted earlier, they can be important neighborhood centers. Libraries have traditionally been part of civic centers and still function well in those locations, bringing after-hours activity in an area that often closes down after business hours. Many libraries have found retail malls ideal locations, scheduling reading hours and preschool activities so parents can drop children off while shopping (Fulton and Jackson 1999, p. 4).

Various organizations provide standards for libraries, such as the American Library Association (http://www.ala.org/) and the Urban Library Council in Evanston, Illinois. In New Jersey, the State Library recommends the square footage shown in table L-1 for libraries based on population served.

LIFE CYCLE

The phases, changes, or stages an organism passes through during its lifetime.

LIFE-CARE COMMUNITIES

See CONTINUING CARE RETIREMENT COMMUNITY (CCRC).

LIFE-CYCLE HOUSING

A variety of housing types that meet the need of households over a normal life span.

Comment: A typical household might start out in a rental apartment, then move to a small detached home or townhouse, then to a larger detached home, then to a townhouse or apartment, and then eventually to an assisted living environment.

LIFT

In a sanitary landfill, a compacted layer of solid waste and the top layer of cover material.

LIGHT INDUSTRY

See INDUSTRY, LIGHT.

LIGHT PLANE

See SKY EXPOSURE PLANE.

LIGHT RAIL TRANSIT (LRT)

See TRANSIT, LIGHT RAIL.

LIGHT TRESPASS

The shining of light produced by a luminaire beyond the boundaries of the property on which it is located.

LIGHTING PLAN

A plan showing the location, height above grade, type of illumination, type of fixture, the source lumens, and the luminous area for each source of light proposed.

Comment: The ordinance should spell out the standards required as part of the lighting plan, including maximum footcandles permitted and location, maximum height of light standard (usually 25 feet maximum in nonresidential areas and 15 feet in residential areas), and requirements for shielding and style of luminaire if in a historic district or part of an overall neighborhood plan. *See* FOOTCANDLE.

LIMITED-ACCESS HIGHWAY

A highway, especially designed for through traffic, over which abutting lot owners have no right to light, air, or direct access.

Comment: Interstate highways, parkways, and freeways are considered limited-access highways.

LIMITS OF CLEARING

The boundaries of that area of land to be cleared of trees and other vegetation in conjunction with a proposed development or land use.

LIMNOLOGY

The study of the physical, chemical, meteorological, and biological aspects of freshwaters.

LINES

See LOT LINE.

LINKAGE PROGRAMS

Developer contributions, either by construction, actual provision of the service, or in-lieu fees, toward community amenities and needs, such as affordable housing, open space, child-care facilities, transit improvements, and/or related community services, in return for obtaining development approval.

Comment: Linkage programs require developers to contribute money for or actually to build housing, transit improvements, recreation, or other amenities as a prerequisite for approvals. In some cases, the linkage programs allow for an increase in allowable density or intensity of development in return for providing the amenity. In order for linkage to work, there should be some relationship to what is being built and what is required—a rational nexus. For example, a new office building may generate a demand for more transit capacity, child care, and affordable housing. The impact can be determined and the linkage computed. Linkage formulas must be permitted by state law, be based on a local ordinance with clear and equitable requirements, and be applied fairly and uniformly.

However, a New Jersey Supreme Court case—*Holmdel Builders Association v. Township of Holmdel*, 583 A.2d 299 (1990) *(Holmdel II)*—appears to reject the rational nexus test for linkage programs relating to affordable housing. The court noted that the rational nexus test was not an appropriate standard to determine compliance with constitutional regional general welfare standards. *See* RATIONAL NEXUS.

LITTORAL

Pertaining to the shore of seas and oceans.

LITTORAL DRIFT

The transportation of grains of sand resulting from water action produced by winds and currents.

LITTORAL LAND

Land that abuts a large body of water, such as an ocean or sea.

LIVING QUARTERS, SEPARATE

Those in which the occupants live separately from any other individuals in the building and which have direct access from outside the building or through a common hall. (Census 2000)

LOADING SPACE

An off-street space or berth used for the loading or unloading of cargo, products, or materials from vehicles.

LOCAL AUTHORITY

Any city, town, village, or other legally authorized agency charged with the administration and enforcement of land-use regulations. *See* MUNICIPALITY.

Comment: In many states, the county or regional planning agencies are charged with the administration and enforcement of land-use regulations.

LOCAL HOUSING AUTHORITY

Any public body authorized to engage in the development or administration of subsidized or public housing.

LOCAL IMPROVEMENT

A public improvement provided to a specific area benefiting that area and usually paid for by special assessment on the benefiting property owners.

LOCAL ROAD

See STREET, LOCAL.

LODGE

(1) The place where members of a local chapter of an association or a fraternal, cultural, or religious organization hold their meetings; (2) the local chapter itself. *See* PRIVATE CLUB.

LODGER

A transient renter whose meals may or may not be included in the rent. *See* BOARDER.

LODGING HOUSE

A facility in which rental sleeping accommodations are provided and in which meals also may be supplied as part of the rent. *See* BOARDINGHOUSE.

LOGGIA

A colonnaded or arcaded space within the body of a building but open to the outside of the building on one side, often at an upper story overlooking a courtyard.

LONG-TERM CARE FACILITY

An institution or a part of an institution that is licensed or approved to provide health care under medical supervision for 24 or more consecutive hours to two or more patients who are not related to the governing authority or its members by marriage, blood, or adoption.

Comment: A long-term care facility may be either a skilled nursing facility, where patients receive a minimum number of hours of nursing care daily (New Jersey requires 2.75 hours), or an intermediate care facility, where patients receive less than the specified number of hours of nursing care daily. Besides nursing homes, other long-term care facilities are governmental medical institutions or nursing units in a home for

226

the aged. Long-term care facilities can provide, in addition to maintenance care, restorative services and specialized services such as intravenous feeding, tube feeding, injected medication, and daily wound care. Hospices are also examples of long-term care facilities. See EXTENDED CARE FACILITY; INTERMEDIATE CARE FACILITY.

LOT
A designated parcel, tract, or area of land established by plat, subdivision, or as otherwise permitted by law, to be separately owned, used, developed, or built upon. *See Figure 10.*

LOT, CORNER
A lot or parcel of land abutting on two or more streets at their intersection or on two parts of the same street forming an interior angle of less than 135 degrees. *See Figures 10 and 101.*

Comment: The major problem with corner lots is the designation of the yards opposite the street frontages. Most ordinances require that the minimum front yard be maintained on both frontages for purposes of providing adequate sight distances, safety, air and light to abutting residences, and for aesthetic considerations. There remains the question of how to treat the two remaining yards. Some ordinances call them side yards and require them to meet the minimum required side yard dimension. Unfortunately, this deprives the corner lot of any adequate backyard area and encroaches on one or both adjacent residences. A better approach is to permit the applicant to designate one of the street frontages as the front, require the house to be built facing the front, and then require the yard opposite the designated front to meet the minimum rear yard requirement. Both street frontages would still meet the minimum required front yard setback, one yard would meet side yard standards, and the lot would have a rear yard. The corner lot would have to be larger than the interior lots to provide the minimum required setbacks.

LOT, DEVELOPABLE
See DEVELOPABLE LAND.

LOT, DEVELOPED
See LOT, IMPROVED.

LOT, DOUBLE FRONTAGE
See LOT, THROUGH.

LOT, FLAG
A lot not meeting minimum frontage requirements and where access to the public road is by a private right-of-way or driveway. *See Figures 10 and 61.*

227

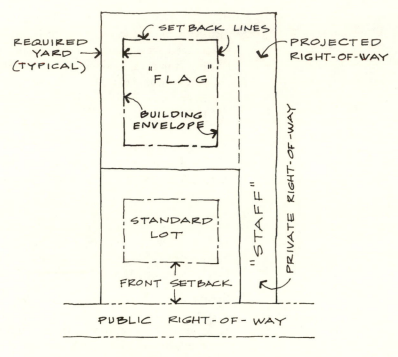

FLAG LOT

FIGURE 61

Comment: Flag lots are usually permitted in rural and developing municipalities to allow development of backland areas while still maintaining their rural character. The usual requirements for a flag lot are as follows: minimum lot area at least twice the area of standard lots in the zone where located, exclusive of the staff connecting the lot to the public road; minimum setbacks from property lines, as opposed to the usual front, side, and rear yard requirements; all setbacks measured from the projected right-of-way; minimum of 20 feet and maximum of 50 feet for the right-of-way; not more than one flag lot for each private right-of-way (the staff), and minimum distance between flag lot right-of-ways at least equal to the minimum lot frontage in the particular zone.

While flag lots can assist in retaining the rural character of an area, they are subject to abuses. The most prevalent is when the flag lot owner wants to further subdivide and use the private right-of-way for access. The municipality then has a major subdivision without adequate access. Many towns do not permit flag lots where the flag lot can be further subdivided.

228

LOT, IMPROVED

A lot with buildings or structures.

LOT, INTERIOR

A lot other than a corner lot. *See Figure 10.*

LOT, ISOLATED

See ISOLATED LOT.

LOT, MINIMUM AREA OF

The smallest lot area established by the zoning ordinance on which a use or structure may be located in a particular district.

LOT, REVERSE FRONTAGE

A through lot with frontage on two parallel streets with vehicular access restricted to only one of the streets. *See* LOT, THROUGH. *See Figures 27 and 62.*

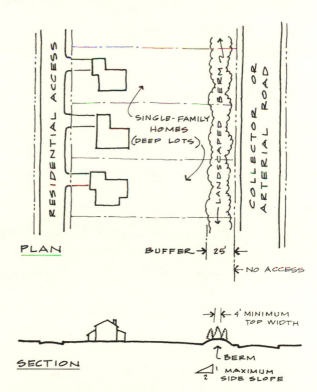

REVERSE FRONTAGE LOTS

FIGURE 62

Comment: As illustrated in figure 62, reverse frontage lot layouts are often used in residential developments abutting an arterial or other high-volume roadway. With the reverse frontage design, vehicular access can be restricted to the lower-volume street frontage, eliminating undesirable driveway access along the higher-volume roadway. In these situations, the through lot may be designed with a greater depth to permit space for a berm and/or landscaped buffer next to the higher-volume roadway.

Yard-setback dimensions for the reverse frontage lot should be consistent with ordinance regulations, although the setback for the restricted access frontage could be designated as a rear yard. The prohibited vehicular access should be a deed restriction on the lot.

LOT, SUBSTANDARD

A parcel of land that has less than the minimum area or minimum dimensions required in the zone in which the lot is located.

LOT, THROUGH

A lot that fronts on two parallel streets or that fronts on two streets that do not intersect at the boundaries of the lot. *See Figure 10.*

LOT, TRANSITION

(1) A lot in a transition zone; (2) a lot in one zoning district abutting another district and designated as a transition lot. *See Figure 63.*

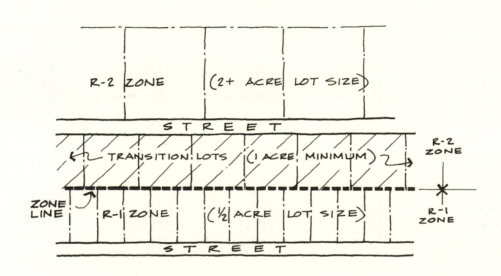

TRANSITION LOT
(RESIDENTIAL EXAMPLE)

FIGURE 63

Comment: Transition lots (or lots in transition zones) serve as logical "change" lots between two zones. For example, a lot between a business and residential zone might allow parking for the business use (with adequate setbacks, buffering, and landscaping) or a higher-density residential use. The zoning ordinance may also establish an intermediate size for the transition lot. For instance, if located between a 40,000-square-foot residential zone and a 20,000-square-foot residential zone, the transition lot might be required to have a minimum of 30,000 square feet. The transition lot also might be part of a lot-averaging design. *See* LOT AVERAGING.

LOT AREA

The total area within the lot lines of a lot, excluding any street rights-of-way.

LOT AVERAGING

A form of development that permits a reduction in individual lot areas and bulk requirements, provided that the number of lots remains the same as permitted without lot averaging.

Comment: Lot averaging has proven to be an excellent and much simpler way of preserving open space than other techniques such as transfer of development rights, which often requires the establishment of sending and receiving zones and the establishment of a transfer bank. Lot averaging is basically the same as cluster development, except that cluster development usually requires that the common open space be designated for the use and enjoyment of the residents and owners of the development and generally is owned by a homeowners association. While lot averaging also allows the open space to be so designated, it also permits, for example, that the open space be permanently deed-restricted for agricultural purposes and sold to a farmer or retained by a single property owner for his or her own open space use.

In Cranbury Township (Middlesex County), New Jersey, the lot-averaging provision has permanently saved considerable acreage for farming. The technique works as follows in the Farm Preservation Zone (areas currently farmed without public water or sewers): The bulk regulations in this zone call for a minimum of 6 acres for each dwelling unit. An applicant wanting to develop a parcel of land using the lot-averaging technique must first lay out the property in a conventional, fully conforming, 6-acre-per-lot subdivision to establish the maximum number of lots that could be devolved without lot averaging. The township then grants a density bonus of 25 percent, provided at least 70 percent of the land is preserved in open space or agriculture. If the parcel is 120 acres, for example, and a fully conforming subdivision resulted in 16 lots (excluding losses from roads and irregularly shaped boundaries), the applicant would be permitted to develop with a 25 percent bonus, or 20 lots. The minimum lot size would be consistent with septic, water treatment, and water requirements. In the example, the actual lot sizes would be between 1 and 1.8 acres. The 70 percent preservation requirement would result in 84 acres saved.

The key to encouraging lot averaging is the bonus provision. It offsets the additional cost of laying out a conventional subdivision plat and any reduction in value by allowing smaller lots. But as builders have pointed out, the local market for 1-acre lots is much greater than for 6-acre lots, so the present value may be as much for the smaller lots as for the larger ones. In addition, the conventional layout required to determine the maximum lot yield does not call for detailed engineering plans.

While the example used is a farm zone, lot averaging works in all residential zones as long as the density in the developed parts of the tract can be accommodated.

LOT COVERAGE

That part of the lot that is covered by impervious surfaces. *See* BUILDING COVERAGE; IMPERVIOUS SURFACE.

LOT DEPTH

The average distance measured from the front lot line to the rear lot line. *See Figure 10.*

Comment: For lots where the front and rear lot lines are not parallel, the lot depth should be measured by drawing several evenly separated lines from the front to rear lot lines, at right angles to the front lot line, and averaging the length of these lines.

LOT FRONTAGE

The length of the front lot line measured at the street right-of-way line. *See Figure 10.*

Comment: On corner lots, each side abutting the street is considered the frontage, and in many ordinances, such lots have two front yards, two side yards, and no rear yards. *See Comment* under LOT, CORNER.

LOT LINE

A line of record bounding a lot that divides one lot from another lot or from a public or private street or any other public space. *See Figure 14.*

LOT LINE, FRONT

The lot line separating a lot from a street right-of-way. *See Figure 14.*

LOT LINE, REAR

The lot line opposite and most distant from the front lot line. In the case of triangular or otherwise irregularly shaped lots, a line 10 feet in length entirely within the lot, parallel to and at a maximum distance from the front lot line. *See Figure 14.*

Comment: The 10-foot minimum length is not sacrosanct. On wider lots, it could be a percentage of the minimum lot width, say 10 percent.

LOT LINE, SIDE

Any lot line other than a front or rear lot line. *See Figure 14.*

LOT OF RECORD

A lot that exists as shown or described on a plat or deed in the records of the local registry of deeds.

LOT WIDTH

The horizontal distance between the side lines of a lot measured at right angles to its depth along a straight line parallel to the front lot line at the minimum required building setback line. *See Figure 10.*

LOW-INCOME HOUSING

Housing that is economically feasible for families whose income level is categorized as low within the standards promulgated by the U.S. Department of Housing and Urban Development (HUD) or the appropriate state housing agency.

Comment: Generally speaking, low income is defined as 50 percent or less of the median family income in a particular market area. Economically feasible can be defined as housing costs between 28 and 30 percent of gross family income. HUD also uses the term "very low" to identify families earning up to 50 percent of the area median family income; "low," 50 to 80 percent; and "moderate," 80 to 120 percent.

LOW-SPEED RURAL HIGHWAY

The access classification for roadways in rural environments where the posted speed limit is 45 miles per hour or less.

LOW-SPEED URBAN HIGHWAY

The access classification for roadways in urban environments where the posted speed limit is 40 miles per hour or less.

LUMBERYARD

An area and structures used for the storage, distribution, and sale of finished or rough-cut lumber and lumber products.

LUMEN

A unit of measure of the quantity of light that falls on an area of 1 square foot, every point of which is 1 foot from the source of 1 candela.

Comment: A light source of 1 candela emits a total of 12.57 lumens.

LUMINAIRE

A complete lighting unit consisting of a light source, pole, and all mounting brackets, if appropriate, and all necessary mechanical, electrical, and decorative parts. (Adapted from Kendig 1980)

M

MADE LAND

Land previously unsuitable for development because of a high water table, open waters, flooding, unstable subsurface conditions, or similar impairments and made suitable by corrective action. *See* FILLING; LAND RECLAMATION.

Comment: Reclaiming land unsuitable for development usually involves filling and draining, activities that require state and often federal permits.

MAGNET STORE

The largest retail establishment in a shopping center, which draws customers and thereby generates business for the remaining stores in the center. *See* ANCHOR TENANT.

Comment: In a regional center, the department store is the magnet. In neighborhood centers, it is the supermarket.

MAIN

The principal artery in any system of continuous piping to which branches may be connected. (N.J.A.C. 5:21-1.4)

MAINTENANCE GUARANTEE

Any security that may be required and accepted by a governmental agency to ensure that necessary improvements will function as required for a specific period of time. *See* PERFORMANCE GUARANTEE.

Comment: The maintenance guarantee takes effect after the municipality has accepted the improvements. The maintenance guarantee usually runs for a period of one to two years. If something malfunctions, the obligor is required to correct the deficiency.

MAJOR LIFE ACTIVITIES

Functions such as caring for oneself, performing manual tasks, walking, seeing, hearing, breathing, learning, and working. *See* AMERICANS WITH DISABILITIES ACT.

MAJOR TRAFFIC GENERATOR

The use or uses that generate a total of 500 or more vehicle trips per day to and from the use or uses.

Comment: The 500-vehicle trip is the generally accepted standard. The developer of a proposed use classified as a major traffic generator would usually be required to undertake impact studies on intersections and roadways surrounding the proposed use.

MALL

(1) A shaded walk or public promenade; (2) a shopping center where stores front on both sides of a pedestrian way, which may be enclosed or open.

MANHOLE

An inspection chamber, located at changes in horizontal and vertical directions for underground utility conduits, whose dimensions allow entry, exit, and working room. (N.J.A.C. 5:21-1.4)

MANSE

See CLERGY RESIDENCE.

MANUFACTURED HOME

A factory-built, single-family structure that meets the Federal Manufactured Home Construction and Safety Standards Act (42 U.S.C. Sec. 5401), commonly known as the *HUD* (U.S. Department of Housing and Urban Development) *Code.* (Sanders 1998)

Comment: Such houses are often referred to as modular homes, and formerly, mobile homes. The latter term was originally coined to describe trailers that were equipped to function as truly mobile homes. The mobile home of years past has long since become a fixed, in-place house that is mobile only at the time it is moved from the factory to the site. Besides losing its mobility, the "mobile home" has also become larger, and the safety and quality have been significantly improved as a result of the passage of the Federal Manufactured Home Construction and Safety Standards Act in 1976. Units built to this code are properly referred to as "manufactured homes" as a result of the 1976 act.

Along with the name change, the appearance of manufactured housing has also changed. Many new manufactured units are designed to look like site-built housing and have pitched roofs and conventional roofing and siding materials. In addition, many manufactured houses are "customized" with site-built amenities, such as patios, garages, and decks.

As manufactured housing has become less mobile, there has been a gradual shift in development approaches from the mobile home park system, where land was rented on a long-term lease, to subdivisions, where lots are purchased. Although some manufactured housing subdivisions have comparatively large lot sizes, attractive developments can be created at densities typical of multifamily housing development if creative design techniques are used. The combined cost savings of manufactured housing and small lot sizes can produce affordable single-family housing. In 1993, the U.S. Census Bureau found that the retail cost of factory-built homes was half that of traditional site-built housing.

Manufactured housing developments usually require special zoning provisions. In many states, however, state planning and zoning enabling legislation has been amended to make double-wide manufactured

237

units on permanent foundations a permitted use in all areas zoned for residential development. *See* FACTORY-BUILT HOUSING, MANUFACTURED HOUSING COMMUNITY; MODULAR HOME; MOBILE HOME.

MANUFACTURED HOUSING COMMUNITY

A private community of single-family homes that are built in accordance with the Federal Manufactured Home Construction and Safety Standards Act, and transported, sited, and installed in compliance with the act and the State Uniform Construction Code. *See* MANUFACTURED HOME.

MANUFACTURING

Establishments engaged in the mechanical or chemical transformation of materials or substances into new products, including the assembling of component parts, the creation of products, and the blending of materials, such as oils, plastics, resins, or liquors.

Comment: The term "manufacturing" covers all mechanical or chemical transformations, whether the new products are finished or semifinished as raw material in some other process. Manufacturing production usually is carried on for the wholesale market rather than for retail sale, although retail sale to the ultimate consumer is becoming more prevalent. Processing on farms is not usually classified as manufacturing if the raw material is grown on the farm. The manufacturing is accessory to the primary use of farming.

MAP, CONTOUR

A map that displays land elevations in graphic form with lines connecting areas of equal elevation. *See* TOPOGRAPHIC MAP. *See Figure 20.*

MAP, OFFICIAL

See OFFICIAL MAP.

MAPPED STREET

A street appearing on the official map of the municipality or county.

Comment: Mapped streets are planned streets. By placing them on the official map, the integrity of the right-of-way is preserved, since most enabling acts prevent the issuance of a building permit for a structure in the bed of a mapped street.

MARGINAL ACCESS STREET

See STREET, MARGINAL ACCESS.

MARINA

A facility for the storing, servicing, fueling, berthing, and securing of boats and which may include eating, sleeping, and retail facilities for owners, crews, and guests.

MARKETABILITY STUDY

A study that measures the need for a particular land use or activity within a defined geographic area.

Comment: The market study, also referred to as market demand, usually involves a proposal to locate a specific use on a specified site. The study determines how many people can be expected to patronize the facility and how many similar facilities are located in the market area.

MARQUEE

Any hood, canopy, awning, or permanent construction that projects from a wall of a building, usually above an entrance.

Comment: Marquees are usually exempt from setback requirements and are allowed to project over the sidewalk, particularly in central business districts. Consideration should be given, however, to potential problems with fire fighting and the need to get ladders and equipment above the first floor. Also, there is the matter of aesthetics, and any permanent marquee extending along the sidewalk in the central business district should be designed and installed in accordance with an overall plan to ensure design continuity.

MARSHLANDS

Low-lying tracts of land characterized by high water tables and soils and extensive vegetation peculiar to and characteristic of wet places. *See* WETLAND, FRESHWATER.

MASKING

Covering over of one sound or element by another.

Comment: Masking is the amount the audibility threshold of one sound is raised by the presence of a second, masking sound. Also used with regard to odors.

MASS

See BUILDING MASS.

MASSAGE

Pressing, squeezing, stretching, or stimulating the face, scalp, neck, limbs, or other parts of the human body with or without cosmetic preparation, either by hand, or with mechanical or electrical appliances.

Comment: Massage is normally part of the services offered by physical therapists, beauty parlors, spas, gyms, or similar establishments. As such, it normally falls into the category of retail services. Many states require separate licenses, requiring exams and experience for personnel giving massages. Others include massage as part of the license granted to physical therapists, barbers, or beauticians.

MASS GATHERING

Any event, held outdoors or in a temporary structure or tent, over a fixed period of time, and attended by 2,000 or more persons over the period the mass gathering is scheduled to run. *See* TEMPORARY OUTDOOR ACTIVITY.

Comment: Mass gatherings may include music festivals, concerts, theatrical exhibitions, public shows, entertainment, amusement, speeches, circuses, carnivals, rallies, swap-and-shop markets, and flea markets. They are distinctly different from events held in permanent outdoor amphitheaters or stadiums, with permanent parking, clearly delineated circulation, and adequate restroom facilities. Many states require a license to be secured from the local government for any mass gathering and often define them in terms of the number of persons expected to attend over a specified period of time (3,000 persons over 18 hours in New Jersey; 5,000 persons over 18 hours in Indiana).

Mass gatherings that are regularly scheduled at a fixed location can be controlled by zoning. Other mass gatherings are probably best regulated by a local licensing ordinance rather than by zoning. But the requirements are similar, whether controlled by zoning or by the issuance of a license. A site plan showing access, parking, and circulation, particularly for emergency vehicles, should be reviewed. Health and sanitary facilities, litter control, police protection, and noise impacts should be considered. Some local ordinances require one parking space for every four persons expected to be in attendance at any one time or provision for shuttle buses to and from nearby parking lots. Health requirements in one ordinance required one toilet for each 250 persons in attendance. Finally, many ordinances require the promoters to post indemnity or performance bonds to protect the local government against personal injuries and property damage. (American Planning Association, "Fireworks, Farmstands, and Concerts—Summer's Here," *Zoning News*, July 1990)

MASS TRANSIT

A public common carrier transportation system having established routes and fixed schedules.

MASTER DEED

A legal instrument under which title to real estate is conveyed and by which a condominium is created and established.

Comment: The master deed is the key document in establishing a condominium. It is required to be filed in the office of the county recording officer. The contents of the master deed are usually prescribed by the appropriate state legislation covering condominium ownership.

Master deeds usually contain the following information:

- A statement placing the land described in the master deed under the provisions of the condominium act
- The official title of the condominium
- A legal description of the land
- A survey of the land showing the improvements to be erected, common elements, and units to be sold, in sufficient detail and shown in their respective locations with dimensions
- Identification of each unit
- A description of the common elements and limited common elements, if there are any
- The proportion of the undivided interests in the common elements, including rights of owners
- Bylaws
- Methods of amending and supplementing the master deed
- The name and nature of the association
- The manner of sharing common expenses
- Whatever other provisions may be desired, such as restrictions or limitations of use, occupancy, transfer leasing, or other disposition of a unit or the limitations on the use of common elements

MASTER PLAN

A comprehensive, long-range plan intended to guide the growth and development of a community or region for a set period of time and which typically includes inventory and analytic sections leading to recommendations for the community's land use, future economic development, housing, recreation and open space, transportation, community facilities, and community design, all related to the community's goals and objectives for these elements.

Comment: The term "master plan" (also known as the general or comprehensive plan) has almost become a word of art. The principle underlying its analysis and preparation is the comprehensive nature of the document, integrating all of the various parts into a single, unified, coherent plan that includes implementation proposals.

State enabling legislation specifies the legal requirements of a master plan, including its preparation, contents, modifications, adoption, and implementation. Although certain plan elements may be required, there are no limits to the number or type of plan elements, area, or subplans that may constitute a master plan. In many states, zoning ordinances must be based on the master plan, and where discrepancies occur, the master plan takes precedence.

MEAN

The average of a series of figures computed by adding up all the figures and dividing by the number in the series.

MEAN HIGH WATERLINE

The line formed by the intersection of the tidal plane of mean high tide with the shore.

MECHANICAL TURBULENCE

The erratic movement of air caused by local obstructions, such as buildings.

MEDIAN

(1) The middle number in a series of items in which 50 percent of all figures are above the median and 50 percent are below; (2) an island in the center of a highway that separates opposing traffic flows.

MEDIAN BARRIERS

See TRAFFIC CALMING.

MEDIAN ISLAND

A barrier placed between lanes of traffic flowing in opposite directions. *See* BARRIER. *See Figure 87.*

MEDICAL BUILDING

A building that contains establishments dispensing health services. *See* HEALTH CARE SERVICES.

MEGACHURCH

A house of worship with a seating or holding capacity of 10,000 or more persons.

Comment: Megachurches (or any large house of worship regardless of the denomination or religion) are a relatively new phenomenon. They draw from a regional area, have a variety of activities that take place over the entire week, and generate significant amounts of traffic.

The size and scope of these megachurches raise serious questions as to their appropriateness in low-density residential areas. In fact, many of them have become established in once-vacant industrial buildings in industrial areas (Schwab 1996).

The federal Religious Land Use and Institutionalized Persons Act of 2000 (Public Law 106-274, 114 Stat. 803, 42 U.S.C. §2000cc et seq.) places severe restrictions on land-use regulations that affect religious institutions. However, given the potential impact of these intense uses on the surrounding areas, reasonable controls on location, access, parking, lighting, signs, hours of operation, noise and buffers—traditional site plan concerns—may be appropriate (Schwab 1996). *See* PLACE OF WORSHIP; RELIGIOUS USE.

MEGAPLEX

A motion picture theatre with 10 or more screens that may include retail stores and restaurants. *See* CINEPLEX; MOTION PICTURE THEATRE.

Comment: Large movie theatres, with 10 (a somewhat arbitrary number) or more screens, are becoming the norm in movie entertainment, often crowding out smaller theatres. They generate a significant amount of traffic, both pedestrian and vehicular, and properly located can become strong anchors in downtown locations and assist in rejuvenating failing commercial centers.

Lincoln, Nebraska, for example, adopted a zoning amendment that essentially restricted movie theatres to commercial districts and the downtown area (sidebar in Langdon 2000). Many megaplexes are designed to include retail stores and service establishments, particularly restaurants. A West Palm Beach, Florida, megaplex includes an on-site child care center to attract parents who might otherwise stay home (Langdon 2000). Attracting megaplexes downtown, however, may require relaxing parking requirements and reducing the "financial, regulatory, political, and physical barriers to downtown infill development (A. Ricker, quoted in Langdon 2000).

As noted in the Langdon article, one of the major hurdles is ". . . how to accommodate large, windowless theatre buildings and hundreds of parking spaces, which make surroundings unappealing for pedestrians." In Miami Beach, the Lincoln Cinema megaplex has a five-story-high lobby facade of colored glass ". . . which dazzles passersby with views of people, activity, and décor. . . . It gives something back to the street" (B. Zyscovich, quoted in Langdon 2000). Parking is designed to bring people to the theatre by walking on sidewalks and by passing shops rather than directly from parking spaces to the theatre.

MEGALOPOLIS

An extended metropolitan area created from the merging of once separate and distinct metropolitan areas.

MEMBERSHIP ORGANIZATION

A group of persons who have come together on a formal basis, usually with bylaws and membership requirements, with the object of promoting the interests of the group's members.

Comment: Membership organizations differ from professional organizations in that anyone who ascribes to the goals and objectives of the organization can become a member. Payment of a membership fee and/or annual dues is usually required. If a requirement of membership is a college degree, passing an exam, or achieving a formal and recognized level of proficiency (master plumber or electrician, for example), the organization is considered a professional organization. Many organizations have two levels of membership: one open to all who support the goals of the organization and a second level achieved through a formal examination process. For example, the American Planning Association (APA) is open to all who pay the membership fee and annual dues. Membership in the American Institute of Certified Planners (AICP), the APA's professional subsidiary, can be achieved only by passing an examination and thus qualifies as a professional organization.

Some organizations do not fit easily into one or the other category, however. For example, military veterans' organizations may require a military affiliation or overseas duty or the winning of certain awards in order to join. These may be more logically classified as clubs or fraternal organizations.

Most membership organizations operate out of office buildings and are treated as such. Others, however, have large buildings designed for their specific use, which often produces a large turnout on meeting nights. In addition, the buildings are often rented out to other organizations for events, parties, weddings, flea markets, and the like. It is doubtful that they belong in residential zones, unless they are located on major streets and careful consideration is given to site plan issues such as landscaping, parking, lighting, and circulation. *See* CLUB; FRATERNAL ORGANIZATION.

MERGED LOTS

Two or more contiguous lots, in single ownership, that individually do not conform to zoning ordinance bulk standards.

Comment: In many states, the doctrine of merger treats separate lots under the same ownership as a single lot if either of the lots fails to meet the zoning requirement for area or frontage. The fact that the lots may have been purchased separately and may have been legally conforming lots at some time does not vest development rights in perpetuity.

244

MESOTROPHIC LAKES

Lakes that are intermediate in characteristics between *oligotrophic* (clear waters and relatively free of nutrients) and *eutrophic* (high levels of growth and nutrients) lakes. *See* EUTROPHIC LAKES; OLIGOTROPHIC LAKES.

METER

A metric scale measure equal to 3.28 feet.

METES AND BOUNDS

A method of describing the boundaries of land by directions (bounds) and distances (metes) from a known point of reference.

METROPOLIS

The major city in a designated area; generally, any large city.

METROPOLITAN AREA

An area whose economic and social life is influenced and boundaries are roughly defined by the commuting limits to the center city.

Comment: While commuting patterns usually define a metropolitan area, other factors can be used, such as newspaper circulation and retail trade areas.

METROPOLITAN STATISTICAL AREA (MSA)

A geographic area consisting of a large population nucleus together with adjacent areas having a high degree of economic and social integration.

Comment: The major purpose of the MSA designation is to provide federal agencies with a common base in tabulating and publishing data for metropolitan areas. Data are available for individual metropolitan areas on population, housing, industry, trade, employment, payrolls, and labor markets. To that end, MSAs are defined in terms of counties and the smallest geographical unit for which a wide range of statistical data can be obtained.

MEZZANINE

An intermediate level between the floor and ceiling of any story and covering not more than 33 percent of the floor area of the room in which it is located. *See Figure 8.*

Comment: In this definition, mezzanines are counted as part of the floor area ratio calculation. The BOCA Code (BOCA 1996) does not include mezzanines in FAR calculations.

MGD

Millions of gallons per day.

MICROBREWERY

See BREW PUB.

MICROWAVE

That part of the electromagnetic spectrum from 2900 megahertz (MHz) and higher.

MID-RISE

A building of three to seven stories. *See* DWELLING, MID-RISE. *See Figure 33.*

MIGRATION

The movement of people from one domicile to another.

Comment: The key word is domicile. It implies a permanent as opposed to a temporary movement, such as daily commuting to a job.

MILE

A linear measure equal to 5,280 feet, 1,760 yards, or 1.6 kilometers.

MILL

One-tenth of a cent.

Comment: The term is still used in matters relating to taxes.

MINE

(1) A cavity in the earth from which minerals and ores are extracted; (2) the act of removing minerals and ores.

MINERAL RIGHTS

One of a number of distinct and separate rights associated with real property that gives the owner of rights certain specified privileges, such as to extract, sell, and receive royalties with respect to the minerals.

Comment: The holder of mineral rights, in some cases, may be able to exercise those rights to the detriment of all other rights. For example, if the mineral rights owner has the right to explore or mine the minerals, it could severely affect the remainder of the land. *See* EXTRACTIVE INDUSTRIES.

MINIMALL

A shopping center of between 80,000 and 150,000 square feet on a site of 8 to 15 acres where tenants are located on both sides of a covered walkway with direct pedestrian access to all establishments from the walkway. *See* SHOPPING CENTER; SHOPPING MALL; SPECIALTY SHOPPING CENTER.

MINIMART

A convenience store that is located on the same lot and is accessory to a gasoline station. *See* RETAIL STORE, CONVENIENCE.

Comment: What goes around comes around, as the saying goes. In the beginning of the automotive age, the general store was the primary source of fuel for the growing fleet of automobiles. One or two pumps located on the curb in front of the general store supplied the fuel. Later, the pumps were moved to the sidewalk and a canopy erected to provide some protection against the weather. The next-to-last scenario was the conversion of the general store into an automobile service station.

But the latest trend is the combination gasoline station and minimart. Many municipalities are still debating the idea of permitting the minimart as an accessory use to the primary gasoline service use. The planning implications have to be considered, such as maximum size, products permitted to be sold, allowing food preparation on the premises, and on-site consumption. There are also concerns for the potential impact on established commercial centers nearby.

Some towns have severely limited the size of the minimart (300 square feet, for example), allowing only prepackaged single-serve snacks, maps, newspapers, and personal hygiene items ("Convenience Stores and Zoning to Go," *Zoning News*, March 1993). Others have taken the position that as long as the site is large enough and the gasoline station represents the principal use, a full convenience store would be allowed.

As noted earlier, the municipality has to decide whether the minimart represents primarily a service to the traveling public or is an end destination in and by itself. For example, if the minimart is located at a gasoline station near an industrial area with warehouses and distribution centers, the minimart could quickly evolve into a restaurant with food preparation and both on- and off-premises consumption. Questions of auto and truck parking, circulation, hours of operation, aesthetics, and design have to be addressed.

There is no consensus on minimart size. Some towns severely limit their size, essentially allowing the owner to bring only the vending machines under cover. Other minimarts vary from 400 to 3,000 square feet and are limited to the sale of prepackaged items, with limited food preparation.

MINI-WAREHOUSE	*See* SELF-STORAGE FACILITY.
MINIMAL ACCESSIBILITY	An environment that affords a handicapped person access with difficulty; the handicapped person may require some assistance.
MINING	The extraction of minerals, including solids, such as coal and ores; liquids, such as crude petroleum; and gases, such as natural gases. *See* EXTRACTIVE INDUSTRIES.
MINOR SUBDIVISION	*See* SUBDIVISION, MINOR.
MINOR TRAFFIC GENERATOR	The use or uses that generate less than a total of 500 vehicle trips per day. *See* MAJOR TRAFFIC GENERATOR.

MIST

Liquid particles suspended in air and formed by condensation of vaporized liquids.

MITIGATION

Methods used to alleviate or lessen the impact of development.

Comment: One of the purposes of requiring an environmental impact statement is to determine the potential impacts from any development proposal and to propose mitigation methods to alleviate and minimize the impacts. These might include soil erosion measures and buffers, replacement of wetlands, or contributions for expanded public facilities.

MIXED-USE DEVELOPMENT (MXD)

The development of a neighborhood, tract of land, building, or structure with a variety of complementary and integrated uses, such as, but not limited to, residential, office, manufacturing, retail, public, and recreation, in a compact urban form.

Comment: Central business districts are examples of MXDs, but they generally develop over long periods of time and often without a plan. A very early example of a planned MXD is Rockefeller Center in New York City. The appearance of developments with several mutually supported activities in a single, compactly configured, integrated project is a relatively recent innovation in urban land use, dating only from the mid-1950s. Early examples of inner-city MXDs include Penn Center in Philadelphia (1953), Midtown Plaza in Rochester (1956), and Charles Center in Baltimore (1957).

Smart-growth advocates cite the advantages of MXDs in reducing traffic congestion by locating homes and jobs within easy commuting distance and integrating shopping and related facilities into residential neighborhoods. Ideally, every neighborhood should be a mixed-use development providing a variety of housing types and sizes and places to work, shop, and recreate.

MIXED-USE ZONING

Regulations that permit a combination of different uses within a single development or zone.

MOBILE HOME

A residential dwelling that was fabricated in an off-site manufacturing facility, designed to be a permanent residence, and built prior to enactment of the Federal Manufactured Home Construction and Safety Standards. *See* FACTORY-BUILT HOUSING; MANUFACTURED HOME; MODULAR HOME.

MOBILE HOME PARK

A site containing spaces with required improvements and utilities that are leased for the long-term placement of manufactured houses. The site may include services and facilities for the residents. *See* MANUFACTURED HOME.

Comment: Mobile home parks, frequently referred to as manufactured housing parks or subdivisions, often are licensed by the municipality or county, and compliance with local regulations is a prerequisite to annual license renewal. The regulations may specify a minimum area for the house pad, such as 4,000 to 5,000 square feet, and other required amenities. The spaces may be rented, owned individually, or sold as condominiums. Mobile home parks usually ban recreational vehicles, campers, or trailers.

MOBILE HOME SPACE

A plat of land for placement of a single mobile home within a mobile home park. *See* PAD.

MOBILE SOURCE

A moving source of pollution, such as an automobile.

MODAL SPLIT

The breakdown of how people travel by type of conveyance.

Comment: An example of a modal split for commuting traffic might indicate 85 percent private auto, 10 percent bus, and 5 percent pedestrian or bike.

MODE

In statistics, the value or number that occurs most frequently in a given series.

MODERATE-INCOME HOUSING

Housing that is economically feasible for families whose income level is categorized as moderate within the standards promulgated by the U.S. Department of Housing and Urban Development (HUD) or the appropriate state housing agency.

Comment: Generally speaking, moderate income is defined as between 50 and 80 percent of the median family income in a particular market area. Economically feasible can be defined as housing costs between 28 and 30 percent of gross family income. HUD also uses the term "very low" to identify families earning 50 percent or less of area median family income; "low," 50 to 80 percent; and "moderate," 80 to 120 percent.

MODULAR HOME

A structure intended for residential use and manufactured off-site in accordance with the local or state code. *See* FACTORY-BUILT HOUSING; MANUFACTURED HOME.

Comment: This definition differs from the one for manufactured home in that it refers to the code that governs the construction of modular homes if other than the Federal Manufactured Home Construction and Safety Standards Code. Where the Code is used, the definition is the same as for manufactured home.

MODULAR-ASSEMBLY-UNIT NEWSRACK

Two or more newsracks assembled in a single housing unit that is supported by one or more pedestals and permanently attached to a sidewalk or concrete pad. *See* NEWSRACK. *See Figure 64.*

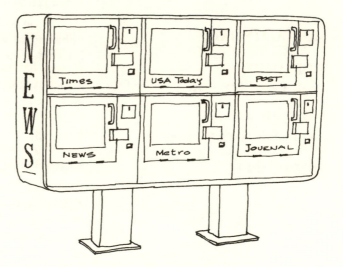

NEWSRACK
MODULAR—ASSEMBLY—UNIT

FIGURE 64

Comment: Modular units are now available in a variety of designs, shapes, and sizes. These units can be selected to reflect community values and eliminate the problem of unsightly clutter and installation control. The illustration shows a double-deck design that requires less sidewalk area; a less-expensive design would be a simple metal rack, elevated about eight inches, and capable of holding several newsracks in place.

MORATORIUM

The legally authorized delay of new construction or development.

Comment: Local moratoriums to halt development activity while local master plans and/or development regulations are prepared or amended are not permitted in many states. However, a recent United States Supreme Court decision on a development moratorium in *Tahoe-Sierra Preservation, Inc. v. Tahoe Regional Planning Agency* (2002) appears to permit such a moratorium. *See Comment* under TAKING.

MORBIDITY RATE

The incidence of a specific disease per specified unit of population.

MORGUE

A place for the storage of human bodies prior to autopsy, burial, or release to survivors.

MORTALITY RATE

The annual number of deaths per thousand population.

MORTUARY

A place for the storage of human bodies prior to their burial or cremation.

MOSQUE

See PLACE OF WORSHIP.

MOTEL

An establishment providing sleeping accommodations for transients.

Comment: There is little distinction between hotels and motels. Traditionally, the motel (motor-hotel) was a one- or two-story, less-expensive accommodation catering to the automobile traveling public, with a majority of all rooms having direct access to the outside without the necessity of passing through the main lobby of the building. Today, rentals range across the entire economic spectrum, multistory structures are common, and motels may offer a full range of services, including restaurants, meeting rooms, entertainment, and recreational facilities. *See* HOTEL.

MOTION PICTURE THEATER

A place where motion pictures are shown to the public for a fee. *See* MEGAPLEX.

MOTOR FREIGHT TERMINAL

See FREIGHT-HANDLING FACILITIES.

MOTOR VEHICLE, ABANDONED

A motor vehicle that 1) is physically inoperable, or missing essential parts to be operable, and has been stored on public property for more than 48 hours; (2) lacks a current license plate and is not stored within a completely enclosed structure or is not currently for sale and stored at a facility licensed for such sales. *See* VEHICLE, JUNK.

MOUNTABLE CURB

See CURB, MOUNTABLE.

MOVING LANE

Any traffic lane where traffic movement is the primary, if not sole, function. (N.J.A.C. 5:21-1.4)

MULCH

A layer of wood chips, dry leaves, straw, hay, plastic, or other material placed on the surface of the soil around plants to retain moisture, to prevent weeds from growing, to hold soil in place, and to aid plant growth.

MULCHING

The application of mulch.

MULTIFAMILY DWELLING

See DWELLING, MULTIFAMILY.

MULTIPHASE DEVELOPMENT

A development project that is constructed in stages, each stage being capable of existing independently of the others.

MULTISERVICE CENTER

A building containing a variety of social services convenient and readily available to the residents of the neighborhood where located.

Comment: Such services may include education, counseling, legal aid, recreation, and health care. It is often associated with and may be located in a church, school, or similar facility. (Schultz and Kasen 1984)

MULTIUSE BUILDING

A building containing two or more distinct uses.

Comment: A multiuse building might include retail stores on the first floor and offices and/or apartments on the upper floors.

MUNICIPALITY

The political subdivision that can adopt and enforce the development ordinances if so empowered by state legislation.

Comment: The development regulations would, under this definition, note the specific legal name of the municipality. In some states, the county or state itself may adopt and enforce development regulations. *See* LOCAL AUTHORITY.

N

Definitions:

National Ambient Air Quality Standards
through
Nursing Home

**NATIONAL AMBIENT
AIR QUALITY STANDARDS**

Standards promulgated by the U.S. Environmental Protection Agency for specified air pollutants, including suspended particulates, sulfur dioxide, carbon monoxide, nitrogen dioxide, ozone, hydrocarbons, and lead. (Schultz and Kasen 1984)

**NATIONAL
ENVIRONMENTAL
POLICY ACT (NEPA)**

A 1969 federal act that established the Council on Environmental Policy and whose purposes include the promotion of efforts to prevent or eliminate damage to the environment and biosphere and to enrich the understanding of the ecological systems and natural resources important to the nation.

**NATIONAL FLOOD
INSURANCE PROGRAM**

A federal program that provides flood insurance.

Comment: See Comment under FLOOD for related definitions.

NATIONAL HISTORIC AREAS

Parts of the National Park System that commemorate historic events, activities, or persons associated with the history of the United States.

Comment: National historic areas include battlefields, monuments, parks, and memorials.

**NATIONAL HISTORIC
PRESERVATION ACT**

A 1966 federal law that established a National Register of Historic Places and the Advisory Council on Historic Preservation and authorized grants-in-aid for historic properties preservation.

**NATIONAL HISTORICAL
LANDMARK**

A site with national historic significance included on the National Register of Historic Places. *See* NATIONAL REGISTER OF HISTORIC PLACES.

**NATIONAL REGISTER OF
HISTORIC PLACES**

The official list, established by the National Historic Preservation Act, of sites, districts, buildings, structures, and objects significant in the nation's history or with unique artistic or architectural value.

Comment: Listing on the National Register does not restrict any activities or actions of the private property owner using private funds. It does, however, place limits on any action of the federal government that might damage the historic nature of the property. Some states have a similar register, and listing on these registers does not apply to private property owners using private money. Only local historic district ordinances can place limits on the actions of a private property owner with respect to a property in that district. *See* HISTORIC AREA; HISTORIC BUILDING; HISTORIC BUILDING

STYLES; HISTORIC PRESERVATION; HISTORIC SITE; NATIONAL HISTORIC PRESERVATION ACT.

NATIVE VEGETATION

See VEGETATION, NATIVE.

NATURAL CONDITION

A condition that arises from or is found in nature and not altered by human intervention.

NATURAL DRAINAGE FLOW

The pattern of surface and stormwater drainage from a particular site before the construction or installation of improvements or prior to any regrading.

NATURAL GRADE

See GRADE, NATURAL.

NATURAL GROUND SURFACE

The ground surface in its original state before any grading, excavation, or filling. *See* GRADE, NATURAL.

NATURAL MONUMENT

(1) A natural feature or object used to define or mark a boundary; (2) any noteworthy natural feature.

NATURAL RECHARGE

Adding water to an aquifer by natural means, such as precipitation, or from lakes and rivers.

NATURAL RESOURCES INVENTORY (NRI)

A survey of existing natural elements, including land, water, air, plant, and animal life, and the interrelationship of these elements.

Comment: The NRI (also known as the environmental resources inventory) usually includes data on soils, geology, topography (including watershed and flood areas), and vegetation. The NRI is an important part of master plan preparation and is useful in the review of subdivision and other development plans. Such studies primarily indicate which areas are environmentally suitable for development and which are not. Depending on study detail, they also can provide: (1) assessment of development capacity; (2) background information useful in the preparation of environmental impact statements; (3) disclosure of current imbalances between development and the environment; and (4) information to residents on the environmental impacts of development.

The NRI is an areawide inventory and, as such, its data may not be sufficiently precise for use in the preparation or detailed review of specific development projects. One of the initial steps in the design review procedure, though, is a check of the proposed plans against the findings of the NRI. This check may provide some design direction or at least alert the reviewing authority to potential environmental problems. This

255

review may also suggest that an environmental impact statement might be necessary.

NATURAL SELECTION

The natural process by which organisms best adapted to their environment survive and those less well adapted are eliminated.

NATURE PRESERVE

An area in which human activities are very limited and where the natural environment is protected from human changes.

Comment: Nature preserves may be large holdings protected by governmental ownership or small parcels restricted by conservation easements. Nature preserve uses are usually limited to hiking and walking trails. *See* CONSERVATION EASEMENT.

NAVIGABLE WATERS

Waterways that are or may be used in their natural state for recreational, travel, or commercial purposes, such as the transporting of goods.

NECKDOWNS

See TRAFFIC CALMING.

NEGATIVE EASEMENT

See EASEMENT, NEGATIVE.

NEIGHBORHOOD

An area of a community with characteristics that distinguish it from other areas and that may include distinct ethnic or economic characteristics, housing types, schools, or boundaries defined by physical barriers, such as major highways and railroads, or natural features, such as water bodies or topography.

Comment: Historically, the neighborhood was defined as the area served by an elementary school, with shopping and recreation facilities to serve neighborhood residents. While the description is probably dated, the neighborhood designation is useful in analyzing the adequacy of facilities and services and in identifying factors affecting the quality of the built environment. In addition, as distinct and identifiable areas, often with their own name, neighborhoods are recognized as fostering community spirit and providing a sense of place—factors recognized as important in community planning. *See* TRADITIONAL NEIGHBORHOOD DEVELOPMENT.

NEIGHBORHOOD BUSINESS AREA

A commercial area, usually located on an arterial or collector street, providing convenience goods and services for residents of the surrounding area. *See* STRIP COMMERCIAL DEVELOPMENT; SHOPPING CENTER.

Comment: The neighborhood business area usually serves residents within a half-mile radius. The stores include food, drugs, hardware, and sundries; services include banks, offices, barber and beauty parlors, cleaners, and laundry facilities. The major characteristic of the neighborhood business area is its scale. It usually does not contain any large stores or uses designed to serve several neighborhoods. Zoning can protect the scale of such areas by placing restrictions on the size of uses.

NEIGHBORHOOD PARK/PLAYGROUND

A park area designed for intense recreational activities including, but not limited to, field games, crafts, playground apparatus, and picnicking.

Comment: The National Recreation and Park Association (NRPA) publishes guidelines and general development standards for a variety of park and recreation facilities. For this use level, NRPA recommends 1.0 to 2.0 acres per 1,000 population, located within safe and easy walking and bike access to the neighborhood population, and which may be developed as part of a local school facility. *See* RECREATION FACILITY.

NEIGHBORHOOD PLAN

The master or specific design plan for a particular neighborhood or district that provides recommended standards and guidelines for future land use and development, open space and recreation areas, streets and circulation, and community facilities. *See* TRADITIONAL NEIGHBORHOOD DEVELOPMENT.

NEIGHBORHOOD SHOPPING CENTER

See NEIGHBORHOOD BUSINESS AREA; SHOPPING CENTER.

NEIGHBORING LOT

The first lot on each side of the subject lot on the same side of the street and any lot that fronts directly across from the subject lot and the lots adjacent thereto.

Comment: The phrase is used in zoning to establish a prevailing setback line or to enforce anti–look-alike clauses. In some ordinances, two lots on either side of the subject lot are used to establish the prevailing setback. When a neighboring lot is vacant, the required setback is assumed and an average distance determines the setback.

NEOTRADITIONAL DESIGN

See TRADITIONAL NEIGHBORHOOD DEVELOPMENT. *See also* White and Jourdan 1997.

NET AREA OF LOT (NET ACREAGE)

The area of the lot excluding those features or areas that the development ordinance excludes from the calculations.

Comment: A development ordinance might exclude, for density or area calculation purposes, undevelopable or critical areas such as floodways, wetlands, areas with steep slopes, or other constrained areas or easements. However, in recent years, court cases have sharply restricted the ability to exclude these lands, particularly where a state land use law defines terms differently. For example, an ordinance might establish the maximum permitted residential density as 15 dwelling units per acre. If the proposed development is located in a state where wetlands cannot be excluded from the area measurement and half of the parcel is wetlands, the density would have to be reduced to 7.5 dwelling units per acre in order to maintain the level of development intensity anticipated by the ordinance.

NET RESIDENTIAL DENSITY

The number of dwelling units relative to the net land area used for residential purposes.

Comment: Net land area used for residential purposes should include local access streets, tot lots or local recreation areas, and a limited amount of open space around the residences. *See* NET AREA OF LOT.

NEW CAR AGENCY

See AUTOMOBILE SALES.

NEW TOWN

A planned community, usually developed on largely vacant land and containing housing, employment, shopping, industry, recreation and open space, and public facilities.

Comment: The term "new town" implies a predetermined population level and phased development over a relatively short period. Reston, Virginia, and Columbia, Maryland, are excellent examples of completed new towns.

NEW URBANISM

See TRADITIONAL NEIGHBORHOOD DEVELOPMENT.

NEWSRACK

One or more self-service or coin-operated boxes, containers, storage units, or other dispensers installed, used, or maintained for the display and sale or distribution of newspapers, periodicals, or other written material. *See* MODULAR-ASSEMBLY-UNIT NEWSRACK. *See Figure 64.*

Comment: Great care must be used in adopting standards to control the location of newsracks located on sidewalks and along public streets. Unreasonable controls, not related to safety, run afoul of First Amendment (freedom of speech) criteria. Where location

258

controls are imposed on newsracks, the basis for the controls has to be carefully documented. For example, accidents attributed to poorly placed newsracks that block drivers' vision would be the kind of documentation needed to support these controls.

Design standards for newsracks are probably defensible, provided they are not overly burdensome and relate to some overall design criteria established for the zone or area where the newsracks are proposed to be located. (Floyd and Reed 1997)

NEWSSTAND

A portable structure, usually not exceeding 100 square feet, from which newspapers, magazines, and other printed material are sold.

Comment: Newsstands usually do not have water or sanitary facilities but may have electricity. They are frequently located on sidewalks at busy intersections, typically in the right-of-way and exempt from the usual building setback requirements. They are often licensed by the municipality.

NIGHTCLUB

An establishment dispensing liquor and meals and in which music, dancing, or entertainment is conducted. *See* TAVERN.

NOISE

(1) Any undesired audible sound; (2) any sound that annoys or disturbs humans or that causes or tends to cause an adverse psychological or physiological effect on humans. (City Code, Dallas, Texas)

Comment: Noise standards are usually not found in zoning or land development ordinances but rather in health ordinances. In addition, many states have adopted noise codes as part of general environmental standards. The state standards often preempt local ordinances or establish maximum noise level standards that municipalities cannot exceed. Where a local ordinance controlling noise is allowed, the traditional definitions used are contained in the American National Standards Institute Standard ANSI S1.1-1971, Acoustical Terminology, as amended.

A local noise ordinance would establish a maximum noise level, usually expressed as an A-weighted sound level in decibels (dBA). While the level varies by jurisdiction, 55 dBA is often cited as the maximum allowed during daylight hours and 45 dBA for evening hours. As noted earlier, many states have established maximum standards that municipalities may not exceed. In addition to maximums, a local ordinance might establish different standards for residential and nonresidential zones and indicate where sound measurements are to be made, for example, at the lot line for industries and zone line for other uses. Finally, an ordinance should distinguish between intermittent and impulsive noise, exempt certain activities (sporting events, occasional outdoor gatherings, and the like), and designate the enforcement officer or office. *See* AMBIENT NOISE LEVEL; A-WEIGHTED SOUND LEVEL; DECIBEL; INTERMITTENT SOUND; INTRUSIVE SOUND; NOISE ATTENUATION; NOISE DISTURBANCE; SOUND-AMPLIFYING EQUIPMENT.

NOISE ATTENUATION

A reduction in the level of a noise source using a substance, material, or surface, such as an earth berm and/or a dense wall. (California General Plan Glossary 1997)

Comment: Jeffrey Grob (in an article entitled "Concrete Examples" in the April 2001 issue of *Planning*), discusses the efficacy, alternatives, and aesthetic issues in noise wall installations along major highways. He notes that "The most effective barriers and those that require the least amount of space are solid walls about a foot thick. Such barriers have a dual effect. They block or deflect sound waves while also eliminating the view of the road. Studies have shown that removing the sound source visually reduces the perceived noise level. Seeing the source of the noise can be almost as distracting as hearing it." (Grob 2001 in Sorvig 2001)

NOISE DISTURBANCE

Any noise exceeding the noise level limits established for the specific zoning district.

NOISE POLLUTION

Continuous or episodic excessive noise in the human environment.

Comment: Noise pollution usually is defined in terms of a maximum decibel level by frequency range.

NOISE WALL

See NOISE ATTENUATION.

NONAMBULATORY HANDICAP

An impairment that, regardless of cause or manifestation, for all practical purposes confines individuals to wheelchairs. *See* AMERICANS WITH DISABILITIES ACT.

NONCONFORMING LOT

A lot, the area, dimensions, or location of which was lawful prior to the adoption, revision, or amendment of the zoning ordinance but that fails by reason of such adoption, revision, or amendment to conform to the present requirements of the zoning district.

NONCONFORMING SIGN

See SIGN, NONCONFORMING.

NONCONFORMING STRUCTURE OR BUILDING

A structure or building, the size, dimensions, or location of which was lawful prior to the adoption, revision, or amendment of the zoning ordinance but that fails by reason of such adoption, revision, or amendment to conform to the present requirements of the zoning ordinance.

NONCONFORMING USE

A use or activity that was lawful prior to the adoption, revision, or amendment of the zoning ordinance but that fails by reason of such adoption, revision, or amendment to conform to the present requirements of the zoning district.

Comment: Ordinances should provide for "certificates of nonconformance" to be issued to property owners and occupants upon application to the zoning officer for a reasonable period (90 to 180 days, for example) after the adoption of a new ordinance or major amendment. The certificate of nonconformance would officially establish the type, extent, and intensity of use taking place on a specific property. It can benefit both the property owner and the zoning authority.

The general policy with respect to nonconforming uses is to provide for their eventual elimination. To accomplish this, most local ordinances impose restrictions on the extent to which a nonconforming use may expand or change. In addition, the ability of the local zoning authority to grant variances for the expansion or change of a nonconforming use is often sharply limited.

A lawful nonconforming use exists when it meets two requirements:

1. It must have existed before the prohibitory regulation was enacted; and

2. The use must have been lawful when the change was enacted.

Thus, a use that was in violation of the zoning ordinance when the ordinance was amended does not gain status as a preexisting and lawful nonconforming use upon adoption of the amendment. It must have been a fully conforming use at the time of the amendment.

There has been considerable case law relating to permissible and impermissible changes in nonconforming uses as well as lawful and unlawful expansions. Mark S.

261

Dennison's "Changing or Expanding Nonconforming Uses" (Dennison 1997) is an excellent article on this subject. It contains case citations and lists permissible and impermissible nonconforming use changes as well as lawful and unlawful nonconforming use expansions based on the cases.

NONCONTIGUOUS PARCEL CLUSTERING

A planning technique that allows one parcel to be preserved in its entirety for farming or open space, while its development rights are transferred to a noncontiguous parcel that is developed at a higher density than otherwise permitted, provided both parcels are considered together as a single cluster development. *See* CLUSTER; CLUSTER SUBDIVISION; LOT AVERAGING.

Comment: The receiving parcel must be suitable for the higher density. In addition, the total number of dwelling units and/or total floor area should not exceed the total allowed on both parcels.

NONPOINT RUNOFF

Surface water entering a channel from no definable discharge source.

NONSLIP

A surface that is tested or approved to be slip resistant by a nationally recognized testing laboratory. *See* AMERICANS WITH DISABILITIES ACT.

NONSTRUCTURAL MANAGEMENT PRACTICES

Controls of stormwater runoff and nonpoint-source pollution such as landscaping techniques, source controls, zoning, setbacks, buffers, or clustering. (N.J.A.C. 5:21-1.4)

NORTH AMERICAN INDUSTRY CLASSIFICATION SYSTEM (NAICS)

A standard code system to describe and classify business establishments based on the activities in which they are primarily engaged.

Comment: The NAICS became the new standard code system in 1997, when it replaced the old Standard Industrial Classification (SIC) system. It classifies business establishments into 20 two-digit broad categories as compared with the 10 divisions in the old SIC. The 20 broad categories are then further subdivided into three-, four-, five-, and six-digit categories. A total of 1,170 different industries and business activities are identified. The sector breakdowns are shown in table N-1.

    The NAICS can be used by planners to develop various land use categories and identify changes of use. A zoning ordinance could identify specific NAICS business sectors or subsectors as permitted uses in

TABLE N-1: NAICS UNITED STATES STRUCTURE

Sector	Name	Sub-sector	Industry Groups	NAICS 5-Digit Industries	U.S. 6-Digit Industries	Total U.S. Industries	New Industries
11	Agriculture, Forestry, Fishing, and Hunting	5	19	42	32	64	20
21	Mining	3	5	10	28	29	—
22	Utilities	1	3	6	6	10	6
23	Construction	3	14	28	—	28	3
31–33	Manufacturing	21	84	184	408	474	79
42	Wholesale Trade	2	18	69	—	69	—
44–45	Retail Trade	12	27	61	18	72	17
48–49	Transportation and Warehousing	11	29	42	25	57	28
51	Information	4	9	28	12	34	20
52	Finance and Insurance	5	11	32	15	42	23
53	Real Estate and Rental and Leasing	3	8	19	9	24	15
54	Professional, Scientific, and Technical Services	1	9	35	17	47	28
55	Management of Companies and Enterprises	1	1	1	3	3	1
56	Administrative and Support and Waste Management and Remediation Services	2	11	29	23	43	29
61	Educational Services	1	7	12	7	17	12
62	Health Care and Social Assistance	4	18	30	16	39	27
71	Arts, Entertainment, and Recreation	3	9	23	3	25	19
72	Accommodation and Food Services	2	7	11	7	15	10
81	Other Services (except Public Administration)	4	14	30	30	49	19
92	Public Administration	8	8	29	—	29	2
	TOTAL	96	311	721	659	1,170	358

Source: NAICS (North American Industry Classification System). 1997. Washington, DC: U.S. Department of Commerce, National Technical Information Service.

appropriate zones. The local ordinance would still control the intensity of development through the bulk regulations. (NAICS 1997)

NUISANCE

A condition or situation that results in an interference with the enjoyment and use of property.

NUISANCE ELEMENT

Any environmental pollutant, such as smoke, odors, liquid wastes, solid wastes, radiation, noise, vibration, glare, or heat.

NURSERY, RETAIL

The growing, cultivation, storage, and sale of garden plants, flowers, trees, shrubs, and fertilizers, as well as the sale of garden tools and similar accessory and ancillary products, to the general public. *See* GREENHOUSE.

Comment: Also known as garden centers, retail nurseries can generate significant volumes of traffic, but only during limited periods, such as the spring planting season and some holidays. Site plan review of parking and circulation should provide safe circulation and convenient parking, keeping in mind, however, the temporary nature of the impact.

Another issue is that of nursery greenhouses. These are enclosed, permanent structures and should be regulated in terms of setbacks, lot coverage, and other bulk controls.

NURSERY, WHOLESALE

The growing, cultivation, storage, and sale of garden plants, flowers, trees, and shrubs to landscapers, developers, builders, and retail nurseries.

Comment: Wholesale nurseries are large-scale operations, encompassing extensive land areas, a considerable amount of mechanical equipment, and selling and delivering large amounts of material to single customers, such as builders and landscapers. Many wholesalers also run retail operations, and most ordinances usually allow some retail sales. From a practical point of view, wholesalers who want to sell to the retail market should be permitted to do so as long as the site plan review process addresses the different impacts of retail operations versus wholesale.

NURSERY SCHOOL

See CHILD-CARE CENTER.

NURSING HOME

See EXTENDED CARE FACILITY; INTERMEDIATE CARE FACILITY; LONG-TERM CARE FACILITY.

O

OBSOLESCENCE

A loss in value due to reduced desirability and usefulness of a structure because its designed construction becomes outmoded. (Johnsich 1991)

OBSTRUCTION

Any dam, wall, embankment, levee, dike, pile, abutment, soil, material, bridge, conduit, culvert, building, wire, fence, refuse, fill, structure, or other matter in, along, across, or projecting into any channel, watercourse, or floodplain that may impede, retard, or change the direction of the flow of water, either in itself or by catching debris carried by such water, or that is placed where the flow of water might carry the same downstream.

OCCUPANCY OR OCCUPIED

The residing of an individual or individuals overnight in a dwelling unit or the storage or use of equipment, merchandise, or machinery in any public, commercial, or industrial building; (2) holding real property by being in possession. (Johnsich 1991)

OCCUPANCY PERMIT

A required permit allowing the use of a building or structure after it has been determined that all the requirements of applicable ordinances have been met.

Comment: The occupancy permit may be a temporary one for a given period of time to permit completion of certain improvements. For example, installation of landscaping may be delayed because of weather or season. Obviously, a temporary permit would not be granted if the unfinished or incomplete improvement is essential to the use or affects health or safety.

One of the problems in granting temporary permits is the difficulty in halting operations or evicting tenants if the temporary permit expires. Consequently, many jurisdictions grant temporary permits reluctantly or not at all.

OCCUPANCY RATE

The ratio of occupied space or dwelling units to total space or dwelling units.

OCCUPANT

The individual, individuals, or entity in actual possession of a premise.

OCCUPATION

Gainful employment in which an individual engages to earn compensation.

ODD-LOT DEVELOPMENT

See INFILL.

ODOROUS MATTER

Any material that produces an olfactory response in a human being.

Comment: Unlike excessive light and noise, which are relatively easy to identify and measure and for which effective limits have been established, odor is difficult to measure and maximum levels of performance hard to establish. Rafson (1999) notes that when we refer to odors, we generally mean unpleasant odors, but some pleasant odors, "if omnipresent," can be an annoyance as well.

Rafson also notes that various odors can be quantified using direct measurements in a laboratory or by indirect odor measurements on-site. In most cases, the measurement uses trained panelists ". . . who identify the level at which they can no longer tell the diluted odor from clean air." This method is called the "Dilutions to Threshold" (D/T) method, using an ASTM International procedure (E-679-91) for measuring odors. Other methods compare the odorous material to an established standard, for example, the amount of odorous material that can be detected by at least 50 percent of a group of observers. Indirect methods use mass spectroscopy and gas chromatography to identify compounds and compare them with standard concentrations.

Developing effective zoning regulations for odors requires expert assistance from scientists with experience in this field.

OFFER

A proposal to enter into an agreement with another party.

OFFICE

A room or group of rooms used for conducting the affairs of a business, profession, service, industry, or government and generally furnished with desks, tables, files, and communication equipment.

Comment: The term "office" is almost generic, not requiring the spelling out of all the functions that may be carried out in an office. Indeed, as modern technology expands, office functions include tasks that in the past would have been considered production, industrial, or commercial. For example, desktop publishing, high-speed data transmission, and large varieties of research are now carried out in offices. While goods or merchandise are sold from offices, the transactions usually take place by phone or data transmission.

OFFICE, HOME

A home occupation in which a part of a dwelling unit is used as the resident's office. *See* HOME OCCUPATION.

OFFICE, PROFESSIONAL

See PROFESSIONAL OFFICE.

OFFICE BUILDING

A building used primarily for conducting the affairs of a business, profession, service, industry, or government, or like activity; it may include ancillary services for office workers, such as a restaurant, coffee shop, newspaper or candy stand, and child-care facilities.

Comment: Office buildings are often classified as Class A, B, or C, which generally refers to the age of the structure and amenities, although a renovated older building could be classified as a Class A building.

Typical controls for offices include floor area ratio (FAR), height, setbacks, impervious surface coverage, parking, lighting, signs, and landscaping requirements. A typical suburban office building FAR may range from .15 to .30. Town and small city FARs range from 1 to 5, with FARs in major cities often in excess of 15.

OFFICE PARK

A development on a tract of land that contains a number of separate office buildings, with accessory and supporting uses, and open space designed, planned, constructed, and managed on an integrated and coordinated basis.

Comment: For mortgage or other reasons, individual buildings and parcels can be subdivided from the entire office park. However, cross easements and agreements on drainage, circulation, maintenance, parking, signage, landscaping, and access must be in place before the subdivision is permitted and made part of the resolution of subdivision approval.

OFFICIAL MAP

An ordinance in map form adopted by the governing body that conclusively shows the location and width of existing and proposed streets, public facilities, public areas, and drainage rights-of-way.

Comment: State regulations vary as to what may be shown on an official map. The purpose is to prevent private development from encroaching on sites for proposed public improvements. However, most states require that governmental entities move to acquire the land within a relatively short period of time (often one year) after approval of a development application for the land. In addition, an option fee may be required for the year. There is often a waiver of taxes on the property during the option period.

OFFICIAL SOIL MAP

Maps that are part of a Soil Conservation Service soil survey that delineates various soil types.

Comment: Soil surveys contain information on soil characteristics, including depth to bedrock, height of water table, slopes, permeability, size of rocks, erodibility, and other characteristics. The soil surveys may also contain aerial photographs on which the locations of the various types of soil within a particular geographic area are shown. More detailed on-site surveys and investigations may be needed to verify the types and locations of soils before a development plan is prepared.

OFFICIAL SOILS INTERPRETATION

The written description of soil types and their characteristics and accompanying maps that are part of a recognized soil survey.

OFF-ROAD VEHICLE

See VEHICLE, OFF-ROAD.

OFFSHORE FACILITIES

Any facility floating or supported on a pier or piers, seaward of the outer harbor line, used to transfer or assemble materials or for construction purposes.

OFF-SITE

Located outside the lot lines of the lot in question but within the property (of which the lot is a part) that is the subject of a development application or within a contiguous portion of a street or other right-of-way. *See Figure 65.*

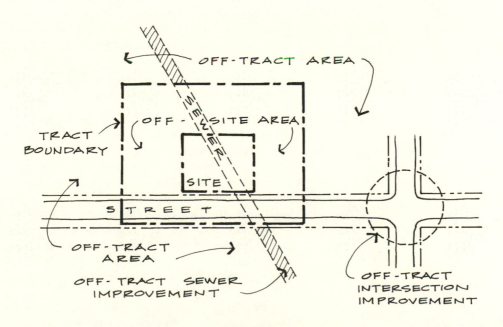

FIGURE 65

269

OFF-SITE IMPROVEMENT

An improvement required to be made off-site as a result of an application for development and including, but not limited to, road widening and upgrading, stormwater facilities, and traffic improvements.

Comment: Off-site improvements are imposed as a condition of development approval. The type and extent of the improvements should be spelled out in the development ordinance. Typically, a proposed development adjacent to a narrow road would be required to widen and improve the road on the development side and install curbs and drains. When the property across from the development is not expected to be improved in the immediate future, though, municipalities often opt for requiring the developer to improve the entire width of the road to a somewhat lesser extent than normally required rather than have one-half the width totally improved and one-half in relatively poor condition.

OFF-SITE PARKING

Parking provided for a specific use but located on a site other than the one on which the specific use is located.

Comment: Many ordinances permit off-site parking provided it is located reasonably close to the use it is designed to serve. A distance of 300 to 400 feet is considered the maximum. Off-site parking offers an advantage in that it encourages a grouping of parking (shared parking) for more than one use. In some cases, shared parking can result in the need for fewer spaces than the sum of individual uses. *See* PARKING, SHARED.

OFF-STREET LOADING

Designated areas located adjacent to buildings where trucks may load and unload cargo.

Comment: A minimum dimension of 14 by 55 feet is needed to accommodate modern tractor-trailers plus maneuvering space. Site design should provide wide aisles, large turning radii, and space for backing up. Since many trucks load and unload throughout the night or early in the morning, and many are refrigerator trucks requiring noisy machinery to be kept going at all times, the nature and location of adjacent uses should be taken into consideration in locating the off-street loading areas. Landscaping, berms, and solid fencing may be needed for buffering.

OFF-STREET PARKING SPACE

A temporary storage area for a motor vehicle that is directly accessible to an access aisle and that is not located on a dedicated street right-of-way. *See Figure 68.*

OFF-TRACT

Not located on the property that is the subject of a development application or on a contiguous portion of a street or other right-of-way. *See Figure 65.*

OFF-TRACT IMPROVEMENT

An improvement required to be made off-tract as a result of an application for development.

Comment: The assessment for off-tract improvements can be complicated. Most state land use laws permit only a proportionate share assessment and require the facility to be improved to have a "rational nexus" to the project. Consequently, a developer cannot, for example, be required to pay for the entire improvement of an intersection that is seriously congested even without the new project. The developers could be made to provide for their fair share of any improvement needed to accommodate the traffic impact of the new development.

"Rational nexus" means that the project has a discernible impact on the facility proposed to be improved. The impact of a major traffic generator on adjacent intersections is obvious. The impact on one 10 miles away probably does not meet the rational nexus test. *See* RATIONAL NEXUS.

OIL CHANGE FACILITY

An establishment that provides the lubrication and/or checking, changing, or additions of those fluids and filters necessary to the maintenance of a motor vehicle.

Comment: The line between "quick lube" establishments and other types of specialized auto maintenance establishments such as tire and muffler shops is quickly becoming blurred. "Service maintenance stations without fuel" may be a more appropriate term.

OLIGOTROPHIC LAKES

Deep lakes that have a low supply of nutrients, contain little organic matter, and are characterized by high water transparency and high dissolved oxygen.

ON-SITE

Located on the lot that is the subject of an application for development. *See Figure 65.*

ON-SITE WASTEWATER DISPOSAL SYSTEM

A set of components or systems that treat, convey, and dispose of domestic wastewater on-site. *See* SEPTIC SYSTEM.

Comment: The system includes septic systems, aerobic treatment systems, activated sludge systems, recirculating sand filters, gravel, pipes, and leach chambers. (Bowers 2001)

ON-STREET PARKING SPACE

A temporary storage area for a motor vehicle that is located on a dedicated street right-of-way. *See Figure 68.*

ON-TRACT

Located on the property that is the subject of a development application or on a contiguous portion of a street or other right-of-way. *See Figure 65.*

ONE HUNDRED PERCENT LOCATION

A real estate term identifying the prime business location usually able to command the highest commercial and office rentals for a particular area or municipality.

ONEROUS

Burdensome or oppressive.

Comment: (1) As a condition of development approval, an onerous requirement is one that has no clear, direct or substantial relationship to the development; (2) in connection with deeds, titles, gifts, or contracts, the consideration given is of greater value than the one received. (Johnsich 1991)

OPACITY

(1) The property of a substance that renders it partially or wholly obstructive to the transmission of visible light; (2) degree of obscuration of light.

Comment: The range of opacity is from 0 to 100 percent. For example, clear glass has 0 percent opacity and a wall has 100 percent opacity.

OPEN BURNING

Uncontrolled burning of wastes in an open area.

OPEN MEETING OR HEARING

A meeting open to the public.

Comment: Open meetings may be required by statute under a "sunshine law." However, the fact that a meeting is required to be open to the public does not necessarily mean that the public can participate. Public participation usually is permitted only at a public hearing, with notice duly posted and advertised.

OPEN SPACE

Any parcel or area of land or water, essentially unimproved and set aside, dedicated, designated, or reserved for public or private use or enjoyment or for the use and enjoyment of owners, occupants, and their guests.

Comment: Open space may include active recreational facilities, such as swimming pools, play equipment for youngsters, ball fields, court games, and picnic tables. The improved recreation facilities, though, would be only a small part of the overall open space. The open space might include incidental parking and access roads.

OPEN SPACE, COMMON   Land within or related to a development, not individually owned or dedicated for public use, that is designed and intended for the common use or enjoyment of the residents of the development and their guests and that may include such complementary structures and improvements as are necessary and appropriate. *See Figure 19.*

OPEN SPACE, NATURAL   An open space area not occupied by any structures or impervious surfaces. See GREEN AREA; GREENBELT.

OPEN SPACE, PRIVATE   Common open space, the use of which is limited to the occupants of a single dwelling, building, or property.

OPEN SPACE, PUBLIC   Open space owned by a public agency and maintained by it for the use and enjoyment of the general public.

OPEN SPACE ELEMENT   That section of the master plan of the municipality or other jurisdiction that provides an inventory of public and private open space lands and proposed goals, policies, and implementation programs for the preservation, acquisition, and management of open space lands.

OPEN SPACE RATIO   Total area of open space divided by the total site area in which the open space is located. *See Figure 66.*

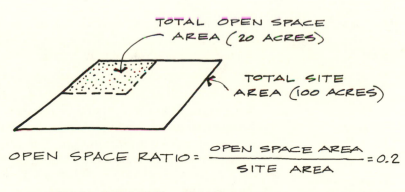

OPEN SPACE RATIO CALCULATION

FIGURE 66

OPTION   An exclusive right to purchase, rent, or sell a property at a stipulated price and within a specified time.

ORDINANCE   A law or regulation adopted by a governing body.

ORGANIC

Referring to or derived from living organisms.

ORGANISM

Any living human, plant, or animal.

ORIENTATION

The placement of a structure on its lot with regard to other structures, natural elements such as sun and wind, and impacts from noise, glare, and similar adverse elements.

ORIGIN AND DESTINATION STUDY

A transportation study that records the location where a trip begins and where it ends.

ORNAMENTAL TREE

A deciduous tree planted primarily for its beauty, color, flower, or leaf, rather than for screening purposes.

Comment: Ornamental trees tend to be smaller at maturity than shade trees. (American Planning Association, *Preparing a Landscaping Ordinance*, Planning Advisory Service Report No. 431, 1990)

OUTBUILDING

A separate accessory building or structure not physically connected to the principal building.

Comment: Outbuildings are smaller than the principal structure and may be used for storage or ancillary purposes. On estates, outbuildings are often the living quarters for employees.

OUTDOOR RETAIL SALES

See RETAIL SALES, OUTDOOR.

OUTDOOR STORAGE

The keeping, in an unenclosed area, of any goods, junk, material, merchandise, or vehicles in the same place for more than 24 hours. *See* RETAIL SALES, OUTDOOR.

Comment: Many ordinances prohibit outdoor storage entirely or allow it only in certain restricted zones and in the rear yard only. In addition, the outdoor storage is required to be screened from public view by a fence, wall, or heavy landscaping. Where allowed, it must be on the same lot as the establishment or use for which it is providing the storage. For especially obnoxious outdoor storage uses such as junkyards, large setbacks from the street, solid fences, and a maximum height of stored material should be required.

There are uses, however, that typically and traditionally include outdoor storage and displays. These include new and used car dealers, agriculture, plant and landscaping establishments, and parking lots. Hardware stores and gas stations often display merchandise outdoors. The local ordinance should establish controls over these uses to ensure they do not become nuisances, pose safety problems, and become aesthetic disasters. These controls should include traditional site plan review, minimum setbacks from street rights-of-way and property lines, sign controls, and landscaping requirements.

OUTFALL

The mouth of a sewer, drain, or conduit where an effluent is discharged into the receiving waters.

OUTLET STORE

See RETAIL OUTLET STORE.

OUTPATIENT FACILITY

See CLINIC.

OVERFLOW RIGHTS

An easement that allows an owner to run excess water onto another's land.

OVERFLOWED LAND

A floodplain or land subject to frequent flooding. *See* FLOODPLAIN.

OVERHANG

The part of a roof or wall that extends beyond the facade of a lower wall (*see Figure 17*).

OVERLAY ZONE

A zoning district that encompasses one or more underlying zones and that imposes additional requirements beyond those required for the underlying zone.

Comment: Overlay zones deal with special situations that are not appropriate to a specific zoning district or that apply to several districts. For example, in all business zones, an overlay provision might require impact fees to provide for traffic improvements. A historic district overlay may cover parts of several zones. An overlay provision covering an entire municipality or specific zoning districts might require that all properties over a certain acreage proposed for higher-density development also provide a percentage of lower-income housing. (American Planning Association, *The Administration of Flexible Zoning Techniques*, Planning Advisory Service Report No. 318, 1976)

OWNER

An individual, firm, association, syndicate, partnership, or corporation having sufficient proprietary interest to seek development of land.

OXIDATION POND

An artificial lake or pond in which organic wastes are reduced by bacterial action.

OZONE

A pungent, colorless, toxic gas.

Comment: Ozone is one component of photochemical smog and is considered a major air pollutant.

P

PACKAGE TREATMENT PLANT *See* ON-SITE WASTEWATER DISPOSAL SYSTEM.

PAD (1) A paved space, with utility connections, in a mobile home park for the parking of a mobile home; (2) the proposed site of a freestanding use within a shopping center. *See* MOBILE HOME SPACE.

PAPER STREET *See* STREET, PAPER.

PARAPET The extension of the main walls of a building above the roof level. *See Figure 17.*

Comment: Parapet walls often are used to shield mechanical equipment and vents. Many ordinances permit a parapet wall to extend beyond the maximum height limits.

PARATRANSIT A form of public transportation service characterized by the flexible routing and scheduling of small vehicles such as taxis, vans, and small buses, to provide shared-occupancy, doorstep, or curbside personalized transportation service.

PARCEL (1) A piece or area of land formally described and recorded with block and lot numbers, by metes and bounds, by ownership, or in such a manner as to specifically identify the dimensions and/or boundaries; (2) informally, as land in general.

Comment: The term is often used generically to describe a piece of land often without specific boundaries, such as "that hilly parcel" or "all agricultural parcels."

PARK, PRIVATE A tract of land owned or controlled and used by specific and designated entities or persons for active and/or passive recreational purposes.

PARK, PUBLIC A tract of land owned by a branch of government and available to the general public for recreational purposes.

Comment: Public parks may also be owned by private entities and made available to the public. For example, a service club or nonprofit institution may dedicate land for park or open space purposes. As long as the land is available to the general public in the same manner as parks owned by a branch of government, it can be considered a public park.

PARK-AND-RIDE FACILITY A parking lot designed for drivers to leave their cars and use mass transit facilities beginning, terminating, or stopping at the park-and-ride facility.

Comment: Park-and-ride facilities are often called "intercept facilities."

PARKING, BANKED

Required parking, the construction of which is permitted to be deferred until needed.

Comment: Many municipalities permit or even encourage a part of the required parking for a development to be landscaped and not constructed until the demand for the parking materializes. The applicant receives all necessary planning and engineering approvals for the banked parking at the time the development receives its original approval. Only when the additional parking is needed, as determined by the applicant or required by the approving authority, is a construction permit secured and the parking installed. The advantages to the municipality are less runoff, more landscaping, and better aesthetics, even if temporary. The applicant saves money by not having to construct the improvement.

PARKING, SHARED

Joint utilization of a parking area for more than one use.

Comment: Shared parking involves parking spaces that are used at different times by different uses. A shared parking space serves several stores so that a vehicle does not have to be moved from place to place. The classic example is the mall movie theater that, because of off-peak-hour use, may not generate any additional parking demand.

Each type of joint use reduces the total number of spaces needed. Shopping center parking is an example of a shared parking facility. Instead of computing the parking requirement for each use, a ratio of parking spaces to total square footage is used. *See* PARKING RATIO.

PARKING ACCESS

The part of a parking lot or parking area that allows motor vehicles ingress and egress from the street. *See Figure 68.*

PARKING AREA

Any public or private area, under or outside of a building or structure, designed and used for parking motor vehicles, including parking lots, garages, private driveways, and legally designated areas of public streets. *See* GARAGE.

PARKING AREA, PRIVATE

A parking area for the exclusive use of the owners of the lot on which the parking area is located or whomever else they permit to use the parking area.

278

PARKING AREA, PUBLIC

A parking area available to the public, with or without payment of a fee.

PARKING BAY

The parking module consisting of one or two rows of parking spaces and the aisle from which motor vehicles enter and leave the spaces. *See Figure 68.*

PARKING LANE

A lane designed to provide on-street parking.

Comment: Parking lanes are usually located on one or both sides of the street. On very wide streets, however, the parking lane can be in the center of the cartway. In areas where traffic volumes are high, parking lanes may be restricted during rush hours and used only for vehicular travel.

PARKING LOOP

A private street with perpendicular parking.

PARKING LOT

An off-street, ground-level open area that provides temporary storage for motor vehicles. *See* PARKING AREA.

Comment: Parking lots may provide access to other uses, such as dwellings, offices, stores, and so on. They are not designed for permanent storage unless permitted by the local ordinance.

PARKING METER

A device operated by the insertion of coins or other acceptable payment method, installed adjacent to a vehicle parking space on streets or parking areas for the purpose of limiting the amount of time a vehicle can park.

Comment: Newer parking meters accept credit cards, and some municipalities are now using single meters for entire parking lots or on-street parking. These meters disperse slips of paper, which are displayed on the dashboard of vehicles and show when the time has expired.

PARKING RATIO

The number of parking spaces required per 1,000 square feet of gross floor area.

Comment: Parking ratios may also be expressed in terms of one space per unit of floor area—for example, one space for each 250 square feet of floor area for offices. Some ordinances base the ratio on net floor area, excluding bathrooms, hallways, and similar areas from the count. Gross floor area is easier to compute and more accurately reflects parking demand. Basements and attics are usually excluded from gross floor area unless they are occupied. However, a basement used for storage frees up other space for workers and thus contributes to the total parking demand. While the general practice is to compute parking ratio on a floor area basis, other standards have been used, such as number of classrooms, hospital beds, or motel rooms. But practices change. For example, a majority of medical and surgical procedures are now accomplished on an outpatient basis, sharply reducing demand for visitor spaces. The ITE handbook, *Trip Generation* (Institute of Transportation Engineers 1997), suggests that local surveys are the most accurate method for determining parking needs.

For nonresidential uses, floor area remains the most widely used standard. Typical ratios for nonresidential uses are as follows:

Use	Parking Ratio (Spaces per 1,000 ft.^{2})
Retail mall	5.5
Retail (individual)	4.5
Wholesale	1.0
Industrial	2.5
General office use	4.0
Medical office	5.0

For residential land uses, most ordinances require a specific number of spaces for each dwelling-unit type. For example:

Dwelling-Unit Type	Spaces Required (per unit)
Single-family	2.5
Town house	2.0
Garden apartment	1.5
High-rise	1.0

The ratios should be adjusted downward, or a cap placed on the number of off-street spaces, when a particular area is served by mass transit, shared parking is available, or the municipality, as a land-use policy, uses on-street parking to meet parking demand. Additional parking, often 10 percent of the required number of spaces, is needed for visitor parking for multifamily developments. Driveway space (10 feet x 20 feet), provided it clears the sidewalk, can be counted toward the required off-street parking for single- or two-family houses. Garages also can be counted as part of the required parking despite the fact that, in many situations, the garage becomes a storage area.

Finally, many municipalities encourage applicants, particularly in the case of nonresidential development, to bank a part of the parking and construct it only when the need is apparent. *See* PARKING, BANKED. (American Planning Association, *Off-Street Parking Requirements: A National Review of Standards*, Planning Advisory Service Report No. 432, 1990)

PARKING SPACE

A space for the parking of a motor vehicle within a public or private parking area. *See* OFF-STREET PARKING SPACE; ON-STREET PARKING SPACE; STALL. *See Figure 67.*

PARKING SPACE, HANDICAPPED

A space in a parking area with stall dimensions, access, and signage conforming to the Americans with Disabilities Act (ADA) or applicable state standards. *See* AMERICANS WITH DISABILITIES ACT (ADA). *See Figure 5.*

PARKING STRUCTURE

A building or structure consisting of more than one level and used to store motor vehicles. *See* GARAGE; GARAGE, MUNICIPAL; GARAGE, PUBLIC.

PAROCHIAL SCHOOL

See SCHOOL, PAROCHIAL.

PARSONAGE

See CLERGY RESIDENCE.

PARTIAL DESTRUCTION

A building or structure that, because of fire, flood, explosion, or other calamity, requires the rebuilding of less than half of the original floor area.

Comment: The rebuilding of partially destroyed buildings becomes an issue when the building or use does not conform to current development regulations. Most ordinances stipulate that if a substantial part of a building or structure is damaged and requires rebuilding, the new structure must meet current requirements. It is difficult to arrive at an enforceable and easily applicable standard that describes the extent of destruction beyond which a nonconforming structure may not be rebuilt. Some ordinances base it on value, others on the amount of floor area that has to be replaced. Many municipalities require a conforming structure when 50 percent of the value or floor area is destroyed. Others permit any damaged or destroyed building to be rebuilt, regardless of the amount of area or percentage of

281

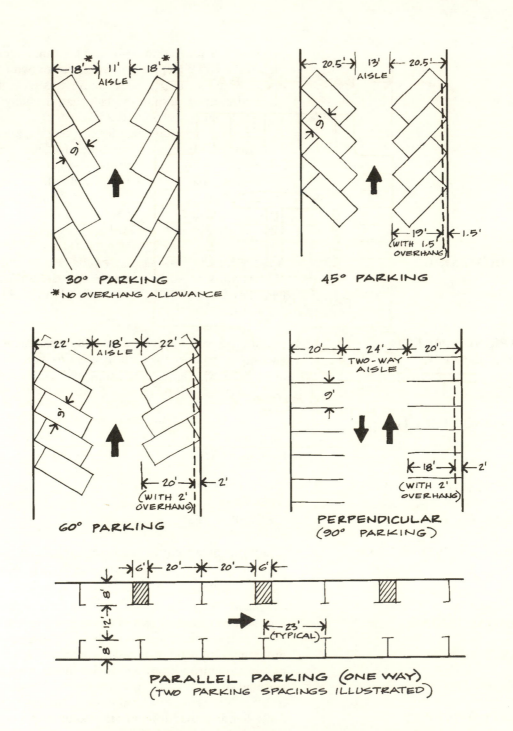

30° PARKING
*NO OVERHANG ALLOWANCE

45° PARKING

60° PARKING

PERPENDICULAR
(90° PARKING)

PARALLEL PARKING (ONE WAY)
(TWO PARKING SPACINGS ILLUSTRATED)

PARKING AREA DIMENSIONS
(FOR STANDARD-SIZE VEHICLES)

FIGURE 67

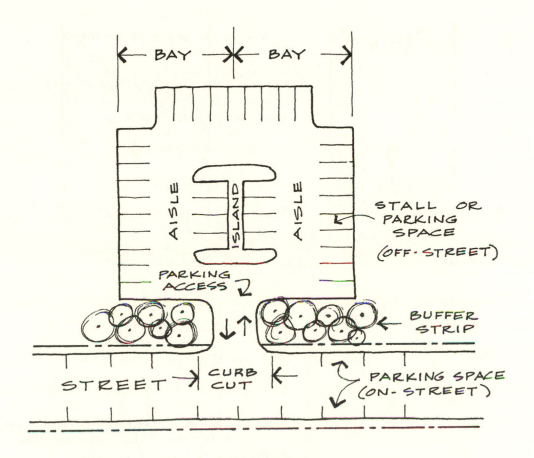

FIGURE 68

value. In the process of application review, the approving authority will often attempt to mitigate some of the zoning deficiencies.

PARTIAL TAKING

The condemnation of part of a property. *See* TAKING.

PARTICULATES

Finely divided solid or liquid particles in the air or in an emission, including dust, smoke, fumes, mist, spray, and fog.

PARTY DRIVEWAY

A single way providing vehicular access to two or more properties. *See* COMMON PASSAGEWAY. *See Figure 3*.

PARTY IMMEDIATELY CONCERNED

For purposes of notice, "party immediately concerned" means any applicant for development, the owners of the subject property, and all owners of property and government agencies entitled to notice under a zoning ordinance, subdivision regulations, or other development regulations.

283

PARTY WALL

A common wall shared by two attached structures, buildings, or dwelling units. *See Figure 3.*

PASEO

A connecting walkway that links streets and parking areas, open plazas, courtyards, and residential and business uses within an urban center.

PASSENGER VEHICLE

See VEHICLE, PASSENGER.

PASSIVE RECREATION

See RECREATION, PASSIVE.

PATH

A cleared way for pedestrians and/or bicycles that may or may not be improved.

PATHOGENIC

Causing or capable of causing disease.

PATIO

See TERRACE.

PATIO HOME

See DWELLING, PATIO HOME.

PAVEMENT

(1) A created surface, such as brick, stone, concrete, or asphalt, placed on the land to facilitate passage; (2) that part of a street having an improved surface.

PAVERS

Preformed paving blocks that are installed on the ground to form patterns while at the same time facilitating pedestrian and vehicular travel.

Comment: Pavers provide an attractive alternative to concrete or asphalt for walkways, driveways, and residential or light-duty parking areas.

PEAK-HOUR TRAFFIC

The highest number of vehicles passing over a designated section of a street during the busiest 1-hour period during a 24-four-hour period.

PEAT

Partially decomposed organic material.

PEDESTRIAN

An individual who travels on foot.

PEDESTRIAN GENERATOR

A development or project that will realize high facility use by people arriving on foot. (N.J.A.C. 5:21-1.4)

Comment: A pedestrian generator can trigger the need for sidewalks in areas where sidewalks are not normally required. For example, in a low-density residential area, sidewalks might not be required if the density is less than one dwelling unit per acre. Construction of a school, a typical pedestrian generator, would permit the approving agency to require sidewalks to be constructed.

PEDESTRIAN MALL

An area of streetlike proportions devoted entirely to pedestrian traffic. *See* MALL.

Comment: Pedestrian malls may be open or enclosed. In urban areas they are often converted streets, with added amenities such as landscaping and street furniture.

PEDESTRIAN SCALE

The proportional relationship between an individual and his or her environment.

Comment: Pedestrian scale is an informal and subjective standard. It suggests that the relationship between the person and his or her environment, whether natural or created, is comfortable, intimate, and contributes to the individual's sense of accessibility.

PEDESTRIAN TRAFFIC COUNT

The number of people who walk past a single point during a specified period of time.

PEDESTRIAN WALKWAY

A right-of-way for pedestrians, separate from vehicular traffic and including access ramps, stairs, mechanical lifts, and routes through buildings and other areas that are available for public use.

PENINSULA

A projection of land surrounded on three sides by water.

PENINSULA LOT

A lot surrounded on three sides by roads. *See Figure 69.*

PENINSULA LOT

FIGURE 69

Comment: Peninsula lots for residential use should be avoided whenever possible. They lack privacy and since they "front" on three streets, front yard setbacks are required on three sides. Accessory structures (sheds, swimming pools, and so on) are prohibited in any of the front yards unless allowed by variance. In addition, the lot is subjected to traffic from three roads and abuts two intersections.

285

PENTHOUSE

An enclosed structure located on the roof of a building. *See Figure 17.*

Comment: Penthouses may be used for a variety of purposes, such as offices, apartments, or for mechanical equipment serving the building. Penthouses housing mechanical equipment are often excluded from building height requirements. Penthouses designed for occupancy, such as offices or apartments, are usually counted as another story although some ordinances allow penthouses to occupy up to 20 percent of the roof area without being counted. They would, however, be included within maximum floor area ratio calculation.

PEOPLE MOVER

A conveyor system designed for carrying pedestrians.

PERCOLATION

Downward flow or infiltration of water through the pores or spaces of rock or soil.

PERCOLATION TEST

A test designed to determine the ability of ground to absorb water and used to determine the suitability of soil for drainage or for septic system use.

PERFORMANCE GUARANTEE

Any security that may be accepted by a municipality to ensure that improvements required as part of an application for development will be satisfactorily completed.

Comment: Performance guarantees may be cash, surety bond, or letter of credit. In fact, the performance guarantee may be any security permitted by state or local ordinance. *See* MAINTENANCE GUARANTEE.

PERFORMANCE STANDARDS

A set of criteria or limits relating to certain characteristics that a particular use or process may not exceed.

Comment: The standards regulate the characteristics of an activity rather than the activity itself. The standards usually cover noise, vibration, glare, heat, air or water contaminants, and traffic. The performance standard approach is based on the technical ability to identify activities by impact and to measure them to determine if they meet ordinance requirements. *See* PERFORMANCE ZONING. (American Planning Association, *Performance Standards for Growth Management*, Planning Advisory Service Report No. 461, 1996)

PERFORMANCE ZONING

Zoning regulations that permit uses based on a particular set of standards rather than on a particular type of use. *See* PERFORMANCE STANDARDS.

PERGOLA

A structure of parallel colonnades supporting an open roof of crossing rafters or trelliswork.

PERIMETER

The boundaries or borders of a lot, tract, or parcel of land.

PERMAFROST

A permanently frozen soil layer.

PERMEABILITY

The speed with which water can drain through soil. *See* PERCOLATION; PERCOLATION TEST.

PERMEABLE PAVEMENT SYSTEM

An alternate or supplemental stormwater management system using cast-in-place or precast modular units, both of which create voids for gravel or grass. *See Figure 70.*

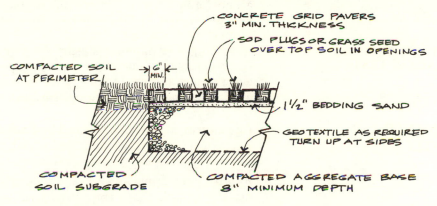

PERMEABLE PAVEMENT SYSTEM
(SECTION)

FIGURE 70

Comment: Cast-in-place systems are very strong when reinforced with welded wire mesh. They are more expensive and labor-intensive than are systems using the precast modular pavers. Plastic flexible systems have less intrinsic strength than concrete pavers, but with adequate base and subgrade preparation, they are fully capable of supporting heavy loads. Flexible pavers are also more easily laid over irregular surfaces.

Grass infill (sodding for plastic, seeding for concrete) is more labor intensive and expensive than gravel. In addition, a period of one to two months is required to allow the grass to become established, and the traffic on grass should not exceed one to two trips per day.

In research reported by Booth and Leavitt (1999), the differences in runoff from permeable and impermeable surfaces is "quite dramatic" and "where soil conditions are suitable, permeable pavements are quite successful at managing runoff from small and moderate storms." The authors note that both types of permeable pavements accomplish the hydrologic goal of infiltration well but point out that they differ in how well they can handle high traffic volumes and in their appearance.

PERMIT

Written governmental permission issued by an authorized official, empowering the holder thereof to do some act not forbidden by law but not allowed without such authorization.

PERMITTED USE

Any use allowed in a zoning district and subject to the restrictions applicable to that zoning district.

PERMITTEE

Any person to whom a permit is issued.

PERPETUITY

Lasting forever; continuous and eternal; unlimited in respect to time. (*Black's* 1999)

PERSON

A corporation, company, association, society, firm, partnership, or joint stock company, as well as an individual, a state, and all political subdivisions of a state or any agency or instrumentality thereof.

PERSONAL SERVICES

Establishments primarily engaged in providing services involving the care of a person or his or her personal goods or apparel.

Comment: Personal services usually include the following: laundry, including cleaning and pressing service; linen supply; diaper service; beauty shops; barbershops; shoe repair; funeral services; steam baths; reducing salons and health clubs; clothing rental; locker rental; porter service; and domestic services.

PERSONAL WATERCRAFT

A small vessel that uses an outboard or inboard motor to power a water jet pump as its primary source of motive power and that is designed to be operated by a person sitting, standing, or kneeling on the vessel.

PERVIOUS SURFACE

Any material that permits full or partial absorption of stormwater into previously unimproved land. *See* IMPERVIOUS SURFACE; PERMEABLE PAVEMENT SYSTEM. *See Figure 56.*

PESTICIDE

An agent used to control pests.

Comment: Pesticides include insecticides for use against harmful insects; herbicides for weed control; fungicides for control of plant disease; rodenticides for killing rats, mice, and such; and germicides used in disinfectant products, algaecides, and slimicides. Some pesticides, particularly if they are misused, can contaminate water, air, or soil and accumulate in humans, animals, and the environment.

PESTICIDE TOLERANCE

A scientifically and legally established limit for the amount of chemical residue that can be permitted to remain in or on a harvested food or feed crop as a result of the application of a chemical for pest-control purposes.

pH

A measure of the acidity or alkalinity of a material, liquid, or solid.

Comment: A pH of 7 is considered neutral. Below 7 is acidic; above 7 is alkaline.

PHARMACY

A place where drugs and medicines are prepared and dispensed. *See* DRUGSTORE.

PHASING

Development undertaken in a logical time and geographical sequence.

Comment: The approving authority must ensure that each phase can exist as a separate entity if the project does not continue to buildout. Improvements for any phase that are geographically located in other phases must be installed and maintained prior to or coincident with construction of the phase to be served. Both objectives can be ensured by establishing deadlines, requiring performance guarantees, and withholding occupancy permits until all required improvements are installed and operating. *See* CONCURRENCY.

PHOTOCHEMICAL SMOG

Air pollution associated with oxidants rather than with sulfur oxides, particulates, or similar materials.

PHYSICAL HANDICAP

A physical impairment that confines a person to a wheelchair; causes a person to walk with difficulty or insecurity; affects the sight or hearing to the extent that a person functioning in a public area is insecure or exposed to danger; causes faulty coordination; or reduces mobility, flexibility, coordination, and perceptiveness to the extent that facilities are needed to provide for the safety of that person. *See* AMERICANS WITH DISABILITIES ACT.

289

PICNIC AREA

A place equipped with tables, benches, grills, and trash receptacles for people to assemble, cook, eat, and relax.

Comment: Picnic areas are passive recreation areas and could include rest rooms, play facilities, and open shelters.

PIER

(1) A column, used to support a structure; (2) any fixed or floating structure for securing vessels, loading or unloading persons or property, or providing access to the water, including wharves, docks, floats, or other landing facilities, and dry docks. (American Planning Association, *Glossary of Zoning, Development and Planning Terms*, Planning Advisory Service Report 491/492, 1999)

PIERHEAD LINE

A line beyond which no structure may extend out into navigable waters.

PILASTER

A column partially embedded in a wall and usually nonstructural.

PILOT PLANT

A facility used to test out concepts and ideas, to determine physical layouts, material flows, type of equipment required, costs, and to secure other information prior to full-scale production.

Comment: The pilot plant is usually an intermediate step between research and full-scale production. It requires monitoring and supervision by other than the usual production personnel and may involve frequent changes in physical layout, natural flow, or even processes. Pilot plants may produce production-grade goods, especially during the latter stages of the pilot process. However, if the pilot plant is switched to full production and operation and used for other than testing, it should be treated as a principal permitted use. Most development ordinances allow some percentage of research facilities, usually not more than 25 percent of the floor area, to be used for pilot plant operations.

PLACE OF WORSHIP

(1) A church, synagogue, temple, mosque, or other facility that is used for prayer by persons of similar beliefs; (2) a special-purpose building that is architecturally designed and particularly adapted for the primary use of conducting formal religious services on a regular basis.

Comment: The major problem associated with places of worship is that very often the accessory uses may create greater impact than the primary use. Places of worship may include schools, meeting halls, recreational facilities, day care, counseling, homeless shelters, and kitchens capable of feeding hundreds of persons. They are often rented out for weddings and other social events. In previous years, churches drew primarily from the neighborhood in which they were located. Today, the area they serve may be considerably larger. Care should be taken in drafting any ordinance regulating places of worship to ensure that the accessory uses do not become nuisances.

While such uses may be desirable in residential areas, conditional use controls on lot size, parking, access, setbacks, and buffering may be appropriate to avoid adverse neighborhood impacts. Depending on a facility's size and outreach, its specific location should be controlled—for example, frontage on a major road or location as a transitional use between a residential and nonresidential zone. *See Comment* under CONDITIONAL USE.

Some places of worship enjoy greater popularity during certain holidays. While it is not necessary to plan for peak use, there should be some consideration given to the several holidays or holy days within the year when occupancy will be two to three times that of normal worship services.

Finally, the recently enacted federal Religious Land Use and Institutionalized Persons Act of 2000 (Public Law 106-274, 114 Stat. 803, 42 U.S.C. §2000cc et seq.) states:

(1) *General Rule*—No government shall impose or implement a land use regulation in a manner that imposes a substantial burden on the religious exercise of a person, including a religious assembly or institution, unless the government demonstrates that imposition of the burden on that person, assembly or institution

(A) is in furtherance of a compelling government interest; and

(B) is the least restrictive means of furthering that compelling governmental interest.

It clearly places the burden on the municipality to prove that any regulation that imposes restrictions on houses of worship is needed and necessary. Some attorneys suggest that it even precludes the prohibition of houses of worship, whether in the form of bulk controls or location. Any restrictions on houses of worship must be carefully documented and spelled out to provide a firm basis in the event of litigation. For a detailed discussion on religious land-use issues, see the September 2001 issue of the American Planning Association's *Land Use and Zoning Digest*, Vol. 53, No. 9.

PLANNED DEVELOPMENT (PD)

An area of a minimum contiguous or noncontiguous size, planned, developed, operated, and maintained as a single entity and containing one or more structures to accommodate retail, service, commercial, industrial, office, and residential uses or a combination of such uses, and appurtenant common areas and accessory uses, customary and incidental to the predominant uses. *See* PLANNED DEVELOPMENT, COMMERCIAL; PLANNED DEVELOPMENT, INDUSTRIAL; PLANNED-UNIT RESIDENTIAL DEVELOPMENT.

Comment: The local land development ordinance should specify the minimum area required for a planned development. Many ordinances require a minimum of 5 acres for planned-unit residential development (PURD), where the predominant use is residential, and 10 acres for other types of planned developments.

All planned developments have a number of features in common, and the definition emphasizes those features. They are planned, developed, operated, and maintained as a single entity. The resolution of approval of a planned development establishes the parameters by which the PD operates, including parking and circulation, landscaping, signage, lighting, security, and waste disposal. Where a lot or parcel in the PD is to be subdivided out for mortgaging or financing purposes (a fairly common occurrence), cross-easements are required to allow all the conditions of approval to be enforced. Where the local ordinance permits noncontiguous lands to be considered as part of the PD, the location and use of the noncontiguous parcels should be rationally related; that is, close enough to permit all the conditions of approval to be uniformly and reasonably applied.

While many ordinances list specific conditions for various types of PDs, the current trend is to consider them all as planned unit developments (PUDs) without any preconditions on the mix of uses. Many PUDs have a mix of housing, office, commercial, and industrial uses, along with retail and service facilities. The local ordinance would still establish maximum floor area ratios (FARs) for nonresidential uses and maximum densities for residential uses, as well as bulk controls, so that the overall intensity of development is controlled. This type of planning requires that the proposed PD be planned and developed within the context of an overall master plan for the municipality.

Since PDs are developed over many years, with a significant upfront expenditure in infrastructure, the local ordinance usually permits approvals extending well beyond the usual 3 to 5 years for preliminary and final approvals for conventional development, with 20 years not uncommon. In addition, the local ordinance permits changes in the mix of uses, based on market demands. If the overall number of dwelling units and the square footage of nonresidential uses remains the same, or is reduced, the changes can be achieved without the necessity of additional expensive and often time-consuming public hearings and the many exhibits required for new applications.

PLANNED DEVELOPMENT, COMMERCIAL (PCD)

An area of at least 10 contiguous or noncontiguous acres in size to be planned, developed, operated, and maintained as a single entity and containing one or more structures with appurtenant common areas to accommodate office, retail, and commercial uses, and other uses incidental to the predominant commercial use.

Comment: The ordinance spells out the details, including limitations on land use and bulk controls. *See Comment* under PLANNED DEVELOPMENT.

PLANNED DEVELOPMENT, INDUSTRIAL (PID)

An area of at least 10 contiguous or noncontiguous acres in size to be planned, developed, operated, and maintained as a single entity and containing one or more structures with appurtenant common areas to accommodate industrial, manufacturing, warehousing, office, retail, and commercial uses, and other uses incidental to the predominant industrial use.

Comment: The ordinance could specify the percentage of land to be used for various uses. For example, it may limit retail use to reduce traffic and may also limit the percentage of warehousing use to encourage office development.

PLANNED-UNIT RESIDENTIAL DEVELOPMENT (PURD)

An area of at least 5 contiguous or noncontiguous acres in size to be planned, developed, operated, and maintained as a single entity and containing one or more residential clusters, which may include appropriate commercial, public, or quasi-public uses primarily for the benefit of the residential development.

293

Comment: The land development ordinance could include limitations on the various housing types to be located in the PURD and the maximum densities permitted by housing type.

PLANNING BOARD

The duly designated planning board of the municipality, county, or region.

Comment: The planning board (also known as planning agency or planning commission) is created by ordinance with the responsibility for reviewing and approving applications for development, preparation of master plans, and other duties as specifically provided for in the state enabling act.

PLANNING OMBUDSMAN

An official appointed by the mayor to help resolve disputes between builders and applicants and the public.

Comment: The ombudsman serves as a facilitator, often gathering facts, presenting positions, suggesting alternatives, and making recommendations to the approving authority. While the definition calls for the position to be filled by the mayor, it can be a planning board appointment or one appointed by the governing body or as specified in the enabling legislation.

PLAT

(1) A map representing a tract of land, showing the boundaries and location of individual properties and streets; (2) a map of a subdivision or site plan.

PLAT, FINAL

A map of all or a portion of a subdivision or site plan that is presented to the approving authority for final approval. *See* FINAL APPROVAL.

Comment: Approval of the final plat usually is granted only on the completion or installation of all improvements or the posting of performance guarantees ensuring the completion or installation of such improvements. The final approval is generally required before property can be transferred or building permits issued.

PLAT, PRELIMINARY

See PRELIMINARY APPROVAL; PRELIMINARY PLAN.

PLAT, SKETCH

A layout of a proposed subdivision, site plan, or development scheme of sufficient accuracy and detail to be used for the purpose of discussion and classification.

Comment: Many planning boards and development review agencies encourage applicants to submit sketch plats or plans for informal, conceptual, and nonbinding reviews prior to the preparation of detailed plans.

PLAYGROUND

An active recreational area with a variety of facilities, including equipment for younger children as well as court and field games. *See* NEIGHBORHOOD PARK/PLAYGROUND; RECREATION FACILITY.

Comment: The playground is usually located next to an elementary school and serves the neighborhood (a half-mile radius). Playgrounds vary in size, depending on the type of equipment and games.

PLAZA

An open space that may be improved and landscaped; usually surrounded by streets and buildings. *See* COURT; SQUARE. *See Figure 14.*

PLOT

(1) A single-unit parcel of land; (2) a parcel of land that can be identified and referenced to a recorded plat or map.

PLUME

The visible emission from a flue or chimney.

POINT OF TANGENCY

The point at which a curved line meets a straight line. *See Figure 26.*

POINT SOURCE

A stationary source of an individual emission, generally of an industrial nature. *See* AREA SOURCE; STATIONARY SOURCE.

POLLUTANT

Any introduced gas, liquid, or solid that makes a resource unfit for a specific purpose.

POLLUTION

The presence of matter or energy whose nature, location, or quantity produces undesired environmental effects.

POPTOPS

Second-story or higher additions, at least one story higher than surrounding structures. *See* COMPATIBLE DESIGN.

PORCH

A roofed, open area, which may be screened, attached to or part of a building, and with direct access to or from it. *See* PORTICO. *See Figure 9.*

POROSITY

A measure of the amount of space between grains or cracks that can fill with water.

PORTICO

(1) An open-sided structure attached to a building and sheltering an entrance or serving as a semienclosed space (Nelessen 1994); (2) a roofed area supported by columns, forming a front porch (Johnsich 1991). *See* PORCH.

POTABLE WATER

Water suitable for drinking purposes.

POWER CENTER

Three or more freestanding, large-scale retail stores with shared parking. *See* RETAIL STORE, LARGE- SCALE.

PPM

Parts per million.

Comment: A measurement commonly used to represent the amount of pollutant concentration in a liquid or gas.

PRECIPITATE

A solid that separates from a solution because of some chemical or physical change.

PRECIPITATION

In pollution control work, any of a number of air pollution control devices, usually using mechanical or electrical means, to collect particulates from an emission.

PREEMPTIVE RIGHT

The right of a riparian owner to a preference in the acquisition of lands under tidewaters adjoining the owner's upland. *See* RIPARIAN LAND.

PREEXISTING USE

The use of a lot or structure prior to the time of the enactment of a zoning ordinance. *See* NONCONFORMING USE.

Comment: Many municipalities, at the time a new zoning or development ordinance is enacted, survey existing uses in order to provide an accurate record of preexisting nonconforming uses. The preexisting nonconforming use, legal prior to the time of the passage of the ordinance but made nonconforming as a result of the ordinance, has a legal right to continue. Future problems arise because of confusion as to the extent and nature of the use at the time of passage. Hence, an inventory is often necessary to ensure that nonconforming uses do not expand illegally.

PRELIMINARY APPROVAL

"Preliminary approval" means the conferral of certain rights prior to final approval, after specific elements of a development plan have been approved by the approving authority and agreed to by the applicant.

Comment: Preliminary approval generally freezes the terms and conditions required of an applicant for a specified period of time, often three to five years. It protects against any changes in zoning or other conditions of approval during that period. Preliminary approval usually involves public hearings and serious planning board input to the design. All specific conditions of approval are spelled out during the preliminary approval phase.

PRELIMINARY FLOOR PLANS AND ELEVATIONS

Architectural drawings, prepared during the early and introductory stages of a project, illustrating the scope, scale, and relation of the project to its site and immediate environs.

PRELIMINARY PLAN

A map or plan, with supporting documentation, showing the proposed layout of the subdivision or site plan that is submitted for preliminary approval. *See* PRELIMINARY APPROVAL.

Comment: While the term is "preliminary," the submission requirements for preliminary plan approval are detailed and extensive. The preliminary plan requires detailed engineering drawings of the proposed development, road profiles, utility layouts, drainage calculations, stormwater control plans, soil erosion and sediment control plans, environmental and community impact statements, and landscaping plans. For site plans, requirements include lighting plans, signage, circulation, parking plans, and building plans and elevations.

PRELIMINARY PLAT

See PRELIMINARY PLAN.

PREMATURE SUBDIVISION

Platted lands, legally filed in the county or state recording office, lacking all or some improvements such as, but not limited to, roads, curbs, sidewalks, and utilities, and not meeting current development standards.

Comment: In many premature or antiquated subdivisions, lots have been sold and some houses constructed, despite a lack of streets or utilities. Current practices have largely eliminated the premature subdivision by requiring improvements to be installed, or bonds posted to ensure their completion, before building permits are issued. Where premature subdivisions do exist, municipalities often use their redevelopment powers to acquire the lands, clear up title problems, and repackage the property for subsequent redevelopment. Some states permit municipalities to require replatting, lot mergers, or automatic street vacation after notice, when certain conditions have been met. These include no lot sales for several years (five, for example), bankruptcy or disappearance of the developer, failure to complete improvements, and a finding of imminent danger to the public health and safety. (American Planning Association, *Zoning News*, April and May 1997 issues)

PREMISES

A lot, parcel, tract, or plot of land together with the buildings and structures thereon.

PRESCRIPTION

The securing of a title to property by adverse possession of land by right of continuous use without protest from the owner. (Johnsich 1991)

Comment: The time period for a prescription is usually 20 years. *See* ADVERSE POSSESSION.

PRESERVATION, HISTORIC

See HISTORIC PRESERVATION.

PRESERVE

Open space that preserves or protects endangered species, critical environmental features, viewsheds, or other natural elements.

PRETREATMENT

In wastewater treatment, any process used to reduce the pollution load before the wastewater is introduced into a main sewer system or delivered to a treatment plant.

PRIMARY TREATMENT

The first stage in wastewater treatment in which substantially all floating or settleable solids are removed by screening and sedimentation.

PRINCIPAL BUILDING

See BUILDING, PRINCIPAL.

PRINCIPAL ENTRANCE

The place of ingress and egress used most frequently by the public.

PRINCIPAL USE

The primary or predominant use of any lot or parcel.

PRIVATE CLUB

A building and related facilities owned or operated by a corporation, association, or group of individuals established for the fraternal, social, educational, recreational, or cultural enrichment of its members and not primarily for profit and whose members pay dues and meet certain prescribed qualifications for membership. *See* LODGE.

Comment: Private clubs may include sleeping and dining facilities for members and guests. In some cases, the dining facilities may be open to the public.

PRIVATE SCHOOL

See SCHOOL, PRIVATE.

PRO RATA

In proportion.

Comment: "Pro rata" refers to improvements required to be constructed by developers that benefit more than one development. For example, when a road or sewer main is extended through several developments, each developer must pay a fair share of the improvement cost.

298

PROBABILITY

A statistical method that calculates the chance that a specific event will occur.

PROCESS WEIGHT

The total weight of all materials, including fuels, introduced into a manufacturing process.

Comment: The process weight is used to calculate the allowable rate of emission of pollutant matter from the process.

PROCESSING

A series of operations, usually in a continuous and regular action or succession of actions, taking place or carried on in a definite manner.

Comment: The term "processing" is usually associated with the chemical transformation of materials or substances into new products and may include the blending and combining of gases and liquids. However, the term also may be applied to a specific industrial or manufacturing operation.

PROCESSING AND WAREHOUSING

The storage of materials in a warehouse or terminal, and where such materials may be combined, broken down, or aggregated for transshipment or storage and where the original material is not chemically or physically changed.

Comment: "Processing and warehousing" is a single term and must be defined as such. Otherwise, the word "processing," which is akin to manufacturing, describes a manufacturing facility, which could also contain warehousing space, not uncommon in a manufacturing operation. The term "processing and warehousing" as defined refers essentially to a storage and shipment place as opposed to a manufacturing establishment.

PROFESSIONAL OFFICE

The office of a member of a recognized profession maintained for the conduct of that profession. *See* HOME OCCUPATION; HOME PROFESSIONAL OFFICE.

PROHIBITED USE

A use that is not permitted in a zone district.

Comment: Older zoning ordinances usually listed those uses specifically prohibited in each zone. New technology often created uses that were clearly inappropriate for certain zones, but because they were not listed as prohibited uses, they became permitted uses. Most ordinances today are permissive ordinances, and a use not specifically permitted is prohibited.

PROJECTION

(1) A prediction of a future state based on an analysis of what has happened in the past; (2) part of a building

or structure that is exempt from the bulk requirements of the zoning ordinance.

Comment: Usually bay windows, steps, and chimneys may project into required yards, and parapet walls and mechanical equipment on roofs may exceed the height limitation.

PROPERTY   A lot, parcel, or tract of land together with the building and structures located thereon.

PROPERTY LINE   *See* LOT LINE.

PROSPECTIVE NEED   A projection of low- and moderate-income housing needs based on the development and growth that are reasonably likely to occur in a region or municipality.

PROTECTIVE COVENANT   *See* RESTRICTIVE COVENANT.

PUBLIC ADMINISTRATION   Legislative, judicial, administrative, and regulatory activities of federal, state, local, and international governmental agencies.

Comment: Government-owned and -operated business establishments are excluded from this category and are classified in accordance with the major activity.

PUBLIC AREAS   Parks, playgrounds, trails, paths, and other recreational areas and open spaces; scenic and historic sites; schools and other buildings and structures; and other places where the public is directly or indirectly invited to visit or permitted to congregate.

Comment: Historically, all public areas were owned by a governmental agency. This is not necessarily the case any longer. For example, malls and shopping areas and private plazas with benches are public areas in the sense that they invite the public in to browse, sit, walk, and congregate. Shopping malls, for instance, have become popular meeting places for people. While legally private property, they are functionally public areas.

PUBLIC ASSEMBLY AREA   Any area where large numbers of individuals collect to participate or to observe programs of participation.

Comment: The most common public assembly areas are auditoriums, stadiums, gymnasiums, or comparable facilities under different names—for example, field house, banquet room, and theater.

PUBLIC BUILDING   (1) Any building used exclusively for public purposes by any department or branch of government; (2)

300

buildings of an institutional nature and serving a public need, such as houses of worship; hospitals; schools; libraries; museums; post offices; police, rescue, and fire stations; and public utilities and services.

PUBLIC DEVELOPMENT PROPOSAL

A master plan, redevelopment plan, capital improvement program, or other land development proposal or plan adopted by the appropriate public agency and including possible implementation options.

Comment: A public development proposal identifies a concept plan, sketch, idea, or suggestion that has moved beyond the preliminary phase toward implementation.

PUBLIC DOMAIN

All lands owned by the government.

PUBLIC DRAINAGE WAY

Land owned or controlled by a governmental agency that is reserved or dedicated for the installation of stormwater sewers or drainage ditches, or is required along a natural stream or watercourse for preserving the channel and providing for the flow of water so as to safeguard the public against flood damage, sedimentation, and erosion.

PUBLIC GARAGE

See GARAGE, PUBLIC.

PUBLIC HEARING

A meeting announced and advertised in advance and open to the public, with the public given an opportunity to talk and participate.

Comment: Public hearings are often required before adoption or implementation of a master plan, project, ordinance, or similar activity that will have an effect on the public.

PUBLIC HOUSING

Housing that is constructed, bought, owned, or rented and operated by a local housing authority for households meeting designated income limits. *See* LOCAL HOUSING AUTHORITY; LOW-INCOME HOUSING.

PUBLIC IMPROVEMENT

Any improvement, facility, or service, together with its associated site or right-of-way, necessary to provide transportation, drainage, utilities, or similar essential services and facilities and that is usually owned and operated by a governmental agency.

Comment: The requirement that public improvements be owned and operated by a governmental agency is changing. Public improvements may be owned by a governmental agency and leased to a private entity to provide the service or operate a facility. Conversely, the government may lease a private facility to carry out a governmental function. In both situations, the improvement, facility, or service is still considered a public improvement.

PUBLIC NOTICE

The advertisement of a public hearing in a paper of general circulation, and through other media sources, indicating the time, place, and nature of the public hearing and where the application and pertinent documents may be inspected.

PUBLIC OPEN SPACE

See OPEN SPACE, PUBLIC.

PUBLIC SERVICE

Relating to the health, safety, and welfare of the population.

Comment: The term is often used in defining inherently beneficial uses or public utilities.

PUBLIC SEWER AND WATER SYSTEM

Any system other than an individual septic tank, tile field, or individual well, that is operated by a municipality, governmental agency, or a public utility for the collection, treatment, and disposal of wastes and the furnishing of potable water.

PUBLIC TRANSIT SYSTEM

Any vehicle or transportation system owned, operated, or regulated by a governmental agency used for the mass transport of people.

PUBLIC UTILITY

A closely regulated enterprise with a franchise for providing to the public a utility service deemed necessary for the public health, safety, and welfare.

Comment: All states regulate public utilities, but the kinds of uses that are classified as a public utility differ from state to state. For example, cellular telephone service is classified as a public utility in New York but not in New Jersey. The threshold question as to whether a use is a public utility is whether it is so defined in the applicable state legislation. When it is, it obviously must be considered a public utility; even if it is not defined as such, it may still be a public utility for zoning purposes if it has the following characteristics:

- Provides a service that is essential to the public health, safety, and general welfare. This critical criterion rules out radio stations, which, while important, are not essential to public health, safety, and general welfare.

- Is regulated by a governmental agency. The regulatory agency may be a federal or state agency.

(In the example of cellular phones, the Federal Communications Commission is the regulatory agency, regardless of whether the state also regulates them.)

- Is granted an exclusive or near-exclusive franchise for a specific geographic area. (At one time, public utilities were given exclusive rights to provide the service in the franchised area. In recent years, more than one utility may be permitted to operate in a geographic area.)

- Is required to provide service to all who apply within its franchised area.

- May have the right of condemnation.

- Is usually exempt from local development requirements or can appeal such requirements to an administrative agency.

PUBLIC UTILITY EASEMENT

A right granted by an owner of property to a public utility or governmental agency to erect and maintain poles, wires, pipes, or conduits on, across, or under the land, for telephone, electric power, gas, water, sewers, or other utility services. *See* EASEMENT, UTILITY.

PUBLIC UTILITY FACILITIES

Buildings, structures, and facilities, including generating and switching stations, poles, lines, pipes, pumping stations, repeaters, antennas, transmitters and receivers, valves, and all buildings and structures relating to the furnishing of utility services, such as electric, gas, telephone, water, sewer, and public transit, to the public.

PUBLIC WORKS

Things constructed by the government at public expense for general public use, such as highways and public buildings. (Johnsich 1991)

PULVERIZATION

The crushing or grinding of material into small pieces.

PUMPING STATION

A building or structure containing the necessary equipment to pump a fluid to a higher level.

PUTRESCIBLE

Capable of being decomposed by microorganisms with sufficient rapidity to cause nuisances from odors or gases.

Q

Definitions:

Quadruplex

through

Quiet Enjoyment

QUADRUPLEX   *See* DWELLING, QUADRUPLEX.

QUARRY   *See* EXTRACTIVE INDUSTRIES.

QUALITY OF LIFE   The attributes or amenities that combine to make an area a desirable place to live.

Comment: Examples of attributes or amenities include the availability of political, educational, and social support systems; good relations among constituent groups; a safe and healthy physical environment; and economic opportunities for both individuals and businesses.

QUARTER-SECTION   A tract of land one-half mile square, 2,640 feet by 2,640 feet, or 160 acres.

QUASI-PUBLIC USE   A use owned or operated by a nonprofit, religious, or eleemosynary institution and providing educational, cultural, recreational, religious, or similar types of programs.

Comment: The term is somewhat antiquated. A quasi-public use should be included under the definition of institutional or public uses.

QUENCH TANK   A water-filled tank used to cool incinerator residues.

QUORUM   A majority of the full authorized membership of a board or agency.

Comment: In general, no public agency meeting may be held in the absence of a quorum, except to adjourn the meeting to a specified date and time. Once a quorum is present, all actions may be taken by a majority vote of those present and eligible to vote. Failure to receive the number of votes required for approval constitutes a denial. In those applications for development in which a simple majority of the vote would suffice, a tie vote amounts to a denial.

A member of a public body who abstains from voting is, under the common law rule, counted toward a quorum and is regarded as having assented to the vote of the majority. However, when a statute requires the *affirmative* vote of a majority to approve a measure, it has been held that one who abstains from voting cannot be considered as having voted affirmatively. (Cox 2003)

QUIET ENJOYMENT   The right of an owner or occupant to the use of property without interference of possession. (Johnsich 1991)

R

RACQUET SPORTS   Court games played with a racquet and ball either indoors or outdoors on various surfaces.

RADIAL STREET SYSTEM   A pattern of streets converging on a central point or
area. *See Figure 71.*

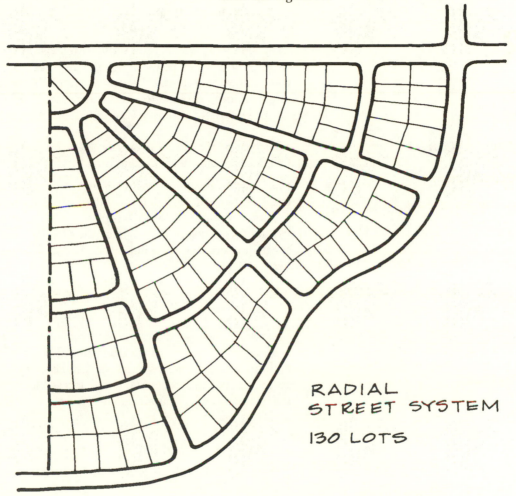

RADIAL
STREET SYSTEM
130 LOTS

FIGURE 71

RADIATION   Energy that propagates through space.

Comment: While lay people use the term with particular reference to ionizing radiation (as produced by
a nuclear reactor, for example), the energy can be in
any form: acoustic (as in ultrasonic radiation), light
(as from a flashlight), high-energy particles (as cosmic
radiation), high energy photons (as X-rays), and radio-
frequency electromagnetic fields.

RADIATION STANDARDS

Regulations that include exposure standards, permissible concentrations, and regulations for transportation of radioactive material.

RADIO AND TELEVISION BROADCASTING STATION

An establishment engaged in transmitting oral and visual programs to the public and which consists of a studio, transmitter, tower, and antenna(s). *See* STUDIO.

Comment: The studio for a radio or television broadcasting station may be located some distance from the transmitter and antenna. The transmitter and antennas must be located close to each other. *See* WIRELESS TELECOMMUNICATIONS TOWERS AND FACILITIES.

RADIO FREQUENCY

That part of the electromagnetic spectrum employed by many communications and broadcast applications.

Comment: The exact frequency range to which this refers is defined variously by different authors. The Federal Communications Commission refers to radio-frequency energy as that part of the electromagnetic spectrum between 300 kilohertz (KHz) and 100 gigahertz (GHz).

RADIOACTIVE WASTES

The by-products of nuclear reactors and military, industrial, and medical activities using radioactive material.

Comment: Disposal and storage of radioactive wastes is a major concern. Storage sites should be safe from natural disasters (such as hurricanes and earthquakes), away from population centers, and accessible without traversing heavily populated areas. (Schultz and Kasen 1984)

RAILROAD YARD

An area for the storage and repair of trains.

Comment: Railroad yards may include open storage yards, rail-switching equipment, roundhouses, and workshops.

RAINFALL, EXCESS

The portion of rainfall that becomes direct surface runoff.

RAISED CROSSWALKS

See TRAFFIC CALMING.

RAISED INTERSECTIONS

See TRAFFIC CALMING.

RAMP

(1) A sloping walkway, roadway, or passage used to join and provide a smooth transition between two levels of different elevations; (2) driveways leading to parking aisles.

Comment: For ramps accessible to the handicapped, the Americans with Disabilities Act specifies a maximum slope of 1 to 12 (8.33 percent).

RANCH
A place where livestock are bred and/or raised but that does not include a concentrated animal feeding operation. *See* CONCENTRATED ANIMAL FEEDING OPERATION.

RANCHETTE
A single dwelling unit occupied by a nonfarming household on a parcel that has been subdivided from agricultural land.

Comment: This term is used by developers to give some cachet to relatively large lots located in rural or exurban areas. To qualify as a farm for tax assessment purposes, state regulations, which often establish minimum acreage and annual farming income, would have to be met.

RASP
A device used to grate solid waste into a more manageable material, ridding it of much of its odor.

RATABLE
An improvement producing revenues to the taxing authority.

RATABLE PROPERTY
Real property subject to tax by a municipality or other taxing district.

RATIONAL NEXUS
A clear, direct, and substantial relationship between a particular development and the off-tract public improvement needs generated by the development.

Comment: Rational nexus is an important method for apportioning the cost of off-tract improvements. *See* LINKAGE PROGRAMS; OFF-TRACT IMPROVEMENT.

RAVINE
(1) A long, deep hollow in the earth's surface; (2) a valley with sharply sloping walls created by the action of stream waters.

RAW LAND
Land in its natural state before development. *See* UNIMPROVED LAND.

RAW SEWAGE
Untreated wastewater.

REAL ESTATE
Land, tenements, and other hereditaments or rights therein, and whatever is made part of or is attached to it by nature or by humans; the land and all improvements thereon. (Johnsich 1991)

REALIGNED INTERSECTION

See TRAFFIC CALMING.

REALLOCATED PRESENT NEED

That part of a municipality's present affordable housing need that is redistributed to other municipalities in the region.

Comment: Affordable housing need consists of a municipality's indigenous or existing need, reallocated present need, and prospective need. The reallocated present need is that part of a region's present need that has been proportionally reallocated from municipalities with obligations in excess of the regional average.

REAR LANE

See ALLEY.

REAR LOT LINE

See LOT LINE, REAR.

REAR YARD

See YARD, REAR.

REASONABLE ACCOMMODATIONS

See HANDICAP.

REASONABLE USE DOCTRINE

A common law principle that prohibits the use of one's property in such a way as to deprive others of the lawful enjoyment of their property.

RECEIVING MUNICIPALITY

A municipality that agrees to assume a part of another municipality's fair share obligation.

Comment: Some states permit one municipality to transfer part of its lower-income housing obligation to another willing municipality for a fee. In New Jersey, these transfers are permitted as part of a "regional contribution agreement." *See* SENDING MUNICIPALITY.

RECEIVING WATERS

Rivers, lakes, oceans, or other water bodies, including underground aquifers, that receive treated or untreated wastewaters.

RECHARGE

The addition to, or replenishing of, water in an aquifer.

RECLAIMED LAND

See MADE LAND.

RECREATION, ACTIVE

Leisure-time activities, usually of a formal nature and often performed with others, requiring equipment and taking place at prescribed places, sites, or fields.

Comment: The term "active recreation" is more a word of art than one with a precise definition. It obviously includes swimming, tennis and other court games, baseball, and track, and other field sports and playground activities. There is a legitimate difference of opinion as to whether park use per se may be considered active recreation, although obviously some parks contain activity areas that would qualify.

RECREATION, PASSIVE

Activities that involve relatively inactive or less energetic activities, such as walking, sitting, picnicking, board and table games.

Comment: The reason for the differentiation between active and passive recreation is their potential impacts on surrounding land uses. Passive recreation can also mean open space for nature walks and observation.

RECREATION FACILITY

A place designed and equipped for the conduct of sports and leisure-time activities. *See* HEALTH CLUB.

Comment: The National Recreation and Park Association publishes general standards for a variety of recreational facilities (see column 1 in table R-1). These standards can be used in all types of jurisdictions. A selective survey of municipalities in New Jersey and the standards they use is shown in column 2. These two sets of standards provide benchmarks, but the specific recreation preferences of residents based on current and future needs should be considered. Accessibility and convenience are important criteria in determining the adequacy of existing facilities. In addition, smaller municipalities with fewer than 5,000 persons may have many of the listed facilities.

RECREATION FACILITY, COMMERCIAL

A recreation facility operated as a business and open to the public for a fee.

RECREATION FACILITY, PERSONAL

A recreation facility provided as an accessory use on the same lot as the principal permitted use and designed to be used primarily by the occupants of the principal use and their guests.

RECREATION FACILITY, PRIVATE

A recreation facility operated by a private organization and open only to bona fide members and guests.

RECREATION FACILITY, PUBLIC

A recreation facility open to the general public.

Comment: Public recreation facilities are usually owned and operated by a governmental agency, but not necessarily so. For example, ball fields owned by industry might be available for public use at certain times.

TABLE R-1: GENERAL STANDARDS FOR RECREATIONAL FACILITIES

Type of Facility	(1) National Recreation and Park Standards[a]		(2) Outdoor Recreation Facility Standards[b]	
Baseball fields	1/5,000	population	1/5,000	population
Basketball courts	1/5,000	population	1/2,000	population
Community centers	1/25,000	population[c]	1/20,000	population
Field hockey fields	1/20,000	population	1/20,000	population
Football fields	1/20,000	population	1/10,000	population
Little League fields	1/5,000	population	1/3,000	population
Paddle tennis courts	No standard		1/5,000	population
Playgrounds/tot lots	No population-based standard		1/1,000	population
Running track (quarter-mile)	1/20,000	population	1/20,000	population
Soccer fields	1/10,000	population	1/4,000	population
Softball fields	1/5,000	population	1/1,500	population
Swimming pools	1/20,000	population	1/20,000	population
Tennis courts	1/2,000	population	1/1,500	population
Trails	1 system per region		1 mile/3,000	population
Volleyball courts	1/5,000	population	1/3,000	population

Sources:

a. National Recreation and Park Association, *Recreation, Park and Open Space Standards and Guidelines.* Alexandria, VA: National Recreation and Park Association, 1983.

b. Standards derived from a variety of municipalities.

c. Joseph DeChiara and Lee E. Koppelman, *Urban Planning and Design Criteria* (New York: Van Nostrand Reinhold, 1982). p. 405.

RECREATIONAL DEVELOPMENT

A residential development planned, maintained, operated, and integrated with a major recreation facility, such as a golf course, ski resort, or marina.

RECREATIONAL VEHICLE

A vehicular-type portable structure without permanent foundation that can be towed, hauled, or driven and is primarily designed as a temporary living accommodation for recreational and camping purposes.

Comment: Recreational vehicles include, but are not limited to, travel trailers, truck campers, camping trailers, and self-propelled motor homes.

RECREATIONAL VEHICLE PARK

Any lot or parcel of land upon which two or more sites are located, established, or maintained for occupancy by recreational vehicles for a fee as temporary living quarters for recreation or vacation purposes. *See* CAMPGROUND.

Comment: Many ordinances define "temporary" in terms of length of continuous occupancy permitted in order to prevent these facilities from becoming permanent homesites. Some developments also contain recreational vehicle parking areas for the use of their residents.

RECTILINEAR STREET SYSTEM

A pattern of streets that is characterized by right-angle roadways, grid pattern blocks, and four-way intersections. *See* GRIDIRON PATTERN. *See Figure 72.*

RECTORY

See CLERGY RESIDENCE.

RECYCLABLE

A waste product capable of being reused or transformed into a new product.

RECYCLING

The process by which waste products are reduced to raw materials and transformed into new and often different products.

Comment: "Recycling" also has a broader meaning, referring to all activities related to recycling, including the collection, separation, and storage of materials.

RECYCLING AND RECOVERY FACILITY

Land and buildings used for the sorting and reshipment of solid waste. *See* RECYCLING CENTER; RECYCLING COLLECTION POINT; RECYCLING PLANT.

Comment: A recent state court decision ruled that recovery of construction material was not an industrial or manufacturing use as provided in the local ordinance, which listed permitted uses as those that ". . . involve a process of manufacturing, fabrication, or production of useful goods" (*Atlantic Container, Inc. vs. Township*

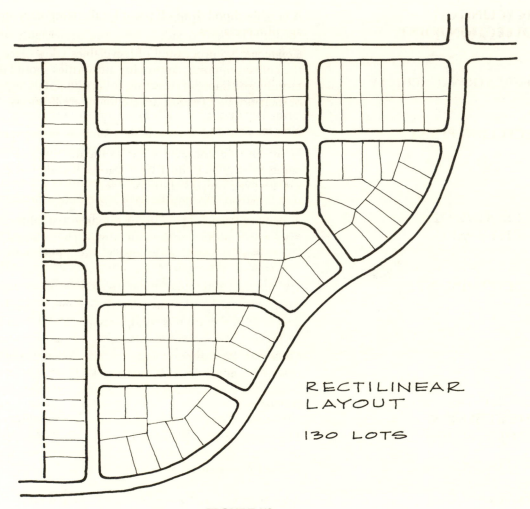

RECTILINEAR
LAYOUT

130 LOTS

FIGURE 72

of Eagleswood Planning Board, Superior Court of N.J., Appellate Division, decided May 18, 1999, 728 A. 2d 849 and reported in *Zoning Digest*, Vol. 52, No. 1, Case #5).

RECYCLING CENTER

A lot or parcel of land, with or without buildings, upon which used materials are separated and processed for shipment for eventual reuse in new products.

Comment: Most recycling centers are publicly owned. If they are privately owned, it may become difficult to distinguish recycling centers from junkyards, with all their attendant problems. All recycling centers should be planned with adequate buffers, unloading areas, and safe and convenient access. Larger ones belong in industrial zones.

RECYCLING COLLECTION POINT

A neighborhood drop-off point for the temporary storage of recyclables.

Comment: No processing of recyclables takes place at the collection point. Approving authorities should determine and approve recycling collection points as part of their review of major development applications.

RECYCLING PLANT

A facility in which recyclables, such as newspapers, magazines, books, and other paper products; glass; metal cans; and other products, are recycled, reprocessed, and treated to return such products to a condition in which they may be used again in new products.

Comment: Recycling plants are intensive uses that generate truck traffic, noise, and waste. They should be located in the heavy (or intensive) industrial district.

REDEVELOPMENT

The removal and replacement, rehabilitation, or adaptive reuse of an existing structure or structures, or of land from which previous improvements have been removed.

Comment: Replacement may include construction of residential, commercial, industrial, public, or other uses as well as provisions for streets, parks, and other public facilities.

REFORESTATION

The planting or replanting of forest plant materials, resulting in the creation of a biological community dominated by trees or other woody plants.

REFUSE

See SOLID WASTE.

REFUSE RECLAMATION

The process of converting solid waste to salable products.

Comment: An example of refuse reclamation is the composting of organic solid waste to yield a salable soil conditioner.

REGION

A geographic area defined by some common feature, such as a river basin, housing market, commutershed, economic activity, or political jurisdiction. *See* HOUSING REGION.

REGIONAL SHOPPING CENTER

See SHOPPING CENTER.

REGULATORY BASE FLOOD

See FLOOD, REGULATORY BASE.

REGULATORY BASE FLOOD DISCHARGE

See FLOOD, REGULATORY BASE DISCHARGE.

315

REGULATORY FLOODWAY *See* FLOODWAY; FLOODWAY, REGULATORY.

REHABILITATION The restoration of a property previously in a dilapidated or substandard condition for human habitation or use, without drastically changing the plan, form, or style of architecture.

REHABILITATION CENTER *See* CONVALESCENT CENTER.

RELICTION An increase in land area by the permanent withdrawal of a water body. (Johnsich 1991)

RELIGIOUS USE A structure or place in which worship, ceremonies, rituals, and education pertaining to a particular system of beliefs are held. *See* PLACE OF WORSHIP; MEGA-CHURCH.

RELOCATE To move an individual, household, use, or building from its original place to another location.

REMEDIATION The action or measures taken, or to be taken, to lessen, clean up, remove, or mitigate the existence of hazardous materials present on a property to such standards or requirements as may be established by federal, state, or local statute or regulation.

REMODEL To construct an addition or alter the design or layout of a building or make alterations or structural changes.

RENT A periodic payment, made by a tenant, to a landlord for the use of land, buildings, structures, or other property, or portions thereof.

RENTAL HOUSING Housing that is occupied by a tenant paying rent to an owner, with no part of the rent being used to acquire equity in the property.

REPAIR, MAJOR Any improvement that requires a building permit or that requires the replacement of a roof, wall, or other major building element. *See* ALTERATION.

Comment: The reason for the distinction between major and minor repairs is to facilitate and expedite minor repairs with a minimum of red tape. Major repairs, on the other hand, should be more carefully reviewed to determine whether existing variances or site plan deficiencies can be ameliorated or reduced as part of the project.

REPAIR, MINOR

Improvements to correct deficiencies resulting from normal wear and tear or improvements not requiring a building permit. *See* REPAIR, MAJOR.

REPLACEMENT COST

The cost of constructing a substitute structure having utility equivalent to the structure being appraised but composed of modern materials according to current standards, design, and layout. (Johnsich 1991)

Comment: Replacement cost is often used as a standard in determining whether a nonconforming structure or use may be rebuilt after a fire. One frequently applied standard is that when the replacement cost is 50 percent or more of the value of the structure after repairs, the structure can be rebuilt only as a conforming one. From a practical point of view, it is often difficult to prevent a structure or use from being rebuilt unless the destruction is total. The approving authority should attempt to reduce the degree of nonconformity in any permitted rebuilding.

The "equivalent" is not necessarily an exact replica of the original. The cost of providing a replica with the same or very similar materials is called "reproduction cost."

RES JUDICATA

Dismissal of an application (or case) on the grounds that it has already been heard and decided.

Comment: In order for the doctrine of *res judicata* to be applicable, the following must be shown:

1. The second application is substantially similar to the first.

2. The same parties or their privies are involved.

3. There must be no substantial change in the application itself or conditions surrounding the property.

4. There must have been a decision on the merits of the first application.

5. Both applications must involve the same cause of action.

(Cox 2003)

RESEARCH LABORATORY

A facility for investigation into the natural, physical, or social sciences, which may include engineering and product development.

Comment: Research laboratories imply physical activities usually associated with "wet" labs or places with running water, gases, special ventilation devices, chemicals, special heating and electrical or electronic equipment, or use of animals or human subjects under controlled conditions.

Research facilities often include pilot plant operations, and development ordinances usually permit a certain percentage of the floor area (25 percent, for example) for pilot plant use. *See* PILOT PLANT.

RESERVATION

(1) A provision in a deed or other real estate conveyance that retains a right for the existing owner even if other property rights are transferred; (2) a method of holding land for future public use by designating public areas on a plat, map, or site plan as a condition of approval.

RESERVOIR

A pond, lake, tank, or basin, natural or man-made, used for the storage, regulation, and control of water.

RESIDENCE

A home, abode, or place where an individual is actually living at a specific point in time.

Comment: One may have a number or residences, but the permanent home is called the "domicile." *See* DOMICILE.

RESIDENCE DISTRICT

An area where the buildings used exclusively for residential purposes occupy more than 50 percent of the total street frontage.

Comment: The term "residence district" is derived from motor vehicle statutes in defining areas where the maximum speed limit is 25 miles per hour. It also provides a specific standard that can be applied in a variety of situations to describe predominantly residential areas.

RESIDENT MANAGER

An agent of the owner of a building, living on the premises, who exercises general supervision of the building.

RESIDENTIAL ACCESS STREET

See STREET, LOCAL.

RESIDENTIAL AREA

A generic term describing an area that gives the impression that it is predominantly a place where people live. *See* RESIDENCE DISTRICT.

Comment: The definition does not provide any standard by which an area is described as residential. It is, at best, a visual impression, and the area may include a significant amount of commercial or industrial uses.

RESIDENTIAL CLUSTER

A form of planned-unit residential development to be built as a single entity and containing residential housing units that have private or public open space area as an appurtenance. *See* CLUSTER.

Comment: The open space may be used for agricultural activities, parks, or recreation. A question that should be addressed during the approval process is whether the open space is restricted to residents of the residential cluster or open to the general public. Another question is whether residents and/or the general public can be charged for the use of facilities such as swimming pools, tennis courts, or golf.

RESIDENTIAL DENSITY

The number of dwelling units per acre of residential land.

Comment: The density must be further defined in terms of net or gross. *See* DENSITY; NET RESIDENTIAL DENSITY.

RESIDENTIAL HEALTH CARE FACILITIES (RHCFs)

Residences usually occupied by the frail elderly that provide rooms, meals, personal care, and health monitoring services under the supervision of a professional nurse and may provide other services, such as recreational, social, and cultural activities, financial services, and transportation.

Comment: RHCFs may be independent facilities but are most often developed in conjunction with long-term care facilities. In many states certificates of need, which are required for an RHCF, are issued only when the RHCF is part of a long-term care facility, although not necessarily on the same lot as the RHCF. RHCFs are almost always licensed by the state, and most have communal dining rooms and other communal space. The professional nurse may be a registered or a licensed practical nurse. In general, all residents must be ambulatory and free of communicable diseases. Rooms and baths may be either private or shared.

RESIDENTIAL UNIT

See HOUSEHOLD.

RESORT

A facility for transient guests where the primary attractions are recreational features or activities.

RESOURCE RECOVERY

The process of obtaining materials or energy, particularly from solid waste.

REST HOME

See NURSING HOME.

319

RESTAURANT

An establishment where food and drink are prepared, served, and consumed, mostly within the principal building. *See* RESTAURANT, TAKE-OUT; RETAIL FOOD ESTABLISHMENT.

Comment: A restaurant may have limited forms of musical entertainment to accompany the dining experience; however, restaurants that provide dancing and stage shows are nightclubs. *See* NIGHTCLUB.

RESTAURANT, DRIVE-IN

See RESTAURANT, TAKE-OUT.

RESTAURANT, OUTDOOR

Any part of a food establishment located outdoors, not used for any other purposes, and open to the sky, with the exception that it may have a retractable awning or umbrellas, and may contain furniture, including tables, chairs, railings, and planters that are readily moveable. (American Planning Association, "Regulating Outdoor Sales," *Zoning News*, April 1995)

Comment: The above definition does not distinguish between outdoor service on private land and that on public land. Most jurisdictions require special licenses or permits to use public land, such as sidewalks, for outdoor sales, including food. Site plan review requirements for both public and private land include access, circulation, signage, noise (including controls on loudspeakers), appearance, and health considerations. Outdoor food service on public land would also include, in addition to license requirements or special permits for using public land, particular attention to public access and circulation, public liability, obstruction to traffic, and blocking access to adjacent buildings.

RESTAURANT, TAKE-OUT

An establishment where food and/or beverages are sold in a form ready for consumption, where all or a significant part of the consumption takes place outside the confines of the restaurant, and where ordering and pickup of food may take place from an automobile.

Comment: "Take-out restaurants" also encompass restaurants that sell food from drive-up windows. One of the zoning problems with these types of restaurants occurs when tables are added for on-premises consumption of food. The additional parking area required is often not available or is otherwise inadequate. In addition, since such uses have drive-up and pickup lanes, circulation, stacking, and safety are major considerations.

Originally, the term "drive-in restaurant" applied mainly to fast-food places where the food was served and eaten in cars on the premises. Many municipalities banned drive-in restaurants because of their nuisance characteristics including litter, glare, noise, and garish architecture. Most of the former "drive-ins" now resemble standard restaurants and are regulated as such. In fact, most restaurants now provide for take-out service.

RESTORATION

The replication or reconstruction of a building's original architectural features.

Comment: "Restoration" is usually used to describe the technique of preserving historic buildings. Rehabilitation, which also accomplishes building upgrading, does not necessarily retain the building's original architectural features. *See* REHABILITATION.

RESTRICTION

A limitation on property, which may be created in a property deed, lease, mortgage, through certain zoning or subdivision regulations, or as a condition of approval of an application for development.

RESTRICTIVE COVENANT

A restriction on the use of land, usually set forth in the deed.

Comment: Restrictive covenants usually run with the land and are binding on subsequent owners of the property. However, some restrictive covenants run for specific periods of time.

RESUBDIVIDE

(1) The further division of lots or the relocation of lot lines of any lot or lots within a subdivision previously approved and recorded according to law; (2) the alteration of any streets or the establishment of any new streets within any subdivision made and approved or recorded according to law, but not including conveyances made so as to combine existing lots by deed or other instrument.

RETAIL, LIFESTYLE CENTER

An unenclosed retail center of between 100,000 and 250,000 square feet without any regional anchor and generally featuring national specialty stores and restaurants, with limited recreational facilities and services, convenient and easily accessible parking, a pedestrian-friendly ambiance, and each store fronting on and having its own entrance on the major circulation street.

Comment: Lifestyle centers are upscale versions of the traditional strip retail center, with greater emphasis on design, building material, landscaping, and street furniture. They attempt to establish a decidedly pedestrian feel, much like the traditional downtown, in a

321

vehicle-oriented suburban setting. Because of their relatively smaller scale and pedestrian-friendly design, they are more likely to gain acceptance in suburban settings than the regional mall. The lifestyle center is popular even in less friendly all-year round climates; for example, Deer Park Town Center in northern Illinois. It appeals particularly to women, who do 70 percent of the family shopping. As noted by one frequent shopper, "It is much easier to pick up or return merchandise in a lifestyle center than in an enclosed mall. You can easily spot the store you want and park close by." The concept is still evolving, and jobs and housing, in an integrated setting, are probably the next step. (Baeb 2002)

RETAIL FOOD ESTABLISHMENT

Any fixed facility in which food or drink is sold primarily for off-premises preparation and consumption.

Comment: A retail food establishment is a grocery store, convenience store, or supermarket. Some supermarkets now prepare and serve meals at lunch counters or tables as an accessory use.

RETAIL FOOD ESTABLISHMENT, MOBILE

A vehicle, usually a van, truck, towed trailer, or pushcart, from which food and beverages are sold.

Comment: Many municipalities choose to regulate these uses by licensing them and requiring compliance with regulations dealing with sanitation, traffic safety, and location. Typical locations are job sites; places of assembly, such as colleges, industries or sports activities; and special events.

RETAIL OUTLET STORE

A retail establishment selling a single manufacturer's product.

Comment: A traditional or conventional retail establishment normally handles a number of different product lines, often of the same product. An outlet store differs in that it handles the products of a single manufacturer and is usually owned by that manufacturer. From a planning and zoning perspective, the major difference is that outlet stores draw from a much larger service area than a typical retail establishment. The service area may vary between 5 and 50 miles. Consequently, much of the traffic generation takes place on weekends, as opposed to the more typical daily or evening traffic flow generated by conventional retail stores.

RETAIL SALES

Establishments engaged in the selling or rental of goods or merchandise (usually to the general public for personal use or household consumption, although they may also serve business and institutional clients) and in rendering services incidental to the sale of such goods.

Comment: Some of the important characteristics of retail sales establishments follow:

- The establishment is usually a place of business and is engaged in activity to attract the general public to buy.

- The establishment buys and receives as well as sells merchandise.

- It may process or manufacture some of the products, such as a jeweler or bakery, for example, but such processing or manufacturing is usually incidental or subordinate to the selling activities.

- Retail establishments sell to customers for their own personal or household use.

An important characteristic of a retail trade establishment is that it buys goods for resale. A farmer, for example, selling goods grown on his own property, would not be classified as a retailer. A farm stand that brings in goods from other farmers could be classified as a retail outlet but more typically is classified as a customary accessory use to a farm. Eating and drinking places also may be classified as retail establishments, although more often they are classified under retail services.

Lumberyards and paint, glass, and wallpaper stores usually are included as retail trade even though a substantial portion of their business may be to contractors. Establishments selling office supplies and equipment are usually classified as retail although they sell to offices and other business establishments.

Finally, there are categories of retail trade that manufacture products and sell them on premises, such as bakeries. If the bulk of the products made in the bakery are sold on premises, it would be classified as retail trade. If the baking includes a large wholesale operation, selling to other stores, or supplying its own outlets, the operation would probably more accurately be classified as manufacturing.

RETAIL SALES, OUTDOOR

The display and sale of products and services, primarily outside of a building or structure, including vehicles; garden supplies, flowers, shrubs, and other plant materials; gas, tires, and motor oil; food and beverages;

boats and aircraft; farm equipment; motor homes; burial monuments; building and landscape materials; and lumberyards. *See* RESTAURANT, OUTDOOR; SIDEWALK SALES.

Comment: The major characteristic of outdoor retail sales establishments is that the material sold is usually stored outdoors and customers examine and inspect the materials outside of a building or structure. Outdoor retail establishments usually have buildings in which sales may be consummated or products displayed; however, most of the items sold outdoors are too large, there are too many of them to be stored indoors, or they require light, air, and water.

From a planning and zoning perspective, site plan considerations include the visual impact of the stored materials, outdoor lighting, signage, noise generation (including amplifiers), banners and attention-gathering devices, vehicular and pedestrian circulation, parking, and litter control.

The outdoor area where the material is stored should be improved or dust free, except for plant materials. The stored material should be kept a reasonable distance from all lot lines, and less "tidy" items, such as building materials and lumber stacks, could be restricted to rear or side yards with adequate screening or fencing. The maximum height of the stored material should be specified.

RETAIL SERVICES

Establishments providing services or entertainment, as opposed to products, to the general public for personal or household use, including eating and drinking places; hotels and motels; finance, real estate, and insurance offices; personal services; theatres; amusement and recreation services; health, educational, and social services; museums; and galleries.

Comment: Services may involve some products, like restaurants, for example. The difference, though, is that the products are part of the overall service and are usually consumed on the premises. Retail services may also include personal services, such as cleaners, shoemakers, and beauty parlors. Services to businesses or industry are not usually included under retail services.

In addition, not all retail services are appropriate in all zones. For example, hotels and large multiplex movie theatres may not be appropriate for neighborhood business zones because of heavy traffic generation and hours of operation. *See* PERSONAL SERVICES; SERVICES.

RETAIL STORE, CONVENIENCE

A retail establishment of up to 5,000 square feet selling primarily food products, household items, newspapers and magazines, candy, and beverages, and a limited amount of freshly prepared foods such as sandwiches and salads for off-premises consumption.

Comment: Convenience food stores are a fast-growing segment of the retail food industry. They are the modern equivalent of the corner grocery store—open long hours, containing a variety of items, providing quick and convenient service, and often touted as being compatible with and logically located in residential neighborhoods.

Convenience stores pose the usual problems of all retail establishments. These include provision of sufficient parking, lighting, litter control, access, and concern for impacts on adjacent residences. The problems are often intensified because these stores usually are open long hours. Site plan review should pay particular attention to hours of operation, lighting impact on surrounding uses, and plans to control litter.

Convenience stores often pose unique challenges, a major one being that of design. Unfortunately, the convenience store is often a concrete-block, flat-roofed, stand-alone, one-story building with windows covered with signs, and lacking any meaningful landscaping. Parking is invariably located directly in the front of the building, disrupting the existing streetscape. Regulations should establish architectural standards, requirements for building materials, respect for existing development context and streetscape, parking layout and location, vigorous enforcement of sign standards, landscaping requirements, and litter control.

If on-site food consumption is allowed, it should be specified in the regulations, with additional requirements for parking. (American Planning Association, *A Survey of Zoning Definitions*, Planning Advisory Service Report No. 421, 1989)

RETAIL STORE, LARGE-SCALE

Retail sales establishments in freestanding industrial-style one-story buildings, with floor areas of approximately 100,000 to 200,000 square feet.

Comment: Large-scale retail stores are commonly referred to as "big-box retailers." Examples are Home Depot, Wal-Mart, Target, and Sam's Club. They are the result of the growth of national chains, with their emphasis on providing value to their customers.

The four major value-retail formats are discount department stores, warehouse clubs, category killers, and outlet stores. The discount department stores include Wal-Mart and Kohl's. Warehouse clubs include

Sam's Club, BJ's, and Costco. Category killers are specialized retail stores such as Toys "R" Us, Barnes & Noble, and Home Depot. Finally, outlet stores are the discount branches of national department stores and manufacturers.

The value retailers are located in conventional regional malls, as freestanding stores, or in power centers and value malls. The power centers usually combine all types of major value retailers and smaller stores. Value malls combine factory outlets, department store outlets, category killers, and large specialty retailers. Value retailers and power centers are usually developed with 250,000 to 750,000 square feet of space in three or more large specialty stores.

Big-box stores usually require sites with maximum access and visibility. Interstate interchanges and major arterials are the preferred locations. However, some of the big-box retailers have also located in downtowns and in industrial and warehousing districts, often adapting size, building, and site design to reflect an area's traditional architecture, scale, and fabric.

If the local master plan and land development ordinance reflect municipal land-use policy to permit big-box development, either as stand-alone buildings or as part of large-scale shopping centers, the following controls should be addressed: minimum and maximum lot and tract size, floor area ratio and impervious coverage, setbacks and buffers, and parking requirements. In general, minimum lot and tract sizes encourage mall-type or center development, while a maximum lot or building size will discourage centers and encourage stand-alone buildings.

Parking requirements for big-box stores, either as stand-alones or in malls, are not too dissimilar from current retail parking requirements, ranging from four to eight parking spaces per 1,000 square feet of gross leasable area. However, some categories of big-box stores, such as warehouse clubs, claim to have half the traffic demand of a conventional shopping center. Big-box retailers do generate significantly more truck traffic than conventional retail establishments. As part of the site plan review process, testimony from qualified traffic engineers can be extremely helpful as to parking demand and truck loading and unloading requirements.

In addition to the conventional controls, design criteria become increasingly more important for big-box buildings. The most frequent complaint is that they look like "big faceless boxes." One publication describes them as "blank, windowless facades, flat roofs, lack of architectural detail, and minuscule, hard to see entries, . . . big box stores are boring at best and future eyesores at worst" (Duerksen 1996). The publication goes on to report how Fort Collins, Colorado, addressed these issues and the controls implemented there to prevent and avoid many of the design deficiencies, as follows:

- Uninterrupted facades in excess of 100 horizontal feet are prohibited. Facades greater than 100 feet in length must incorporate recesses and projections along at least 20 percent of the length of the facade. Windows, awnings, and arcades must total at least 60 percent of the facade length abutting a public street.

- Smaller retail stores that are part of a larger principal building are required to have display windows and separate outside entrances.

- Greater architectural interest in the main structure is encouraged by directing the use of a repeating pattern of change in color, texture, and material modules. The ordinance requires that one of these elements shall repeat horizontally and all elements shall repeat at intervals of no more than 30 feet, either horizontally or vertically.

- Variation in rooflines is required to reduce the massive scale of these structures and add visual interest. Roofs must have at least two of the following features: parapets concealing flat roofs and rooftop equipment, overhanging eaves, sloping roofs, and three or more roof slope planes.

The Fort Collins ordinance, as reported by Duerksen, requires that each principal building have a clearly defined, highly visible customer entrance with features such as canopies or porticos, arcades, arches, wing walls, and integral planters.

Color and materials are also carefully addressed in the Fort Collins ordinance. For example, smooth-faced concrete block, tilt-up concrete panels, or prefabricated steel panels are prohibited as the predominant exterior building materials. Brick, wood, sandstone, or other native stone and tinted or textured concrete masonry units are encouraged.

Facade colors are required to be of low reflectance, subtle, neutral and earth-tone colors. The use of high-intensity colors, metallic colors, black, or fluorescent colors is prohibited.

327

The Fort Collins ordinance addresses the relationship of the superstores to the surrounding community and public streets and calls for berms and landscaping to buffer the stores from adjacent residential uses.

Pedestrian circulation features require sidewalks of at least 8 feet in width along all lot sides that abut a public street and a continuous internal pedestrian walkway from public sidewalks to the principal customer entrance. The internal walkway requires landscaping, benches, and other such materials and facilities for no less than 50 percent of its length. Internal pedestrian walkways must provide weather-protection features such as an awning within 30 feet of all customer entrances, and the internal pedestrian walkways must be distinguished from driving surfaces through the use of special paving brick or scored concrete to enhance pedestrian safety and the attractiveness of the walkways.

Finally, the Fort Collins ordinance allows only 50 percent of the required off-street parking for the entire property to be located between the front facade of the principal building and the primary abutting street.

An excellent discussion of all aspects of big-box retail development, and from which much of the first part of this commentary was derived, is contained in a memo entitled "Big Box Retail" (New Jersey Office of State Planning 1995). As noted above, the summary of the Fort Collins ordinance pertaining to big-box retailers is contained in Duerksen 1996.

RETAIL WAREHOUSE OUTLET

A retail use operating from a warehouse as an accessory use to the principal warehouse use.

Comment: The individual terms are easily understood: a retail store in a warehouse. The major problem is how to regulate these uses, since they can cause relatively low-intensity warehouse uses and districts to become high-traffic, very intensive retail centers. Reasonable controls include the following:

- The retail establishment is accessory to and incidental to the principal warehouse use.
- The maximum area within the warehouse that can be used for retail sales is a small percentage of the warehouse and a small area (10 percent and 2,500 square feet, whichever is less, for example).
- Controls on the size and location of signs should be included in the ordinance.
- Adequate parking, in accordance with retail standards, is required for the retail space (often five spaces per 1,000 square feet of retail space).

RETAINING WALL

A structure that is constructed between lands of different elevations to stabilize the surfaces, prevent erosion, and/or protect structures. *See Figure 16.*

RETENTION BASIN

A pond, pool, or basin used for the permanent storage of water runoff.

Comment: Retention basins differ from detention basins in that the latter are temporary storage areas. Retention basins have the potential for water recreation and water-oriented landscaping since the water remains. Both types of basins provide for the controlled release of the stored water, and they may permit ground water recharge. Retention basins are usually not considered an impervious surface unless the bottom has a plastic or other impervious membrane.

RETIREMENT COMMUNITY

Any age-restricted development, which may be in any housing form, including detached and attached dwelling units, apartments, and residences, offering private and semiprivate rooms.

Comment: The 1988 amendments to the Federal Fair Housing Act provide guidance on age restrictions. These amendments stipulate that a community will be considered to be "housing for the elderly," and therefore exempt from lawsuits for discriminating against children, if the minimum age for all residents is 62 years, or 55 years for one resident of each of 80 percent of the units, provided that "significant facilities and services for the elderly are provided." The term "significant facilities and services" is not specifically defined in the regulations that implement the amendments and, therefore, has been determined on a case-by-case basis as litigation has arisen.

Housing in retirement communities usually provides one-level living, or elevators in multistory buildings, and usually includes other features designed to increase safety and amenities for the elderly, such as grab bars in the bathrooms, nonskid flooring, and higher levels of lighting. The housing may also be adaptable to use by the physically impaired and, accordingly, may be built with features such as wider doorways and elevators that can accommodate wheelchairs.

Retirement communities vary from those that provide only one type of housing and one level of service to communities that provide a range, from apartments for independent living to residences for assisted living (which includes meals, personal care, housekeeping, and some health services) to long-term bed care. *See*

ADULT RETIREMENT COMMUNITY; ASSISTED LIVING FACILITY; CONGREGATE RESIDENCES; CONTINUING CARE RETIREMENT COMMUNITY; HOUSING FOR THE ELDERLY; RESIDENTIAL HEALTH CARE FACILITIES.

RETURN

The line between the mean high waterline and the seaward extension of a permitted structure, such as a bulkhead.

REUSE

See ADAPTIVE REUSE.

REVERBERATION

The persistence of sound in an enclosed or confined space after the sound source has stopped.

REVERSE FRONTAGE

See LOT, REVERSE FRONTAGE.

REVERSE OSMOSIS

An advanced method of wastewater treatment relying on a semipermeable membrane to separate waters from pollutants.

REVERSION

The return of real estate to its original owner or owner's heirs.

Comment: Many donations of land to a governmental agency specify that if the property is not used for the purpose for which it was donated, it reverts back to the owner. Another type of reversion is a street that may have been platted but never constructed and that is subsequently vacated by the municipality. The unused right-of-way reverts back to abutting land owners.

REZONE

To change the zoning classification of particular lots or parcels of land.

REZONING APPLICATION

A request for a change in zone to permit new uses or prohibit one or more current uses or to amend the current requirements.

Comment: Some state enabling legislation will often specify how a request for a zone change is accomplished. But even in states without formal procedures, the courts have often upheld reasonable procedures designed to allow requests to be considered (*see TWC Realty v. Zoning Bd. of Adj.*, 315 N.J. Super. 205, 215 [Law Div. 1998)] aff'd o.b. 321 N.J. Super. 216 [App. Div. 1999]). A reasonable procedure would have the applicant apply to the planning board as a first step and the planning board then examine the request in terms of (1) consistency with the master plan; (2) changed circumstances either in the area or the nature of the new use; and (3) appropriateness of the zone for the proposed change. The planning board would then consider the request at a public meeting and forward a recommendation to the governing body.

RIDE SHARING

The cooperative effort between two or more people to travel together, usually to and from work.

Comment: Car pools, vanpools, and bus pools are all examples of ride sharing.

RIDGE LINE

(1) The intersection of two roof surfaces forming the highest horizontal line of the roof; (2) the highest elevation of a mountain chain or line of hills. *See Figure 73.*

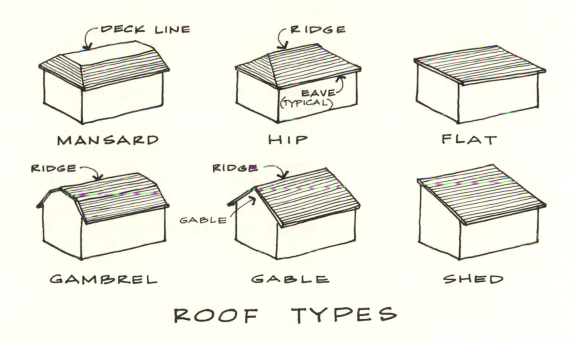

ROOF TYPES

FIGURE 73

RIDING ACADEMY

An establishment where horses are boarded and cared for and where instruction in riding, jumping, and showing is offered and where horses may be hired for riding. *See* AGRICULTURE; BOARDING STABLE; FARM OR FARMLAND; HORSE FARM.

RIGHT OF ACCESS

The legal authority to enter a property.

Comment: In privately owned property, right of access usually means access to a public road. In rented property, right of access also could mean the landlord's right to enter the property to make repairs.

RIGHT-OF-WAY (ROW)

(1) A strip of land acquired by reservation, dedication, prescription, or condemnation and intended to be occupied by a street, crosswalk, railroad, electric transmission lines, oil or gas pipeline, water line, sanitary storm sewer, or other similar uses; (2) generally, the right of one to pass over the property of another. *See Figure 1.*

RIGHT-OF-WAY LINES

The lines that form the boundaries of a right-of-way. *See Figure 1.*

RIGHT TO FARM

Public policy designed to protect farmers against municipal regulations, private nuisance suits, and unnecessary constraints on essential agricultural management practices, if these practices are consistent with federal and state law and are not a threat to the public health and safety.

Comment: The right-to-farm policy is usually implemented by adopting municipal ordinances listing permitted farming activities. A typical right-to-farm ordinance would include provisions allowing farming to take place on "holidays, Sundays, and weekdays, at night and in the day," and providing that "the noise, odors, dust, and fumes that are caused by them are also specifically permitted as part of the exercise of this right." (Township of Cranbury, N.J. Code, Chapter 81, Farming)

The Cranbury ordinance defines the right to farm to "include the use of large irrigation pumps and equipment, aerial and ground seeding and spraying, large tractors, numerous farm laborers and the application of chemical fertilizers and products for the control and elimination of insects, pests, weeds, fungus and other substances injurious to the farming process or for the purpose of producing from the land agricultural products such as vegetables, grains. . . . This right to farm shall also include the right to use land for grazing by animals, subject to the restrictions contained elsewhere in this Code for raising livestock" (ibid., §81-2).

Finally, as if to reemphasize the point, the right-to-farm ordinance states: "It is expressly found that whatever temporary inconveniences may be caused to others by such uses and activities so conducted, they are more than offset by the benefits from farming to . . . community . . . and to society in general . . ." (ibid., §81-4).

RINGELMANN SMOKE CHART

A scale for grading the density of smoke as published by the United States Bureau of Mines or any chart, recorder, indicator, or device that is approved by the Bureau or appropriate state department as the equivalent for the measurement of smoke density.

Comment: There is some indication that the Ringelmann chart is being phased out and replaced by more modern devices. Many agencies still use the Ringelmann chart, and the definition covers all situations.

RIPARIAN GRANT

The grant by the state of lands below the mean high waterline, usually beginning at the shore and extending outward to the center of the stream or some predetermined line.

RIPARIAN LAND

Land that is traversed or bounded by a natural watercourse or adjoining tidal lands.

RIPARIAN RIGHTS

Rights of a landowner to the water on or bordering his or her property, including the right to make use of such waters and to prevent diversion or misuse of upstream water.

RIVER

A natural stream of water, of greater volume than a creek, flowing in a more or less permanent bed or channel, between defined banks or walls, with a current that may be either continuous in one direction or affected by the ebb and flow of the tide.

RIVER BASIN

The total area drained by a river and its tributaries. *See* BASIN.

ROAD

See STREET.

ROD

A lineal measure equal to 16.5 feet or 5.5 yards.

Comment: This surveyor's measure is no longer used. Four rods equal 1 chain. Ten chains by 10 chains equals 10 acres. *See* CHAIN.

ROOF

The outside top covering of a building. *See Figure 73.*

ROOF, FLAT

A roof that is not pitched and the surface of which is generally parallel to the ground. *See Figure 73.*

ROOF, GABLE	A ridged roof forming a gable at both ends of the building. *See Figure 73.*
ROOF, GAMBREL	A gabled roof with two slopes on each side, the lower steeper than the upper. *See Figure 73.*
ROOF, HIP	A roof with sloping ends and sides. *See Figure 73.*
ROOF, MANSARD	A roof with two slopes on each of four sides, the lower steeper than the upper. *See Figure 73.*
ROOF, SHED	A roof with one slope. *See Figure 73.*
ROOMER	*See* BOARDER.
ROOMING HOUSE	*See* BOARDINGHOUSE.
ROOMING UNIT	Any habitable room or group of rooms forming a single habitable unit, used or intended to be used for living and sleeping but not for cooking or eating.
ROOMS, COMBINED	Two or more adjacent habitable spaces which by their relationship, planning, and openness permit their common use.
ROOMS, HABITABLE	A space used for living, sleeping, eating or cooking, or combinations thereof, but not including bathrooms, toilet compartments, closets, halls, storage rooms, laundry and utility rooms, basement recreation rooms, and similar spaces.
ROUNDABOUTS	*See* TRAFFIC CALMING.
ROW HOUSE	An attached dwelling separated from others in a row by a vertical unpierced wall extending from basement to roof. *See* DWELLING, TOWN HOUSE.
	Comment: Row houses are urban housing types, usually on their own lots with little or no front yard and a small, enclosed rear yard.
RUBBISH	A generic term for solid waste, excluding food waste and ashes, taken from residences, commercial establishments, and institutions.
RUMMAGE SALE	The sale by a school, religious institution, trust association, fund or foundation, organized and operated for religious, charitable, scientific, community, or educational purposes, of tangible personal property to obtain money for some charitable purpose.

334

RUN WITH THE LAND

A covenant or restriction to the use of land contained in a deed and binding on the present and all future owners of the property.

Comment: For example, a restriction never to divide the land into more lots is incorporated in a deed and the prohibition against subdivision is said to "run with the land," since future owners also are bound by the restriction.

RUNOFF

The portion of rainfall, melted snow, irrigation water, and any other liquids that flows across ground surface and eventually is returned to streams. *See Figure 6.*

RURAL AREA

A sparsely developed area, with a population density of fewer than 100 persons per square mile, where the land is undeveloped or primarily used for agricultural purposes.

RURAL ROAD

See STREET, RURAL.

S

SALE

The exchange of goods, services, or property for money or some other consideration.

SALINE LAND

Land with a high salt content that makes it unsuitable for agricultural cultivation.

SALINITY

The degree of salt in water.

SALTWATER INTRUSION

The invasion of salt water into a body of fresh water, occurring in either surface or ground water bodies. *See Figure 4.*

Comment: Saltwater intrusion or infiltration is generally caused by overpumping or overdrawing fresh water from an aquifer.

SALVAGE

The utilization of waste materials. *See* REFUSE RECLAMATION.

SALVAGE YARD

A facility or area for storing, selling, dismantling, shredding, compressing, or salvaging scrap, discarded material, or equipment. *See* JUNK; JUNKYARD.

SAME OWNERSHIP

Properties owned or controlled by the same individual, corporation, partnership, or other entity.

Comment: Multi-building or multi-tract developments may be subdivided in several corporate names or owned by subsidiaries of the parent company. This definition clarifies the intent of considering all such parcels as a single parcel for zoning purposes.

SAMPLING

A statistical technique that involves selecting a small, random, stratified percentage of a group; analyzing it; and then drawing certain conclusions about the group.

SANDPIT

See EXTRACTIVE INDUSTRIES.

SANITARY LANDFILL

A site for solid waste disposal. *See* DUMP.

SANITARY LANDFILLING

A planned method of solid waste disposal in which the solid waste is spread in thin layers, compacted to reduce its volume, and covered with earth.

SANITARY SEWAGE

Any liquid waste containing animal or vegetable matter in suspension or solution or the water-carried waste resulting from the discharge of toilets, laundry tubs, washing machines, sinks, dishwashers, or any other source of water-carried waste of human origin or containing putrescible material.

SANITARY SEWERS

Pipes that carry domestic or commercial sanitary sewage and into which storm, surface, and ground waters are not intentionally admitted. *See* COMBINED SEWERS; SEWER.

SANITATION

The control of all the factors in the physical environment that exercise or can exercise a deleterious effect on human physical development, health, and survival.

SANITARIUM

A hospital used for treating chronic and usually long-term illnesses.

SATELLITE DISH ANTENNA

A parabolic or dish-shaped antenna designed to receive radio waves.

Comment: Many local ordinances have attempted to control the location and size of satellite dish antennas for aesthetic reasons. Recent court cases have ruled that Federal Communications Commission regulations have preempted local control over these devices or at least require them to be treated as any other antenna (*Alsan Technology v. Zoning Board of Adjustment*, 235 N.J. Super. 471; *Nationwide v. Zoning Board of Adjustment*, 243 N.J. Super. 18).

Local control of satellite antennas may be upheld if the local ordinance is crafted to meet the following three-point test:

1. The ordinance should not differentiate between satellite dish antennas and other types of antennas.

2. There should be a reasonable, clearly defined health, safety, and/or aesthetic objective as the basis for the ordinance.

3. The ordinance should not impose unreasonable limitations on reception or impose costs on the user disproportionate to total investment in antenna equipment and installation.

SATELLITE OFFICE

(1) An office used by employees who are telecommuting; (2) a branch office or facility of a company or governmental agency.

Comment: With respect to zoning, there is no reason to distinguish between satellite offices and any other types of business office use. *See* TELECOMMUTING.

SAUNA

A steam bath or heated bathing room used for the purpose of bathing and relaxation, with steam or hot air used as a cleansing and relaxing agent.

SCALE

(1) The relationship between distances on a map and actual ground distances; (2) the proportioned relationship of the size of parts to one another. *See Figure 7.*

Comment: Map scale is usually represented by a graphic scale (a visual bar) or by a ratio (or representative fraction), indicating that, for example, 1 inch (on the map) equals 1 mile (on the ground). Because maps are often enlarged or reduced, the bar scale should be used, since it is not affected by map enlargement or reduction. *See* AREA SCALE.

SCALE OF DEVELOPMENT

The relationship of a particular project or development, in terms of its size, height, bulk, intensity, and aesthetics, to its surroundings.

SCATTERED-SITE HOUSING

Subsidized housing located on dispersed vacant sites in substantially built-up areas.

Comment: The theory behind scattered-site housing is the location of subsidized units throughout established neighborhoods as opposed to concentrating the units in one area. *See* INFILL.

SCENIC AREA

An open area, the natural features of which are visually significant or geologically or botanically unique.

Comment: Conservation easements are often used to preserve scenic areas. *See* EASEMENT, CONSERVATION.

SCENIC CORRIDOR

An area visible from a highway, waterway, railway, or major hiking, biking, equestrian trail, or publicly accessible right-of-way that provides vistas over water and across expanses of land, such as farmlands, woodlands, coastal wetlands, or mountaintops or ridges. *See* VIEWSHED.

Comment: Scenic vistas also provide views of the built environment, such as an urban skyline.

SCENIC EASEMENT

An easement designed to limit development in order to preserve a viewshed or scenic area. *See* EASEMENT, CONSERVATION.

SCENIC OVERLOOK

A designated area, usually at the side of a road, where a scenic area or viewshed can be observed. *See* VIEWSHED.

SCENIC ROADWAY

An official designation for roadways that cross areas of natural beauty, including open space areas, farmlands, forests, and/or scenic vistas.

Comment: Scenic roadway designation can provide the rationale for special design guidelines relating to land use, building design, sign standards, landscaping, and view protection.

SCHEMATIC DRAWING　　*See* PLAT, SKETCH.

SCHOOL　　Any building or part thereof that is designed, constructed, or used for education or instruction in any branch of knowledge.

Comment: The above definition includes all types of schools, such as business and trade schools, schools of art, dance, theatre, culture, and the martial arts, as well as academic institutions. Local ordinances can further define the kinds of schools that might be allowed in specific areas, for example, only elementary and secondary schools in residential areas. In many states regulations affecting schools must be applied uniformly to private and public schools. *See Roman Catholic Diocese of Newark v. Borough of Ho-Ho-Kus*, 202 A.2d 161 (1964).

SCHOOL, ELEMENTARY　　Any school that is licensed by the state and meets the state requirements for elementary education.

SCHOOL, PAROCHIAL　　A school supported, controlled, and operated by a religious organization. *See* SCHOOL, PRIVATE.

SCHOOL, PRIVATE　　Any building or group of buildings, the use of which meets state requirements for elementary, secondary, or higher education and which does not secure the major part of its funding from any governmental agency.

SCHOOL, SECONDARY　　Any school that is licensed by the state and authorized to award diplomas for secondary education.

SCHOOL, VOCATIONAL　　*See* VOCATIONAL SCHOOL.

SCHOOL DISTRICT　　The specific jurisdiction administered by the elected or appointed body of a state, county, or other local governmental unit to provide educational services to its resident population.

SCRAP　　Discarded or rejected materials that result from manufacturing or fabricating operations.

SCREENING　　(1) A method of visually shielding or buffering one abutting or nearby structure or use from another by fencing, walls, berms, or densely planted vegetation;

(2) the removal of relatively coarse floating and/or suspended solids by straining through racks or screens.

SCRUBBER

An air pollution control device that uses a liquid spray to remove pollutants from a gas stream by absorption or chemical reaction.

SEA LEVEL

The level of the ocean between high and low tides, which is used as a reference for all land elevations. *See* CONTOUR LINE; INTERTIDAL AREA.

SEASHORE

The area where the land meets the sea or ocean.

SEASONAL DWELLING UNIT

A dwelling unit that lacks one or more of the basic amenities or utilities required for all-year or all-weather occupancy.

Comment: In resort or seashore areas, municipalities may grant dwelling-unit certificates of occupancy that place limits on their occupancy during certain periods of time. For example, houses that lack heating might not be certified for use during winter months.

Many municipalities also recognize that houses originally built for seasonal use eventually become all-year-round dwellings and require all dwellings to be fully certified.

SEASONAL STRUCTURE

A temporary covering erected over a recreational amenity, such as a swimming pool or tennis court, for the purpose of extending its use to cold-weather months or inclement conditions.

Comment: The problem with seasonal structures is that they often become permanent, and where an open tennis court, for instance, is acceptable, one with a plastic structure to extend the season may be visually objectionable.

SEASONAL USE

A use carried on for only a part of the year.

Comment: Typical seasonal uses are recreational activities such as outdoor swimming or skiing, but they also include farm stands and Christmas tree sales. Zoning regulations should consider the fact that the use is in place or being used for only a relatively small part of the year. Bulk controls can be waived or relaxed for many of these uses, although some site plan review may be needed to ensure adequate parking and safe circulation.

SEAWALL

A wall or embankment that acts as a breakwater and is used to prevent beach erosion.

341

SECOND-HOME COMMUNITY

A development consisting of vacation homes or resort residences not used as the principal domicile.

SECONDARY TREATMENT

Wastewater treatment beyond the primary state in which bacteria consume the organic parts of the wastes.

Comment: This biochemical action is accomplished by use of trickling filters or the activated sludge process. Effective secondary treatment removes virtually all floating and settleable solids and approximately 90 percent of both BOD (biological oxygen demand) and suspended solids. Customarily, disinfection by chlorination is the final state of the secondary treatment process. *See* TERTIARY TREATMENT.

SECTION OF LAND

Measured as 640 acres, 1 square mile, or 1/36th of a township. *See* QUARTER SECTION.

SEDIMENT

Deposited silt that is being or has been removed by water or ice, wind, gravity, or other means of erosion. *See* SILT.

SEDIMENT BASIN

A barrier or dam built across a waterway at suitable locations to retain sediment.

SEDIMENTATION

(1) The depositing of earth or soil that has been transported from its site of origin by water, ice, wind, gravity, or other natural means as a product of erosion; (2) in wastewater treatment, the settling out of solids by gravity.

SEDIMENTATION TANKS

In wastewater treatment, containers where the solids are allowed to settle or to float as scum.

Comment: The scum is skimmed off and settled solids are pumped to incinerators, digesters, filters, or other means of disposal.

SEEPAGE

Water that flows through the soil.

SEEPAGE PIT

A covered pit with open, jointed lining through which septic tank effluent or other liquid waste may seep or leach into the surrounding soil.

SELF-STORAGE FACILITY

A building or group of buildings containing separate, individual, and private storage spaces of varying sizes available for lease or rent for varying periods of time.

Comment: In the 1970s, when self-storage facilities first became popular, they were often classified as miniwarehouses and limited to industrial and warehouse zoning districts. The modern self-storage facility is a multistory retail service use, located in a commercial corridor and serving individuals and small businesses within a 5-mile radius.

Self-storage facilities are very low traffic generators, requiring little permanent parking, often as little as one parking space per 50 to 100 rental units for one-story buildings. Two-story buildings may require elevator access, and more parking spaces around the elevators may be needed. Many have resident managers living in on-site apartments; the newer facilities rely on enhanced automated operational and security systems.

Access is provided to the rental units from driveways, so the width between buildings should be at least 20 feet. Many self-storage facilities are not particularly attractive because they are often flat-roofed, one-story structures arranged in long, monotonous rows. Newer facilities have two stories and direct access to the units from enclosed corridors. The outer walls have significant areas of glass and other architectural treatment. Heavy perimeter landscaping may be the best way to break up building appearance, along with substantial setbacks from lot lines.

Local ordinances should address security, landscaping, fencing, lighting, and height, as well as wall treatment. The use of the storage spaces should also be regulated. Most ordinances specify that the use is for dead storage only, and flammable or hazardous chemicals and explosives are prohibited. Arlington, Texas, prohibits the following uses in self-storage facilities:

- Auctions; commercial, wholesale, or retail sales; or miscellaneous or garage sales.

- The servicing, repair, or fabrication of motor vehicles, boats, trailers, lawn mowers, appliances, or other similar equipment.

- The operation of power tools, spray-painting equipment, table saws, lathes, compressors, welding equipment, kilns, or other similar equipment.

- The establishment of a transfer and storage business.

- Any use that is noxious or offensive because of odors, dust, noise, fumes, or vibrations.

Some self-storage facilities have open areas where boats, vacant trailers, and recreation vehicles may be stored. The local ordinance should specify whether this type of storage is permitted. (American Planning Association, *Standards for Self-Service Storage Facilities*, Planning Advisory Service Report No. 396, 1986)

SEMIAMBULATORY HANDICAP

An impairment that causes individuals to walk with difficulty or insecurity.

Comment: Individuals using braces or canes; arthritics; spastics; and those with pulmonary and cardiac ills may be semiambulatory.

SEMIDETACHED

See DWELLING, SINGLE-FAMILY SEMIDETACHED.

SEMIFINISHED PRODUCT

The end result of a manufacturing process that will become a raw material for an establishment engaged in further manufacturing.

Comment: The above definition, derived from NAICS (1997), includes the following illustration of a semi-finished product:

> The product of the alumina refinery is the input used in the primary production of aluminum; primary aluminum is the input to an aluminum wire drawing plant; and aluminum wire is the input of a fabricated wire product manufacturing establishment. (NAICS 1997)

SENDING MUNICIPALITY

A municipality that transfers a portion of its fair share obligation to another willing municipality.

Comment: In New Jersey, a municipality, usually a suburban town, may transfer up to 50 percent of its low- and moderate-income housing obligation to a municipality, usually an urban center, that is willing to accept the units. The transfer usually involves a payment to help construct the low- or moderate-income unit or to rehabilitate a substandard unit. In New Jersey, for example, that cost in 2002 was between $25,000 and $30,000 per unit. *See* RECEIVING MUNICIPALITY.

SENIOR CITIZEN HOUSING

Housing designed for, and occupied by, at least one person 55 years of age or older per dwelling unit, and which has significant facilities and services specifically designed to meet the physical or social needs of older persons as described in §100.306, "Significant Facilities and Services Specifically Designed for Older Persons," 24 C.F.R. part 100 (Department of Housing and Urban Development—Housing for Older Persons) or any amendments thereto. *See* HOUSING FOR THE ELDERLY.

SENSE OF PLACE

The characteristics of an area that make it readily recognizable as being unique and different from its surroundings and having a special character and familiarity. (Schultz and Kasen 1984) *See* CHARACTER; COMMUNITY OF PLACE.

344

SEPARATE OWNERSHIP

See SAME OWNERSHIP.

SEPARATE LIVING QUARTERS

See LIVING QUARTERS, SEPARATE.

SEPTIC SYSTEM

An underground system with a septic tank used for the decomposition of domestic wastes. *See* ON-SITE WASTE-WATER DISPOSAL SYSTEM. *See Figure 28.*

Comment: Bacteria in the wastes decompose the organic matter, and the resultant sludge then settles to the bottom of the septic tank. The effluent flows through perforated pipe and into the ground. Sludge must be pumped out at regular intervals.

SEPTIC TANK

A watertight receptacle that receives the discharge of sewage from a building, sewer, or part thereof and is designed and constructed so as to permit settling of solids from this liquid, digestion of the organic matter, and discharge of the liquid portion into a disposal area. *See Figure 28.*

SERVICE STATION

See AUTOMOBILE SERVICE STATION.

SERVICES

Establishments primarily engaged in providing assistance, as opposed to products, to individuals, business, industry, government, and other enterprises.

Comment: The general category of services includes hotels and other lodging places; personal, business, repair, and amusement services; health, legal, engineering, and other professional services; educational services; membership organizations; and other miscellaneous services.

The above definition includes all types of services and would be appropriate for intensive commercial and retail districts, such as the central business district of an urban area. Development ordinances should specify different types and scale of services appropriate for neighborhood or local business areas. *See* BUSINESS SERVICES; PERSONAL SERVICES; RETAIL SERVICES; SOCIAL SERVICES.

SET-ASIDE

The percentage of housing units devoted to low- and moderate-income households within an inclusionary development.

Comment: The minimum required set-aside varies by state. In Florida, for example, the percentage is lower than 20 percent, and there is no requirement for a 50 percent low and 50 percent moderate split. In New Jersey, the minimum set-aside is 20 percent, with 10 percent for moderate-income and 10 percent for low-income households. *See* INCLUSIONARY DEVELOPMENT.

SETBACK

The distance between the building and any lot line. *See Figure 14.*

Comment: The minimum setbacks in a zoning ordinance define the building envelope and establish the required yards—front, rear, and side. The ordinance should also indicate what may be permitted in which yards, such as parking, fences, accessory buildings, patios, swimming pools, and other recreational uses. Certain projections, such as uncovered walks, chimneys, bay windows, and stoops, are usually exempt from setback requirements, although limits may be set.

SETBACK LINE

That line that is the required minimum distance from any lot line and that establishes the area within which the principal structure may be erected or placed. *See* BUILDING LINE. *See Figure 14.*

SETTLEABLE SOLIDS

Bits of debris and fine matter heavy enough to settle out of wastewater.

SETTLING CHAMBER

In air pollution control, a device used to reduce the velocity of flue gases, usually by means of baffles, promoting the settling of fly ash.

SETTLING TANK

In wastewater treatment, a tank or basin in which settleable solids are removed by gravity.

SEWAGE

The total of organic waste and wastewater generated by residential, industrial, and commercial establishments.

SEWER

Any pipe or conduit used to collect and carry away sewage or stormwater runoff from the generating source to treatment plants or receiving water bodies.

Comment: A sewer that conveys household, commercial, and industrial sewage is called a sanitary sewer; if it transports runoff from rain or snow, it is a storm sewer. A combined sewer is one in which stormwater runoff and sewerage are transported in the same pipe.

SEWER SYSTEM AND TREATMENT

Devices for the collection, treatment, and disposal of sewage. *See* COMBINED SEWERS; INTERCEPTOR SEWER; LATERAL SEWERS; OUTFALL; PACKAGE TREATMENT PLANT; PRIMARY TREATMENT; SANITARY SEWAGE; SANITARY SEWERS; SECONDARY TREATMENT; SEPTIC SYSTEM; SEWER; TERTIARY TREATMENT.

SEWERAGE

(1) All effluent carried by sewers, whether it is sanitary sewage, industrial wastes, or stormwater runoff; (2) the entire system of sewage collection, treatment, and disposal.

SEX SHOP

See ADULT USE.

SHADE TREE

A tree, usually deciduous, planted primarily for its overhead canopy.

SHADOW PATTERN

(1) The impact of shade cast by a structure or building on surrounding areas during the day and over various seasons; (2) the pattern of light or shade cast by an object.

SHARED DRIVEWAY

A single driveway serving two or more adjoining lots.

Comment: A shared driveway may cross a side lot line, enabling a lot without direct highway access to have access to the highway. Shared driveways require access easements.

SHARED HOUSING

See HOUSING, SHARED.

SHARED PARKING

See PARKING, SHARED.

SHED

An accessory structure or building used primarily for storage purposes.

Comment: In general, sheds should be restricted to rear or side yards, and the local ordinance should establish limits on their size and minimum setbacks from all lot lines.

SHEETFLOW

The flow of surface water runoff over a broad expanse of land.

SHELTERED CARE FACILITY

See BOARDING HOME FOR SHELTERED CARE.

SHIELD

A wall that protects persons from harmful radiation released by radioactive materials.

SHOPPING CENTER

A group of commercial establishments planned, constructed, and managed as a total entity, with customer and employee parking provided on-site, provision for goods delivery separated from customer access, aesthetic considerations and protection from the elements, and landscaping and signage in accordance with an approved plan.

347

Comment: Shopping centers are further defined by size and the area their shoppers come from:

- A superregional center includes retail, office, and service uses, occupies more than 100 acres, has four or more anchor stores, and contains more than 1 million square feet of gross leasable space.

- A regional shopping center contains a wide range of retail and service establishments, occupies 50 to 100 acres of land, has at least one or more anchor stores, and contains more than 400,000 square feet of gross leasable space. It draws its clientele from as much as a 45-minute drive away.

- A community shopping center features a discount store or supermarket, contains approximately 150,000 square feet of gross leasable area, and has a site area of 10 to 25 acres. Its clientele draw is approximately a 10-minute drive from the center.

- A neighborhood shopping center generally offers goods necessary to meet daily needs, occupies up to 10 acres, has up to 100,000 square feet of gross leasable area, and draws its clientele from a 5-minute driving radius from the center.

See MINIMALL; RETAIL OUTLET STORE; RETAIL STORE, LARGE-SCALE; SPECIALTY SHOPPING CENTER.

SHOPPING MALL

A shopping center with stores on both sides of an enclosed or open pedestrian walkway.

SHOULDER

That part of the roadway contiguous with the traveled way for accommodation of stopped vehicles, emergency use, and lateral support of base and surface courses.

SHRUB

A woody plant, smaller than a tree, consisting of several small stems from the ground or small branches near the ground. It may be deciduous or evergreen. (American Planning Association, *Preparing a Landscaping Ordinance*, Planning Advisory Service Report No. 431, 1990)

SIDE YARD

See YARD, SIDE.

SIDEWALK

A paved, surfaced, or leveled area, paralleling and usually separated from the traveled way, used as a pedestrian walkway.

Comment: The New Jersey Residential Site Improvement Standards (RSIS) (NJDCA 2000; NJ Administrative Code,

Title 5, Chapter 21) recommend that sidewalks in residential developments have a minimum width of 4 feet, and 6 feet where sidewalks abut the curb and perpendicularly parked cars overhang the sidewalk. The Standards call for a wider width near pedestrian generators and employment centers. A minimum of 5 feet is generally recommended to allow two adults to walk side by side. The New Jersey Department of Transportation (NJDOT 1996) guidelines recommend 8 to 10 feet for centers (growth areas) designated in the New Jersey State Development and Redevelopment Plan (2002) and 13 feet for urban areas.

The RSIS does not specify any minimum distance between the curb and sidewalk. In urban areas and areas of higher density, the sidewalk should be right up to the curb. In other areas, the NJDOT guidelines recommend a setback from the curb of at least 4 feet and preferably 8 feet to permit a physical separation from the roadway. The setback allows for car-door opening and plantings.

The RSIS requires sidewalks in developments in excess of one dwelling unit per acre, and where the development or project is within 2,500 feet of a train station, public school, school bus route, existing recreational, business, or retail use of a site where such is permitted by existing zoning. The RSIS also requires sidewalks where the proposed street connects to or extends existing streets that have sidewalks on both sides of the street.

The RSIS also mandates sidewalks where the net density of the development exceeds 0.5 dwelling units per acre and the development is located within 2 miles of a school. Sidewalks are not required on rural streets or rural lanes and are not required in alleys. In blocks greater than 600 feet long, 10-foot pedestrian-way easements may be required by the approving authority through the center of the block.

Finally, sidewalks should be required on arterial and collector roads. These roads carry considerable traffic and often connect employment areas with business and retail uses. The lack of sidewalks forces workers to use vehicles to drive relatively short distances to get to restaurants and shopping. Wide sidewalks, a minimum of 8 feet, should be set back 10 feet from the roadway to encourage safe pedestrian travel.

SIDEWALK CAFÉ

A restaurant with tables on the sidewalk in front or on the side of the premises. *See* RESTAURANT, OUTDOOR.

Comment: Municipalities that permit outdoor cafés usually do so by special permit or licensing, since the space occupied by tables is often part of the right-of-way. In considering outdoor cafés, the width of the sidewalk becomes a crucial criterion to ensure adequate pedestrian circulation.

SIDEWALK DISPLAY

The outdoor display of merchandise for sale by a business use.

SIDEWALK SALES

Retail sales of a short-term and temporary nature conducted on the sidewalk or adjacent to the indoor establishment of the tenant or owner without permanent improvement made to the site.

Comment: The local ordinance should specify those zones in which sidewalk sales are permitted, such as commercial or business zones, and how long and how many times a year they are allowed. For example, a typical restriction might limit sidewalk sales to not more than four times a year for periods not exceeding seven days. In addition, other restrictions might include how much area can be devoted to the sales. Daytona, Florida, for example, requires that the display area not be greater than 10 percent of the lot or parcel area or 500 square feet, whichever is smaller. Maintaining pedestrian circulation is a critical consideration in allowing sidewalk sales. Site plan review considerations also include liability issues, aesthetics, clean-up provisions, lighting, and signs. Many municipalities require sidewalk sales to be licensed or classify them as conditional uses and require the applicant to secure a special permit.

SIGHT TRIANGLE

A triangular-shaped portion of land established at street intersections in which nothing is erected, placed, planted, or allowed to grow in such a manner as to limit or obstruct the sight distance of motorists entering or leaving the intersection. *See Figures 1 and 74.*

Comment: Also known as a sight easement.

SIGN

Any object, device, display, or structure, or part thereof, situated outdoors or indoors, that is used to advertise, identify, display, direct, or attract attention to an object, person, institution, organization, business, product, service, event, or location by any means, including words, letters, figures, design, symbols, fixtures, colors, illumination, or projected images. *See Figure 75.*

Comment: Ordinances usually exclude from the definition of signs national or state flags, window displays

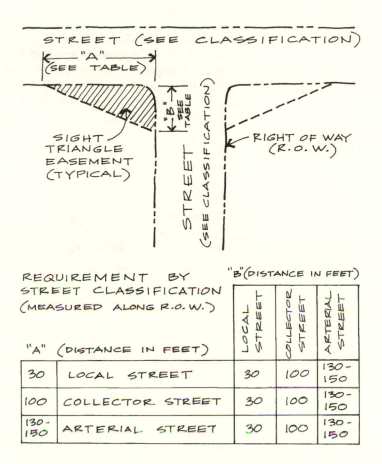

REQUIREMENT BY
STREET CLASSIFICATION
(MEASURED ALONG R.O.W.)

"A" (DISTANCE IN FEET)		"B"(DISTANCE IN FEET)		
		LOCAL STREET	COLLECTOR STREET	ARTERIAL STREET
30	LOCAL STREET	30	100	130-150
100	COLLECTOR STREET	30	100	130-150
130-150	ARTERIAL STREET	30	100	130-150

SIGHT TRIANGLE

FIGURE 74

(but not window signs), graffiti, athletic scoreboards, or the official announcements or signs of government. (American Planning Association, *The Mechanics of Sign Control*, Planning Advisory Service Report No. 354, 1980; *Sign Regulation for Small and Midsize Communities: A Planners Guide and Model Ordinance*, Planning Advisory Service Report No. 419, 1989)

SIGN, ANIMATED OR MOVING

Any sign or part of a sign that changes physical position or light intensity by any movement or rotation or that gives the visual impression of such movement or rotation.

SIGN, AWNING

A sign that is mounted, painted, or attached to an awning or other window or door canopy that is otherwise permitted by ordinance. *See Figure 75.*

351

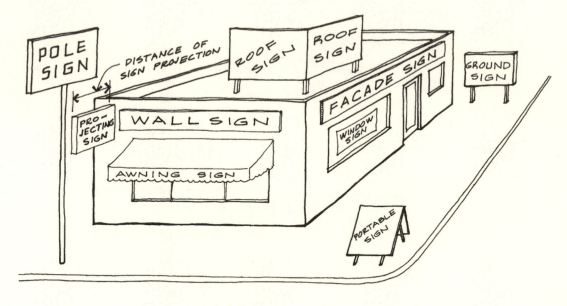

SIGN TYPES

FIGURE 75

Comment: A recent merchandising trend in downtown and commercial centers is the installation of translucent awnings across an entire store frontage. These often brightly colored, transparent awnings, with lighting from below and integral signage, are used to draw shopper attention. In these circumstances the sign area could be interpreted to include the entire awning area. *See* AWNING, ILLUMINATED.

SIGN, BANNER

A temporary sign of cloth or similar material that celebrates an event, season, community, neighborhood, or district and is sponsored by a recognized community agency or organization. *See Figure 76.*

Comment: Banner signs are often attached to lampposts in local business districts and provide an attractive streetscape feature celebrating the seasons, holidays, or special community-wide events.

SIGN, BENCH

A sign painted on, located on, or attached to any part of the surface of a bench, seat, or chair placed on or adjacent to a public place or roadway.

SIGN, BILLBOARD

A commercial sign that directs attention to a business, commodity, service, or entertainment conducted, sold,

352

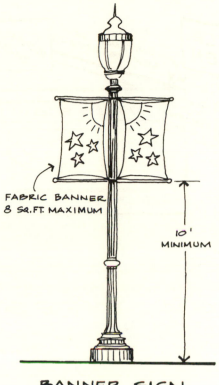

FABRIC BANNER
8 SQ.FT. MAXIMUM

10'
MINIMUM

BANNER SIGN

FIGURE 76

or offered at a location other than the premises on which the sign is located.

Comment: Billboards are also known as "off-premises" or "off-site" signs because they generally advertise a product or service available at another location. This definition identifies billboards as commercial signs, referring to the content of the sign message. In many communities, billboards are prohibited in all zoning districts, largely for aesthetic reasons, regardless of sign content. However, such outright prohibition, particularly for noncommercial message signs, raises serious constitutional issues and would require very careful ordinance drafting and support. It would be more appropriate to restrict such signs to specific zones and regulate their size, lighting, and placement accordingly. For an excellent discussion of the legal issues of billboard regulation, *see* American Planning Association, *Aesthetics, Community Character, and the Law*, Planning Advisory Service Report No. 489/490, 1999.

SIGN, BLADE

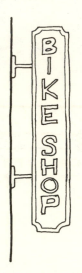

A vertically oriented wall sign. *See Figure 77.*

BLADE SIGN
(PROJECTING SIGN)

FIGURE 77

SIGN, BULLETIN BOARD

A sign that identifies an institution or organization on whose premises it is located and that contains the name of the institution or organization, the names of individuals connected with it, and general announcements of events or activities occurring at the institution, or similar messages.

SIGN, BUSINESS

A sign that directs attention to a business or profession conducted, or to a commodity or service sold, offered, or manufactured, or to an entertainment offered on the premises where the sign is located.

SIGN, CANOPY

A sign attached to the underside of a canopy. *See Figure 78.*

SIGN, CONSTRUCTION

A temporary sign erected on the premises where construction is taking place, during the period of such construction, indicating the names of the architects, engineers, landscape architects, contractors or similar artisans, and the owners, financial supporters, sponsors, and similar individuals or firms having a role or interest with respect to the structure or project.

SIGN, DIRECTIONAL

Signs limited to directional messages such as "one way," "entrance," and "exit."

354

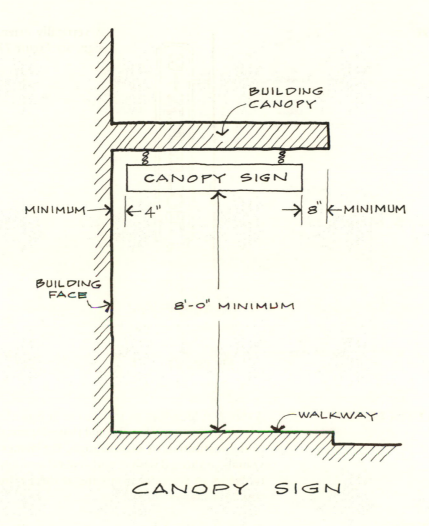

BUILDING CANOPY

CANOPY SIGN

MINIMUM → |← 4" 8" |← MINIMUM

BUILDING FACE →

8'-0" MINIMUM

WALKWAY

CANOPY SIGN

FIGURE 78

Comment: In multibuilding projects, the name of a business may also be included on the sign.

SIGN, DIRECTORY A sign listing the tenants or occupants of a building or group of buildings and that may also indicate their respective professions or business activities. *See Figure 79.*

SIGN, FACADE *See* SIGN, WALL.

SIGN, FACE The area or display surface used for the message.

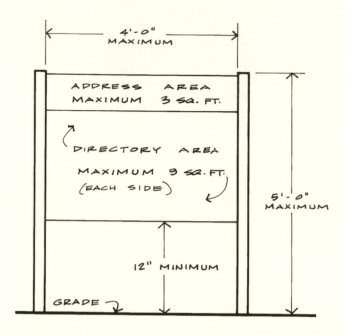

DIRECTORY GROUND SIGN DIMENSIONS
(DOUBLE POLE SUPPORT)

FIGURE 79

SIGN, FIGURATIVE

FIGURATIVE SIGN
(PROJECTING SIGN)

Figure-shaped signs that identify a specific type of business through the use of objects as graphic symbols. *See Figure 80.*

FIGURE 80

SIGN, FLASHING

Any directly or indirectly illuminated sign that exhibits changing natural or artificial light or color effects by any means whatsoever.

SIGN, FREESTANDING

Any nonmovable sign not affixed to a building.

Comment: Freestanding signs are usually pole signs, ground signs, and construction signs. Aesthetically, pole signs tend to be the most offensive in terms of height, size, and design. The preferable alternative to the pole sign is the ground sign.

SIGN, GOVERNMENTAL

A sign erected and maintained pursuant to and in discharge of any governmental functions or required by law, ordinance, or other governmental regulation.

SIGN, GROUND

A freestanding sign, other than a pole sign, in which the entire bottom is in contact with or is close to the ground. *See Figure 75.*

Comment: Also known as a pedestal or monument sign.

SIGN, HANGING

A freestanding sign supported by the extended arm of a single post, with the top edge of the sign face not exceeding 8 feet above grade level. *See Figure 81.*

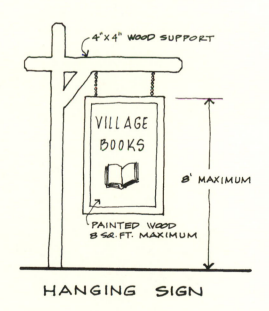

FIGURE 81

**SIGN,
HOLIDAY DECORATION**

Temporary signs, in the nature of decorations, and customarily and commonly associated with any national, local, or religious holiday.

**SIGN,
HOME OCCUPATION**

A sign containing only the name and occupation of a permitted home occupation.

SIGN, IDENTIFICATION

A sign giving the nature, logo, trademark, or other identifying symbol; address; or any combination of the name, symbol, and address of a building, business, development, or establishment on the premises where it is located.

SIGN, ILLUMINATED

A sign lighted by, or exposed to, artificial lighting either by lights on or in the sign or directed toward the sign.

Comment: The regulation of sign illumination is a most important element in sign control. The key to such regulation is the zone district itself and the carefully enunciated community design objectives for that district. In a New Jersey case (*State v. Calabria, Gillette Liquors*, 301 N.J. Super. 96 [Law Div. 1997]), the court applied the test enunciated in *Virginia State Bd. of Pharmacy v. Virginia Citizens Consumer Council*, 425 U.S. 748 (1976) as follows:

(i) whether the restriction is justified without reference to the content;

(ii) whether the restrictions serve a significant governmental interest; and

(iii) whether the restrictions leave open ample alternative channels for communication of the information at issue.

The New Jersey case was an outright ban on neon signs, and the court concluded that "The municipality's interest in aesthetics, while proper, was not advanced by an outright ban on the use of neon illumination rather than by some form of other restriction on the use of such lighting" (Cox 2003, p. 789). The court found "The municipality's expert's conclusory allegation, lacking facts or explanation, was insufficient to support the conclusion that neon in and of itself could not otherwise be regulated to meet the municipality's aesthetic standards. Ibid. at 105–108" (Cox 2003, p. 789).

However, a prohibition on the use of neon signs in a designated historic district is likely to be upheld, and reasonable limitations on the size and use of neon signs in other areas may be appropriate.

SIGN, INFLATABLE

Any display capable of being expanded by air or other gas and used on a permanent or temporary basis to advertise a product or event.

SIGN, LANDMARK

Any sign of artistic or historic merit, uniqueness, or of extraordinary significance to the community as may be identified by the local historical commission or other official agency.

SIGN, MARQUEE

Any sign made a part of a marquee and designed to have changeable copy, either manually or electronically. *See* MARQUEE.

SIGN, MEMORIAL

A sign, tablet, or plaque memorializing a person, event, structure, or site.

SIGN, MONUMENT

See SIGN, GROUND.

SIGN, NAKED LIGHT DISPLAY

A string of lights or any unshielded light used to attract attention.

SIGN, NAMEPLATE

A sign, located on the premises, giving the name and/or address of the owner or occupant of a building or premises.

SIGN, NEON

A sign consisting of glass tubing, bent to form letters, symbols, or other shapes and illuminated by neon or a similar gas through which an electric voltage is discharged.

Comment: See discussion under SIGN, ILLUMINATED.

SIGN, NONCONFORMING

A sign lawfully erected and maintained prior to the adoption of the current ordinance that does not conform with the requirements of the current ordinance.

Comment: If permitted by state law, nonconforming signs can be phased out over a period of time. This requires the establishment of an amortization schedule, commensurate with the sign's initial cost and current value. For more information *see* American Planning Association, *Sign Regulation for Small and Midsize Communities: A Planners Guide and a Model Ordinance*, Planning Advisory Service Report No. 419 (1989) and *Aesthetics, Community Character, and the Law*, Planning Advisory Service Report No. 489/490 (1999).

SIGN, OFF-PREMISES

See SIGN, BILLBOARD.

SIGN, OFFICIAL

Any sign installed by a governmental agency and intended to direct or control traffic; identify streets, parks, and historical events; or to provide other information deemed necessary by that official agency.

SIGN, ON-SITE INFORMATIONAL

A sign commonly associated with, and not limited to, information and directions necessary or convenient for visitors coming on the property, including signs marking entrances and exits, parking areas, circulation direction, restrooms, and pickup and delivery areas.

SIGN, OPEN HOUSE

Temporary, off-premises signs used to direct prospective purchasers to a house for sale.

Comment: This type of sign is often improperly placed in the public right-of-way; the ordinance should place restrictions on their number, size, placement, use, frequency, and duration.

SIGN, PEDESTAL

See SIGN, GROUND.

SIGN, POLE

A sign that is mounted on a freestanding pole or other support so that the bottom edge of the sign face is 6 feet or more above grade. *See Figure 75.*

SIGN, POLITICAL

A temporary sign announcing or supporting political candidates or issues in connection with any national, state, or local election.

Comment: Political signs can be regulated, but not prohibited, regardless of the type of area or particular zoning district. The most appropriate regulations are those that limit such signs to private property and prohibit placement in public rights-of-way and attachment to utility poles and traffic signs and devices. The ordinance should require removal within a specified period of time following completion of the political event or election.

SIGN, PORTABLE

Any sign not permanently attached to the ground or other permanent structure, or a sign designed to be transported, including, but not limited to, signs to be transported on wheels; sandwich board signs; and signs on balloons and umbrellas. *See Figure 75.*

Comment: The prohibition of portable signs for aesthetic purposes has been upheld by the courts. *See* American Planning Association, *Sign Regulation for Small and Midsize Communities: A Planners Guide and a Model Ordinance*, Planning Advisory Service Report No. 419 (1989) and *Aesthetics, Community Character,*

360

and the Law, Planning Advisory Service Report No. 489/490 (1999).

SIGN, PRIVATE SALE OR EVENT

A temporary sign advertising private sales of personal property, such as "house sales," "garage sales," "rummage sales," and the like, or private not-for-profit events, such as picnics, carnivals, bazaars, game nights, art fairs, craft shows, and Christmas tree sales.

SIGN, PROJECTING

A sign that is wholly or partly dependent upon a building for support and that projects more than 12 inches from such building. *See Figure 75.*

Comment: Also known as a shingle sign. *See Figure 82.*

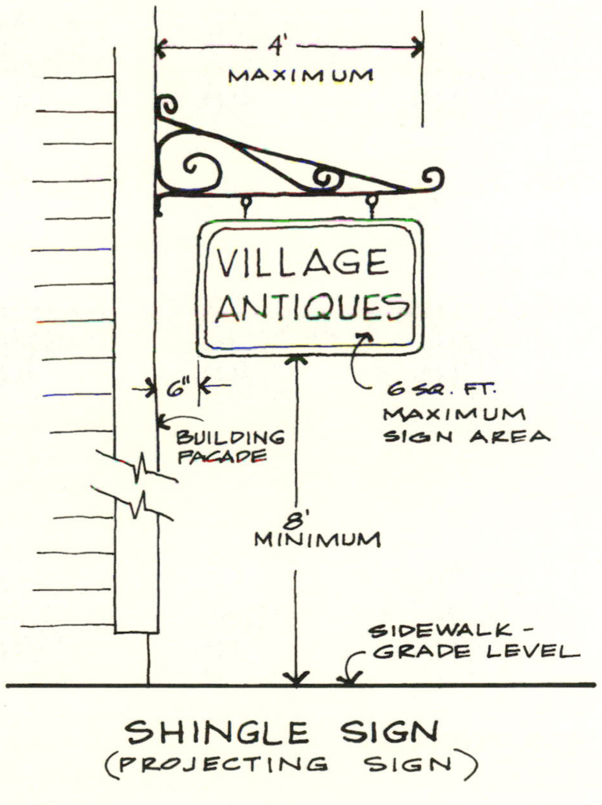

SHINGLE SIGN
(PROJECTING SIGN)

FIGURE 82

SIGN, REAL ESTATE

A sign pertaining to the sale or lease of the premises, or a portion of the premises, on which the sign is located.

SIGN, RESIDENCE DESIGNATION

A sign or nameplate indicating the name and/or address of the occupants of a residential property.

361

SIGN, ROOF

A sign that is mounted on the roof of a building or that is wholly dependent upon a building for support and that projects above the top edge or roof line of a building with a flat roof, the eave line of a building with a gambrel, gable, or hip roof, or the deck line of a building with a mansard roof. *See Figure 75.*

SIGN, SEARCHLIGHT DISPLAY

Any use of lighting intended to attract the general public by the waving or moving of light beams.

SIGN, SIDEWALK

Any temporary freestanding display located on the sidewalk or sidewalk area adjacent to a public roadway or storefront.

SIGN, SUSPENDED

A sign hanging from a marquee, awning, or porch.

SIGN, TEMPORARY

A sign or advertising display constructed of cloth, canvas, fabric, plywood, or other light material and designed or intended to be displayed for a short period of time.

SIGN, VEHICLE

A sign on a vehicle not customarily and regularly used to transport persons or properties.

SIGN, VENDING MACHINE

Any sign, display, or other graphic attached to or part of a coin-operated machine dispensing food, beverages, or other products.

SIGN, WALL

A sign fastened to, or painted on, the wall of a building or structure in such a manner that the wall becomes the supporting structure for, or forms the background surface of, the sign and that does not project more than 12 inches from such building or structure. *See Figure 75.*

SIGN, WINDOW

A permanent sign that is painted or mounted onto a windowpane, or that is hung directly inside a window solely for the purpose or effect of identifying any premises from the sidewalk or street; or a temporary sign advertising special sales, events, or products.

Comment: Unlimited window signs, both permanent and temporary, can result in a cluttered, unattractive appearance for the premises. Most sign regulations limit signs to 15 or 20 percent of window area.

SIGN AREA

The entire face of a sign, including the advertising surface and any framing, trim, or molding but not including the supporting structure. *See Figure 83.*

Comment: Figure 83 illustrates the measurement of a wall sign area where there is no defined sign background.

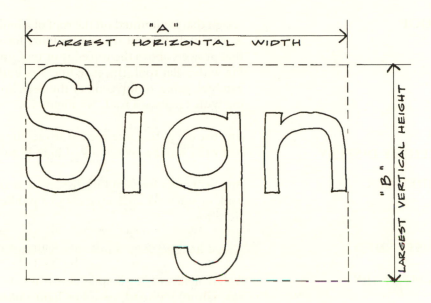

"A"
LARGEST HORIZONTAL WIDTH

"B"
LARGEST VERTICAL HEIGHT

MEASUREMENT OF WALL SIGN AREA WHERE
THERE IS NO DEFINED SIGN BACKGROUND

"A" x "B" = SIGN AREA

FIGURE 83

For those signs with a defined background (such as sign frame, trim, molding, or color panel) the calculated sign area should include the defined background. The area for a sign with more than one face is usually computed by adding together the area of all sign faces visible from any one point. For double-sided identical signs, only one side constitutes total sign area.

SIGN CONTROL

Regulations on the number, size, location, height, color, materials, lighting, and content of signs.

Comment: Sign controls are difficult to prepare, enact, and enforce. Planning Advisory Service Report 489/490 offers important guidelines, as follows:

- First Amendment restrictions must be observed. Restrictions on speech are valid only if the regulation seeks to implement a substantial government interest, directly advances that interest, and reaches no farther than necessary to accomplish the given objective.

- Time, place, and manner restrictions generally are valid. Examples of potentially appropriate subjects for regulation include size, shape, color, height, flashing, placement, orientation, and number.

- A sign ordinance should clearly state the purposes for which it is being adopted. The promotion of aesthetic objectives alone is sufficient justification for regulating signs.

- An ordinance that is part of a comprehensive city beautification effort (including, for example, preservation, scenic roadway protection, or street tree planting) is more likely to withstand judicial scrutiny than an ordinance disconnected from other city policies and regulations.

- A distinction can be made between on-premises and off-premises signs (billboards), and the latter may be banned entirely, but care should be taken in carving out exceptions within those two categories. Unexplained differences in treatment of different kinds of noncommercial signs have been particularly troublesome to some courts.

- A total community-wide ban on political and ideological signs is likely to be unconstitutional.

- All signs can be prohibited in special areas in a community, such as historic districts, but great care should be taken in doing so, particularly in commercial zones and with respect to noncommercial signs.

- Conditional permit systems for signs must be guided by clear, definite, objective standards that prevent unbridled discretion in the hands of local officials.

- Post-campaign and post-event removal requirements are permissible, as are inspection and removal fees, if reasonably related to actual administrative costs.

- "Problem" signs, such as portable signs, can be regulated strictly, but the grounds for the special treatment should be rooted in the public welfare and should be made explicit.

- When drafting amortization provisions, be sure the amortization period selected is long enough to allow the sign owner to recoup his investment and make a profit; five- to eight-year periods have been upheld by the courts.

(American Planning Association, *Aesthetics, Community Character, and the Law*, Planning Advisory Service Report No. 489/490 [1999], pp. 99, 100)

Some of the more specific controls are as follows:

- *Number*: Most ordinances permit only one free-standing sign per lot, if they allow any, regardless of the number of establishments on the lot. If a lot has more than one frontage, a freestanding sign for each frontage might be appropriate.

- *Location*: Freestanding signs should be set back at least 5 to 10 feet from the right-of-way and out of the sight easement if the property is on a corner lot or there is a driveway. A ground sign for large industrial or office properties is the recommended freestanding-type sign. An entrance sign on an island in the main driveway eliminates the need for a sign on each side of the driveway.

- *Area*: Wall signs, if allowed, should be based on a percentage of the building facade, with a maximum size. The percentage is often set at 5 to 10 percent of the principal ground-level facade, with a maximum of 60 square feet. Window signs, whether temporary or permanent, should be included in the maximum permitted sign area. The area of freestanding signs, particularly those on major arterials or highways, depends on the actual average speed limit of traffic and the nature of the land uses along the road. A maximum letter size of 12 inches for highways with speeds of 50 miles per hour or more would probably result in a sign size of between 75 and 100 square feet.

- *Height*: The maximum height of the top of signs should not exceed the height of the principal structure on the site, or 20 feet, whichever is lower. No signs should be permitted above the roofline.

- *Multiple-building campuses*: In industrial and office parks and shopping centers, the overall sign program should be carefully coordinated as an approved sign plan. The plan would include a sign design theme that covers location, color, size, lettering, material, content, and lighting. In a multi-tenanted industrial park, for example, there would normally be a single entrance sign and, before the first intersection within the park, a directional sign indicating the location of all the buildings and their tenants. Smaller direction signs (6 square feet or less) around each building would indicate parking, loading, and unloading areas. In a single-tenant building, one freestanding sign, preferably a ground sign, should be permitted. In a multitenanted building, a directory sign should be located at the entrance to each building. Wall signs should be avoided, but a letter or number (spelled out) at or near the top of the building, and referred to in the main directional sign near the entrance, would be allowed.

- *Flags, banners, and pennants*: Banners and pennants are designed for instant attention. They can create a carnival-like atmosphere and should be banned except for carnivals, special temporary events, or the opening of new establishments and should require a special permit establishing sign size, location, and duration. Well-designed banner signs that identify and celebrate a community, local business district, or other special district can be attractive streetscape elements and should be encouraged. *See Figure 76.*

National flags are another matter. Many businesses, particularly car dealers, are now featuring enormous garrison-size flags on very high flagpoles. While national flags are exempt from sign controls, the height of the poles should be restricted to the maximum height of buildings in the district.

SIGN ENHANCEMENT FEATURE

Any portion of a sign structure intended to improve the physical appearance of a sign, including roofs, moldings, railroad ties, lattice, or other decorative features. *See Figure 84.*

SIGN ENHANCEMENT FEATURES
(WITH 24 SQ. FT. GROUND SIGN)

FIGURE 84

Comment: It is not unusual for a pole or freestanding sign to be "enhanced" with decorative elements or features to increase its attention-drawing capacity while not exceeding the ordinance sign size limitation. A comprehensive sign ordinance can include regulations on the extent of allowable sign enhancement features.

SIGN PROJECTION

On a sign attached to a wall, the distance from the exterior wall surface to the sign element farthest from such surface. *See Figure 75.*

SIGNAL SPACING

The distance between traffic signals along a roadway.

SIGNIFICANT INCREASE IN TRAFFIC

Vehicular use exceeding the previously anticipated two-way traffic generated by the greater of:

1. One hundred trips during the peak hour of the highway or the development

2. Ten percent of the previously anticipated daily movements.

Comment: The two standards (100 trips and 10 percent) are those used by the New Jersey State Department of Transportation for their highway access calculations. The term "anticipated" means that the actual and projected trips are modeled using methods in the *Trip Generation Handbook* (Institute of Transportation Engineers 1997). A significant increase in traffic triggers more study and possibly the need for improvements to the highway system.

SILT

Finely divided particles of soil or rock, often carried in cloudy suspension in water and eventually deposited as sediment.

SILVICULTURE

The development and/or maintenance of a forest or wooded preserve.

SIMILAR USE

A use that has the same characteristics as the specifically cited use in terms of trip generation and type of traffic, parking, and circulation; utility demands; environmental impacts; physical space needs; and market area. *See* CHANGE OF USE.

Comment: The term "same" refers to the range of impacts of all the previously cited uses as opposed to one specific standard for each characteristic.

SINGLE OWNERSHIP

See SAME OWNERSHIP.

SINGLE-FAMILY DWELLING

See DWELLING, SINGLE-FAMILY DETACHED; DWELLING, SINGLE-FAMILY SEMIDETACHED.

SINGLE-ROOM OCCUPANCY (SRO)

A housing type consisting of one room, often with cooking facilities and with private or shared bathroom facilities.

Comment: The closest models to an SRO are hotels and

apartment buildings composed entirely of studio apartments. Some cooking facilities in the room and a private bathroom are desirable; shared showers are acceptable. SROs may have the potential to meet some of the need for lower-cost housing and housing for the homeless, without the use of direct subsidies. However, some relaxation of zoning, parking, and building requirements may be needed to bring costs down. (Gallagher 1993)

SINKING

A method of controlling oil spills that employs an agent to entrap oil droplets and sink them to the bottom of the body of water.

SITE

Any plot or parcel of land or combination of contiguous lots or parcels of land. *See Figure 65.*

SITE IMPROVEMENTS

Construction of, or improvement to, streets, access roadways, parking facilities, sidewalks, drainage structures, and utilities in connection with any development. (N.J.A.C. 5:21-1.4)

SITE PLAN

The development plan for one or more lots on which is shown the existing and proposed conditions of the lot, including topography, vegetation, drainage, floodplains, wetlands, and waterways; landscaping and open spaces; walkways; means of ingress and egress; circulation; utility services; structures and buildings; signs and lighting; berms, buffers, and screening devices; surrounding development; and any other information that reasonably may be required in order for an informed decision to be made by the approving authority.

Comment: Many ordinances classify small site plans (5 acres or less in rural areas, less in urban areas, or less than a specific square footage of building area) as minor site plans and relieve the applicant of some of the submission requirements.

SITE PLAN REVIEW

The review of a site plan for any public or private project by the designated review agency for the local jurisdiction.

Comment: Site plan review generally refers to a method authorized in the local development ordinance whereby a committee of the local planning board, or the board itself, reviews applications for development using established standards and criteria. Site plan review of development applications is necessary because, for example, although the proposed development may include the number and size of parking spaces required

368

in the development ordinance, it does not ensure that such spaces will function properly.

Although the local planning board is responsible for the approval of site plans, the actual task of review may be undertaken by a committee of the board or by a special committee with particular expertise in plan review. Committee members should include the municipal planner or consultant, municipal engineer, and representatives of municipal agencies such as the environmental commission. Often the planning board attorney is on the committee. *See* TECHNICAL COORDINATING COMMITTEE.

The review procedure itself should be a systematic process that starts with the overall design concept and ends with design details, such as the size and type of curbs and sidewalks, and should include the following steps.

- Site inspection
- Overall design concept
    - Land use (contextual) relationships (to off-site areas)
    - Local Master Plan conformance
    - Utility considerations (need and available capacity)
    - Overall circulation (site access)
    - Support facilities (schools, shops, police, fire, and the like)
- Internal site-use relationships
- Evaluation of environmental impact
- Analysis of on-site circulation
- Site design details
    - Parking layout
    - Landscape design
    - Lighting
    - Signage
    - Street furniture

The authority for site plan review is found in state planning laws authorizing development ordinances. Site plan review standards must be in conformance with state law and any guidelines established by the courts in land-use decisions. Site design standards must have a reasonable relationship to the public health, safety, or general welfare, or other proper police power objectives.

SKATEBOARD PARK

A building, structure, or open area containing or developed with slopes, hills, passageways, and other challenges for skateboard users.

Comment: Rental or sale of skateboards and related equipment may be included, and a user fee may be charged.

SKETCH PLAN

See PLAT, SKETCH.

SKI AREA

An area developed for snow skiing, with trails and lifts, and including ski rental and sales, instruction, and eating facilities.

SKI RESORT

A ski area that also includes sales, rental, and service of related equipment and accessories, eating places, residences, and hotels and motels. *See* SKI AREA.

SKILLED NURSING FACILITY

See LONG-TERM CARE FACILITY.

SKIMMING

The mechanical removal of oil or scum from the surface of water.

SKY EXPOSURE PLANE

A theoretical plane beginning at a lot line or directly above a street line at a height set forth in the ordinance and rising over a slope determined by an acute angle measured down from the vertical as set forth in the ordinance. *See Figure 85*.

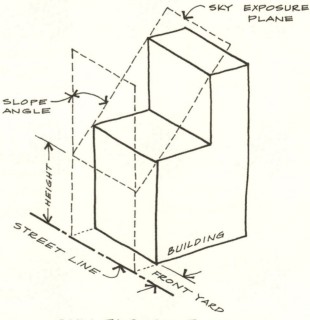

SKY EXPOSURE PLANE

FIGURE 85

370

SLOPE

Comment: Sky exposure plane controls regulate the bulk and height of tall structures such that a predetermined level of natural light will be available to the adjacent street or other public space.

The deviation of a surface from the horizontal, usually expressed in percent or degrees. *See* GRADE. *See Figure 46.*

Comment: Slope percent is computed by dividing the vertical distance by the horizontal distance times 100. For example, a parcel of land 150 feet in length that rises 12 feet in height has a slope of 8 percent:

$$12 \div 150 \times 100 = 8 \text{ percent}$$

See TOPOGRAPHY; CONTOUR LINE.

SLOUGH

Low-lying muddy ground, wetlands, or marshy area. *See* WETLANDS.

SLUDGE

Solids removed from sewage during wastewater treatment.

Comment: Sludge is disposed of by incineration, dumping, or burial.

SLUM

See BLIGHTED AREA.

SMART GROWTH

Policies, legislation, regulations, procedures, and strategies that attempt to achieve more compact, efficient, mixed-use development, tied to existing infrastructure and facilities by using such techniques as transfer of development rights, growth boundaries, targeted public and private investments, impact fees, open space and farmland preservation, and flexible zoning and subdivision regulations within established parameters.

Comment: Smart growth is the antithesis of sprawl, promoting development patterns that are economically sound, environmentally responsible, and socially just. Smart growth shares many of the principles found in traditional neighborhood design including:

- A mix of land uses: stores, jobs, and homes
- A range of housing types, sizes, and costs
- A variety of transportation choices including accessible public transit
- Compact, safe, and walkable neighborhoods
- Distinctive communities with a strong sense of place

- The preservation of open space, farmland, and critical environmental areas

- A focus of public investment on existing community assets

- Citizen participation in development decisions

(Downs 2001; Duany et al. 2000; Meck 2002)

SMOG
Generally used to mean an equivalent of air pollution, particularly associated with oxidants.

SMOKE
(1) Solid particles generated as a result of the incomplete combustion of materials containing carbon; (2) gas-borne and airborne particles arising from a process of combustion in sufficient numbers to be observable, exclusive of visible condensed water vapor.

SNOUT HOUSE
A house with a front entrance garage that occupies more than 50 percent of the house frontage and/or protrudes more than 10 feet from the rest of the house facade.

Comment: Snout houses dominate their lots and create unattractive "garage door" streetscapes. One approach is to require all front entrance garages to occupy less than 50 percent of the house frontage and not protrude more than 10 feet closer to the street than the rest of the frontage. Other restrictions call for locating the front door not more than 8 feet from the front of the garage. (Knack 2001)

SNOWMOBILE
A self-propelled vehicle designed for travel on snow or ice or a natural terrain and steered by wheels, skis, or runners. *See* VEHICLE, OFF-ROAD.

SOCIAL SERVICES
Establishments providing assistance and aid to those persons requiring counseling for job training, employment, psychological problems, or learning and physical disabilities.

Comment: This major group also includes organizations soliciting funds for these and related services. Additionally, it includes child day-care services, nurseries as well as residential care, and special categories for persons with limited ability for self-care but for whom medical care is not a major requirement.

SOIL
All unconsolidated mineral and organic material, of whatever origin, that overlies bedrock and can be readily excavated.

SOIL CEMENT

A mixture of portland cement and soil.

SOIL CONDITIONER

A biologically stable organic material, such as humus or compost, that makes soil more amenable to the passage of water and to the distribution of fertilizing material, providing a better medium for necessary soil bacteria growth.

SOIL CONSERVATION DISTRICT

A geographic area, usually a county, in which professionals provide advice to communities, agencies, and individuals within the jurisdiction and review development proposals for soil erosion and sedimentation control measures.

Comment: The soil conservation district concept began in 1936 and is used by the U.S. Department of Agriculture to administer its programs relating to water and soil.

SOIL ENGINEER

A professional engineer who is qualified by education and experience to practice applied soil mechanics and foundation engineering.

SOIL EROSION

See EROSION.

SOIL EROSION AND SEDIMENT CONTROL PLAN

Strategies and procedures that describe necessary land treatment measures for minimizing soil erosion and sedimentation. *See* EROSION; SEDIMENTATION.

SOIL MAP

A map indicating the names and spatial distribution of soil types on a site and including information relating to soil characteristics such as slope, depth to seasonal high water, depth to bedrock, permeability, natural drainage class, stoniness, and flood and stream overflow hazard.

Comment: The data source for maps showing the soil types and locations of a given area is usually the official soil maps prepared by the Soil Conservation Service of the U.S. Department of Agriculture. The information provided in the official soil maps is field-compiled by the Soil Conservation Service by testing at selected locations. However, soil maps developed from this base for use in development applications must be field-checked for accuracy and adjusted if warranted, especially in cases involving the delineation of areas where development is precluded or limited.

SOIL REMOVAL

See EXTRACTIVE INDUSTRIES.

SOLAR ACCESS

A property-owner's right to have the sunlight shine on the owner's land. *See* SKY EXPOSURE PLANE.

Comment: The enforcement of this right is through the zoning ordinance that establishes height and setback requirements. Applicants may be asked to present sun-shadow diagrams to permit an agency to determine if solar access will be impaired.

SOLAR COLLECTOR

A device or combination of devices, structure, or part of a device or structure that transforms direct solar energy into thermal, chemical, or electrical energy.

SOLAR ENERGY SYSTEM

A complete design or assembly consisting of a solar energy collector, an energy storage facility (where used), and components for the distribution of transformed energy.

SOLAR SKY SPACE

The space between a solar energy collector and the sun that must be free of obstructions that shade the collector to an extent that precludes its cost-effective operation.

Comment: Increasingly, planners will be asked to develop zoning requirements that protect the solar sky space. It can be done through minimum setback requirements and sky exposure planes. Site plan review might also require a shadow analysis to ascertain whether or not any proposed tree plantings, landscaping, or structures will block off solar collectors. For single-family and two-family homes, which are usually excluded from site plan review, the construction code official or building inspector should be given guidelines as to what may be permitted and minimum setbacks needed in order to ensure a functioning solar collector.

SOLAR SKY SPACE EASEMENT

A right, expressed as an easement, covenant, condition, or other property interest, in any deed or other instrument executed by or on behalf of any landowner, that protects the solar sky space of an actual, proposed, or designated solar energy collector at a described location by forbidding or limiting activities or land uses that interfere with access to solar energy.

Comment: The solar sky space must be described either as the three-dimensional space in which obstruction is prohibited or limited, or as the times of day in which direct sunlight to the solar collector may not be obstructed, or as a combination of the two methods.

SOLID WASTE

Unwanted or discarded material, including waste material with insufficient liquid content to be free flowing.

Comment: Solid waste may be categorized as follows:

- *Agricultural*—solid waste that results from the raising and slaughtering of animals and the processing of animal products and from orchard and field crops
- *Commercial*—waste generated by stores, offices, and other activities that do not actually turn out a product
- *Industrial*—waste that results from industrial processes and manufacturing
- *Institutional*—waste originating from educational, health care, and research facilities
- *Municipal*—residential and commercial solid waste generated within a community
- *Pesticide*—the residue from the manufacturing, handling, or use of chemicals intended for killing plant and animal pests
- *Residential*—waste that normally originates in a residential environment, sometimes called "domestic solid waste"

SOLID WASTE DISPOSAL

The ultimate disposition of solid waste that cannot be salvaged or recycled.

SOLID WASTE MANAGEMENT

A planned program providing for the collection, storage, and disposal of solid waste, including, where appropriate, recycling and recovery.

SOLID WASTE TRANSFER FACILITY

A place where solid waste materials are taken from a collection vehicle, temporarily stored or stockpiled, and ultimately moved to another facility.

SOOT

Agglomerations of tar-impregnated carbon particles that form when carbonaceous material does not undergo complete combustion.

SORORITY HOUSE

See FRATERNITY HOUSE.

SOUND

See NOISE.

SOUND-AMPLIFYING EQUIPMENT

Any machine or device that amplifies sound.

Comment: Ordinances usually exclude standard automobile radios when heard only by the occupants of the vehicle in which installed, warning devices on emergency vehicles, and horns or other warning devices on other vehicles used for traffic safety purposes. It does include remotely located loudspeakers attached to and operated from a vehicle.

SPECIAL ASSESSMENT

A fee levied by a local authority for the financing of a local improvement that is primarily of benefit to the landowners who must pay the assessment.

SPECIAL IMPROVEMENT DISTRICT (SID)

A district, with the power to levy taxes, created by legislative act, petition, or vote of the residents or owners for a specific purpose.

Comment: Special improvement districts have been very effective in assisting in the revitalization of local business areas. Their work primarily focuses on cleanliness and safety but also includes recommendations on building facades and signage, coordinating special events and programs, streetscape improvement, development of off-street parking, liaison with officials and elected representatives, and providing district maintenance. Some SIDs deploy "community service representatives," uniformed individuals who "serve as the eyes and ears for police and other code enforcement agencies." An important reason for the effectiveness of SIDs is their ability to tax themselves and channel the additional revenues into programs directly benefiting the district. (Levy 2001)

SPECIAL EXCEPTION USE

See CONDITIONAL USE.

SPECIAL USE PERMIT

A permit issued by the proper governmental authority that must be acquired before a special exception use can be implemented. *See* CONDITIONAL USE PERMIT.

SPECIALTY FOOD STORE

A retail store specializing in a specific type or class of foods, such as an appetizer store, bakery, butcher, delicatessen, fish market, or gourmet shop.

SPECIALTY SHOPPING CENTER

(1) A shopping center whose shops cater to a specific market and are linked together by an architectural, historical, or geographic theme or by a commonality of goods and services; also known as a theme or fashion center; (2) a retail center of between 100,000 and 200,000 square feet consisting mostly of small shops with distinctive, one-of-a-kind merchandise with emphasis on arts and crafts supplied locally. *See* MINI-MALL; SHOPPING CENTER.

SPECIFICATIONS

Detailed instructions that designate the quality and quantity of materials and workmanship expected in the construction of a structure.

SPECIMEN TREE

A particularly impressive or unusual example of a species because of its size, shade, age, or any other trait that epitomizes the character of the species. (American Planning Association, *Preparing a Landscaping Ordinance*, Planning Advisory Service Report No. 431, 1990)

SPEED HUMPS

See TRAFFIC CALMING.

SPEED TABLES

See TRAFFIC CALMING.

SPEED-CHANGE LANE

An auxiliary lane, deceleration lane, or acceleration lane, including tapered areas, primarily for the deceleration or acceleration of vehicles entering or leaving the through-traffic lanes.

SPILLWAY

A passageway through which excess water escapes from a water body.

SPILLWAY, EMERGENCY

A constructed or natural channel whose function is to pass the design storm flows in the event the principal channel fails to operate as designed or is blocked.

SPLIT LOT ZONING

A lot or single parcel of land located in two or more zones.

Comment: As a general rule, a lot should be located in a single zone. Occasionally, because of topography or platting that took place before modern subdivision techniques, single lots may be in two or more zones. One way to overcome the problem is to permit a zone line to be shifted to the lot line if the lot line and zone line are within 25 feet of each other.

A common example is a through lot, with half of the lot fronting on a commercial street and zoned for commercial use and the rear fronting on a residential street and zoned residential. In this example, the shifting of the lot line may not be a practical way to reconcile the problem. The lot, for example, might be too deep and the lot line and zoning boundary not be within 25 feet of each other. In addition, if the lines were shifted arbitrarily, it might result in an inappropriate mix of land uses.

If the zone line is maintained, and the lot remains split, all use and bulk requirements for the specific zone apply only to that part of the lot in that zone. The land area in the residential zone cannot be used to determine the floor area for the commercially zoned parcel, and the land in the commercial part of the lot cannot be used to establish the number of dwelling units to be built on the residential part of the lot. In addition, the setback lines are measured from the zone boundary line. If the ordinance calls for a rear yard setback of 50 feet for the commercial property, that setback is measured from the zone boundary line dividing the lot.

There are exceptions, however. For example, in *AMG Associates v. Tp. of Springfield*, 65 N.J. 101 (1974) the New Jersey Supreme Court (state's highest court) ruled that a property owner could use the rear part of his property, which was zoned residential, to provide parking for the commercial use on the front of the property. But in this situation, the residentially zoned parcel could be accessed only through the commercial part of the lot, and the residentially zoned part was less than the minimum required for residential development. In this case, a variance would have been justified on the basis of hardship, since the strict application of the law would have rendered the rear portion unusable.

SPOIL

Dirt, rock, or waste material that has been removed from its original location or materials that have been dredged from the bottoms of waterways.

SPOT ZONING

Rezoning of a lot or parcel of land to benefit an owner for a use that is incompatible with surrounding land uses and that does not further the comprehensive zoning plan.

Comment: Spot zoning per se may not be illegal; it may only be descriptive of a certain set of facts and consequently neutral with respect to whether it is valid or invalid. Hagman (1975) states that spot zoning is invalid only when all the following factors are present: (1) A small parcel of land is singled out for special and privileged treatment; (2) the singling out is not in the public interest but only for the benefit of the land owner; and (3) the action is not in accord with a comprehensive plan. *See Kozesnik v. Township of Montgomery,* 24 N.J. 154, 131 A.2d 1 (1957); *Borough of Cresskill v. Borough of Dumont,* 15 N.J. 238, 104 A.2d 441 (1954); and *Jones v. Zoning Board of Adjustment of Long Beach Twp.,* 32 N.J. Super. 397, 108, 498 (1954).

SPRAWL

Poorly planned, auto-dependent growth, usually of a low-density, single-use nature, in previously rural areas and some distance from existing development and infrastructure.

Comment: Sprawl is typically an automobile-dependent, single-use, resource-consuming, discontinuous, low-density development pattern. (*New Jersey State Development and Redevelopment Plan* 2002) Urban sprawl is now recognized as a direct result of national policies that encourage the dispersal of urban growth and is being challenged by proponents of "smart growth." *See* SMART GROWTH. *See also* Duany et al. 2000.

SQUARE

A public open space in a developed area. *See* COURT; PLAZA.

SQUATTER

A person who settles on land without the permission of the owner.

STABILIZATION

As pertaining to streets, the ability of a surface to resist deformation from imposed loads.

Comment: Stabilization can be accomplished by adequate thickness of asphalt base and surface course, dense graded aggregates, cement-treated soil aggregates, or concrete or precast masonry units set on a base course. (N.J.A.C. 5:21-1.4)

STABILIZED BASE COURSE (BITUMINOUS)

Soil aggregate and bituminous material uniformly mixed and placed on a previously prepared surface.

STABILIZED EARTH

Earth or soil, strengthened usually by the mixing of cement or lime with the original material. *See* SOIL CEMENT.

Comment: The mixing achieves increased strength, thereby reducing shrinkage and movement. (N.J.A.C. 5:21-1.4)

STABILIZED TURF

Established, mowable vegetation.

STABLE

A structure that is used for the shelter or care of horses and cattle.

STACK

A smokestack, vertical pipe, chimney, flue, conduit, or opening designed to exhaust gases and suspended particulate matter into the outdoor air.

STADIUM

A large open or enclosed place used for games and major events and partly or completely surrounded by tiers of seats for spectators.

Comment: Stadiums may include restaurants and retail stores as accessory to the principal use.

STAGGERED WORK HOURS	Work schedules that permit employees to arrive and leave at different hours, either individually or by department.
STALL	The parking space in which vehicles park. *See Figures 67 and 99.*
	Comment: The sizes of stalls vary. The typical automobile stall is 9 by 20 feet. However, where there is a large turnover and drivers have packages, such as in a shopping center, a 10- by 20-foot space may be more appropriate. The wider stall permits easier vehicular access for shoppers burdened with packages. In low-turnover situations, an 8.5- by 20-foot stall may suffice. If spaces are assigned, compact car parking can be as small as 7 by 17 feet. Where vehicles can overhang a curb, the stall depth can be reduced by 2 feet. The typical parallel parking space is 8 feet by 23 feet. *See* PARKING SPACE.
STANDARD OF LIVING	A measure of the adequacy of necessities and comforts in an individual's daily life in reference to the general populace.
STANDPIPE	*See* WATER TOWER.
STATIONARY SOURCE	A nonmobile emitter of pollution. *See* AREA SOURCE; POINT SOURCE.
STEEP SLOPE	Land areas where the slope exceeds 20 percent.
	Comment: Use of the 20 percent figure is somewhat arbitrary. The major point is that construction on slopes in excess of 20 percent requires additional safeguards against erosion and other potential problems. Some ordinances reduce the allowable intensity of development on steep slopes.
STORAGE, OUTDOOR	*See* OUTDOOR STORAGE.
STORM SEWER	A conduit that collects and transports runoff.
STORMWATER DETENTION	Any storm drainage technique that retards or detains runoff, such as a detention or retention basin, parking lot or rooftop detention, porous pavement, dry wells, or any combination thereof. *See* DETENTION BASIN; RETENTION BASIN.
STORMWATER MAINTENANCE FACILITIES	The various improvements, such as swales, curbs, catch basins, trunk sewers, collector sewers, detention and retention basins, comprising the system that accommodates and controls stormwater runoff. *See* STORMWATER DETENTION.

Comment: While there is agreement as to what elements the stormwater maintenance system consists of, responsibility for their maintenance often generates controversy. Generally speaking, improvements on private property are the responsibility of the private party. From time to time, however, improvements on private property are taken over by a public entity because of public safety and health concerns. For example, a detention basin serving a large drainage area might become the maintenance responsibility of the public entity because of flooding concerns beyond the private property that the basin serves.

In cases where the public assumes the maintenance of these facilities on private property, access easements from the public road to the facilities should be provided and the facility itself included in a dedication, either by subdivision or easement, to the public entity.

STORMWATER MANAGEMENT

The control and management of stormwater to minimize the detrimental effects of surface water runoff.

Comment: For new development, stormwater management regulations usually apply only to any net increase in stormwater runoff generated by such development activity.

STORY

That portion of a building included between the surface of any floor and the surface of the floor next above it, or if there is no floor above it, then the space between the floor and the ceiling next above it and including basements used for the principal use. *See Figure 8.*

STORY, HALF

A space under a sloping roof that has the line of intersection of the roof and wall face not more than 3 feet above the floor level and in which space the possible floor area with headroom of 5 feet or less occupies at least 40 percent of the total floor area of the story directly beneath. *See Figure 86.*

STREAM

A watercourse having a source and terminus, banks, and channel through which waters flow at least periodically.

Comment: Streams usually empty into other streams, rivers, lakes, or the ocean but do not lose their character as a watercourse even though the water may dry up.

STREAM CORRIDOR

Any river, stream, pond, lake, or wetland, together with adjacent upland areas, that supports protective bands of vegetation that line the water's edge.

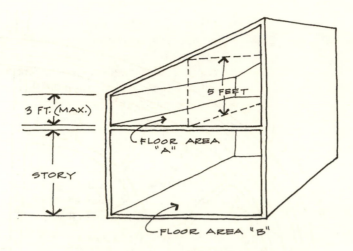

3 FT. (MAX.)

5 FEET

FLOOR AREA "A"

STORY

FLOOR AREA "B"

IF FLOOR AREA "A" IS AT LEAST
40% OF FLOOR AREA "B" —
THEN "A" IS A HALF STORY.

FIGURE 86

STREET

Any vehicular way that is (1) an existing state, county, or municipal roadway; (2) shown upon a plat approved pursuant to law; (3) approved by other official action; (4) shown on a plat duly filed and recorded in the office of the county recording officer prior to the appointment of a planning board and the grant to such board of the power to review plats; (5) shown on the official map or adopted master plan. It includes the land between the street lines, whether improved or unimproved.

STREET, COLLECTOR

A street that collects traffic from local streets and connects with minor and major arterials. *See* BOULEVARD. *See Figure 87.*

Comment: Collector streets generally carry traffic within, but usually not between, neighborhoods. They do provide access to abutting land uses. Traffic volumes may vary between 1,500 and 5,000 vehicles per day (ADT) but may drop as low as 1,000 and go as high as 7,500, depending on the density and type of development. In some cases, where volumes are high, it may be useful to break down the category into "minor" and "major" collectors. Major collectors should not be used to provide access to abutting properties, and parking is usually prohibited.

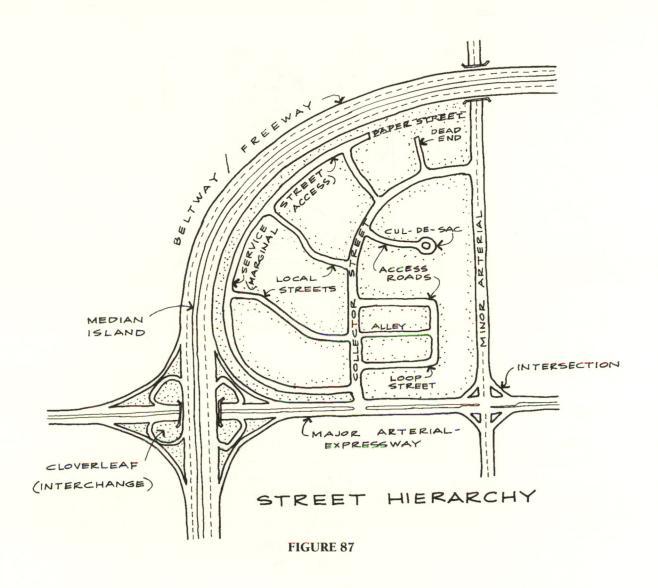

STREET HIERARCHY

FIGURE 87

STREET, CUL-DE-SAC

A street with a single common ingress and egress and with a turnaround at the end. *See Figures 87, 88, 89, 90, and 91.*

Comment: Cul-de-sacs, by eliminating through traffic, provide a safe place for young children to play and can foster neighborhood social interaction. However, most designs do not encourage walking and biking, particularly when compared to the traditional neighborhood grid design. This deficiency can be remedied by including pedestrian and bikeway connections from the end of the cul-de-sac to the neighborhood grid system, open spaces, and to other cul-de-sacs.

383

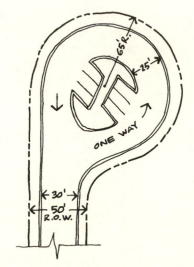

LARGE DIAMETER CUL-DE-SAC
(WITH CENTER ISLAND PARKING)

FIGURE 88

STREET, DEAD-END

A street with a single common ingress and egress. *See* STREET, CUL-DE-SAC. *See Figure 87.*

STREET, DUAL

A street with opposing lanes separated by a median strip, center island, or other form of barrier, which cannot be crossed except at designated locations.

STREET, EXPRESSWAY

A divided, multilane major arterial street for through traffic with partial control of access and with grade separations at major intersections. *See Figure 87.*

STREET, FREEWAY

A limited-access highway with no grade crossings. *See Figure 87.*

STREET, IMPROVED PUBLIC

Any street that complies in width and construction with municipal standards, or a street meeting lesser standards that the municipality agrees to accept.

STREET, LOCAL

A street that provides frontage for access to abutting lots and carries slow-speed traffic primarily having a destination or origin on the street itself. *See Figure 87.*

Comment: Local streets are also known as residential access or neighborhood streets and are the lowest order of residential street, other than a rural street. They usually have rights-of-way of up to 50 feet and cartways of 24 to 28 feet with sidewalks and curbs. Parking is

384

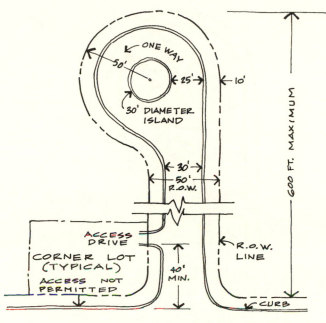

STANDARD CUL-DE-SAC
(SINGLE-FAMILY DEVELOPMENT)

MAXIMUM LENGTH - 600 FT.
MAXIMUM LOTS - 12

CENTER ISLAND STANDARDS:
- GRANITE BLOCK CURB
- 4 TREES
- MAINTENANCE BY LOT OWNERS

FIGURE 89

usually permitted on both sides of the street. *See* STREET, CUL-DE-SAC; STREET, LOOP.

STREET, LOOP

A local street that has its only ingress and egress at two points on the same collector street. *See Figure 87.*

STREET, MAJOR ARTERIAL

A street that connects and distributes traffic to and from minor arterials, with access control, channelized intersections, and restricted parking. *See Figure 87.*

Comment: Major arterials carry regional traffic between communities at higher speeds and with traffic volumes in excess of 10,000 vehicles per day (ADT).

STREET, MARGINAL ACCESS

A service street that runs parallel to a higher-order street, such as an arterial street or expressway, and that provides access to abutting properties. *See Figure 87.*

Comment: Marginal access streets may be designed as a residential access, collector, or arterial street, depending on traffic volumes.

385

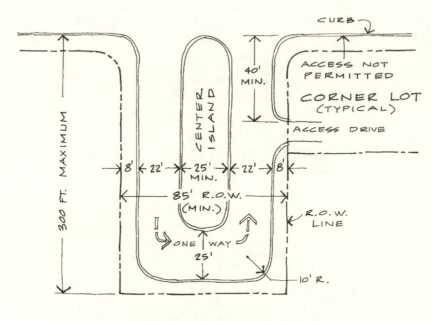

LONG LOOP CUL-DE-SAC
(SINGLE-FAMILY DEVELOPMENT)
MAXIMUM LENGTH - 300 FT.
MAXIMUM LOTS - 12

CENTER ISLAND STANDARDS
- GRANITE BLOCK CURB
- 10 TREES

FIGURE 90

STREET, MINOR ARTERIAL

A street that interconnects and links major arterials and distributes traffic to and from collector streets. *See Figure 87.*

Comment: Minor arterials overlap major collectors to some extent. Traffic volumes range between 5,000 and 10,000 vehicles per day (ADT) with speeds of 30 to 35 miles per hour.

STREET, MULTIFAMILY ACCESS

A type of private residential street serving multifamily development that is either a loop street or a connecting street between streets and that permits nonparallel on-street parking that is accessed from the traveled way.

Comment: The distinguishing element that defines multifamily access streets is that nonparallel on-street parking, accessed from the traveled way, is permitted. The requirement for a loop or connecting street is to

386

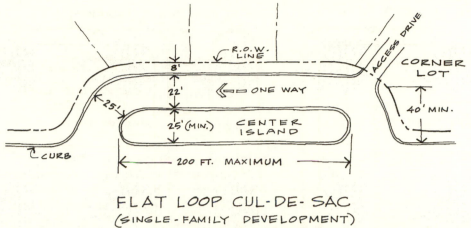

FLAT LOOP CUL-DE-SAC
(SINGLE-FAMILY DEVELOPMENT)
MAXIMUM LENGTH - 200 FT.
MAXIMUM LOTS - 6

CENTER ISLAND STANDARDS
  - GRANITE BLOCK CURB
  - 6 TREES

FIGURE 91

differentiate the multifamily access street from the typical parking lot in a multifamily development. The usual pavement width for the access street traveled way, exclusive of the perpendicular parking spaces, is 24 feet, with curbs and sidewalks required.

STREET, PAPER

A street that has never been built but is shown on an approved plan, subdivision plat, tax maps, or official map.

STREET, PRIVATE

A street that has not been accepted by the municipality or other governmental entity.

Comment: Private streets may be used by the public, often as access to a development, industrial plant, or shopping area. Some states permit the municipality to remove snow on private streets without affecting their status.

STREET, RURAL

A road primarily serving as access to abutting building lots in areas with densities of less than one dwelling unit per acre.

Comment: Rural streets usually have rights-of-way of 40 feet and cartways of 18 to 20 feet without curbs and sidewalks. Parking may be permitted on one side of the street only.

STREET, SERVICE

See STREET, MARGINAL ACCESS.

STREET BEAUTIFICATION

Improving the appearance of a street in accordance with a plan, including, but not limited to, the installation of landscaping, benches, street lighting, sidewalks, wastebaskets, and signage.

STREET CAPACITY

See CAPACITY, ROADWAY.

STREET FURNITURE

Constructed, above-ground objects, such as outdoor seating, kiosks, bus shelters, sculpture, trash receptacles, planters, bollards, fountains, and telephone booths, that have the potential for enlivening and giving variety to streets, sidewalks, plazas, and other outdoor spaces open to and used by the public.

Comment: Street furniture can include, but is generally distinct from, street hardware. *See* STREET HARDWARE.

STREET HARDWARE

Mechanical and utility systems, usually located within a street right-of-way, such as hydrants, manhole covers, tree grids, traffic signals, lighting standards, and directional signs.

STREET HIERARCHY

The system by which roads are classified according to their purpose and the travel demand they serve. *See Figure 87*.

Comment: The State of New Jersey has established site improvement standards, including street hierarchy standards, for all residential development. The purpose of these largely performance-based engineering standards is to help streamline the development approval process while eliminating unnecessary building costs.

The residential street hierarchy under the New Jersey standards is based on the maximum average daily traffic (ADT) for each street type. For example, the ADT for "residential access" and "residential neighborhood" streets is 1,500. For larger-volume "minor collector" and "major collector" streets, the respective maximum ADTs are 3,500 and 7,500. For each of the many street types there are specific standards for cartway and right-of-way widths, curb or shoulders, sidewalks, and parking lanes. The range of cartway widths for all street types is from 9 feet (a one-way alley) to 30 feet (a neighborhood street with two 8-foot parking lanes and one 14-foot moving lane). (NJDCA 2000, N.J.A.C. 5:21-1)

STREET LINE

See RIGHT-OF-WAY LINES.

STREETSCAPE

A design term referring to all the elements that constitute the physical makeup of a street and that, as a group, define its character, including building frontage; street paving; street furniture; landscaping, including trees and other plantings; awnings and marquees; signs; and lighting. (Schultz and Kasen 1984)

STRIP COMMERCIAL DEVELOPMENT

Commercial or retail uses, usually one-story high and one-store deep, that front on a major street.

Comment: Strip commercial development is typically characterized by street-frontage parking lots serving individual stores or strips of stores. Some older commercial strips, however, are dependent on on-street parking and, in some cases, parking lots interspersed among or positioned behind the buildings. Strip commercial developments differ from central business districts and shopping centers in at least two of the following characteristics: (1) There are no provisions for pedestrian access between individual uses; (2) the uses are only one-store deep; (3) the buildings are arranged linearly rather than clustered; and (4) there is no design integration among individual uses.

While strip commercial developments are universally criticized as ugly, the problem with them may be inadequate local regulations. For example, landscaped parking lots, including trees and landscaped island separations between bays, can significantly improve overall appearance and soften building impact. Other requirements that significantly improve the aesthetics of these uses include peaked rather than flat roofs, wide sidewalks abutting the storefronts with canopy or roof overhangs over pedestrian areas, and controlled and integrated signage. Features such as kiosks, benches, and sculpture can help humanize and make these developments more attractive.

In addition, adjacent residential areas can be shielded from strip commercial uses by requiring walls and berms with heavy landscape treatment. Functional and attractive pedestrian access from adjacent residential areas should be provided.

STRIP MINING

A process of recovering ore or fuel deposits by mechanically scraping the overhanging rock and strata.

Comment: Strip mining is also known as surface mining.

STRIP ZONING

See STRIP COMMERCIAL DEVELOPMENT.

STRUCTURAL ALTERATION

Any change in either the supporting members of a building, such as bearing walls, columns, beams, and girders, or in the dimensions or configurations of the roof or exterior walls.

STRUCTURE

A combination of materials that form a construction for use, occupancy, or ornamentation whether installed on, above, or below the surface of land or water.

Comment: By this definition, all buildings are structures; however, not all structures are buildings. *See* BUILDING.

STUB STREET

A street that is designed to be extended when the adjacent property is developed.

STUD FARM

A farm where a stallion stands at stud and mares are bred to him, and where breeding, pasturing, and foaling may take place. *See* HORSE FARM.

STUDIO

(1) The workshop of an artist, sculptor, photographer, or craftsperson; (2) a place for radio or television production; (3) a place where movies are produced. *See* ARTIST STUDIO.

Comment: The studio for radio or television broadcasting is that part of the station from which the signal originates. It could be an office or a home and is often separate and some distance from the transmitter and antennas.

From a zoning perspective, the local ordinance should clearly identify the type of studio permitted. Workshops of craftspersons, for instance, would be appropriate for residential areas, as would small studios for radio productions. Large-scale television or movie production studios clearly belong in nonresidential areas.

STUDIO APARTMENT

See DWELLING UNIT, EFFICIENCY.

SUBDIVIDER

Any person having an interest in land that is the subject of an application for subdivision. *See* APPLICANT.

SUBDIVISION

The division of a lot, tract, or parcel of land into two or more lots, tracts, parcels, or other divisions of land for sale, development, or lease.

Comment: Many state enabling laws exclude certain subdivisions from this definition. For example, in New Jersey, the following are not considered subdivisions, providing no new streets are created: (1) divisions of land for agricultural purposes where all resulting parcels are 5 acres or larger in size; (2) divisions of property by testamentary or intestate provisions; (3) divisions of property upon court order, including, but not limited to, judgments of foreclosure; and (4) conveyances so as to combine existing lots by deed or other instruments.

SUBDIVISION, ANTIQUATED

See PREMATURE SUBDIVISION.

SUBDIVISION, CLUSTER

See CLUSTER SUBDIVISION.

SUBDIVISION, CONSOLIDATION

The combining of individual recorded lots to form a single tract in single ownership. *See* ASSEMBLAGE; CONSOLIDATION.

SUBDIVISION, MAJOR

Any subdivision not classified as a minor subdivision.

SUBDIVISION, MINOR

A subdivision of land that does not involve any of the following: (1) the creating of more than the maximum number of lots specifically permitted by ordinance as a minor subdivision; (2) a planned development; (3) any new street; or (4) the extension of any off-tract improvements.

Comment: Many ordinances further restrict minor subdivisions to land incapable of further subdivision. Any parcel that could be further subdivided would be classified as a major subdivision. The purpose is to ensure that required improvements are installed and are not avoided by a series of minor subdivisions.

SUBDIVISION, PREMATURE

See PREMATURE SUBDIVISION.

SUBGRADE

The prepared surface upon which pavements and shoulders are constructed.

SUBMERGED LAND

Those lands situated below the mean low waterline or all of the lands covered by the mean high waterline.

SUBSIDENCE

The gradual sinking of land as a result of natural or artificial causes.

SUBSIDIZED HOUSING

Housing priced below market cost as a result of the use of subsidies and limited to occupancy by households in specified income ranges. *See* LOW-INCOME HOUSING; MODERATE-INCOME HOUSING; PUBLIC HOUSING.

Comment: Subsidized housing is usually restricted to households earning 80 percent or less of the median income of the area in which the housing is located. Rental and sales prices are usually based on the income of the occupant. The U.S. Department of Housing and Urban Development regulations for rental housing stipulate that rents, including utilities, cannot exceed 30 percent of the occupant's gross annual income. In New Jersey, where subsidized housing is often made available on a sales basis, mortgage principal and interest, condo fees (if applicable), taxes, and insurance cannot exceed 28 percent of the occupant's income.

SUBSOIL

The layer of soil just below the surface of the ground.

SUBSTANDARD STRUCTURE/DWELLING

A term used in the 1960s and preceding the U.S. *Census of Housing* to indicate a lack of some or all plumbing facilities and/or the presence of physical inadequacies. *See* DEFICIENT UNIT.

SUBSTANTIAL IMPROVEMENT

Any extension, repair, reconstruction, or other improvements of a property, the cost of which equals or exceeds 50 percent of the fair market value of a property either before the improvement is started or, if the property has been damaged and is being restored, before the damage occurred.

Comment: "Substantial improvement" is often used to define the point beyond which a nonconforming use or structure cannot be repaired. The Federal Insurance Administration also requires flood-proofing measures to be installed when a structure in a floodway undergoes "substantial improvement."

SUBSTANTIALLY DIFFERENT

See CHANGE OF USE.

SUBSURFACE DISPOSAL SYSTEM

A collection of treatment tanks, disposal areas, holding tanks and ponds, surface spray systems, cesspools, wells, surface ditches, alternative toilets, or other devices and associated piping designed to function as a unit for the purpose of disposing of wastes or wastewater on or beneath the surface of the ground. *See* SEPTIC SYSTEM; WASTEWATER SYSTEM.

SUBURBAN AREA

A predominantly low-density residential area located immediately outside of an urban area or a city and associated with it physically and socioeconomically.

Comment: Suburban areas have population densities ranging from 500 to 1,000 persons per square mile.

392

SUITABLE SITE

A site that is adjacent to compatible land uses, has access to appropriate streets, and is consistent with state environmental policies.

Comment: The above is the definition of the New Jersey Council on Affordable Housing for sites suitable for lower-income housing. The broad criteria have been further refined in a series of court cases by judges and planners. In *Orgo Farms and Greenhouses v. Colts Neck Township*, 192 N.J. Super. 559 (1984), and *Orgo Farms and Greenhouses v. Colts Neck Township*, 204 N.J. Super. 585 (1985), the court cited the importance of state and regional planning designations for growth and limited-growth areas as criteria in determining suitable sites. The court-appointed planning master in the same case proposed five criteria as tests for suitable sites: (1) regional accessibility; (2) proximity to goods and services; (3) availability of water and sewers; (4) environmental suitability; and (5) land-use compatibility.

Another special master added further criteria, as follows: (1) has access to appropriate streets; (2) avoids historic sites; (3) avoids restricted agricultural lands; (4) avoids wetlands and required buffers; (5) avoids flood hazard areas; (6) avoids steep slopes (in excess of 15 percent); (7) avoids reserved recreation, conservation, and open space; (8) has clear title, free of encumbrances that would preclude the development of low- and moderate-income housing; (9) lacks intangible factors likely to delay or hinder development of low- and moderate-income housing; and (10) is owned by or under contract or sale to a developer who is ready, willing, and able to build a substantial amount of low- and moderate-income housing.

SULFUR DIOXIDE (SO$_2$)

A heavy, pungent, colorless gas, formed primarily by the combustion of fossil fuels, that damages the respiratory tract as well as vegetation and certain materials and is considered a major air pollutant.

SUMMER CAMP

A location away from home, often in a rural or country setting, where campers spend all or part of the summer living in tents, barracks, or dormitories, participating in organized activities, sports, and arts and crafts, and usually eating together in a central dining facility.

Comment: The term "summer camp" may be a misnomer, since these facilities operate throughout the year in all seasons and many are located in urban areas. Some are geared to the elderly or the physically or mentally handicapped. Housing includes "camp-type" dormitories and cabins.

SUMP

A depression or tank that serves as a drain or receptacle of liquids for salvage or disposal.

SUPERMARKET

A retail establishment primarily selling food as well as other convenience and household goods.

Comment: Supermarkets usually vary in size, from approximately 35,000 square feet to 70,000 square feet, and provide parking at a ratio of about five to six off-street spaces per 1,000 square feet of gross leasable space. The larger supermarkets include branch banking facilities, video rentals, and eating areas.

SURFACE COURSE

The placement of asphalt or concrete on the previously prepared base course.

SURFACE WATER

Water on the earth's surface exposed to the atmosphere as rivers, lakes, streams, and oceans. *See* GROUND WATER.

SURGICAL CENTER

An outpatient facility for medical procedures and simple surgery.

Comment: Surgical centers are more elaborate than a doctor's office but less equipped and more limited in the services they perform than a hospital. The maximum stay at an outpatient surgical center is 23 hours.

SURROGATE

A census indicator of deficient housing used in the calculation of present need.

Comment: Surrogates for deficient housing include age of structure, no elevators in a mid-rise building, no central heat, overcrowding, nonexclusive use of complete plumbing facilities, inadequate kitchen facilities, and access. Usually any deficiency, together with age, constitutes evidence of deficient housing.

SURVEILLANCE SYSTEM

(1) A monitoring system to determine environmental quality; (2) a monitoring system to maintain security.

Comment: Surveillance systems are established to monitor all pollution and other aspects of progress toward attainment of environmental standards. Surveillance systems identify potential episodes of high pollutant concentrations in time to take preventive action.

SURVEY

(1) The process of precisely ascertaining the area, dimensions, and location of a piece of land; (2) determining the characteristics of persons, land, objects, buildings, or structures by sampling, census, interviews, observations, or other methods.

394

SUSPENDED SOLIDS

Small particles of solid pollutants in sewage that contribute to turbidity and that resist separation by conventional means.

Comment: The examination of suspended solids and the BOD (biological oxygen demand) test constitute the two main determinations for water quality performed at wastewater treatment facilities.

SUSTAINABLE DEVELOPMENT

Development that maintains or enhances economic opportunity and community well-being while protecting and restoring the natural environment upon which people and economies depend. (Schwab and Brower 1997)

SWALE

Low-lying or depressed land area commonly wet or moist, which can function as an intermittent drainageway. (N.J.A.C. 5-21-1.4)

SWIMMING POOL

A water-filled enclosure, permanently constructed or portable, having a depth of more than 18 inches below the level of the surrounding land, or an above-surface pool, having a depth of more than 30 inches, designed, used, and maintained for swimming and bathing.

Comment: The 18-inch exclusion would be effective in permitting landscaping and other shallow, not-for-swimming, pools. The 30-inch height for surface pools marks the usual break between portable and non-portable pools beyond which some codes require fencing and gates.

SYNDICATE

A group formed to combine capital or other assets for future investment.

SYNERGISM

The cooperative action of separate substances so that the total effect is greater than the sum of the effects of the substances acting independently.

T

Definitions:

Tailings
through
Two-Family Dwelling

Figures:

TAILINGS

Second-grade or waste material derived when raw material is screened or processed.

TAKING

To take, expropriate, acquire, or seize property without compensation. *See* EMINENT DOMAIN; JUST COMPENSATION.

Comment: The question of taking has become increasingly important as a result of a number of U.S. Supreme Court decisions since 1987, including *First English Evangelical Lutheran Church v. County of Los Angeles* (1987); *Nollan v. California Coastal Comm'n* (1987); *Keystone Bituminous Coal Ass'n v. DeBenedictis* (1987); and *Lucas v. South Carolina Coastal Council* (1992).

The cases are complicated and in some cases contradictory. In *Keystone,* for example, the Court appeared to suggest that if the regulations serve broad public purposes and permit reasonable economic use of property, they are legal. In *Nollan,* on the other hand, the Court seemed to say that the broad public benefit is narrow and has to be carefully considered. In *Lutheran,* the Court indicated that if the regulations are too restrictive or excessive, the entity harmed can secure damages for the time the regulations were in effect. In *Lucas,* the Court established guidelines to determine if a regulatory taking had occurred:

- Is there a denial of economically viable use of the property as a result of the regulatory imposition?

- Does the property owner have distinct investment-backed expectations?

- Is the property owner's interest derived from state property law and not within the power of the state to regulate under the state's common law nuisance doctrine?

More recently, in *Tahoe-Sierra Preservation Council, Inc. v. Tahoe Regional Planning Agency* (2002), the Court changed direction, ruling that a government-imposed moratorium on development, even one that lasts for years, does not automatically amount to a taking of private property for which taxpayers must compensate landowners.

The Court has now made it clear that the distinction between a physical and a regulatory taking remains a vital one. Regulations that permanently deprive property of all value are a taking; regulations that are temporary or allow some economic use of a property are not. The decision reaffirms the doctrine known as the "parcel as a whole" rule. Under this rule the analysis of whether a regulation that affects only part of a property, such as a wetlands, constitutes a taking must take into account the regulatory impact on the property as a whole and not just on the regulated portion. See Meltz et al. 1999.

TANK FARM

An open-air facility containing large, above-ground containers for the bulk storage of material in liquid, gaseous, powder, or pellet form.

TAVERN

An establishment in which alcoholic beverages are served, primarily by the drink, and where food or packaged liquors may also be served or sold.

Comment: Liquor laws vary by state, and the above definition may not be applicable in all states or areas. Zoning regulations should make a distinction between taverns that have live entertainment or permit dancing and those that do not. Those with live entertainment and dancing may require considerably more parking and need additional setbacks because of noise.

TAX ABATEMENT

Full or partial exemption from real estate taxes for a defined period of time.

Comment: Tax abatements can be used for a variety of purposes, including encouraging development, historic preservation, natural resource conservation, urban redevelopment, enterprise zones, or some other public objective. In many states, tax abatements are limited to those uses or geographic areas listed in applicable state legislation.

TAX-EXEMPT PROPERTY

Property that, because of its ownership or use, is not subject to property taxation.

TAX MAP

The recorded map of delineated lots or tracts in a municipality showing boundaries, bearings, sizes, and dimensions, including the block and lot numbers.

Comment: The tax map shows individual parcels of land that are duly recorded in the office of the county (usually) recording office. It may include ownership and use.

TECHNICAL COORDINATING COMMITTEE (TCC)

A committee consisting of one or more persons to review all applications for development. *See* DESIGN REVIEW; DESIGN STANDARDS; SITE PLAN REVIEW.

Comment: TCCs may also be known by a variety of other names, such as the development review committee, application review committee, technical review team, or professional staff review. The TCC, if permitted by enabling legislation and established by the municipality, can save both applicants and approving authority time, money, and energy. The exact makeup of the TCC and members' duties should be carefully spelled out in the land development ordinance.

In general, TCCs may consist of the municipal engineer, planner, planning board or zoning board attorney, building inspector, zoning official and one or two members of the approving authority (planning board or zoning board). The members are usually appointed by the approving authority chairman, although the engineer and planner are often specified by ordinance as ex-officio members.

Their job may consist of any one or more of the following:

- Determine whether the application is a minor or major development application
- Determine compliance with municipal development standards and regulations
- Make recommendations on the design and technical elements of any application
- Determine whether the application is complete and ready for public hearing
- Conduct formal hearings on minor development applications

The TCC meetings are less formal than the planning board meeting and, as a result, allow for informal exchanges of ideas and recommendations on design and layout to make the application more acceptable to the municipality. TCCs usually do not get involved in policy matters such as when variances are requested. They generally confine themselves to the technical aspects of the application.

In some states, TCCs can approve minor applications for development. In such situations, more formal procedures, including hearings, notices, and the publication of decisions, are often required.

TELECOMMUNICATIONS CELL SITE

See WIRELESS TELECOMMUNICATIONS TOWERS AND FACILITIES.

TELECOMMUTING

An arrangement for performing work at a location other than the primary work location, such as at home or in a satellite office, and sending and receiving material by phone, e-mail, or other electronic means.

TEMPORARY OUTDOOR ACTIVITY

Happenings that are carried out primarily out-of-doors for a fixed period of time; these include flea markets, fireworks, displays, speeches, farm stands, seasonal sales, swap and shop markets, racing meets, circuses, carnivals, concerts, and parades. *See* MASS GATHERING.

Comment: Some forms of temporary outdoor activities are clearly addressed by zoning. These include weekend flea markets, farm stands, racing meets, and so forth. Others are more transitory, such as parades, carnivals, and fireworks, and are probably best controlled by permit or license from the municipality.

TEMPORARY PERMIT

Authorization for a land-use activity for a limited period of time.

Comment: The local zoning ordinance should spell out what activities can be authorized by a temporary permit, what municipal official or office can issue the temporary permit, and what is required to be submitted for the temporary permit.

Activities usually covered by temporary permits include yard sales, construction trailers, temporary signs, carnivals and circuses sponsored by nonprofit organizations, and seasonal or outdoor sales.

The usual officials authorized to issue the temporary permit are the zoning officer, planner, or municipal engineer. Material to be submitted usually includes a site plan showing access, parking, location, use of structures, and where appropriate, lighting, sanitary facilities, and security arrangements. Some ordinances require the posting of bonds to ensure compliance with the provisions of the grant of the temporary permit. (Jaffee 1999)

TEMPORARY PROTECTION

Stabilization of erosive or sediment-producing areas by temporary measures until permanent measures are in place.

TEMPORARY RETAIL FOOD ESTABLISHMENT

A retail food establishment that operates at a fixed location for a temporary period of time in connection with a fair, carnival, circus, picnic, concert, public exhibition, or similar transitory gathering.

Comment: Temporary retail food establishments are accessory to the principal permitted use, for instance, a fair or carnival.

TEMPORARY STRUCTURE

A structure that is erected without any foundation or footings and is removed when the designated time period, activity, or use for which the temporary structure was erected has ceased.

TEMPORARY USE

A use established for a limited duration with the intent to discontinue such use upon the expiration of the time period.

Comment: Temporary uses usually do not involve the construction or alteration of any permanent building or structure, although the authorization of the temporary use does not necessarily preclude such construction.

TENANT

An occupant of land or premises who occupies, uses, and enjoys real property for a fixed time, usually through a lease or rental arrangement with the property owner.

TENEMENT HOUSE

A multifamily dwelling most commonly associated with low-income families and generally characterized as an aging, often substandard structure.

TENNIS COURT

An improved area used for playing tennis.

Comment: In residential areas, the site plan concerns are lighting, buffers, and setbacks.

TERMINAL

(1) A place where transfers between modes of transportation take place; (2) a terminating point where goods are transferred from a truck to a storage area or to other trucks or another form of transportation. *See* DISTRIBUTION CENTER; TRUCK TERMINAL; WAREHOUSE.

TERMINAL VISTA

See VISUAL TERMINATION.

TERRACE

A level, landscaped, and/or surfaced area, also referred to as a patio, directly adjacent to a principal building at or within 3 feet of the finished grade and not covered by a permanent roof.

TERTIARY TREATMENT

Wastewater treatment, beyond the secondary or biological stage, that includes removal of nutrients, such as phosphorus and nitrogen, and a high percentage of suspended solids.

TEXTURE

The quality of a surface, ranging from mirror-finish smooth to coarse and unfinished.

TEXTURED PAVEMENT

See TRAFFIC CALMING.

THEATER

A building or part of a building used to show motion pictures or for drama, dance, musical, or other live performances.

THEATER, DRIVE-IN

An open lot devoted primarily to the showing of motion pictures or theatrical productions on a paid-admission basis to patrons seated in automobiles.

Comment: Drive-in theaters are usually temporary uses until demand for other, more remunerative uses materializes. Drive-in theaters include refreshment stands and amusement rides. Since drive-in theaters operate only at night, many sites are used for other purposes during the day, such as flea markets.

THEME PARK

An entertainment or amusement facility built around a single theme that may be historical, architectural, or cultural. *See* AMUSEMENT PARK.

THEORETICAL DRIVEWAY LOCATION

The center of the highway frontage of any lot; used to calculate whether a lot is conforming for highway access purposes.

Comment: Used in highway access ordinances.

THERMAL POLLUTION

Degradation of water quality by the introduction of a heated effluent.

Comment: Thermal pollution is primarily the result of the discharge of cooling waters from industrial processes, particularly from electrical power generation.

THREATENED SPECIES

Wildlife species that may become endangered if conditions surrounding them begin or continue to deteriorate and that are so designated by a governmental agency.

THROUGH LOT

See LOT, THROUGH.

TIDE

A periodic rise and fall of the surface of ocean waters caused by gravitational pull.

TIDE LAND

Land between low and high tide. *See* INTERTIDAL AREA. *See Figure 11.*

TILLABLE LAND

Fertile land that can be cultivated.

TIMBERLAND

Land covered by harvestable trees and wooded areas.

T-INTERSECTION

An at-grade intersection where one of the intersecting legs is perpendicular to the other two.

TOPOGRAPHIC MAP

A map of a part of the earth's surface showing elevations from sea level or some other fixed reference point.

Comment: Topographic maps often include natural and artificial features, such as structures, rivers, and wooded areas. *See* MAP, CONTOUR.

TOPOGRAPHY

The physical land surface relief describing terrain elevation and slope. *See* CONTOUR LINE.

TOPSOIL

(1) The natural, undisturbed surface layer of soil having more organic material than subsequent layers, having a pH of 5.0 to 7.5, and being suitable for satisfactory growth and maintenance of permanent, locally adapted vegetation; (2) where the original surface layer has been removed, the reapplication of soil material used to cover an area so as to improve soil conditions for establishment and maintenance of adapted vegetation. (NJDCA 2000, N.J.A.C. 5:21-1)

Comment: The above source also provides standards for when the surface layer has been removed and new soil material brought in, as follows: " . . . the new soil must be friable, loamy soil, reasonably free of debris, objectionable weeds and stones, have a natural pH of 5.0 to 7.5, have an organic matter content greater than 2.0 percent and contain no toxic substances which may be harmful to plant growth."

Topsoil usually has a depth of 6 to 10 inches, although it may be less in certain regions and more in others. Since topsoil is needed to support plant growth and is relatively poor in terms of providing a stable base for buildings or structures, builders will often scrape off the topsoil on a construction site and stockpile it on the site until the final permanent landscaping phase of development, when it is re-spread. Many local ordinances prohibit the export of topsoil from building sites.

TOT LOT

An improved and equipped play area for small children, usually up to elementary school age.

Comment: Tot lots generally do not exceed 2,500 square feet and are usually equipped with swings, sandboxes, and recreation facilities suitable for small children. They include benches and tables and are usually fenced.

TOURISM

The attracting and serving of people visiting an area for recreation and vacations.

TOURIST HOME

See BED AND BREAKFAST.

403

TOWER, AMATEUR RADIO

A tower with one or more antennas connected to radio equipment operated by a licensed amateur radio operator in accordance with applicable FCC laws and regulations.

Comment: An application to install an amateur radio tower often provokes opposition because of real or perceived interference problems, potential dangers to health, and aesthetic considerations. Because amateur radio towers are usually much lower than cellular towers, opposition is usually local in nature, often limited to the street or immediate neighborhood surrounding the tower.

The Federal Communications Commission (FCC) regulates amateur radio licensing and operations, including operating frequencies, maximum radio frequency emissions, and interference. In 1985, the FCC issued a limited federal preemption of amateur radio antennas (FCC PRB-1, 101 FCC. 2d 952 [September 16, 1985]). PRB-1 states that local governments must reasonably accommodate amateur operations, but they may still zone for height, safety, and aesthetic concerns. Any regulations affecting aesthetics, location, height, and screening must "reasonably accommodate such communications and must represent the minimum practicable regulation to accomplish the stated purpose." (American Planning Association, *Aesthetics, Community Character, and the Law*, Planning Advisory Service Report No. 489/490, 1999, p. 121)

Amateur radio operators provide important, recognized communication support services to government and private relief agencies in times of major local and national disasters. They also provide assistance to citizens in forwarding "health and welfare" messages during periods when normal communication facilities are unavailable. To protect this valuable resource, many states have enacted specific laws providing limits on the types of controls local government can enact affecting the placement, screening, or height of amateur radio antenna support structures. Approximately 13 states have such legislation in place, with others (New York, Nevada, Wisconsin) considering legislation.

Local ordinances should consider addressing the issue directly. For example, antennas, as permitted accessory uses, could be restricted to rear and side yards with reasonable setbacks from property lines. Landscaping can be required around the base of the tower, including the planting of trees that would provide some screening. In addition, a building permit from the local building department would be appropriate to ensure that the structure is erected in a safe manner. Finally, the maximum height could be established at 75 feet, which experts suggest is needed to ensure communication reliability for certain frequencies. Anything higher would require a variance. Towers on top of buildings would have to meet the maximum established for buildings in the particular zone.

These controls address issues of safety and aesthetics while still providing a reasonable accommodation for amateur radio.

TOWER, ANTENNA

A structure that is intended to support antennas and related equipment used to transmit and/or receive telecommunications signals.

TOWER, COMMERCIAL COMMUNICATIONS

A transmission tower that either (1) serves an individual user and is not available to the general public; (2) is privately owned and operated for the purpose of leasing tower space to others; and/or (3) is a single-purpose facility and not part of a cell site network.

TOWN

(1) A developed community, smaller than a city and larger than a village; (2) in some states, a description of the form of local government.

Comment: *The New Jersey State Development and Redevelopment Plan* (2002) defines a town as having an urban density of more than 1,000 persons per square mile and interrelated mixed uses.

TOWN CENTER

See CENTRAL BUSINESS DISTRICT.

TOWN SQUARE

The traditional center of a village or town, usually surrounded by governmental, religious, and cultural buildings.

TOWN HOUSE

See DWELLING, TOWN HOUSE.

TOWNSHIP

(1) A unit of territory 6 miles square and containing 36-mile-square sections; (2) in some states, a description of the form of local government.

TOXIC SUBSTANCES

Any combination of pollutants, including disease-carrying agents, that, after discharge and upon exposure, ingestion, inhalation, or assimilation into any organism, can cause death or disease, mutations, deformities, or malfunctions in such organisms or their offspring, and that adversely affect the environment.

TOXICITY

The quality or degree of being poisonous or harmful to plant or animal life.

TRACE METALS

Metals, usually insoluble, found in small quantities in air, water, or other materials.

TRACT

An area, parcel, site, piece of land, or property that is the subject of a development application. *See Figure 65.*

TRADITIONAL NEIGHBORHOOD DEVELOPMENT (TND)

An approach to land-use planning and urban design that promotes the building of pedestrian-friendly neighborhoods with a mix of uses, housing types and costs, lot sizes and density, architectural variety, a central meeting place such as a town square, a network of narrow streets and alleys, and defined development edges. *See* NEIGHBORHOOD.

Comment: Traditional neighborhood development de-emphasizes dependence on the automobile by employing mixed land-use patterns that afford residents the opportunity to live, work, play, and shop within their own neighborhood. It is based on the form and design of older towns and cities. Porches, detached garages, alleys, and residences over retail uses are encouraged. Traditional neighborhood design promotes mass transit alternatives by allowing higher densities.

TND zoning controls will not necessarily produce their stated objectives. But Hinshaw (2000) suggests that such ordinances can be tilted toward good development by adhering to the following five principles:

1. Respect for existing scale and proportions

2. A close relationship to the street, which ensures the continuity of the townscape

3. The mixing of different uses, both vertically and horizontally

4. Minimum intrusiveness from parking

5. A variety of attractive and accessible public spaces

TRAFFIC CALMING

The use of traffic management measures such as changes in existing street alignment, installation of barriers and diversions, and other physical measures to reduce traffic speeds and/or volumes in the interest of street safety and neighborhood amenity. (Knack 1998)

Comment: Traffic calming has the objective of reducing the negative effects of motor vehicle use on the quality of life in a residential neighborhood by altering driver behavior and thereby improving living conditions for area residents. Traffic calming includes both volume-control devices and speed-control devices. Volume-control devices largely divert traffic in order to reduce or eliminate through traffic. Speed-control devices have the objective of slowing traffic in a given neighborhood. Both types of devices are physical in nature, ranging from speed humps or bumps in streets to street closures or diversions. Examples of traffic-calming devices are defined here and illustrated in *Figures 92* and *93.*

FULL CLOSURES (cul-de-sacs/dead ends): Barriers or turnarounds placed across a street to completely close it to through traffic except for connecting pedestrian or bicycle pathways.

HALF-CLOSURES (partial closures/one-ways): Barriers that block travel in one direction for a short distance on otherwise two-way streets.

DIAGONAL DIVERTERS (full diverters/diagonal road closures): Barriers placed diagonally across an intersection, blocking through movement.

MEDIAN BARRIERS (median diverters/island diverters): Raised islands located along the centerline of a street and continuing through an intersection so as to block through movement at a cross street.

FORCED-TURN ISLANDS (forced-turn channelizations/right-turn islands): Raised islands on approaches to an intersection that block certain vehicular movements.

SPEED HUMPS (road humps/indulations): Rounded, raised areas placed across the road to slow traffic.

SPEED TABLES (trapezoidal humps/speed platforms): Flat-topped speed humps, often with a brick or other textured surface on the flat section.

RAISED CROSSWALKS (raised crossings): Speed tables with crosswalk markings and signage providing pedestrians with a level street crossing.

RAISED INTERSECTIONS (raised junctions): Flat, raised areas covering entire intersections, with ramps at all approaches and often with a textured surface on the flat section.

TEXTURED PAVEMENTS: A textured or rough road surface of brick or stone that slows traffic while adding an aesthetic dimension to the street environment.

TRAFFIC CIRCLES (rotaries/intersection islands): Raised islands, placed in intersections, around which traffic is forced to circulate.

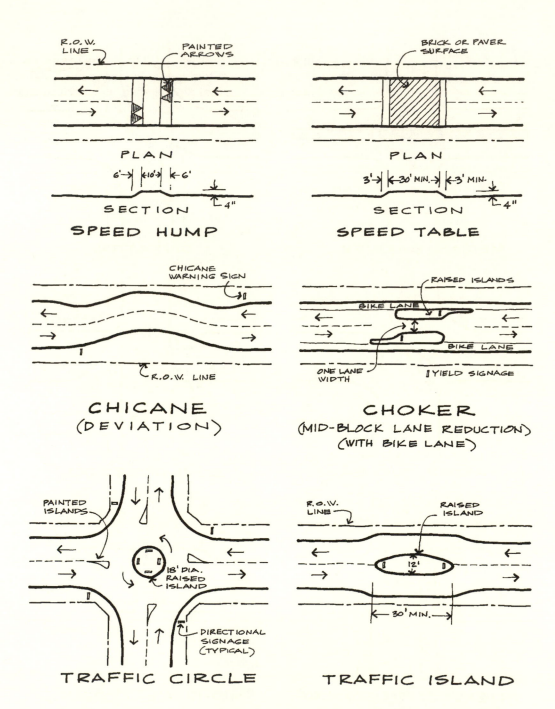

SPEED HUMP

R.O.W. LINE
PAINTED ARROWS
PLAN
6' 10' 6'
SECTION
4"

SPEED TABLE

BRICK OR PAVER SURFACE
PLAN
3' 30' MIN. 3' MIN.
SECTION
4"

CHICANE
(DEVIATION)

CHICANE WARNING SIGN
R.O.W. LINE

CHOKER
(MID-BLOCK LANE REDUCTION)
(WITH BIKE LANE)

RAISED ISLANDS
BIKE LANE
BIKE LANE
ONE LANE WIDTH
YIELD SIGNAGE

TRAFFIC CIRCLE

PAINTED ISLANDS
18' DIA. RAISED ISLAND
DIRECTIONAL SIGNAGE (TYPICAL)

TRAFFIC ISLAND

R.O.W. LINE
RAISED ISLAND
12'
30' MIN.

TRAFFIC-CALMING MEASURES
(SPEED-CONTROL DEVICES)

FIGURE 92

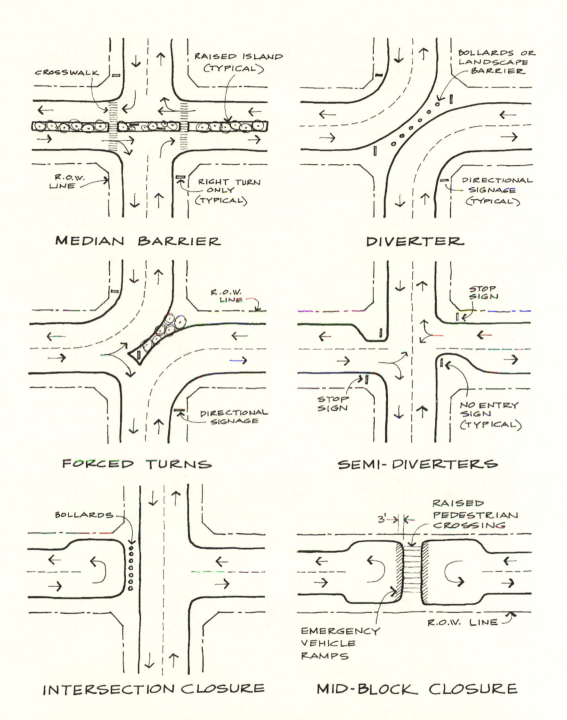

MEDIAN BARRIER

DIVERTER

FORCED TURNS

SEMI-DIVERTERS

INTERSECTION CLOSURE

MID-BLOCK CLOSURE

TRAFFIC-CALMING MEASURES
(VOLUME-CONTROL DEVICES)

FIGURE 93

ROUNDABOUTS (rotaries): Traffic circles for higher-volume streets.

CHICANES (deviations/serpentines/twists): Curb extensions or islands that alternate from one side to the other, forming S-shaped roadways.

REALIGNED INTERSECTIONS (modified intersections): Changes in alignment that convert T-intersections with straight approaches into curving streets meeting at right angles.

NECKDOWNS (nubs/bulbouts/intersection narrowing): Curb extensions at intersections that reduce roadway width.

CENTER ISLAND NARROWING (mid-block medians/median chokers): Raised islands located along the center line of a street that narrow the street at that location.

CHOKERS (pinch points/constrictions/mid-block narrowing): Curb extensions on one or both sides of the street that narrow the street at that location.

TRAFFIC CIRCLES

See TRAFFIC CALMING.

TRAFFIC COUNT

A tabulation of the number of vehicles or pedestrians passing a certain point during a specified period of time.

TRAFFIC DEMAND MANAGEMENT

Strategies aimed at reducing the number of vehicle trips, shortening trip lengths, and reducing trips during peak hours.

Comment: These strategies encourage the use of mass transit, car pools, vanpools, bicycling, and walking and typically focus on the home-to-work commute. They also include efforts to provide housing close to jobs to shorten trip lengths. The strategies usually require the joint cooperation of developers, employers, and local governments.

TRAFFIC GENERATOR

A use in a particular geographic area that is likely to attract substantial vehicular or pedestrian traffic into the area.

TRAFFIC GROWTH RATE

The rate at which traffic volumes are projected to increase over a period of time, expressed as a percentage that is compounded annually.

TRAFFIC IMPACT STUDY

A report analyzing anticipated roadway conditions before and after proposed development. (American Planning Association, *Traffic Impact Analysis*, Planning Advisory Service Report No. 387, 1984)

Comment: The report may include an analysis of mitigation measures and a calculation of fair-share financial contributions. Mitigation measures may include road widenings, intersection improvements, and traffic control devices.

TRAILER

A structure standing on wheels, towed or hauled by another vehicle, and used for short-term human occupancy, carrying of materials, goods, or objects, or as a temporary office.

Comment: Development ordinances may allow for trailers on work sites to be used as temporary offices.

TRANSFER OF DEVELOPMENT RIGHTS (TDR)

The removal of the right to develop or build, expressed in dwelling units per acre or floor area, from land in one zoning district, and the transfer of that right, to land in another district where such transfer is permitted. *See* DENSITY TRANSFER. *See Figure 94.*

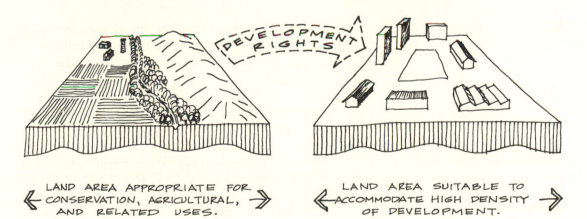

PRESERVATION ZONE
EXISTING PERMITTED LOW DEVELOPMENT DENSITY REDUCED FURTHER BY TRANSFER OF DEVELOPMENT RIGHTS TO TRANSFER ZONE.

TRANSFER ZONE
ZONING REGULATIONS ALLOW DENSITY INCREASE TO ACCOMMODATE DEVELOPMENT RIGHTS ACCEPTED FROM THE PRESERVATION ZONE.

LAND AREA APPROPRIATE FOR CONSERVATION, AGRICULTURAL, AND RELATED USES.

LAND AREA SUITABLE TO ACCOMMODATE HIGH DENSITY OF DEVELOPMENT.

TRANSFER OF DEVELOPMENT RIGHTS

FIGURE 94

411

Comment: TDR, or transfer of development credits, is a development tool used to preserve open space, farmland, water resources, or vistas in one area and to direct development to other, more suitable areas. In urban areas, TDR has been used for historic preservation. TDR permits an owner of real property to sell the development rights associated with that property (the preservation or sending zone) to the owner of another property (the transfer or receiving zone) in return for compensation. Regulations governing the transfer zone would allow an increase in development intensity to accommodate the added development, all in accordance with the local master plan. *See* LOT AVERAGING.

TRANSFER STATION

An intermediate destination for solid waste.

Comment: Transfer stations may include separation of different types of waste and aggregation of smaller shipments into larger ones. They may also include compaction to reduce the bulk of the waste. These facilities are intensive uses and are properly located in heavy industrial zones. They are usually necessary because garbage trucks that pick up from houses are unsuitable for long, over-the-road hauls to distant landfills or other facilities for solid waste disposal.

TRANSIT, LIGHT RAIL (LRT)

Electrically self-propelled passenger vehicles that operate entirely or substantially in mixed traffic and in nonexclusive at-grade rights-of-way.

TRANSIT-ORIENTED DEVELOPMENT (TOD)

The concentration of development at nodes along public transit corridors, either light rail or bus routes.

Comment: TODs are designed to maximize transit ridership by locating employment and housing within walking distance (up to 2,000 feet) of a transit stop. Urban TODs are located on main transit routes (bus and rail) and have high-density housing and employment. Neighborhood TODs should be located on a feeder bus line and contain lower-density housing and local retail/services only. *See Figure 95.*

TRANSIT SHUTTLE

Transit service that travels over a short route or one that connects two transit systems or centers.

TRANSIT STOP

Facilities at selected points along transit routes for passenger pickup, drop-off, and waiting.

TRANSITION ZONE

A zoning district that permits uses compatible with uses permitted in two adjacent zones that, without the

412

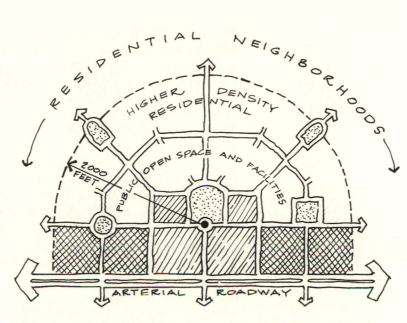

TRANSIT-ORIENTED DEVELOPMENT
CONCEPT PLAN BY PETER CALTHORPE

● TRANSIT STOP EMPLOYMENT

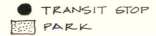 PARK ▨ COMMERCIAL

FIGURE 95

transition zone, could be considered incompatible with each other. *See Figure 96.*

Comment: Low-density, multifamily zones between commercial and single-family zones are an example of transition zones.

TRANSITIONAL AREA

(1) An area in the process of changing from one use to another or changing from one racial or ethnic occupancy to another; (2) an area that acts as a buffer between two land uses of different intensity and compatibility.

Comment: A transitional area—more specifically, a transitional use area—may be, for example, the land area between a business area along a street frontage and the adjacent residential area. Many development ordinances establish transitional districts that permit either residential or some less-intensive commercial use to be located between the two different land uses. The less-intensive commercial use might be a small office building or institutional use.

TRANSITIONAL CARE CLINIC

A facility operated as an accessory use in connection with, and on the premises of, a transitional care home to provide physical, social, and psychological therapy or counseling by qualified personnel, whose patients are limited to those who have recently resided in the transitional care home or to families of those who are residing in or have recently resided in a transitional care home.

TRANSITIONAL CARE HOME

A facility in which individuals live for a short period while receiving physical, social, or psychological therapy and counseling to assist them in overcoming physical or emotional problems.

Comment: The transitional care home is a form of halfway house. Residents do not require segregation from society and require only short-term shelter away from their usual residences. Professional therapy and counseling are done on a more intensive basis than is permitted in an outpatient facility. In zoning, these facilities usually function as boarding homes. *See* BOARDING HOME FOR SHELTERED CARE.

TRANSITIONAL USE

A permitted use or structure of an intermediate intensity of activity or scale and located between a more-intensive and less-intensive use. *See* TRANSITIONAL AREA. *See Figure 96.*

Comment: Some random examples of transitional uses include professional offices located between retail and residential uses; two-family and townhouse units located between single-family detached and apartment blocks; and private clubs or low-intensity recreational uses between industrial and residential uses.

TRANSPORTATION CORRIDOR

A combination of principal transportation routes involving a linear network of one or more highways of four or more lanes, rail lines, or other primary and secondary access facilities that support a development corridor.

TRANSPORTATION DEMAND MANAGEMENT PLAN

A system of actions and timetables to alleviate traffic problems through improved management of vehicle trip demand.

Comment: The transportation demand management plan's objective is to decrease the number of vehicles on the road by one or more of the following methods: increase in parking fees; requiring businesses to encourage ride sharing; allowing flexible work times and schedules, or other programs, designed to reduce the

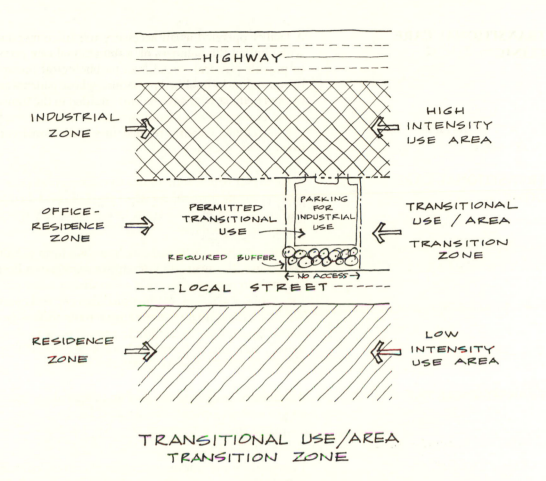

INDUSTRIAL ZONE

HIGH INTENSITY USE AREA

OFFICE-RESIDENCE ZONE

PERMITTED TRANSITIONAL USE

PARKING FOR INDUSTRIAL USE

TRANSITIONAL USE / AREA

TRANSITION ZONE

REQUIRED BUFFER

← NO ACCESS →

---- LOCAL STREET -----

RESIDENCE ZONE

LOW INTENSITY USE AREA

TRANSITIONAL USE/AREA
TRANSITION ZONE

FIGURE 96

number of people who commute independently or during peak travel times.

TRANSPORTATION MANAGEMENT ASSOCIATION (TMA)

(1) A group of employers, developers, building owners, and local government officials working together to solve local transportation problems and establish transportation policies for their employees and the area; (2) a nonprofit corporation that arranges transportation services, including, but not limited to, public transportation, vanpools, carpools, and bicycling, to corporations, employees, individuals, and other groups.

TRANSPORTATION SERVICES, ACCESSORY

Establishments furnishing services incidental to transportation, such as forwarding and packing services and the arranging of passenger or freight transportation.

415

TRANSPORTATION SERVICES, LOCAL

Establishments primarily engaged in furnishing local and suburban passenger transportation, including taxicabs, passenger transportation charter service, school buses, and terminal and service facilities for motor vehicle passenger transportation.

TRANSPORTATION SYSTEMS MANAGEMENT

Modifications to the existing road system to make it work more efficiently.

Comment: Improvement options include closing side streets, prohibiting left turns, eliminating on-street parking, improving the coordination and timing of traffic lights, and lane dedication for high-occupancy-vehicle (HOV) use.

TRANSSHIPMENT

(1) The act of transferring freight between two modes of transport, such as from a truck to a railroad car; (2) the act of transferring freight from long-haul trucks to local delivery vehicles.

Comment: Transshipment may include aggregating or breaking down shipments into larger or smaller ones.

TRAP

A fitting or device so designed and constructed as to provide, when properly vented, a liquid seal that will prevent the back passage of air without materially affecting the flow of sewage or wastewater.

TRASH ENCLOSURE

An accessory use or structure where trash and/or recycling material containers or any other type of waste or refuse containers are stored. *See Figure 30.*

Comment: The local ordinance should include specific design requirements for trash enclosures including location, materials, gates, and screening. For large-scale developments, the enclosure should be roofed, and enclosure design should reflect principal building architecture and materials.

TRAVEL CENTER

See GASOLINE STATION AND CONVENIENCE CENTER.

TRAVEL PLAZA

See TRUCK STOP.

TRAVEL TRAILER

A recreational vehicle that is towed by a car or a truck. *See* RECREATIONAL VEHICLE.

TRAVELED WAY

That part of the roadway used for the movement of vehicles.

416

TREE HOUSE

A structure built above ground level, using a tree for part of its support, and not designed for continuous habitation.

TREE, PROHIBITED

Any tree species that, by the nature of its fruit, root system, brittleness of wood, or susceptibility to disease, is not permitted for use in proposed development projects or as a replacement tree.

TREE PROTECTION

Measures taken, such as temporary fencing and the use of tree wells, to protect existing trees from damage or loss during construction. *See Figures 97 and 98.*

Comment: The local land development ordinance should require, as part of the landscaping plan for major developments, a tree protection plan to be submitted showing which trees are proposed to be protected and the method to be used to provide the protection.

TRICKLING FILTER

A device for the biological or secondary treatment of wastewater consisting of a bed of rocks or stones that supports bacterial growth and permits sewage to be trickled over the bed, enabling the bacteria to break down organic wastes.

TRIP

A single or one-way motor vehicle movement either to or from a subject property or study area. *See Figure 57.*

TRIP DISTRIBUTION

The measure of the number of vehicles or passenger movements that are or will be made between geographic areas. (Schultz and Kasen 1984)

TRIP ENDS

The total of single or one-direction vehicle movements entering and leaving a specified land use or site over a designated period of time. *See Figure 57.* (Adapted from Institute of Transportation Engineers 1997)

TRIP GENERATION

The total number of vehicle trip ends produced by a specific land use or activity.

Comment: The Institute of Transportation Engineers (1997) reports the results of more than 3,000 trip generation studies undertaken in its *Trip Generation* publication. The book provides estimates on the number of vehicle trips likely to be generated by a particular land use in terms of a number of variables, such as the square footage of the structure, size of parcel, and number of employees.

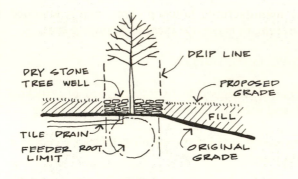

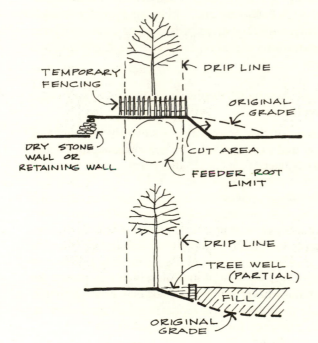

DRY STONE TREE WELL

DRIP LINE

PROPOSED GRADE

TILE DRAIN

FEEDER ROOT LIMIT

FILL

ORIGINAL GRADE

TEMPORARY FENCING

DRIP LINE

ORIGINAL GRADE

DRY STONE WALL OR RETAINING WALL

CUT AREA

FEEDER ROOT LIMIT

DRIP LINE

TREE WELL (PARTIAL)

FILL

ORIGINAL GRADE

TREE PROTECTION

FIGURE 97

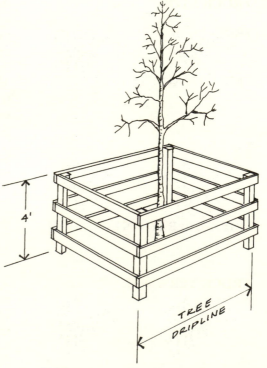

4'

TREE DRIPLINE

TREE PROTECTION

FIGURE 98

418

TRIPLE-WIDE UNITS

Three manufactured housing components, attached side to side, to make one complete housing unit.

TRIPLEX

See DWELLING, TRIPLEX.

TRUCK CAMPER

A structure designed to fit into the bed of a pickup truck and used for temporary shelter and sleeping.

TRUCK ROUTE

Streets designated for use by all vehicles exceeding a certain weight.

Comment: Truck routes generally follow major arterials through industrial areas, bypassing retail, commercial, and residential areas and avoiding areas with large concentrations of people, such as schools and cultural centers.

TRUCK SALES

The sale of vehicles primarily designed to carry cargo and material.

Comment: Truck sales often involve the assembly of chassis and cabs and may be more appropriate in an industrial zone.

TRUCK STOP

Any building, premises, or land in which or upon which a business or service involving the maintenance, servicing, storage, or repair of commercial vehicles is conducted or rendered, including the dispensing of motor fuel or other petroleum products directly into motor vehicles and the sale of accessories or equipment for trucks and similar commercial vehicles, and which may include overnight accommodations and restaurant facilities primarily for the use of truck crews.

Comment: Recent trends in this industry include enlarging the market to more than just over-the-road trucks. Facilities for campers and recreation vehicles are now provided and attempts have been made to attract families on vacations. More franchised food establishments are the norm. "Truck stops" are now more commonly known as "travel plazas."

TRUCK TERMINAL

An area and building where trucks load and unload cargo and freight and where the cargo and freight may be broken down or aggregated into smaller or larger loads for transfer to other vehicles or modes of transportation.

Comment: Truck terminals are basically transshipment facilities and often include the storage or parking of trucks awaiting cargo as well as facilities for servicing of trucks. Storage facilities such as warehouses, incidental to the principal use, may also be part of a truck terminal.

Truck terminals are similar to distribution centers and warehouses except they usually serve many manufacturing firms and are owned and operated by trucking companies. There are two types of terminals. "End-of-line" terminals serve a small geographic area, often a city or metropolitan area. "Branch bulk" terminals serve large regional areas. Freight may be stored on the site until a full truckload for a specific area has been aggregated. Truck terminals generate more truck traffic than warehouses or distribution centers, but usually at off-peak hours. *See* DISTRIBUTION CENTER; WAREHOUSE.

TURBIDITY

A thick, hazy condition of air or water produced by the presence of suspended particulates or other pollutants.

TUTORING

The provision of instruction to students.

Comment: Tutoring is usually considered a home occupation. The local ordinance should specify the type of tutoring permitted, such as academic subjects, art, music or dance, and the number of students permitted at any one time.

TWO-FAMILY DWELLING OR DUPLEX

See DWELLING, TWO-FAMILY.

U

Definitions:

Underground Utilities
through
Utility Services

UNDERGROUND UTILITIES

The placement of electric, telephone, cable, and other utilities, customarily carried on poles, in underground vaults or trenches.

UNDERSIZED ISOLATED LOT

See ISOLATED LOT.

UNDERUTILIZED LAND

Land parcels with any of the following characteristics:

- More than 80 percent of the parcel in a non-building use, such as surface parking or storage yard
- Land parcels containing structures that are at least 50 percent vacant
- Land parcels with buildings with a floor area ratio of less than .10
- Land parcels with buildings that are abandoned, dilapidated, or otherwise seriously impaired by physical deficiencies.

Comment: The definition is useful in determining the redevelopment potential of a tract of land. The percentages should be adjusted to meet local needs and conditions.

UNDEVELOPED LAND

Land in its natural state before development.

UNDIVIDED HIGHWAY

A highway without any center island, median, or barrier.

UNIFORMITY

The requirement that all properties in a zoning district be treated alike.

UNIMPROVED LAND

Land without building and structures. *See* RAW LAND.

UNIQUE NATURAL FEATURE

That part of the natural environment that is rare or not duplicated in the community or region.

UNIVERSITY

See COLLEGE.

UNSIGHTLY AREAS

(1) Areas outside of a building where machinery or equipment is repaired, stored, and/or serviced; (2) outside trash storage areas; (3) loading docks; (4) outdoor vehicle storage areas; (5) utility facilities.

Comment: Unsightly areas, as defined, can be the subject of specific regulations to restrict their locations and/or provide for screening. For example, loading and unloading docks can be restricted to those sides of buildings that keep them from being visible from the street.

Outside trash storage areas can be required to be screened with fencing or landscaping.

UPLAND

(1) Land elevated above surrounding lands; (2) any nonwetland area.

UPZONE

To reduce the intensity of use by decreasing allowable density or lowering the floor area ratio or otherwise increasing bulk requirements.

Comment: This term and its counterpart, "downzone," are often misused and have certain class distinctions. It would be more accurate to use terms such as "more restrictive," "less restrictive," "more intense," or "less intense." *See* DOWNZONE.

URBAN

All population and territory within the boundaries of urbanized areas and the urban portion of places outside of urbanized areas that have a decennial census population of 2,500 or more. (U.S. Census Bureau)

URBAN AREA

A highly developed area that includes, or is appurtenant to, a central city or place and contains a variety of industrial, commercial, residential, and cultural uses. *See* URBANIZED AREA.

Comment: Densities of urban areas are usually 2,000 persons per square mile with central cities of 50,000 persons or more.

URBAN CENTER

(1) An area of statewide importance; (2) a large settlement that has a high intensity of population and mixed land uses, including industrial, commercial, residential, and cultural uses; (3) the historical focus in the major urban areas of the state. (*New Jersey State Development and Redevelopment Plan* 2002)

URBAN CONTEXT

The combination of buildings, structures, and streetscape elements that form a distinct neighborhood or section of a city or urban place. *See* DEVELOPMENT CONTEXT.

URBAN DESIGN

(1) The process of organizing the contextual elements of the built environment such that the end result will be a place with its own character or identity; (2) planning the development of the built environment in a comprehensive manner to achieve a unified, functional, efficient, and aesthetically appealing physical setting. (Schultz and Kasen 1984) *See* BUILDING MASS; BUILDING SCALE; COMMUNITY DESIGN PLAN; DESIGN

STANDARDS; DEVELOPMENT CONTEXT; HARMONIOUS RELATIONSHIP; HUMAN SCALE; URBAN CONTEXT.

Comment: Although often associated with the practice of architecture, the discipline of urban design is unique. While architects are concerned primarily with the design of individual buildings, urban designers are concerned with developing contextual design guidelines for all buildings. Architects are concerned with a specific product within a client's specific time frame; urban designers deal with uncertain futures and indefinite periods of time. Urban design is largely a public activity because it is concerned not only with building form but also with the spatial element created by groups of buildings. Architecture, on the other hand, is largely a private activity because its primary concern is with individual building form. *See* Hedman 1984.

URBAN FRINGE

The closely settled territory adjacent to the central place(s) of an urbanized area.

Comment: The census blocks that constitute the urban fringe generally have an overall population density of at least 1,000 people per square mile of land area. (U.S. Census Bureau)

URBAN GROWTH BOUNDARY

(1) A perimeter drawn around an urban growth area (American Planning Association, *Growing Smart* project); (2) a boundary, often parcel-specific, marking the outer limit beyond which urban development will not be permitted (California Planning Roundtable).

Comment: This is a planning tool that has the aim of discouraging urban sprawl by containing urban development during a specific period; its location may be modified over time.

URBAN HOMESTEADING

A program for selling vacant, usually substandard urban housing to people who will rehabilitate and occupy such housing.

URBAN RENEWAL

A program for the physical improvement of primarily urban areas through comprehensive planning and governmental assistance to effect rehabilitation and redevelopment.

URBAN RUNOFF

Stormwater from city streets, gutters, and paved surfaces.

Comment: Urban runoff usually contains a significant amount of litter and organic and bacterial wastes. *See* RUNOFF.

URBAN SERVICE BOUNDARY	A defined region, not always coincidental with a municipality's corporate boundary, which delineates the geographical limit of government-supplied public facilities and services.
URBAN SERVICES	Utilities, such as water, gas, electricity, and sewer, and public services, such as police, fire, schools, parks, and recreation, provided to an urbanized or urbanizing area.
URBAN SPRAWL	*See* SPRAWL.
URBANIZED AREA	An area consisting of a central place(s) and adjacent urban fringe that together have a minimum residential population of at least 50,000 people and generally an overall population density of at least 1,000 people per square mile.
USE	The purpose or activity for which land or buildings are designed, arranged, or intended or for which land or buildings are occupied or maintained.
USE, ACCESSORY	*See* ACCESSORY USE.
USE, CONDITIONAL	*See* CONDITIONAL USE.
USE, EXISTING	*See* EXISTING USE.
USE, INHERENTLY BENEFICIAL	*See* INHERENTLY BENEFICIAL USES.
USE, INSTITUTIONAL	*See* INSTITUTIONAL USE.
USE, PERMITTED	*See* PERMITTED USE.
USE, PRINCIPAL	*See* PRINCIPAL USE.
USE, RELIGIOUS	*See* RELIGIOUS USE.
USE, TEMPORARY	*See* TEMPORARY USE.
USE, TRANSITIONAL	*See* TRANSITIONAL USE.
USE VARIANCE	*See* VARIANCE, USE.
USER CHARGES	A requirement of government under which those who benefit directly from a particular service pay all or part of the cost.
	Comment: User charges are not new, but the types and extent are increasing. Impact fees are similar except that

they are usually paid by the developer and are included in the sale or rental cost of the project.

UTILITY, PRIVATE OR PUBLIC

(1) Any agency that, under public franchise or ownership, or under certificate of convenience and necessity, or by grant of authority by a governmental agency, provides the public with electricity, gas, heat, steam, communication, transportation, water, sewage collection, or other similar service; (2) a closely regulated enterprise with a franchise for providing a needed service. *See* PUBLIC UTILITY.

UTILITY BOX

Electric transformers, switch boxes, telephone pedestals and telephone boxes, cable television boxes, traffic control boxes, and similar devices.

UTILITY CORRIDORS

Rights-of-way or easements for utility lines on either publicly or privately owned property.

UTILITY EASEMENT

See EASEMENT, PUBLIC UTILITY.

UTILITY SERVICES

The generation, transmission, and/or distribution of electricity, gas, steam, communications, and water; the collection and treatment of sewage and solid waste; and the provision of mass transportation.

V

VACANCY

Any unoccupied land, structure, building, or part thereof that is available and suitable for occupancy.

VACANCY RATE

The number of uninhabited dwelling units that are available and suitable for occupancy expressed as a percentage of the total number of dwelling units.

Comment: "Vacancy rate" may also apply to nonresidential use and is usually expressed as a percentage of unoccupied floor area to total floor area. *See* OCCUPANCY RATE.

VACANT LAND

(1) Land that is undeveloped and unused; (2) any nonresidential areas with significant amounts of land not covered by nonstructural, impervious surfaces; (3) land suitable for redevelopment. *See* UNDERUTILIZED LAND; UNDEVELOPED LAND; UNIMPROVED LAND.

VACATION HOME

A second home, owned or rented, usually used seasonally, and located in an area with nearby recreational opportunities or amenities.

VALLEY

(1) A stretch of lowland lying between mountains or hills; (2) the land area drained or watered by a major river system.

VALUE MALL

See RETAIL STORE, LARGE-SCALE.

VAN

(1) A closed vehicle with a capacity of approximately 8 to 12 passengers; (2) a self-propelled recreation vehicle containing sleeping facilities but not bathroom or cooking facilities; (3) a large truck for carrying cargo or freight.

VANPOOLING

A share-the-expense method of commutation for people who work in the same place and have the same work hours.

Comment: Vanpools differ from carpools in that the employer or sponsoring organization usually provides the passenger vans that are used in the program. In addition, vans used for vanpooling may be registered as such with the state.

VAPOR

The gaseous phase of substances that are normally either liquids or solids at atmospheric temperature and pressure; for example, steam and phenolic compounds.

VAPOR PLUME

Stack effluent consisting of condensed flue gas or flue gas made visible by condensed water droplets or mist.

VAPORIZATION

The change of a substance from the liquid to the gaseous state.

VARIANCE

Permission to depart from the literal requirements of a zoning ordinance.

VARIANCE, BULK

A departure from any provision of a zoning ordinance except use. *See* VARIANCE, HARDSHIP.

VARIANCE, HARDSHIP

A departure from the provisions of a zoning ordinance relating to setbacks, side yards, frontage requirements, and lot size that, if applied to a specific lot, would significantly interfere with the use of the property.

Comment: The hardship variance is granted because strict enforcement of the zoning ordinance as it applies to a specific lot would present practical difficulties in the use of the property. Hardship relates to the physical characteristics of the property, and without the variance, the property becomes unusable.

In *Brandon v. Montclair* (124 N.J. 135), the New Jersey Supreme Court characterized hardship as "whether the . . . restriction, viewing the property in the setting of its environment is so unreasonable as to constitute an arbitrary and capricious interference with the basic right of private property."

Hardship may also be used to justify a use variance. For example, in cases involving obsolete uses or outdated structures, a hardship variance may be justified so that the building can be adapted or used for a different purpose. Another example of hardship as a basis for a use variance is split lot zoning, where the zone line runs through the center of the property and a part of the property is rendered useless.

VARIANCE, PLANNING

A variance granted for bulk relief that would result in an opportunity for improved zoning and planning that would benefit the community.

Comment: The planning variance is a relatively new concept that recognizes that special reasons or hardship do not always exist when relief from the bulk requirements is being sought. Granting of the variance might result in benefits to the community. Examples include protecting environmentally sensitive areas by allowing a building to be built closer to a side or front yard line than the ordinance provides, reducing the size of parking spaces to provide more parking for an existing use, and increasing setbacks on one side and encroaching on another to provide more light and air to an adjacent building.

The tests of the planning variance are:

- The variance relates to a specific parcel of land.

- The variance advances the purposes of the state enabling legislation.

- The variance can be granted without substantial detriment to the public good.

- The benefits of the deviation would substantially outweigh any detriment.

- The variance would not substantially impair the intent and purposes of the zone plan and zoning ordinance.

(Cox 2003)

VARIANCE, USE

A variance granted for a use or structure that is not permitted in the zone.

Comment: States that permit use variances impose stringent requirements. In New Jersey, the applicant must prove special reasons. Special reasons may be that the use is inherently beneficial, such as a hospital, school, or church, or generally that the use would help advance the purposes of planning as set forth in the state enabling legislation. Hardship may also constitute a special reason. In addition to special reasons, the applicant must prove that if granted, the use will not substantially impair the intent and purpose of the zone plan and ordinance and will be without substantial detriment to the public good.

VEGETATION

(1) Trees, shrubs, groundcovers, vines, grasses (both lawn and ornamental types), herbaceous perennials, biennials, annuals, bulbs, ferns, mosses, and lichens; (2) a living organism belonging to the vegetable kingdom, as distinguished from the animal kingdom, having rigid cell walls and characterized by growth chiefly from the syntheses of simple, usually inorganic food materials from soil, water, and air. (*Funk & Wagnalls* 1968)

VEGETATION, EXOTIC

Vegetation that occurs naturally in another part of the world and does not occur locally.

Comment: Introduction of exotic vegetation has been both accidental and intentional. Although many exotic plants have been used successfully, some exotic species have become nuisances because of their rapid reproduction and the lack of natural pests or diseases in the area to which they have been introduced. Other exotic species are highly susceptible to such pests and diseases. *See* VEGETATION, NATIVE.

VEGETATION, INDIGENOUS

Vegetation existing in a specific geographic area at the present time.

VEGETATION, NATIVE

Vegetation that exists naturally, without intervention by humans, in a specific geographic area. Also, vegetation that would exist naturally in an area if not for human intervention.

Comment: All plants, except those that have been genetically modified by human actions, are native in some location; therefore, it is important that the geographic area be specified. Also, many plants that have been introduced into an area, either intentionally or accidentally, have become naturalized. Such plants are not normally considered native. The use of native vegetation has increased in recent years for reasons of habitat protection, enhancement, and restoration; preservation of regional character; superior adaptability to climate and soil conditions; and resistance to harmful insects and diseases in the area. *See* VEGETATION, EXOTIC.

VEGETATION, NATIVE AND INDIGENOUS

Vegetation that occurred naturally in a specific geographic area or was introduced into the area by humans.

Comment: Native and indigenous vegetation is often specified as replacement vegetation in conservation areas and easements or as part of a landscape plan for development. The specific geographic area may be as small as the municipality but usually encompasses much larger areas, such as the Northwest, Southeast, and so on. The agricultural extension service of the state department of agriculture or local nurseries can be helpful in providing lists of native and indigenous vegetation for the specific geographic area. *See* VEGETATION, EXOTIC; VEGETATION, INDIGENOUS; VEGETATION, NATIVE.

VEGETATION MAP

A pictorial depiction of the location and type of plant materials that appear in a given land area. (Schultz and Kasen 1984)

VEGETATIVE PROTECTION

Stabilization of erosive or sediment-producing areas by covering the soil with permanent or short-term seeding, mulching, or sodding.

VEHICLE, INOPERABLE

Any vehicle that, while at present inoperable, is in a condition whereby repairs to the same could be made to place it in operating condition without exceeding its present estimated value and repair.

VEHICLE, JUNK

Any rusted, wrecked, damaged, dismantled or partially dismantled, inoperative, or abandoned motor vehicle in such a condition that it is economically infeasible to restore the vehicle to an operating condition.

Comment: "Economically infeasible" means that the cost of restoring the vehicle to an operating condition exceeds the market value of the vehicle.

VEHICLE, MOTOR

A self-propelled device licensed as a motor vehicle and used for transportation of people or goods over roads.

VEHICLE, OFF-ROAD (ORV)

Vehicles, including dune buggies and all-terrain vehicles, snowmobiles, trail bikes, mopeds, and motor bikes, designed for use on unimproved surfaces.

Comment: ORVs are also known as all-tract vehicles. As recreational vehicles, the ORVs can be detrimental to the landscape and trails. Many of them are noisy and pose dangers to wildlife.

VEHICLE OVERHANG

The portion of a vehicle extending beyond the wheel stops or curbs (*see Figures 67 and 99*).

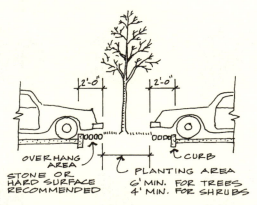

VEHICLE OVERHANG - PARKING ISLAND

FIGURE 99

Comment: In parking lot design, the depth of the parking stall can be reduced by 2 feet if curbing is used in place of wheel stops and allowance is made for the overhang. Since the overhanging car can interfere with pedestrian travel, the adjacent sidewalks should be made wider by at least 2 feet.

432

VEHICLE, PASSENGER

A motor vehicle with no more than two axles and/or four wheels, not more than 4,500 pounds in gross weight, and designed primarily for the transport of persons.

VEHICLE, RECREATIONAL

See RECREATIONAL VEHICLE.

VEHICLE SALES AREA

An open area, other than a right-of-way or public parking area, used for display, sale, or rental of new or used vehicles in operable condition and where no repair work is done.

VEHICLE TRIP

A motor vehicle moving from an origin point to a destination point. *See* TRIP.

VENDING MACHINE

Any unattended self-service device that, upon insertion of money, credit cards, token, or similar means, dispenses something of value including food, beverages, goods, and merchandise. *See* NEWSRACK.

Comment: Vending machines typically dispense soft drinks, but increasingly they are larger in size and offer food and convenience items. These super vending machines, known as automated convenience stores, can be most effective in high-density pedestrian areas, such as business and office locations. Outdoor vending machines can generate problems in terms of location, appearance, number, signs, and lighting. Zoning regulations should include the following with regard to vending machines:

- They are prohibited in historic districts.

- They are allowed as principal permitted or accessory uses in areas with high pedestrian activity, such as office and business zones.

- They are allowed as accessory uses to specific permitted uses, such as gas stations or newsstands.

- They are placed where they will not impede pedestrian or vehicular traffic flows.

- In developed areas with established setbacks, vending machines (other than newsracks) should not be permitted to encroach into the setback.

- Signs should be limited and lights designed to control spillage.

- There should be special controls and design standards for newspaper vending machines as discussed under the definition of NEWSRACK.

**VERNAL POOL
OR HABITAT**

A wetland or water that is a confined basin depression without a permanent flowing outlet, supports species

433

adapted to reproduce in ephemeral aquatic conditions, maintains ponded water for at least a portion of the year, and is free of fish or dries up at some time during the year.

Comment: Species that inhabit vernal pools include amphibians such as frogs and salamanders. Vernal pools are afforded protection from development in many states.

VEST-POCKET PARK

A small land area, usually in a built-up neighborhood, developed for active or passive recreation.

VESTED RIGHT

A right that cannot be changed or altered by changes in regulation.

Comment: A development application that has been granted approval has a vested right for a certain period of time. During that period of time, changes in zoning do not apply to the development.

VETERINARY HOSPITAL

A place where animals are given medical care and the boarding of animals is limited to short-term care incidental to the hospital use.

Comment: Some veterinary hospitals are associated with animal boarding, breeding, and/or laboratories. A zoning ordinance should distinguish between veterinary hospitals, which can be located in any nonresidential area, and animal care facilities, which may or may not include a medical treatment component. Facilities that breed and/or board animals, particularly dog kennels, need special noise-deadening construction and/or deep open-space buffering to avoid sound transmission beyond property boundaries.

VICARAGE

See CLERGY RESIDENCE.

VIDEO VIEWING BOOTHS

See ADULT USE.

VIEW PROTECTION REGULATION

Requirements to ensure that development does not interfere with scenic views. *See* VIEWSHED. (*See* American Planning Association, *Aesthetics and Land-Use Controls: Beyond Ecology and Economics*, Planning Advisory Service Report No. 399, 1986; *Aesthetics, Community Character, and the Law,* Planning Advisory Service Report No. 489/490, 1999.)

Comment: As noted in PAS 489/490, to deflect potential taking claims, view protection ordinances often allow for, or encourage, mechanisms to transfer development out of protected areas, including cluster development and transfer of development rights.

VIEWSHED

An elevated or unobstructed location, position, or area that permits an unhindered panoramic vista of particular interest or pleasure or unique view to or from a particular point. *See* VISTA. *See Figure 100.*

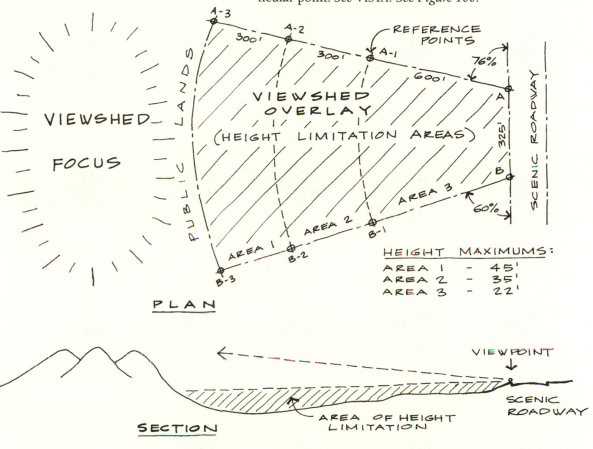

PLAN

SECTION

VIEWSHED RESTRICTIONS
(SCHEMATIC EXAMPLE)

FIGURE 100

Comment: Viewsheds may be identified as part of a comprehensive community design study, master plan, or as part of a development application. Viewsheds may be protected from loss or damage by appropriate development regulations such as special viewshed protection easements, viewshed protection regulations, building setbacks, floor area ratio limits, height restrictions, or similar bulk controls. The community design study, which should be part of the local master plan, provides the basis for the regulations that implement viewshed preservation. Viewshed protection regulations should limit obstructions to the viewpoint area and also include development controls within the viewshed vista area itself.

435

VILLAGE

A small, compact center of predominantly residential character with a core of mixed-use commercial, residential, and community services. *See* NEIGHBORHOOD.

Comment: Mary Winder, for the Heritage Group of Sarasota County, Florida, describes the role of neighborhoods in achieving the traditional village form, as follows:

> The principles call for each neighborhood to have a central area of mixed uses, an interconnected street network, and walkable distance. The walkability standard limits the area of a neighborhood to a quarter-mile radius based on a standard of a five-minute walk. This standard results in an area of 125 acres. In some cases, the size might go up to 200 acres due to special environmental characteristics such as wetlands. The principles call for the neighborhood center to contain a mix of uses, including apartments and townhouses. The overall housing density should be at least three dwelling units per acre and preferably four to six. (These density standards would produce 375 to 750 dwelling units in a 125-acre neighborhood.) There should be an integrated network of streets to facilitate driving, walking, and biking. There should also be locations for civic buildings and spaces such as schools and parks. (Winder 2001)

VISIONING

The master plan process by which a community articulates its desired future image and expresses it in the form of words and graphics. *See* COMMUNITY DESIGN PLAN; COMMUNITY CHARACTER.

Comment: The visioning process should begin with a visual assessment that includes all of the visual assets and liabilities within the community and end in a vision statement that describes in narrative and illustrative form the desired future image of the community. (Hunterdon County [NJ] Planning Board 2000)

VISTA

A unique view to or from a particular point.

Comment: The view may be one of great natural beauty, farmlands, settlements (such as villages), or spectacular urban scenes. Many ordinances attempt to develop vista protection provisions to ensure that unique vistas are preserved and not encroached upon by development. *See* VIEWSHED.

VISUAL COMPATIBILITY

See HARMONIOUS RELATIONSHIP.

VISUAL IMPACT

A modification or change that could be incompatible with the scale, form, texture, mass, or color of the natural or built environment. *See* HARMONIOUS RELATIONSHIP.

VISUAL OBSTRUCTION

Any structure, such as a fence or wall, or natural feature that limits visibility.

Comment: Visual obstructions can be a hazard at street intersections where they interfere with traffic visibility. Many ordinances include requirements for sight easements to restrict visual obstructions.

VISUAL TERMINATION

(1) A building, structure or other surface or streetscape element terminating a view; (2) the placement of a building or structure for the purpose of spatial enclosure, providing a visual focal point, or giving enhanced recognition to the building or structure by such placement.

VOCATIONAL SCHOOL

A secondary or higher education facility primarily teaching usable skills that prepares students for jobs in a trade and meeting the state requirements as a vocational facility.

VOIR DIRE

A preliminary examination to test the competence of a witness or evidence. (*Black's* 1999)

Comment: A traditional method used in courts or before agencies to disqualify experts or to limit their areas of testimony.

VOLATILE

Evaporating readily at a relatively low temperature.

W

Definitions:

Wading Pool

through

Working Drawings

WADING POOL

An above-ground or in-ground structure containing less than 18 inches of water.

WAIVER

Permission to depart from the requirements of an ordinance with respect to the submission of required documents. *See* EXCEPTION.

Comment: The terms "waiver" and "exception" are often used interchangeably. There are differences, however. "Waiver" refers to the submission of required documents; an "exception" is for relief of design standards or other nonzoning requirements in the ordinance. (Waiver of zoning requirements usually requires a variance.)

For example, an applicant may request a waiver of the requirement to submit an environmental impact statement for a small, isolated lot and request an exception to the sidewalk requirement if there are no sidewalks in the area. Cox (2003) notes that a request for a waiver or exception requires the approving agency to make findings and conclusions in order to "permit proper judicial review."

WALK-UP

An apartment building of more than two stories that is not equipped with an elevator.

WALK-UP ESTABLISHMENT

An establishment that by design of its physical facilities, service, or packaging encourages or permits pedestrians to receive a service or obtain a product without entering the establishment.

WALL

(1) The vertical exterior surface of a building; (2) one of the vertical interior surfaces that divide a building's space into rooms.

WAREHOUSE

A building used primarily for the storage of goods and materials. *See* DISTRIBUTION CENTER; TRUCK TERMINAL.

Comment: In addition to the storage of goods and materials, modern warehouses function as distribution centers. Products are received, broken down into smaller quantities, often reassembled, and then reshipped. In the modern warehouse, the holding time is generally short.

Truck terminals differ from both warehouses and distribution centers, although they have certain common characteristics. The function of the truck terminal is to move packages on a contingent basis. Packages are picked up from a given geographic area at different addresses, often by smaller trucks, and then reassembled for shipment by larger trucks for delivery to other geographical areas. Common carriers may pick up tractor-trailer loads from specific manufacturers and then break down the load for subsequent delivery. They may also pick up from different locations, aggregate the loads at their terminals, send them out (often by air), and then break down loads for delivery.

Warehouse and distribution centers employ very few workers; a ratio of one worker per 5,000 square feet of building area is not uncommon. Buildings often contain from 3 to 5 percent office space. Large companies may use small areas within the warehouse for other functions, such as employee training. These can be considered customary accessory uses. In addition, some retail activities may take place but under very strict controls. *See* RETAIL WAREHOUSE OUTLET.

The major planning issue with respect to warehouses (and distribution centers) is that the industry trend is for larger and larger buildings. One-million-square-foot buildings are no longer uncommon. For obvious reasons, interchange areas on major highways are highly desirable locations for these activities.

Municipalities can mitigate and reduce the visual impact of large-scale warehouses by requiring site improvements and building wall treatment. These include the following:

- Extensive use of landscaping and berms to shield and break up building mass

- Variations and articulation to overall building facades by changes in the facade plane

- Use of subdued wall coloration, patterning, texture, and reveals

- Creating or enhancing topographical changes on the site to create visual interest and provide shielding

- Adding elements that draw focus, introduce scale, and provide three-dimensional effects

One New Jersey municipality (Cranbury Township, Middlesex County), experiencing a large influx of very large warehouse buildings, amended its land development ordinance to address the visual impact of these buildings. The ordinance requires staggered building walls. The staggered walls must include a setback or bump-out of at least 4 feet, a minimum of 50 feet in length, at least every 150 to180 feet, depending on bay width.

Other requirements include use of painted panels, reveals, awnings or canopies, wall openings, wall texture changes, changes in building height, and variations in roof lines. Building entries and building corners must be readily identifiable through the use of canopies, marquees, architectural treatments, and the use of different materials, such as glass.

The ordinance also requires that the front and two side elevations of all buildings and structures be constructed of brick, architectural block, architectural precast concrete, or tilt-up construction using similar material of equally high quality and aesthetic value. Utility-standard concrete panels or masonry units may be used on rear elevations and/or loading dock areas only if the rear elevations and loading docks are not visible from any public right-of-way after berming, fencing, or landscape treatment.

Color and texture are addressed. Texture patterns must be provided to create shadow patterns to reduce the visual impact and mass of the building. Variations in color are to be kept to a minimum, and accent colors should be consistent in color, size, and location on all buildings in the industrial park.

Location and siting requirements mandate that all buildings front on internal roadways. To the extent practical, warehouses located along arterial roads must be situated so that they are perpendicular to, or at an angle to, the arterial road, with the short side of the building parallel or at an angle to the road. Loading and unloading bays in multiple-building industrial parks are required to be located between the buildings so that a single means of ingress and egress serves both buildings.

Extensive landscaping is required for these large warehouses. Applicants are required to present computer-generated plans showing how the landscaping looks at various time intervals.

WAREHOUSE OUTLET   *See* RETAIL WAREHOUSE OUTLET.

WAREHOUSING, PRIVATE   A building used primarily for the storage of goods and materials by the owner of the goods or operated for a specific commercial establishment or group of establishments in a particular industrial or economic field.

WAREHOUSING, PUBLIC   A building used primarily for the storage of goods and materials and available to the general public for a fee.

Comment: Public warehouses may be bulk warehouses, such as those with tank storage; commodity warehouses, such as grain elevators; refrigerated warehouses;

or general-merchandise warehouses. *See* SELF-STORAGE FACILITY.

WASTE

1. *Bulk waste*—Items whose size precludes or complicates their handling by normal collection, processing, or disposal methods

2. *Construction and demolition waste*—Building materials and rubble resulting from construction, remodeling, repair, and demolition operations

3. *Hazardous waste*—Wastes that require special handling to avoid illness or injury to persons or damage to property

4. *Special waste*—Wastes that require extraordinary management

5. *Wood pulp waste*—Wood or paper fiber residue resulting from a manufacturing process

6. *Yard waste*—Plant clippings, prunings, and other discarded material from yards and gardens

WASTELAND

Land that is barren and uncultivated.

WASTEWATER

(1) Water carrying wastes from homes, businesses, and industries that is a mixture of water and dissolved or suspended solids; (2) excess irrigation water that is runoff to adjacent land. *See* GREYWATER.

WASTEWATER MANAGEMENT PLAN

A description of existing and future wastewater-related jurisdictions, wastewater service areas, and selected environmental features and domestic treatment works subject to approval by the appropriate state agency.

WASTEWATER SYSTEM

Any device or system in public or private ownership used in the storage, treatment, recycling, or reclamation of sewage generated by two or more individual units of development. (*New Jersey State Development and Redevelopment Plan* 2002)

WATER BODIES

Any natural or artificial collection of water, whether permanent or temporary.

WATER-CARRYING CAPACITY

The ability of a pipe, channel, or floodway to transport flow as determined by its shape, cross-sectional area, bed slope, and coefficient of hydraulic friction.

WATERCOURSE

Any natural or artificial stream, river, creek, ditch, channel, canal, conduit, culvert, drain, waterway, gully, ravine, or wash in which water flows in a definite

442

direction or course, either continuously or intermit-tently; has a definite channel, bed, and banks; and includes any area adjacent thereto subject to inundation by reason of overflow or floodwater.

WATER POLLUTION

The addition of pollutants to water in concentrations or in sufficient quantities to result in measurable degradation of water quality.

WATER QUALITY CRITERIA

The levels of pollutants that affect the suitability of water for a given use.

Comment: Generally, water-use classification includes public water supply, recreation, propagation of fish and other aquatic life, agricultural use, and industrial use.

WATER QUALITY MANAGEMENT PLAN (WQMP)

The identification of strategies, policies, and procedures for managing water quality and wastewater treatment and disposal in a geographical area.

Comment: A plan for water quality management contains four major elements:

1. The use to be made of water (recreation, drinking water, fish and wildlife propagation, industrial, or agricultural)

2. Criteria to protect the water to keep it suitable for use

3. Implementation plans (for needed industrial-municipal waste treatment improvements) and enforcement plans

4. An antidegradation statement to protect existing high-quality waters

WATER RIGHTS

A property owner's right to use surface or underground water from adjacent lands.

Comment: The western and eastern United States have different water laws. Riparian rights are applicable mainly to eastern areas. Western law generally provides that the first to claim the water has the use of it. *See* RIPARIAN RIGHTS.

WATER SUPPLY SYSTEM

The system for the collection, treatment, storage, and distribution of potable water from the source of supply to the consumer.

WATER TABLE

The upper surface of ground water or the level below which the soil is seasonally saturated with water.

WATER TOWER

A water storage facility, usually above ground and often spherical or cylindrical in shape.

WATER TRANSPORTATION

Establishments engaged in freight and passenger transportation on the open seas or inland waters and in the furnishing of incidental services, such as lightering, towing, and canal operation.

Comment: This major group includes excursion boats, sightseeing boats, and water taxis, as well as cargo and hauling operations.

WATERFRONT PROPERTY

A property that has frontage on a water body.

WATERS OF THE UNITED STATES

Waters including territorial seas, navigable waters including tidal waters, and their tributaries, including lakes, rivers, and streams, and wetlands adjacent to these waters.

Comment: Placement of dredged or fill material in "Waters of the United States" is regulated by the U.S. Army Corps of Engineers under Section 404 of the Clean Water Act.

WATERSHED

The drainage area that collects and drains runoff to a receiving body of water. *See* BASIN; DRAINAGE AREA; RIVER BASIN.

WAYFINDING SYSTEM

A comprehensive and coordinated signage system that provides coherent regulatory and directional signs.

Comment: The wayfinding system should be based on an overall design theme that is consistent in colors, sizes, and types of signage and is aesthetically pleasing, easily recognizable, and pedestrian-oriented. It should be part of the comprehensive design plan for residential neighborhoods as well as business districts. The system should serve to integrate and facilitate various modes of transportation and be expandable to new venues. (Finucan 1999)

WEAVING

The crossing of two or more traffic streams traveling in the same general direction along a significant length of highway without the aid of traffic control devices.

WELL

A hole or shaft sunk into the earth to tap an underground supply of water.

WETLAND BUFFER

Abutting areas that surround and protect a wetlands from adverse impacts to its function and values.

WETLAND, COASTAL

A wetland that is regularly flowed by the tides, with inundation frequency ranging from twice daily to twice monthly.

Comment: The U.S. Army Corps of Engineers regulates activities in coastal wetlands under Section 404 of the Clean Water Act and Section 10 of the Rivers and Harbors Act.

WETLAND, DEGRADED

(1) A wetland in which there is impaired surface water flow or ground-water hydrology, or excessive drainage; (2) a wetland that has been partially filled or excavated and/or contaminated with hazardous substances; (3) a wetland that has an ecological value substantially less than that of undisturbed wetlands in the region.

Comment: Improvement of the ecological value and restoration of wetland hydrology to degraded wetlands is termed "enhancement" and is a form of wetland mitigation.

WETLAND, FRESHWATER

An area that is inundated or saturated by surface water or ground water at a frequency and duration sufficient to support—and that under normal circumstances does support—a prevalence of vegetation adapted for life in saturated soil conditions.

Comment: Wetlands are identified by one of three parameters: certain soil types, aquatic plants, and hydrology. Recent federal and state legislation makes the filling or dredging of wetlands extremely difficult. Many states also require buffer or transition areas to provide additional protection to wetlands.

WETLAND MITIGATION

Activities carried out in order to compensate for freshwater wetlands or state open-waters loss or disturbance caused by regulated activities.

Comment: Wetland mitigation may include creation, restoration, enhancement, and preservation of high-quality wetlands and uplands.

WETLAND SWALE

A freshwater wetland that is a linear topographic depression that conveys surface water runoff, generally not more than 50 feet wide and draining an area of less than 50 acres.

Comment: Under the New Jersey Freshwater Wetland Protection Act, no transition area is required adjacent to most swales, and they may be filled under a general permit in some circumstances.

WETLAND TRANSITION AREA

A buffer of upland adjacent to a wetland that serves to minimize adverse impacts on the wetland or serves as an integral component of the wetland ecosystem.

Comment: Transition areas can filter out pollutants from upland areas before they would enter a wetland. Transition areas can also serve as wildlife corridors and sanctuary for wildlife during times of wetland inundation. Activities in transition areas are regulated under state and local wetland protection programs. Transition-area widths may vary depending on the quality of the wetland. In New Jersey, wetland transition areas may range from 50 to 150 feet under the New Jersey Freshwater Wetlands Protection Act, and they may be as much as 300 feet in the New Jersey Pinelands.

WETLANDS

See WETLAND BUFFER; WETLAND, COASTAL; WETLAND, DEGRADED; WETLAND, FRESHWATER; WETLAND MITIGATION; WETLAND SWALE; WETLAND TRANSITION AREA.

WHARF

See PIER.

WHEEL STOPS

See BUMPERS.

WHOLESALE TRADE

Establishments or places of business primarily engaged in selling merchandise to other businesses, including retailers, industrial, commercial, institutional, or professional business users, other wholesalers, or acting as agents or brokers and buying merchandise for, or selling merchandise to, such individuals or companies.

Comment: Lumber, plywood, and millwork yards, such as building materials establishments, are generally classified as wholesale unless the primary operation is directly to the general public rather than to building contractors. In such cases, they are classified as retail operations.

WILDLIFE HABITAT

Land set aside for animal habitat.

WINDBREAK

Berms, vegetation, landscaping, fences, or a combination of all four to provide a barrier against wind, snow, dust, or other natural elements.

WINDROWING

Composting employing large rows of shredded waste, turned from time to time to encourage aeration.

WIRELESS TELECOM-MUNICATIONS TOWERS AND FACILITIES

(1) A parcel of land containing a tower, sending and receiving antennas attached to the tower, and a prefabricated or modular structure or cabinets containing electronic equipment; (2) a Federal Communications

WIRELESS TELECOM-MUNICATIONS TOWERS AND FACILITIES (continued)

Commission (FCC)–licensed facility, designed and used for the purpose of transmitting, receiving, and relaying voice and data signals from various wireless communication devices and equipment. For purposes of this ordinance, amateur radio transmission facilities and facilities used exclusively for receive-only antennas are not classified as wireless telecommunications towers and facilities.

Comment: The definition applies to all personal wireless services covered in the Federal Telecommunications Act of 1996 (§332(c)(7))—"the Act." The Act defines personal wireless services as including commercial mobile services, which in turn is defined to cover cellular telephone services, personal communications services, all types of mobile radio, and paging services. It does not include any amateur radio facility that is owned and operated by a federally licensed amateur radio station operator or is used for "receive only" or noncellular telephone service facilities. For purposes of zoning definitions, the more familiar "cellular antenna tower site" is often used, although the site may also contain equipment designed to provide other commercial mobile services.

For a new tower location the parcel of land is usually small, often 10,000 to 20,000 square feet in area. The tower may be 80 to 200 feet high, or even higher, depending on the area to be served, local topography, and the equipment to be placed on the tower. The shorter towers are usually monopoles; the higher towers usually employ a lattice design.

Telecommunication sites can also be located in or on new or existing buildings. The antennas can be located on the roof or flush with the facade, and the electronic equipment placed inside the building. In some cases, the antennas themselves can be located in "alternative tower structures," such as artificial trees, clock towers, silos, steeples, flag poles, and similar structures that camouflage or conceal the presence of antennas or towers.

Antennas are usually panel types, about 8 to 12 inches in width and 3 to 6 feet in height, but may also include whip antennas (6 to 15 feet in height) and satellite dish antennas.

The modular unit may vary between 400 and 1,200 square feet in area and contains the electronic equipment to enable the system to operate effectively. The equipment can also be located in secure existing buildings. Since the units are unstaffed, there is no traffic activity except for periodic maintenance.

The major conflict between service providers and municipalities is one of aesthetics and the appropriateness of the proposed site for the facility. The Act specifically excludes any denials based on health considerations if the emission from the facility complies with FCC emission regulations.

Since the Act states that state and local government regulations cannot unreasonably prohibit personal wireless services or discriminate between providers (Section 704(c)(7)), municipalities should plan for this use and, if possible, the specific location where these facilities can be located. With the exception of certain existing towers, buildings, and structures, the exact location would probably not be known until more-specific site location studies related to coverage and capacity are undertaken, usually by the provider.

Certainly, existing wireless telecommunications towers represent the most logical location for any proposed new facilities. All approvals of a tower site should provide that the owner/operator must make space available at a "reasonable" fee for any subsequent applicants. Other existing structures that are logical locations for cellular antennas include water towers and industrial and commercial building roofs. Many towns encourage their location on municipally owned land where appropriate, because of lease fees as well as an opportunity to relocate municipal radio facilities to the new, often higher tower.

These uses can also be accommodated in industrial and commercial zones, and remote areas or sites, away from existing residences, although mid-rise and high-rise residential buildings are also logical locations. Other possible locations include the interior of church steeples, water tanks, barn silos, fire and clock towers, utility poles and towers, billboards, and lighting standards.

When these facilities are located on existing buildings, placing the equipment toward the center of the roof and erecting parapet walls can reduce the visual impact.

While there has been some controversy regarding parks and forests as possible sites for these uses, the fact remains that the visual and aesthetic impact in these areas is less than in built-up areas, and the trees effectively block at least part of the view of the tower.

Applicants can provide, through the use of either photography or computer graphics, what the view of a proposed tower will be from various locations in the community.

Safety and environmental factors also are legitimate concerns with respect to these facilities. Although the

WIRELESS TELECOM-MUNICATIONS TOWERS AND FACILITIES (continued)

possibility of the tower collapsing is slight (all are built to BOCA National Building Code standards), setbacks should be established to provide some protection from ice or falling debris. Studies have shown that debris usually falls within 50 percent of the tower's height (Abrams 1998, p. 4). The Act provides for environmental impact assessments when the tower is proposed for areas with endangered species or critical habitats, when it could affect historic sites, impact wetlands, or cause water diversion or deforestation.

Coloration and landscaping are legitimate concerns and are part of the site plan review process. Landscaping around the site can screen street-level visual impacts. While some attempts have been made to incorporate the antennas in fake trees, the result has been less than satisfactory and often draws attention to the obvious.

Wireless telecommunications facilities generate no traffic, noise, lighting, odor, or other adverse impacts. Abrams suggests that they be considered in three broad zoning categories as follows:

1. As permitted uses
   a. On existing structures such as towers and buildings
   b. When located in industrial or commercial areas
   c. When located within moderate- to large-sized public parkland areas or other appropriate public facilities areas, such as maintenance depots or storage areas

2. As special exception and conditional uses when located in
   a. Residentially zoned or developed areas
   b. Agricultural and farmland preservation areas
   c. Areas with transitional zoning and development
   d. Historic districts and sites

3. As prohibited in environmentally sensitive areas such as floodplains, wetlands, and areas with steep slopes and erodible soils

Still, approval of these facilities is not a given. The Act provides that state and local governments must act on requests for siting permits within a reasonable time, put denials in writing, and support the decision by substantial evidence contained in a written record (paragraph 7). The denial must be based on specific, not general concerns. Among the reasons for denial: The service can be provided by (1) less-intrusive means;

(2) a lower tower; or (3) use of an existing structure or an "alternative structure." The local government can deny an application for more towers than the minimum required to provide wireless services (*Sprint Spectrum, L.P. v. Willoth*, U.S. Court of Appeals for the Second Circuit; reported in Lawlor 1999).

For additional materials on cellular towers and facilities, *see*: Abrams 1998, p. 3, and American Planning Association, *Aesthetics, Community Character, and the Law*, Planning Advisory Service Report No. 489/490 (1999), Chapter 6, Telecommunications Facilities.

WORKING DRAWINGS

Detailed, precise drawings by an engineer or architect from which construction may be undertaken.

Comment: Working drawings for buildings are required for issuance of a building permit. For roads and other structures, working drawings are usually required as part of the final process.

Y

YARD

An open space that lies between the principal building or buildings and the nearest lot line. *See* BUILDABLE AREA; LOT LINE; YARD, REQUIRED; YARD DEPTH; YARD LINE. *See Figures 14 and 101.*

Comment: Uses and structures that are typically permitted in required residential yards include accessory structures and swimming pools (rear or side yards only), patios and open porches, bay windows, open steps, driveways, fences, and permitted signs and lighting. In nonresidential zones, parking lots are typically permitted in side and rear yards, usually with requirements for setbacks and buffers from adjoining properties.

YARD, FRONT

A space extending the full width of the lot between any building and the front lot line and measured perpendicular to the building at the closest point to the front lot line.

Comment: Note that this term defines a space and not a required setback. The definition specifies that the line of measurement is perpendicular to the building and extends to the lot line. If the line of measurement were perpendicular to the lot line, there would be problems with pie-shaped and irregular lots.

Typically, many ordinances require that the minimum required yard remain open and unoccupied, regardless of whether the principal structure is set farther back than required. Other ordinances allow parking in the front yard provided the parking is set back beyond the minimum front yard setback.

YARD, REAR

A space extending across the full width of the lot between the principal building and the rear lot line and measured perpendicular to the building to the closest point of the rear lot line. *See Comment* under YARD, FRONT.

YARD, REQUIRED

The minimum open space between a lot line and the yard line within which no structure is permitted to be located except as provided in the zoning ordinance. *See Figure 101.*

YARD, SIDE

A space extending from the front yard to the rear yard between the principal building and the side lot line and measured perpendicular from the side lot line to the closest point of the principal building.

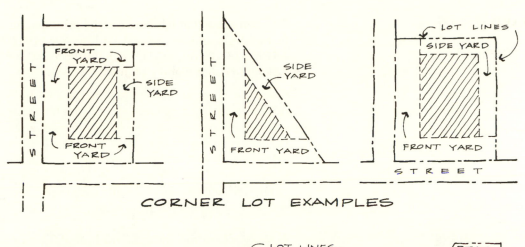

CORNER LOT EXAMPLES

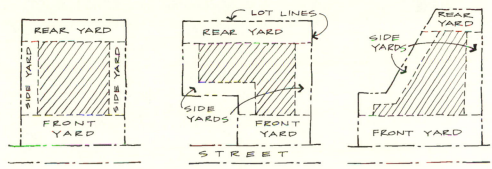

INTERIOR LOT EXAMPLES

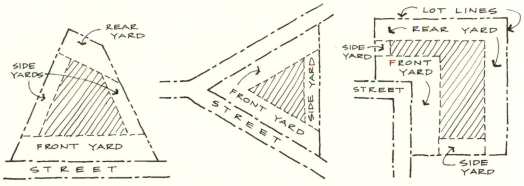

ODD-SHAPED LOT EXAMPLES

REQUIRED YARDS

BUILDING (ZONING) ENVELOPE
(TWO DIMENSIONAL)

FIGURE 101

453

YARD DEPTH

The shortest distance between a lot line and a yard line.

YARD LINE

A line drawn parallel to a lot line at a distance therefrom equal to the depth of the required yard. *See Figure 14.*

YARD SALE

See GARAGE SALE.

YOUTH CAMP

Any parcel or parcels of land having the general characteristics of a camp as the term is generally understood, used wholly or in part for recreational or educational purposes and accommodating five or more children under 18 years of age for a period of, or portions of, two days or more; the term includes a site that is operated as a day camp or as a resident camp.

YOUTH HOSTEL

An establishment providing transient, overnight accommodations, typically characterized by low cost, shared use of a self-service kitchen, common areas, sleeping rooms, and bathroom facilities.

Comment: While primarily youth- and student-oriented, these facilities cater to all age groups. In addition to the dormitory-style accommodations, private rooms and baths are often available. Establishments meeting the standards of the International Youth Hostel Federation (IYHF) in terms of facility standards, operating policies, and programs display the blue triangle logo with a hut-and-tree trademark and receive the seal of approval of the IYHF. (Canon 2003)

Z

ZIPPER LOT

A division of property using zero lot line design with offset rear-lot lines to permit each lot a more usable rear yard. *See Figure 102.*

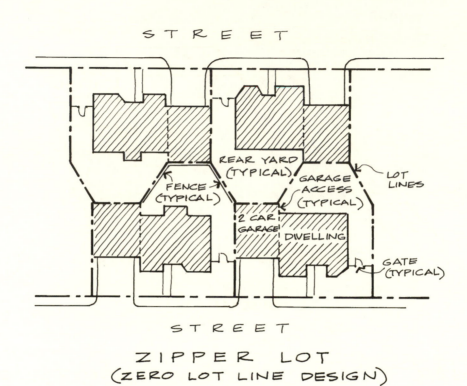

FIGURE 102

ZONE

A specifically delineated area or district in a municipality within which uniform regulations and requirements govern the use, placement, spacing, and size of land and buildings. *See* FLOATING ZONE; TRANSITION ZONE.

ZONING

The delineation of districts and the establishment of regulations governing the use, placement, spacing, and size of land and buildings.

ZONING BOARD

See BOARD OF ADJUSTMENT.

ZONING DISTRICT

See ZONE.

ZONING ENVELOPE

The three-dimensional space within which a structure is permitted to be built on a lot; it is defined by maximum height regulations, minimum yard setbacks, and sky exposure plane regulations when applicable. *See Figure 103.*

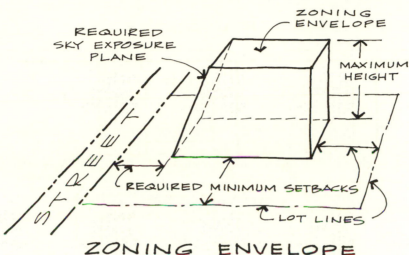

ZONING ENVELOPE

FIGURE 103

ZONING MAP

The map or maps that are a part of the zoning ordinance and delineate the boundaries of zone districts.

ZONING OFFICER

The administrative officer designated to administer the zoning ordinance and issue zoning permits.

Comment: In many smaller communities, the building inspector or construction official is also the zoning officer.

ZONING PERMIT

A document signed by a zoning officer, as required in the zoning ordinance, as a condition precedent to the commencement of a use or the erection, construction, reconstruction, restoration, alteration, conversion, or installation of a structure or building, which acknowledges that such use, structure, or building complies with the provisions of the municipal zoning ordinance or authorized variance therefrom.

Comment: Where a building permit is required, the building permit often includes a zoning permit.

ZOO

A place where animals are kept, often in a combination of indoor and outdoor spaces, and are viewed by the public.

457

References

Abrams, Stanley D. 1998. "Update on the 1996 Telecommunications Act: Personal Wireless Services." *Land Use Law & Zoning Digest* (April).

American Planning Association. 1992. "APA Recommends Proactive Regulation of Electromagnetic Fields." *Zoning News* (August), p. 13.

Babcock, Richard F., and Fred P. Bosselman. 1973. *Exclusionary Zoning: Land Use Regulation and Housing in the 1970s*. New York, NY: Praeger.

Baeb, Edie. 2002. "Upstart Mall Holds Its Own." Reported in *Crain's Chicago Business* (July 8), p. 3.

Barrette, Michael. 1996. "Hog-Tied by Feedlots." *Zoning News* (October).

Black's Law Dictionary (Bryan A. Garner, ed.). 7th ed. 1999. St. Paul, MN: West Group.

Blakeley, Edward J., and Mary Gail Snyder. 1997. *Fortress America: Gated Communities in the United States*. Washington, DC: The Brookings Institution, 1997.

Booth, Derek B., and Jennifer Leavitt. 1999. "Field Evaluation of Permeable Pavement Systems for Improved Stormwater Management." *Journal of the American Planning Association* 65, 3 (Summer).

Bowers, Fred H. 2001. *A Protocol for Testing, Assessing and Approving Innovative or Alternative Onsite Wastewater Disposal Systems*. Trenton, NJ: New Jersey Department of Environmental Protection, Division of Wastewater Quality.

Brennan, Dean, and Al Zelinka. 1997. "Safe and Sound." *Planning* 64, 8 (August).

Building Officials and Code Administrators (BOCA). 1996. *The Boca National Energy Conservation Code 1996: Model Building Regulations for the Protection of Public Health, Safety and Welfare*, 8th ed.

Burchell, Robert W., and David Listokin. 1980. *The Practitioner's Guide to Fiscal Impact Analysis*. New Brunswick, NJ: Center for Urban Policy Research.

California General Plan Glossary. 1997. Palo Alto, CA: California Planning Roundtable.

Canon, John. 2003. Interview by the authors with John Canon, Hosteling International–USA, Silver Spring, Maryland.

Census 2000 (U.S.). Washington, DC: U.S. Department of Commerce, Bureau of the Census.

Coffee Creek Center Design Code Book. 2003. Chesterton, IN: Lake Erie Land Company.

Connor, Susan M. 1998. "How the Federal Fair Housing Act Protects Persons with Handicaps in Group Homes." *Land Use Law* (January).

Corum, Vance; Marcie Rosenzweig; and Eric Gibson. 2001. *The New Farmers Market*. Auburn, CA: New World Publishing.

Cox, William M., with Donald M. Ross. 2003. *New Jersey Zoning and Land Use Administration*. Newark, NJ: Gann Law Books.

DeChiara, Joseph, and Lee E. Koppelman. 1982. *Urban Planning and Design Criteria*. New York. NY: Van Nostrand Reinhold.

Dennison, Mark S. 1996. "Zoning and the Comprehensive Plan." *Zoning News* (August).

Dennison, Mark S. 1997. "Changing or Expanding Nonconforming Uses." *Zoning News* (March).

Downs, Anthony. 2001. "What Does 'Smart Growth' Really Mean?" *Planning* (April).

Duany, Andres; Elizabeth Plater-Zyberk; and Jeff Speck. 2000. *Suburban Nation: The Rise of Sprawl and the Decline of the American Dream*. New York, NY: North Point Press (Farrar, Straus and Giroux).

Duerksen, Christopher. 1996. "Site Planning for Large-Scale Retail Stores." *PAS Memo*. Chicago, IL: American Planning Association. April.

Finucan, Karen. 1999. "Way to Go." *Planning* (November).

Floyd, Charles F., and O. Lee Reed. 1997. "Controlling Newsbox Clutter." *Land Use Law* (September).

Frej, Anne, et al. 2001. *Business and Industrial Development Handbook*. Washington, DC: Urban Land Institute.

Frizell, David J., and Harry S. Pozycki, Jr. 1989. *New Jersey Practice*. Volume 36, *Land Use Law*. St. Paul, MN: West Publishing.

Fulton, William, and Chris Jackson. 1999. "Let's Meet at the Library." *Planning* (May).

Funk & Wagnalls Standard College Dictionary. 1968. New York, NY: Funk & Wagnalls.

Gallagher, Mary Lou. 1993. "A Small Room at the Inn." *Planning* (June).

Grob, Jeffrey. 2001. "Concrete Examples." In Kim Sorvig (2001), "A Sound Solution?" *Planning* (April).

Hagman, D. G. 1975. *Urban Planning and Land Development Control Law*. St. Paul, MN: West Publishing.

Hedman, Richard. 1984. *Fundamentals of Urban Design*. Chicago, IL: Planners Press.

Hinshaw, Mark. 2000. "Rezone or Dezone." *Planning* (June).

Hunterdon County (New Jersey) Planning Board. 2000. *Preserving Community Character in Hunterdon County: A Community Design Handbook*. Flemington, NJ: Hunterdon County Planning Board. February.

Institute of Real Estate Management of the National Association of Realtors. 1985. *Income/Expert Analysis, Office Buildings, Downtown and Suburban*. Chicago, IL: IREM.

Institute of Transportation Engineers (ITE). 1997. *Trip Generation*. 6th ed. Washington, DC: Institute of Transportation Engineers. (*Editor's note:* ITE published the seventh edition of *Trip Generation* in December 2003 as the present book was in press.)

Jaffee, Martin. 1999. "The Case for Temporary Permits." *Land Use Law* (February).

James Duncan and Associates. 1996. *Planning for Agricultural Land Preservation in Minnesota: A Handbook for Planning under Minn. Statutes, Chapter 40A*. Report prepared with Iowa State University for the Minnesota Department of Agriculture.

Johnsich, John Robert. 1991. *The Real Estate Dictionary of Terms and Definitions*. 3d ed. Sacramento, CA: Real Estate Publishing Co.

Kelly, Eric Damian. 1999. "Beyond Regulation: Implementing Comprehensive Plans in the New Millennium." *Law and Zoning Digest* 51, 5 (May).

Kendig, Lane, with Susan Connor, Cranston Byrd, and Judy Heyman. 1980. *Performance Zoning*. Chicago, IL: Planners Press.

Knack, Ruth Eckdish. 1998. "Drive Nicely." *Planning* (December).

Knack, Ruth Eckdish. 2001. "Love Me, Love My Garage." *Planning* (June).

Knack, Ruth Eckdish. 2002. "Dense, Denser, Denser Still." *Planning* (August).

Langdon, Philip. 2000. "Flix, Nix, Stix: Megaplex Theaters Go Downtown." Planning (August).

Lardner/Klein Landscape Architects, P.C. 1998. *Summary Report: Simsbury Center Design Charrette*. Alexandria, VA.

Lawlor, Jim. 1999. "Act Two for Telecommunications." *Planning* (September).

Levy, Paul R. 2001. "Making Downtown Competitive." *Planning* (April).

Linowes, Lisa. 1985. "Farmers Markets." American Planning Service, Planning Advisory Service Memo (July).

Listokin, David. 1976. *Fair Share Housing Allocation*. New Brunswick, NJ: Center for Urban Policy Research.

Listokin, David, and Carole Walker. 1989. *The Subdivision and Site Plan Handbook*. New Brunswick, NJ: Center for Urban Policy Research.

Little, Charles E. 1990. *Greenways for America*. Baltimore, MD: Johns Hopkins University Press.

Lynch, Kevin, and Gary Hack. 1984. *Site Planning*. Cambridge, MA: MIT Press.

Mallach, Alan. 1984. *Inclusionary Housing Programs: Policies and Practices*. New Brunswick, NJ: Center for Urban Policy Research.

Mandelker, Daniel R. 1994. "Zoning Discrimination Against Group Homes under the Fair Housing Act." *Land Use Law* (November).

Mandelker, Daniel R., and William R. Ewald. 1988. *Street Graphics and the Law*. Chicago, IL: Planners Press.

McCarty, Kathryn Shane, ed. 1991. *Local Officials Guide: Complying with the Americans with Disabilities Act of 1990*. Washington, DC: National League of Cities.

McGowan, Leslie, and Betty Richter-Reba. 1998. "'Buy-Downs': A New Direction in Affordable Housing." *New Jersey Planners' Journal* 4, 2 (Summer).

Meck, Stuart, ed. 2002. *Growing Smart Legislative Guidebook: Model Statutes for Planning and the Management of Change*. Chicago, IL: American Planning Association.

Meltz, Robert; Dwight H. Merriam; and Richard Frank. 1999. *The Taking Issue: Constitutional Limits on Land Use Control and Environmental Regulation.* Washington, DC: Island Press.

Merriam, Dwight H., and Herbert J. Sitkowski. 1999. "The Seven-Nun Conundrum: Seeking Divine Guidance in the Definition of 'Family.'" *Land Use Law* (June).

Morgan, M. Granger. 1989. *Electric and Magnetic Fields from 60 Hertz Electric Power: What Do We Know About Possible Health Risks?* Pittsburgh, PA: Department of Engineering and Public Policy, Carnegie-Mellon University.

Nelessen, Anton C. 1994. *Visions for a New American Dream: Process, Principles, and an Ordinance to Plan & Design Small Communities.* Chicago, IL: American Planning Association.

The New Lexicon Webster Dictionary of the English Language. Bernard S. Cayne, ed. 1989. New York, NY: Lexicon Publications.

New Jersey Council on Affordable Housing. 1993. *Substantive Rules of the New Jersey Council on Affordable Housing* (NJAC 5:93-1.3). Trenton, NJ: New Jersey Department of Community Affairs, Council on Affordable Housing.

New Jersey Department of Community Affairs (NJDCA), Division of Codes and Standards. 2000. *Residential Site Improvement Standards (RSIS).* Trenton, NJ: NJDCA.

New Jersey Department of Transportation (NJDOT). 1996. *Pedestrian Compatible Planning and Design Guidelines.* Trenton, NJ: NJDOT. April.

New Jersey Office of State Planning. 1995. Memo, "Big Box Retail." Vol. 1, No. 2. Trenton, NJ: Office of State Planning. December.

New Jersey Office of State Planning. 1996. Memo, "Historic Preservation." Vol. 2, No. 3. Trenton, NJ: Office of State Planning. April.

New Jersey State Development and Redevelopment Plan. 2002. Trenton, NJ: New Jersey State Planning Commission.

Newman, Oscar. 1996. *Creating Defensible Space.* Washington, DC: U.S. Department of Housing and Urban Development.

North American Industry Classification System (NAICS). 1997. Washington, DC: Executive Office of the President, Office of Management and Budget.

President's Advisory Commission on Regulatory Barriers to Affordable Housing. 1991. *"Not in My Back Yard": Removing Barriers to Affordable Housing.* Report to President Bush and Secretary Kemp by the Advisory Commission. HUD-5806. Rockville, MD.

Rafson, Harold J. 1999. "About Odor." *Zoning News* (December).

Rose, Jerome G., and Robert E. Rothman, eds. 1977. *After Mount Laurel: The New Suburban Zoning.* New Brunswick, NJ: Center for Urban Policy Research.

Sawicki, David S. 1989. "The Festival Marketplace as Public Policy: Guidelines for Future Policy Decisions." *Journal of the American Planning Association* 55, 3 (Summer).

Schultz, Marilyn Spigel, and Vivian Loeb Kasen. 1984. *Encyclopedia of Community Planning and Environmental Management.* New York, NY: Facts on File.

Schwab, Anna K., and David J. Brower. 1997. "Sustainable Development: Implementation at the Local Level." *Land Use Law* (April).

461

Schwab, James. 1996. "Zoning and Big Box Religion." *Zoning News* (November).

Schwab, James. 1998. *Planning and Zoning for Concentrated Feed Lot Operations.* Planning Advisory Service Report 482 (Chicago, IL: Planners Book Service).

Schwanke, Dean. 1987. *Mixed-Use Development Handbook.* Washington, DC: Urban Land Institute.

Shirley, Lori. 1999. "Chesapeake Challenge." *Planning* (August).

SmartCode©. 2003. Unified development ordinance developed by Duany Plater-Zyberk & Company, Miami, Florida. Viewable at http://www.smartcode.org/.

Sorvig, Kim. 2001. "A Sound Solution?" *Planning* (April).

Thompson, Laura. 1997a. "The Conflict at the Edge." *Zoning News* (February).

Thompson, Laura. 1997b. "Zoning for Dual Fueling." *Zoning News* (August).

Toenjes, L. P. 1989. *Building Trades Dictionary.* Homewood, IL: American Technical Publishers.

Transportation Research Board, National Research Council. 2000. *Highway Capacity Manual.* Washington, DC: Transportation Research Board.

Watershed Watch. 2001. Stony Brook-Millstone Watershed Association, Pennington, New Jersey. June.

White, S. Mark, and Dawn Jourdan. 1997. "Neo-Traditional Development: A Legal Analysis." *Land Use Law* (August).

Williams, Norman Jr. 1977. "On 'From *Mount Laurel*: Guidelines on the Regional General Welfare,'" in J. G. Rose and R. E. Rothman (1977), *After Mount Laurel: The New Suburban Zoning.* New Brunswick, NJ: Center for Urban Policy Research.

Winder, Mary. 2001. Speech before The Heritage Group, Sarasota, Florida. June 4.

Ziegler, Edward H. Jr. 1991. *Rathkopf's The Law of Zoning and Planning.* New York, NY: Clark Boardman.

AMERICAN PLANNING ASSOCIATION, *PLANNING ADVISORY SERVICE (PAS) REPORTS*
(Listed by author's name; PAS Report number follows bibliographic data.)

American Society of Planning Officials. 1955. *Zoning Ordinance Definitions.* 72.

Bergman, David. 1991. *Off-Street Parking Requirements: A National Review of Standards.* 432.

Browne, Carolyn. 1980. *The Mechanics of Sign Control.* 354.

Burrows, Tracy. 1989. *A Survey of Zoning Definitions.* 421.

Davidson, Michael, and Fay Dolnick, eds. 1999. *A Glossary of Zoning, Development and Planning Terms.* 491/492.

deGrogh, Teresa, and Rachel German. 1986. *Standards for Self-Service Storage Facilities.* 396.

Duerksen, Christopher J. 1986. *Aesthetics and Land-Use Controls: Beyond Ecology and Economics.* 399.

Duerksen, Christopher J., and R. Matthew Goebel. 1999. *Aesthetics, Community Character, and the Law*. **489/490**.

Fleming, Robert Lee. 1994. *Saving Face: How Corporate Franchise Design Can Respect Community Identity*. **452**.

Hinshaw, Mark L. 1995. *Design Review*. **454**.

Glassford, Peggy. 1983. *Appearance Codes for Small Communities*. **379**.

Greenberg, Froda, with Jim Hecimovich. 1984. *Traffic Impact Analysis*. **387**.

Kelly, Eric Damian, and Connie Cooper. 2000. *Everything You Always Wanted to Know About Regulating Sex Businesses*. **495/496**.

Kelly, Eric Damian, and Gary J. Reso. 1989. *Sign Regulation for Small and Midsize Communities: A Planners Guide and a Model Ordinance*. **419**.

Martz, Wendelyn A., with Marya Morris. 1990. *Preparing a Landscape Ordinance*. **431**.

Meshenberg, Michael J. 1976. *The Administration of Flexible Zoning Techniques*. **318**.

Meshenberg, Michael J. 1976. *The Language of Zoning: A Glossary of Words and Phrases*. **322**.

Porter, Douglas, ed. 1996. *Performance Standards in Growth Management*. **461**.

Sanders, Welford. 1998. *Manufactured Housing: Regulation, Design Innovations, and Development Options*. **478**.

Schwab, James. 1993. *Industrial Performance Standards for a New Century*. **444**.

Schwab, James. 1998. *Planning and Zoning for Concentrated Feed Lot Operations*. **482**.

Land Measures

	Equals
1 mile	5,280 feet 1,760 yards 320 rods 80 chains
1 chain	66 feet 100 links 4 rods
1 rod	25 links 16.5 feet 1 perch 1 pole
1 link	7.92 inches
1 township	36 sections
1 full section	640 acres
1 square mile	640 acres 1 full section
1 acre	43,560 square feet 4,840 square yards 160 square rods 10 square chains
1 square chain	10,000 square links
1 square rod	30.25 square yards
1 square yard	9 square feet
1 square foot	144 square inches